The United States
and the Global Struggle
for Minerals

The United States and the Global Struggle for Minerals

Alfred E. Eckes, Jr.

UNIVERSITY OF TEXAS PRESS
Austin and London

Library of Congress Cataloging in Publication Data

Eckes, Alfred E., 1942–
    The United States and the global struggle for
minerals.

    Bibliography: p.
    Includes index.
    1. Natural resources—United States. 2. Mines
and mineral resources—United States. 3. United
States—Foreign relations. I. Title.
HC103.7.E26   333.8'0973   78-11082
ISBN 0-292-78506-2

Copyright © 1979 by the University of Texas Press

Printed in the United States of America

Contents

Introduction

DURING 1973 a series of unsettling economic and political events drove home to Americans how reliant this country was on imported nonrenewable resources. The huge American economy began to overheat; prices of raw materials and industrial commodities such as aluminum, rubber, copper, and scrap steel, climbed precipitously. From 1947 to 1971, the wholesale prices of nonfood raw materials, except fuels, increased only 21 percent, but in the next two years these prices jumped ahead 46 percent. As shortages emerged in basic commodities, a second unforeseen catastrophe hit. War broke out in the Middle East, and Arab oil-producing nations promptly used their petroleum weapon. They sliced oil production, quadrupled prices, and embargoed fuel exports to the Atlantic industrial nations, especially to the Netherlands and the U.S.[1]

As members of the Organization of Petroleum Exporting Countries (OPEC) successfully flexed their energy muscle, other envious raw-material exporting nations watched in awe. Leaders of these underdeveloped nations calculated the prospects for similar concerted action to drive up prices of copper, bauxite, and other vital raw materials. In the industrial nations purchasing agents listened intently, interpreting these events as presaging other shortages. In opting to build up business inventories, the agents helped tighten commodity prices and exacerbate the shortages they hoped to avoid. Within government ministries public officials calculated their own options, considering how to counter threats from an increasingly militant Third World.[2]

The events of 1973–1974 appeared to reveal two underlying perils to the American economy—resource exhaustion and supply disruptions. The first had begun to worry scientists before the surge in commodity prices. A team of systems analysts at the Massachusetts Institute of Technology studied implications of sustained exponential economic growth (that is, economic expansion at a constant percentage) and finite nonrenewable resources. In a controversial report, *The Limits of Growth*, they warned in 1972 that "the earth's interlocking resources—the global system of nature in which we live—probably cannot support present rates of economic and population growth much beyond the year 2100, if that long, even with advanced technology." In what was essentially a sophisticated, updated version of the Reverend Thomas Malthus' exhaustion thesis, the academic researchers forecast the dire consequence of reaching the limits to growth on this planet—"a rather sudden and uncontrollable decline in both population and industrial capacity."[3]

This important study quickly encountered serious criticisms from other specialists who did not share the authors' pessimistic outlook. For instance, economist Lester Brown accepted the notion of gradually rising prices for raw materials, but he rejected the notion of imminent exhaustion. As he put it, the "U.S. and the world are moving from an age of relative resource abundance to an era of relative resource scarcity." While rejecting the catastrophic-breakdown thesis, Brown believed that the problems of managing scarcity would dictate important changes in the way Americans dealt with resource problems. No longer could this country simply satisfy its voracious industrial appetite by consuming only the highest-quality and most easily accessible ores.[4]

Concern about unfavorable long-term trends coincided with new anxieties about short-term dislocations. This country's growing dependence on imported materials heightened its economic and political vulnerability to external shocks. By 1985, it seemed the U.S. would depend on imports for more than half of its petroleum and natural gas supplies. Also, more than half of this country's supplies of nine basic industrial raw materials, including iron ore, bauxite, and tin, would come from abroad. Such a heavy reliance on foreign suppliers, especially underdeveloped nations, was an invitation to future embargoes and price-gouging, and these pressures could jeopardize national security. C. Fred Bergsten, a young economist with a flair for dramatizing issues, created vibrations in Washington with an important article warning the U.S. could soon be pressured to "compromise its positions on international and economic issues."[5]

To many who discussed the dangers of resource exhaustion and the perils of product diplomacy, these problems seemed unique to the 1970s. In fact, the themes underlay twentieth century international relations, and the latest events had earlier analogues. During World War I and its aftermath many American policymakers also believed this country was running out of domestic oil, ironically at the time automobile magnate Henry Ford demonstrated his own confidence in the future by mass-producing gasoline-using automobiles. Then, during the mid-1920s, Secretary of Commerce Herbert Hoover and his subordinates battled against cartels, operating with the backing of foreign governments, a situation bearing some similarity to the OPEC actions of 1973–1974.

Competition for scarce resources remained a source of international discord in the 1930s. "Have-not" nations, like Germany, Italy, and Japan, listed their raw-material deficiencies as reasons for employing military forces to seize foreign territory. World War II did not end the national competition for stable resources; rather the problems continued into the cold war. Certainly the Soviet Union and the U.S. were relatively more self-sufficient than Japan or the West European powers, but each had certain deficiencies. Thus their competition for influence along the Eur-Asian periphery included a contest for control of vital minerals in Africa and Southeast Asia. Since these resources were the industrial lifeblood of Western Europe and Japan, both Moscow and Washington recognized that the battle for materials could determine the outcome of the Soviet-American rivalry.

In brief, this book explores how natural resource considerations have influenced American foreign relations since World War I. Too often historians have neglected this important theme, and my account represents one effort to correct this imbalance. Inevitably, close attention to resources gives the work a determinist tone, but I do not support the proposition that *only* natural resources structure the underlying competition among nations. Obviously, other economic and political factors help shape circumstances, and individual decisionmakers usually have a measure of latitude to choose among policy options and to time their own initiatives. For instance, even Adolf Hitler, one of the most single-minded national leaders, had a fundamental choice, as he perceived it. Germany could either expand to acquire essential materials, or she could accept a subordinate status in Europe, lacking adequate living space and resources while remaining reliant on her national rivals for essential materials.[6]

Necessarily I have established certain arbitrary limits for my research and writing. For one thing, this work does not purport to present an exhaustive and comprehensive study of individual materials. These industrial materials frequently differ so much among themselves that no synthesis can present adequately the complicated problems of exploration, production, and marketing. Also, for purposes of organization I have excluded agricultural commodities and energy materials—including atomic power. A number of historians have probed these themes, and several other books are in preparation. The present study is selective in another way: it rests primarily on official documents, many of them previously unavailable to outside investigators in archives and federal depositories. Much of the World War II and more recent narrative rests on recently opened archival materials not utilized in previously published accounts. Finally, while documents remain the principal way, and most reliable method, for a diplomatic historian to reconstruct the past, it is important to recognize certain limitations. Frequently, written records distort as well as illuminate, for sometimes officials who write memoranda for government files are more concerned with influencing later historical accounts than with shaping national policy. Where possible I have sought to compensate for these evidential problems, through oral interviews and the use of a wide variety of archival materials, such as the office files of participants.

Like other historians working in recent U.S. history, I owe a large debt to many knowledgeable archivists and librarians who directed my attention to relevant documents. My special thanks go to John E. Taylor of the Modern Military Branch, U.S. National Archives, who was extraordinarily helpful in suggesting records collections bearing on this subject. Also, Robert Wood of the Herbert Hoover Library, William Emerson and Donald Schewe of the Franklin D. Roosevelt Library, and Susan Jackson of the Dwight D. Eisenhower Library offered important assistance.

Several others made major contributions to the research. U.S. Rep. Samuel L. Devine suggested a number of important documents and generously offered his own perceptions of the legislative process. Also, the U.S. Bureau of Mines responded quickly to requests for minerals statistics. In particular, I appreciate the efforts of V. Anthony

Cammarota, Jr., John M. Hague, Keith L. Harris, R. A. Heindl, F. L. Klinger, and Harold J. Schroeder in providing data for the appendixes.

Grants from the Ohio State University Graduate School and the Eleanor Roosevelt Institute facilitated travel to archives and reproduction of documents.

For reading and criticizing chapter drafts, I am indebted to John Gaddis, Walt W. Rostow, and Marvin Zahniser. Beatrice Romeo and Phyllis Tietzel aided in preparing the manuscript for publication, while Jerilynn Cornish effectively located materials in the Ohio State University and checked footnotes. Finally, Mary Erler patiently and meticulously edited copy for the University of Texas Press.

The United States
and the Global Struggle
for Minerals

Chapter One
World War I
and the Global Scramble
for Resources

"MINERALOGY and geography elucidate history, for the one helps to explain the forces which have moved the seat of empire, the other the obstacles which have fixed its course by determining the path of least resistance," wrote Brooks Adams in 1902. The author, the visionary grandson of President John Quincy Adams, perceived more clearly than his contemporaries how possession of rich and abundant natural resources shaped the emergence of the United States as a global power after the Civil War. His interpretation of global events was a variety of determinism, the doctrine that environmental and physical conditions shape events.[1]

After World War I as scholars and policymakers reconstructed the origins and consequences of the recent conflict, a number of explanations competed for attention in the intellectual marketplace. In Germany political and military geographers turned to "geopolitics," the interrelationship of politics and geography, both for explanation of their nation's defeat and for a blueprint to future national vindication. The young Adolf Hitler revealed the influence of geopolitical thinking on his own perspective in *Mein Kampf* where he looked to the East for additional living space to make Germany a world power. Elsewhere, economic determinism offered a convenient explanation. Some American historians and journalists claimed that sinister economic interests, particularly bankers and munitions makers, bore heavy responsibility for involving the U.S. in a major war which, the writers claimed, did not directly threaten the security of the Western Hemisphere.[2]

To minerals specialists these deterministic explanations concerned with living space and economic forces conveniently ignored the real "foundations of power": how natural resources and human talents defined the competitive struggle for prestige and prosperity among independent nations. One historian of mining, T. A. Rickard, became so incensed at the general disregard for how minerals shaped the movement of civilization that he concluded a two-volume study of *Man and Metals* with this assertion: The miner "left his mark, as the herald of empire and the pioneer of industry. Trade follows the flag, but the flag follows the pick."[3]

Three geologists who served in the U.S. government during World War I seized upon Brooks Adams' interest in minerals as a dominant factor in global relations and sought to awaken public and official interest in natural resource issues. Their vigorous efforts influenced the evolution of official policy along internationalist lines. Professor Charles K. Leith, a prominent structural and economic geologist from the University of Wisconsin, was a prolific writer and persistent advocate of international arrangements to regulate the global struggle for minerals. Leith, the protege of world renowned geologist Charles Van Hise, who incidentally served as president of the University of Wisconsin, himself acted as mineral adviser to the Shipping and War Industries Boards during World War I. Although nominally a Republican, Leith not only advised the American Commission to Negotiate Peace and travelled to the Paris Peace Conference but also campaigned for international collaboration. Convinced officials in the U.S. government lacked sufficient experience with the critical aspects of global minerals problems and exhibited inadequate concern for them, Leith sought to inform the attentive public by participating in international studies conferences, organizing government studies, and preparing articles for prestigious journals like *Foreign Affairs.*[4]

George Otis Smith and Josiah E. Spurr also emphasized the critical role of mineral resources in shaping international politics, and they, like Leith, worked to awaken American leaders to this country's resource deficiencies during the interwar period. As director of the U.S. Geological Survey for over twenty years, until 1930, Smith had a unique opportunity both to encourage studies of national mineral resources within the Washington bureaucracy and to direct his agency's efforts away from theoretical research toward practical problems. Spurr approached his task differently. Briefly involved in geological survey work, as well as wartime minerals mobilization, he concentrated professionally on mining consulting, editing, and teaching. As president of the Mining and Metallurgical Society of America and as editor of the *Engineering and Mining Journal* (1919–1927), Spurr sponsored professional activities designed to encourage minerals specialists and policymakers to consider America's natural resource problems in a global context.[5]

For Leith, Smith, and Spurr personal experiences in the progressive era and the war strengthened the conviction that governments must hereafter conserve mineral resources and pursue policies intended to achieve the advantages of resource interdependence. Like other conservationists in the progressive period who exhibited concern about misuse of forests, water, soil, and other natural resources, these minerals specialists exhorted Americans to use nonrenewable resources efficiently. While recognizing that minerals were more exhaustible and irreplaceable than forests or soils, Leith and his associates did not oppose growth or economic development. Rather, they encouraged these, providing existing resources were utilized efficiently. Most important for foreign policy, the three understood heavy mineral usage would exhaust America's rich natural endowments, and they anticipated the U.S. would become more and more dependent on foreign suppliers for high-quality ores. This trend, they all understood, foreshadowed intense competition among industrial nations for overseas raw materials. And, based on Germany and Japan's aggressive quest for raw materials during and after World War I, the experts foresaw—accurately as it turned out—the national competition for strategic materials underlying, and perhaps thwarting, efforts to stabilize Europe and restore global prosperity.

To the postwar minerals determinists, like Leith and his colleagues, the struggle for minerals lay at the center of many festering political controversies. For instance, the longstanding Franco-German competition for Alsace-Lorraine Spurr interpreted as "a struggle for the greatest iron deposits of Europe and the second largest in the world, which gave Germany her immense growth and power, and may now transfer that wealth and power to France." Similarly, he described the controversy between Poland and Germany for Upper Silesia as more than a conflict over nationalistic sentiment, or even territory. It "concerns the greatest coal field of Europe as well as great deposits of lead and zinc." A victory for Poland would permit it to rival Germany in wealth and importance, he said; a German loss would make that nation a second-rate power. Discussion of such territorial issues in terms of freely expressed wishes of the native population was tantamount to the "same order of fitness as tossing a coin for it." According to Spurr's line of analysis, populations shifted—at one time primarily German, at another moment largely Polish—but coal deposits remained fixed. To clarify the importance of these strategic areas, we "should in place of Silesia say Coal, in the place of Alsace-Lorraine, Iron, and so on." It was characteristic of minerals specialists, like Spurr and Leith, that their sympathies lay less with the ideology of national self-determination, a theme central to Woodrow Wilson's proposals for a new global order, than with the conservationist view that resources should be utilized efficiently everywhere both for the benefit of future generations and to produce the most efficient use of global resources.[6]

In particular, Leith railed at critics of foreign mineral exploitation, who advocated political controls on resource development but are "the very people" who "go right on buying household utilities and automobiles which create the demand, without realizing that they are just as responsible as any one else for demand and thus for exploitation." Given the irregular distribution of key minerals around the world, Leith considered a certain amount of interference with national sovereignty inevitable and necessary for human progress. "The United States," he said, "is and must continue to be one of the world's chief exploiters."[7]

If World War I and its antecedents offered abundant data appearing to confirm how natural resource problems contributed to international rivalries, the underlying concept of environmental determinism had nineteenth century roots. Both the classical economists, especially David Ricardo and Thomas Malthus, and natural scientists like Charles Darwin, believed natural resources limited human progress. For Ricardo depletion of physical materials led to rising costs, in turn forcing basic adjustments in the human ecosystem, while to Malthus population growth and resource use led inexorably to physical exhaustion and mass starvation. Darwin's *On the Origin of Species* also rested firmly on a foundation of "environmental determinism" containing Malthus' interpretation of population pressure against finite resources. And in this intellectual milieu it is not surprising that American historian Frederick Jackson Turner constructed his famous "frontier thesis," an interpretation of the U.S. experience based in large part on prevailing assumptions that the physical environment shaped the development of social and political institutions.[8]

But at the turn of the century the prevailing view was that America's physical abundance assured a bright future. Banker Frank Vanderlip wrote in 1902 that there was one fundamental reason why the U.S. appeared inevitably destined to lead the world in the coming commercial struggle. "Of all nations the United States has the most unbounded wealth of natural resources," he said. "We have hardly comprehended the inevitable advantages which those resources are to give us." Soon, however, Theodore Roosevelt and the conservation movement helped demolish the deep-seated belief in unlimited natural resources and awakened interest in conserving scarce domestic resources for the use of future generations. President Roosevelt, a skillful advocate of executive action, dramatized conservation issues when he convened a White House Conference in May 1908, and later authorized a National Conservation Commission report. "Conservation of our resources is the fundamental question before this nation, and . . . our first and greatest task is to set our house in order and begin to live within our means," the president asserted.[9]

Claiming wasteful utilization of minerals cost hundreds of human lives and $300 million annually, Roosevelt encouraged the National Conservation Commission to make a complete inventory of natural resources. This study, conducted under the direction of forester Gifford Pinchot, reported that the nation resembled a man who, given a fortune, spent it recklessly, never asking the amount of his inheritance or how long it might last. Pinchot's study counseled efficiency, use of substitutes and low-grade ores, and better cooperation with foreign nations, but it introduced no hard evidence of imminent metals shortage. Both in iron and copper, the principal metals studied, United States domestic reserves seemed adequate for years to come. Ironically, in view of later shortages, the report rejected the argument that a nation should preserve existing copper reserves for future use, when their value is an unknown quantity. Instead, it was better to "extract the ore at as rapid a rate as possible when profit is assured." In policy-oriented terms, then, the National Conservation Commission report failed to anticipate growing dependence on foreign supplies—especially such ferroalloys as manganese, chromium, nickel, and tungsten. Nor did the report urge government intervention to build up public stockpiles or to secure mines abroad in order to supplement declining domestic reserves.[10]

Concerned primarily with national efforts to reduce natural resource waste, especially to guard streams, protect forests, and save the soil, the progressive-era conservation movement left an enduring imprint. For one thing, the leading conservation advocates, although not generally economists, grasped the principles of scarcity discussed in the writing of Ricardo and Malthus. Doubtful about the prospects of relying on technological progress, including use of low-grade ores and substitute materials, the conservationists remained pessimistic about the prospects for avoiding rising costs and resource exhaustion. In particular, they discounted the capability of the free market to adapt to rising costs and shifting technology, and so they prescribed governmental intervention to keep shortsighted private enterprise from exhausting abundant, accessible, high-quality materials. After World War I, incidentally, scientists like Leith, trained in the progressive-conservationist tradition, would continue to advocate expanded governmental intervention at home and abroad to prevent mineral waste and to protect external sources of supply.[11]

Conservationists and policymakers generally considered resource issues in a national context before World War I. They understood the link between minerals and industrial prosperity, but to residents of mineral-rich America domestic reserves seemed sufficient to satisfy requirements of an expanding population and of economic growth, providing the present generation guarded against waste and encouraged efficient utilization of available materials. And by available objective measures the United States did have a commanding resource position in 1913, which protected it against the perils of international commerce and outside political pressures. This country had diversified, high-quality reserves of energy as well as ferrous and nonferrous minerals. According to specialists, coal and iron were the foundations of twentieth century industrial civilization, and in 1913 the U.S. produced nearly as many tons of these two materials as Great Britain, France, and Germany combined. Sixty-four percent of the world's petroleum production came from the U.S. Indeed, this country held first place in the production of thirteen of the thirty most important mineral commodities—coal, iron, copper, lead, zinc, silver, tungsten, molybdenum, petroleum, natural gas, arsenic, phosphate, and salt. By contrast, the major European belligerents—Germany,

France, and Great Britain—lacked diversified holdings of high-quality resources. It is true that Germany ranked first as a global producer of potash, an important fertilizer, and that France stood first in bauxite production, but these two powers lacked a dominant position in any other vital mineral. The United Kingdom itself did not rank among the leading world producers of any vital materials, but the British Empire, including Britain's overseas dependencies, had important supplies of resources, such as copper, nickel, and tin, that would benefit London in time of war providing the English-speaking empire retained control of the seas.[12]

Some officials in Washington appreciated the significance of this advantageous situation. George Otis Smith, director of the Geological Survey, boasted that the U.S. was "not only the world's greatest producer of mineral wealth, but, so far as estimates of the earth's treasures have shown," it possessed "greater reserves of most of the essential minerals than any other nation." In dollar value U.S. mineral production amounted to nearly $2.5 billion annually, a sum smaller than domestic agricultural output but considerably larger than the value of mineral production in other leading industrial nations. Government experts knew that the U.S. mined 40 percent of the world's coal and 65 percent of its petroleum. Also they recognized that the U.S. supplied 40 percent of the world's iron ore, furnished 55 percent of all copper, and produced 30 percent of lead and zinc. With such a strong mineral position the Geological Survey exhibited little concern about U.S. dependence on foreign suppliers for some imported materials, because this country held abundant undeveloped supplies of some minerals, such as low-grade manganese, that might be extracted during an extended emergency. Only in nitrates, potash salts, tin, nickel, and platinum did the U.S. apparently lack supplies commensurate with anticipated needs. "Probably no other nation in the world so nearly approaches absolute independence in respect to mineral resources," Smith concluded.[13]

Because this country had vast quantities of undeveloped minerals, some government officials initially saw World War I as an opportunity to achieve even greater mineral self-sufficiency. President Wilson's Secretary of the Interior, Franklin K. Lane, argued that the European war, by interfering with manufacturing and interrupting imports, would help stimulate the production of domestic minerals and the discovery of new reserves, thus leaving a permanent benefit—that is, reducing U.S. reliance on potentially undependable foreign sources of supply. "When they [businessmen] have found the domestic supply and begin its use," Lane said, "they will not return to dependence upon the foreign supply, and thereafter good or bad times in the United States, so far as the maintenance of industries is concerned, will be more independent of foreign complications." [14]

Policymakers in Washington, as in capitals of other nations directly affected by the conflict, were slow to recognize how technological change and expanding trade had interlocked national economies, altered requirements for strategic materials needed in manufacturing armaments, and changed the conduct of warfare. Since the major powers last engaged in a major conflict a century before, industrial nations had become less self-sufficient and much more dependent on foreign suppliers for food, fuels, and industrial raw materials. Britain, for example, was a leading producer of copper, lead, and tin in the nineteenth century, but heavy use depleted these reserves so that domestic copper production was insignificant after 1885. And the exploitation of lead and tin mines peaked in the early 1870s, so that the United Kingdom became a heavy importer of both minerals. As for iron, the backbone of the steel industry, production reached a peak during the 1880s, not to be surpassed for more than a half century when the disruption of World War II forced even greater reliance on Britain's ores. In 1913 both Britain and Germany were heavily dependent on outside iron shipments, the United Kingdom importing 7,561 metric tons, 47 percent of domestic production, and Germany buying abroad 11,406 metric tons, an amount equal to 40 percent of home production. [15]

In another way technology had changed warfare. Before the mid-nineteenth century national power depended less on the availabilities of resources for mechanized industry and urban populations than on the qualities of soldiers engaged in hand-to-hand fighting. But the growth of the iron and steel industry altered the old ways of warfare and elevated the importance of minerals, especially iron and coal. As geographers observed, it was no accident that the U.S. emerged as a great industrial power in the previous century, for it had the advantages of iron in northern Minnesota and coal in western Pennsylvania. Elsewhere, other industrial centers emerged in

England and in the region encompassing the Ruhr and eastern France, all near supplies of coal and iron.[16]

Early in the twentieth century the four major industrial centers—Britain, France, Germany, and the United States—became more dependent on transoceanic supplies than previously. On the one hand expansion of steel production depleted Britain's limited reserves of iron and placed heavy demands on her small deposits of other metals, including copper, zinc, lead, and tin. Along with depletion of high-quality ores, shifting technology also prompted Britain and other industrial nations to look outward for crucial raw materials. The revolution in steel-making technology, initiated with Sir Robert Hadfield's development of a special manganese steel in 1898, led to production of other ferroalloys, using metals previously utilized primarily in scientific laboratories. Chromium, nickel, and tungsten, the new alloys essential for production of specialty steels needed in warfare, came from remote colonial areas, accessible only to long-distance shipping. France and Britain, long the major European naval powers, possessed the world's principal deposits of chromium (a hard, corrosion-resistant metal used to manufacture alloy steels for such military applications as projectiles, armor plate, and cannon linings) in New Caledonia and Rhodesia. The same two maritime powers had dominant political control over nickel deposits in Sudbury, Ontario, and New Caledonia, an island in the southwest Pacific Ocean. Used as an alloy for steel, nickel proved tougher, more elastic and shock resistant, than ordinary carbon steel. Finally, tungsten, another vital steel-making alloy, existed extensively in China and certain other areas of eastern Asia as well as the Western Hemisphere. This metal, employed militarily for high-speed tool steel, did not exist in Europe to any significant degree, except on the Iberian peninsula.[17]

As sometimes happens, technological developments ran ahead of political and military planning, for in 1914 not even the usually thorough German general staff understood how reliant their nation's arms industry was on foreign supplies, which were vulnerable to maritime controls. For instance, Germany obtained its principal supplies of tungsten from Burma where British companies recovered the wolfram ore. Ironically, although the British Empire had ample supplies of wolfram, in 1914 the British steel industry depended on Ger-

many to treat the wolfram ore and supply tungsten needed for manufacture of high-speed tools. Since it possessed a powerful navy and a
flexible industrial system, Britain stood to benefit more in wartime
from this situation than its rival Germany. During the global struggle
the United Kingdom would develop its own tungsten processing
facilities, and employ its superior naval strength to shut off Germany
from these prewar sources of wolfram ore in the British Empire.[18]

Along with the fact that new metals technology imposed greater
interdependence on the European nation-state system, the growth of
world trade along the lines of comparative advantage imposed an
unprecedented degree of economic integration, with its own wartime
perils. Germany, for instance, imported 25 percent of its iron ore and
lead consumption and about 78 percent of its copper. Much of Germany's supplies of lead and zinc came from Australia, a member of
the British Commonwealth. It is estimated that 40 percent of 10 million German industrial workers owed their jobs directly to imported
raw materials in 1914.[19]

Historical interpretations of the causes of World War I do not
emphasize the importance of natural resources in Germany's decision
to mobilize, so much as they stress political and military considerations. Nevertheless, German historian Fritz Fischer presents convincing evidence that his country's decision for war was a desperate bid
for world status equal to European neighbors Britain and France.
And he demonstrates that Germany's war aims included specific
raw-material objectives: possession of iron-rich French Lorraine,
iron, coal, and manganese from the Ukraine, along with other resources from Belgium, Turkey, and African colonies. For Germany
the Balkan crisis of 1914 presented an opportunity to acquire a raw-
material–rich empire comparable to the empires of its leading rivals.[20]

If the competition for secure sources of raw materials contributed to international tensions and helped ignite a global war, the
military control of natural resources influenced the outcome of World
War I. Both Britain and Germany quickly adopted the latest technology of economic warfare to weaken their rivals and produce internal economic disruption and turmoil. The belligerents employed
the established techniques of economic warfare, such as the blockade and blacklist, to curtail shipments from overseas colonies and
neutrals; and they deployed new military technology, such as the
mine and the submarine. These expedients, applied at first selectively

and then indiscriminately as the rivals maneuvered for military advantage, provoked diplomatic controversies with neutrals like the United States who asserted their rights under existing interpretations of international law to trade with all belligerents. For Germany, who lacked control of the sea lanes and naval superiority, the submarine served as a knockout weapon to disrupt Britain's extended supply lines. And, while Britain suffered heavy shipping losses in 1917 and early 1918, her development of the convoy system helped combat the submarine threat and keep open the critical transatlantic supply lines. As a result, beleaguered London continued to obtain manganese from India, chromite from Rhodesia and Turkey, and nickel from Canada. A strong sea position also enabled the United Kingdom to obtain nitrates from Chile, needed to manufacture high explosives, chemicals, and fertilizer, while Germany, cut off from these overseas supplies, allocated resources at home to development of a nitrogen-fixation process, permitting scientists to remove this element from the air. Ironically, German capital owned one-third of Chile's production capacity, but Germany's ownership of foreign materials was no substitute for Britain's sea strength.[21]

While the Kaiser's submarines torpedoed Britain's merchant shipping and came close to strangling the island empire in 1917, London's system of trade controls proved a more effective weapon than seapower in this war of attrition. Germany had not prepared adequately for a prolonged war and its available supplies proved inadequate in certain key materials. Like the U.S., Germany lacked adequate supplies of ore with more than 30 percent manganese, a metal essential for producing high-quality steel. Fortunately for the war effort Germany captured some manganese during its invasion of Belgium and possessed in 1914 a two-years' supply. In addition, the principal member of the Central Powers learned how to conserve manganese in steel production and also discovered how to employ low-quality manganese ore from domestic reserves. As a result, German steel production continued at a satisfactory level for most of the war. Similarly, the Kaiser's industries avoided serious shortages of lead, zinc, and aluminum, all materials with important military applications, since neighboring Belgium and Switzerland provided some quantities of these.[22]

The British system of trade controls handicapped German war production most, however, in copper, tin, and nickel, critical materials available only in adequate quantity outside Europe. Unable to purchase and take delivery of Chilean copper, or to obtain similar supplies from the U.S., the world's leading producer at that time, Germany simply allowed its industrial equipment to deplete as it substituted zinc and aluminum and requisitioned all available domestic goods for conversion to military uses. Tin presented an even more difficult problem for the Berlin government, since the only supplies of this metal came from non-European sources, especially the Dutch East Indies and Bolivia. Unable to circumvent the British system of shipping controls, Germany failed to obtain tin from its longtime supplier, Bolivia, and instead the belligerent nation looked for second-best solutions. German engineers substituted aluminum for tin wherever possible, and German scientists learned how to recover tin from solder. Germans collected empty tin cans and even requisitioned bells and pipe organs to meet urgent defense needs.[23]

Throughout World War I supplies of nickel were scarce in Germany, as Britain successfully shut off trade from Canada and New Caledonia. At one point in 1916 Germany even dispatched the submarine merchantman *Deutschland* to the U.S. to obtain a cargo of tin and three hundred tons of precious nickel. This was possible because Canada sent its nickel matte to the U.S. for refining by the International Nickel Company. News of the German ploy so angered Canada that it compelled the International Nickel Company to establish a separate refinery in Canada, so that hereafter Britain's North American dominion could control politically the ultimate use of its own natural resources.[24]

More important than minerals sanctions in defeating Germany were controls on shipments of food. Indeed, German commentators accused the Allies of imposing a "hunger blockade" as part of economic warfare, and the Germans asserted these restrictions burdened Germany with more civilian casualties than archrival England. However Allied historians respond that Germany was relatively self-sufficient in food, and that famine resulted from a misguided set of government policies. For instance, the Kaiser's surrogates erred in allocating unduly large quantities of foodstuffs to the armed forces at the expense of civilian consumption and they mistakenly withdrew too much labor from agriculture to meet industrial and military requirements. Historians also say the German government made inadequate preparations for war, failing to stockpile fertilizers, and it displayed too little interest in maintaining discipline and order in the domestic economy.[25]

How did the European war affect the North American minerals industry and U.S. interests? Initially, war conditions disturbed metals markets—driving up the prices of materials in short supply, such as antimony, quicksilver, and platinum, and pushing down prices for copper and lead. In balance, European war orders provided a healthy stimulus to the minerals industry—especially for petroleum and copper, two of the most essential war materials, of which, the U.S. was the world's leading producer. The cost of a barrel of high-grade Pennsylvania crude oil jumped upward from $1.88 to $4.00 between 1914 and 1918. And copper doubled in price between 1914 and 1916.[26]

Modern warfare depended, increasingly, on the gasoline engine and electrical equipment, and to meet these needs the United States provided 65 percent of the world's petroleum requirements and 80 percent of the Allies' oil requirements. In this first mechanized war the availability of American oil determined whether the submarine, tank, and airplane, the latest implements of military technology, functioned effectively. And copper, useful both as a conductor of electricity and as casing for ammunition, also gained an expanded wartime market. The U.S., which previously produced more of this red metal than the rest of the world combined, supplied 60 percent of the global copper production from its domestic reserves and another 20 percent from American-owned mines in the Western Hemisphere. In the course of only four years, 1914–1918, the world produced six million tons of copper, more than half the total nineteenth century production, but at substantially higher prices which encouraged copper expansion in Africa and Latin America. As the chief supplier of petroleum and copper the U.S. benefited from war orders, but rapid depletion of home reserves to meet foreign military requirements aroused concern in Washington. The director of the U.S. Geological Survey, for instance, predicted this country's domestic oil reserves would last only eighteen years more. It appeared that America's resource base was one of the war's casualties.[27]

Interestingly, the wartime surge in commodity prices coincided with the final phase of a long-term upswing. Economist N. D. Kondratieff, who developed a theory of long waves, believed that capitalist economies are subject to fifty-year cycles in output and prices, and the period 1914–1920 coincided with a peak similar to other raw-materials peaks in the 1870s and early 1970s, but with an intermediate peak about 1950. Kondratieff himself seemed to discount such exogenous factors as wars to explain these price fluctuations, but he never elaborated his own explanation. Certainly, war was not solely responsible for the surge in commodity prices, because the costs of fuels and metals were rising before the outbreak of World War I, especially in 1912 and 1913. Yet the world political conflict did seem to reinforce this upward price trend, pushing metals prices to a peak in 1917. Undoubtedly, the sudden upward shift in demand caused by wartime purchasing requirements fueled the rise in metals prices. In petroleum the price surge did not end with World War I but continued into the 1920s, reflecting the perceived shortage of petroleum after World War I demand hastened depletion of U.S. oil fields.[28]

Wartime dislocations also caused serious problems elsewhere in the metals industry—especially for zinc, a widely used metal employed along with copper to make brass. In 1913 the U.S. had produced and consumed about 35 percent of the world's zinc output. But other large quantities of zinc-ore concentrate travelled from ore deposits in Australia, Spain, and Italy to zinc smelters in northern Europe along the Belgian frontier. When the outbreak of fighting and disruption of international trade left a shortage of zinc smelting capacity, and when smelting margins soared from $10 per ton to more than $100 per ton in June 1915, American producers doubled their smelting capacity in two years. As a result, U.S. exports of zinc climbed from only 15,000 tons in 1913 to 200,000 tons in 1916. But this rapid expansion left an oversupply of smelting capacity at the end of the war. The contraction harmed American smelters, in particular, for they failed to consolidate a hold on the world market during World War I when the North Americans declined to offer long-term purchase contracts for high-grade Australian ore.[29]

A different type of problem emerged with ferroalloys and certain other metals which the U.S. normally imported in large quantity. Under the stimulus of higher prices resulting from expanded demand for war materials and from shortages of shipping space, the American mining industry boosted its production of high-cost, low-grade, small-quantity deposits, especially of chromite, tungsten, quicksilver, manganese, and antimony. The problems of domestic manganese and chromite producers reflected these trends. Before the war the U.S. imported almost all its manganese from India, Brazil, and Russia, for nearly fourteen pounds of high-grade manganese was required to produce a single ton of steel. Greater demand for steel to manufacture armaments as well as the closing of the Dardanelles, which left Russia without a gateway to ship its manganese to the industrial West, prompted consuming nations, including the U.S., to search in desperation for alternative supplies. This country quadrupled its imports from Brazil—from 114,000 long tons in 1914 to 513,000 long tons in 1917—and also developed Cuba as a secondary source of manganese ore in the Western Hemisphere. It was difficult and dangerous to rely on Brazilian supplies exclusively, for German submarine attacks on American shipping and inadequate supplies of coal for transporting the Brazilian manganese to ocean ports endangered this supply line early in 1917. As a result domestic producers, sheltered from foreign competition, sought to take advantage of higher manganese prices. Indeed, while the average price jumped from $10.39 per long ton in 1914 to $35.00 per long ton in 1918, domestic production climbed to the point where it actually supplied 38 percent of this country's high-grade manganese needs, a truly remarkable performance for an industry nonexistent in 1913.[30]

The chromite situation resembled that of manganese. In 1913 the U.S. produced less than 1 percent of its chromite requirements, importing the remainder from New Caledonia and Rhodesia. As the average domestic price jumped upward from $14.75 in 1914 to $47.99 in 1918, and as wartime government bureaucracies sought to hold down imports in order to save scarce shipping, domestic chromite production climbed disproportionately to the point where the U.S. soon supplied 44 percent of its own consumption. In both mining industries—chromium and manganese—a combination of wartime shortage and government policies intended to conserve shipping stimulated high-cost domestic production. And as the war moved to a conclusion, the miners looked to Congress for protection against low-cost foreign competition and for other sorts of relief.[31]

Domestic miners had reason for complaint. Hastily created government agencies, intended to regulate the private sector and coordinate economic mobilization, first encouraged the domestic minerals industry to expand production of low-grade ores and then, without adequate warning or provisions for adjustment assistance, permitted

imports to undercut the new American producers. Part of this con-
fusion and contradiction grew out of a conflict between the War
Shipping Board and the War Industries Board. Initially, the Committee on Mineral Imports and Exports, an affiliate of the shipping
board, had forbidden certain mineral imports—chromite, pyrite, and
manganese among others—in order to conserve shipping space in the
face of an aggressive German submarine campaign in 1917. Professional geologists like Charles Leith advocated this position, recognizing it would stimulate development of lower-grade domestic ores
during the military emergency. The net effect, Leith later claimed,
was "the saving during 1918 of upward of one million tons of shipping and the promulgation of official acts, which, had the war continued, would have saved more than two million tons of shipping in
1919."[32]

Geologists like Leith and Spurr, who labored to conserve shipping
space and stimulate the rapid building of a domestic minerals industry, resented the hasty action of Bernard Baruch, powerful chairman of the War Industries Board, who took a contradictory course
of action. Concerned about boosting total supplies at minimum cost,
Baruch forced a showdown with the Committee on Mineral Imports
and Exports, and the South Carolina financier authorized the use of
neutral shipping for obtaining high-grade foreign ores as well as for
importing these metals as ballast and backhaul on outbound ships.
More sensitive to the difficulties of the infant U.S. mining industry
than to the problems of obtaining high-quality raw materials for industrial consumers of manganese and chromium, Spurr criticized
Baruch's moves as "opportunism," but he conceded "Mr. Baruch
was a good provider." Unfortunately, "what he provided for in the
way of copper still hangs over the world's copper markets as the
surplus stocks." The flood of chromite imports, which Baruch encouraged, frustrated Interior Department efforts to stimulate domestic production and it left many domestic miners with a bitter memory
and a conviction that Washington had deceived the minerals industry
when it encouraged rapid expansion to meet wartime shortages.[33]

Fundamentally, the controversy was this: whether to stimulate
domestic high-cost production behind the shipping embargo as an
emergency measure or to rely instead on limited imports plus domestic production. It involved a clash between the Interior Department,
a proponent of domestic production and a strong, self-reliant miner-

War Industries
mining concerns.
problems of its
special interests
er, the War In-
of utilizing low-
ality steel. The
ought to develop
dizing home pro-
oided overexpan-
e minerals prices
Not surprisingly,
partment believed
mmendations. For
r Clarkson, wrote
licy was . . . fully
ruch and the War
d thus embittering
expand production
Washington as the
urgently for tariff

d Western minerals
the federal govern-
fully persuaded Con-
ganese imports, even
ically less than 1 per-
was the War Miner-
more important mea-
e, pyrite, manganese,
government for re-
n had awarded over

rces for war use had
States. First, scientists
itical implications of
d of competing nation-
s situation objectively,
telligent decisions, the

geologists conducted a W
Bureau of Mines, which
concerning political and co
terials. These accounts, whi
Lansing took to Paris for
Washington for the first ti
industries, both in this coun t
lay back of this capital.''
Spurr drew from the invest
United Kingdom had a stro
"A combination of these tw
world control of minerals,
trol." [36]

Second, what American
to those involved in domestio
time skeleton organizations a
himself concluded this count r
and stockpile vital raw materi
And third, the minerals
al assets and understood the
dence in a world where crucia
manganese, all vital to steel pr
deposits, hoped to advise Pro
Allied leaders during the Paris
construct a better world than t
other experts discussed raw-m
the British government in Wa
sentatives knowledgeable and f
national minerals problems. Rec
possessed more than a dozen
minerals—needed by the Centra
proposed an arrangement amon
surpluses of these key materials
In brief, the British visualized
strument for compelling the Ge
have according to the desires o
parallel interest in minerals contr
ment, Leith drew unfavorable co

chromite producers reflected these trends. Before the war the U.S. imported almost all its manganese from India, Brazil, and Russia, for nearly fourteen pounds of high-grade manganese was required to produce a single ton of steel. Greater demand for steel to manufacture armaments as well as the closing of the Dardanelles, which left Russia without a gateway to ship its manganese to the industrial West, prompted consuming nations, including the U.S., to search in desperation for alternative supplies. This country quadrupled its imports from Brazil—from 114,000 long tons in 1914 to 513,000 long tons in 1917—and also developed Cuba as a secondary source of manganese ore in the Western Hemisphere. It was difficult and dangerous to rely on Brazilian supplies exclusively, for German submarine attacks on American shipping and inadequate supplies of coal for transporting the Brazilian manganese to ocean ports endangered this supply line early in 1917. As a result domestic producers, sheltered from foreign competition, sought to take advantage of higher manganese prices. Indeed, while the average price jumped from $10.39 per long ton in 1914 to $35.00 per long ton in 1918, domestic production climbed to the point where it actually supplied 38 percent of this country's high-grade manganese needs, a truly remarkable performance for an industry nonexistent in 1913.[30]

The chromite situation resembled that of manganese. In 1913 the U.S. produced less than 1 percent of its chromite requirements, importing the remainder from New Caledonia and Rhodesia. As the average domestic price jumped upward from $14.75 in 1914 to $47.99 in 1918, and as wartime government bureaucracies sought to hold down imports in order to save scarce shipping, domestic chromite production climbed disproportionately to the point where the U.S. soon supplied 44 percent of its own consumption. In both mining industries—chromium and manganese—a combination of wartime shortage and government policies intended to conserve shipping stimulated high-cost domestic production. And as the war moved to a conclusion, the miners looked to Congress for protection against low-cost foreign competition and for other sorts of relief.[31]

Domestic miners had reason for complaint. Hastily created government agencies, intended to regulate the private sector and coordinate economic mobilization, first encouraged the domestic minerals industry to expand production of low-grade ores and then, without adequate warning or provisions for adjustment assistance, permitted

imports to undercut the new American producers. Part of this con-
fusion and contradiction grew out of a conflict between the War
Shipping Board and the War Industries Board. Initially, the Committee on Mineral Imports and Exports, an affiliate of the shipping
board, had forbidden certain mineral imports—chromite, pyrite, and
manganese among others—in order to conserve shipping space in the
face of an aggressive German submarine campaign in 1917. Professional geologists like Charles Leith advocated this position, recognizing it would stimulate development of lower-grade domestic ores
during the military emergency. The net effect, Leith later claimed,
was "the saving during 1918 of upward of one million tons of shipping and the promulgation of official acts, which, had the war continued, would have saved more than two million tons of shipping in
1919."[32]

Geologists like Leith and Spurr, who labored to conserve shipping
space and stimulate the rapid building of a domestic minerals industry, resented the hasty action of Bernard Baruch, powerful chairman of the War Industries Board, who took a contradictory course
of action. Concerned about boosting total supplies at minimum cost,
Baruch forced a showdown with the Committee on Mineral Imports
and Exports, and the South Carolina financier authorized the use of
neutral shipping for obtaining high-grade foreign ores as well as for
importing these metals as ballast and backhaul on outbound ships.
More sensitive to the difficulties of the infant U.S. mining industry
than to the problems of obtaining high-quality raw materials for industrial consumers of manganese and chromium, Spurr criticized
Baruch's moves as "opportunism," but he conceded "Mr. Baruch
was a good provider." Unfortunately, "what he provided for in the
way of copper still hangs over the world's copper markets as the
surplus stocks." The flood of chromite imports, which Baruch encouraged, frustrated Interior Department efforts to stimulate domestic production and it left many domestic miners with a bitter memory
and a conviction that Washington had deceived the minerals industry
when it encouraged rapid expansion to meet wartime shortages.[33]

Fundamentally, the controversy was this: whether to stimulate
domestic high-cost production behind the shipping embargo as an
emergency measure or to rely instead on limited imports plus domestic production. It involved a clash between the Interior Department,
a proponent of domestic production and a strong, self-reliant miner-

als industry, and the temporary mobilization czar, the War Industries Board, which reflected industrial needs more than mining concerns. Each agency tended, naturally enough, to reflect the problems of its leading constituency, and neither sought to advance special interests over the national interest, as they perceived it. Rather, the War Industries Board was concerned about exorbitant costs of utilizing low-quality American ores for production of high-quality steel. The Bureau of Mines and the Geological Survey both sought to develop a consistent minerals policy, one which while subsidizing home producers for the extent of the war emergency still avoided overexpansion and surplus supply, which could only reduce minerals prices sharply and dislocate the domestic mining industry. Not surprisingly, both the War Industries Board and the Interior Department believed postwar experiences justified their own earlier recommendations. For instance, Baruch's principal defender, Grosvenor Clarkson, wrote that the "wisdom of the War Industries Board policy was . . . fully justified." And, not surprisingly, Spurr blamed Baruch and the War Industries Board for disrupting minerals prices, and thus embittering miners whom the government had encouraged to expand production of low-grade ores at premium prices. Identifying Washington as the source of their problems, the miners petitioned urgently for tariff protection and federal compensation.[34]

With the political muscle of a well-organized Western minerals bloc, domestic producers gained some relief from the federal government. For instance, manganese producers successfully persuaded Congress to clamp a 1 cent per pound duty on manganese imports, even though before the war the U.S. produced domestically less than 1 percent of this ferroalloy required. Also important was the War Minerals Relief Act, a measure passed as a rider to a more important measure, but one that enabled producers of chrome, pyrite, manganese, and tungsten to docket 1,268 claims against the government for relief. By September 1926, the claims commission had awarded over $7 million, dealing with claimants liberally.[35]

These experiences with mobilizing resources for war use had several salutary consequences for the United States. First, scientists and some policymakers confronted the political implications of mounting economic interdependence in a world of competing nation-states. Anxious to evaluate the global minerals situation objectively, so that top-level policymakers might make intelligent decisions, the geologists conducted a War Minerals Investigation, directed by the Bureau of Mines, which generated a series of professional studies concerning political and commercial control of important war materials. These accounts, which, incidentally, Secretary of State Robert Lansing took to Paris for postwar peace deliberations, informed Washington for the first time "what capital controlled key mineral industries, both in this country and abroad, and what political control lay back of this capital." Perhaps the most important conclusion Spurr drew from the investigation was that both the U.S. and the United Kingdom had a strong grip on the world's mineral industries. "A combination of these two countries would amount to a practical world control of minerals, and, with France, a little stronger control."[36]

Second, what American involvement in World War I revealed to those involved in domestic mobilization was the need for peacetime skeleton organizations and systematic planning. Bernard Baruch himself concluded this country should keep arms plants in readiness and stockpile vital raw materials.

And third, the minerals professionals who studied world mineral assets and understood the implications of economic interdependence in a world where crucial ores, such as chromium, nickel, and manganese, all vital to steel production, came from only two or three deposits, hoped to advise President Woodrow Wilson and other Allied leaders during the Paris peace deliberations of 1919. Eager to construct a better world than the one that erupted in 1914, Leith and other experts discussed raw-material issues with representatives of the British government in Washington and found the king's representatives knowledgeable and forward-thinking with regard to international minerals problems. Recognizing, for instance, that the Allies possessed more than a dozen essential commodities—including six minerals—needed by the Central Powers in normal times, the British proposed an arrangement among the Allies to distribute exportable surpluses of these key materials in a fashion likely to ensure peace. In brief, the British visualized raw-materials controls as a potent instrument for compelling the Germans to pay reparations and to behave according to the desires of the victors. Unable to generate a parallel interest in minerals controls at high levels of the U.S. government, Leith drew unfavorable comparisons between British concern and his own government's apathy. "It is of interest to note that high officials of the British government then saw and probably still see the significant relations of raw materials to world peace. There is indication that the British government is using such information intelligently in guiding its own course in world affairs," he said later.[37]

Because Leith would later serve as minerals adviser to the American peace delegation and would accompany President Wilson to Paris, his thoughts on postwar relationships deserve careful examination. Basically, he was a careful thinker, one aware of the interrelated scientific, political, and economic issues at stake. The Wisconsin geologist realized that the U.S. faced a critical choice. Should it continue wartime efforts to achieve the greatest possible level of self-sufficiency? Or should the U.S.—either for direct material benefit or as a contribution to global stability in the postwar years—help underwrite some type of international solution, permitting maximum resource specialization among independent nations and perhaps involving provisions for joint minerals controls designed to discourage outbreak of a future war?

On the one hand, there were powerful and appealing arguments for self-sufficiency. Shipping controls and government minerals policy encouraged domestic producers of manganese, chromium, tungsten, and other materials to expand production from low-grade ores; but now, as the hostilities ceased, these high-cost producers faced stiff foreign competition and wanted Congress to grant permanent protection from low-cost foreign minerals. Leith knew, in addition, that this country far more than other nations could protect its vital resource interests outside a League of Nations peace structure, for the U.S. had a potential exportable surplus of minerals approximating $1 billion. This country, by contrast, imported only about $175 million annually in minerals. Against America's strong position as a rich supplier of energy and other raw materials, Britain, France, and Italy had a greater dependence on outside suppliers. Together these states exported $325 million and imported $265 million in minerals. But, without the U.S. continuing to buy the cheapest and highest quality materials on the world market, not only would the U.S. have trouble selling its own exports but also foreign nations would encounter export difficulties. Recognizing that minerals and trade restrictions invited conflict among nations, Leith analogized that if each state of the U.S. sought to become self-sustaining in minerals, "the result would be to increase largely the chances of interstate friction and to lower efficiency in the United States as a whole."[38]

Believing that protectionism contradicted the basic principles of international specialization, Leith also conceded the U.S. had an obligation to provide temporary assistance to minerals producers who had invested heavily in Western mines during the military emergency. And, so long as shipping remained in short supply and rates stayed high, this factor would offer a measure of temporary protection to bulky commodities like manganese, though not to high-priced minerals like tungsten. What Leith feared, however, was that legitimate appeals for tariff protection to shelter some sectors of the mining industry would become generalized, complicating efforts to revive international trade along the lines of greatest efficiency.

After weighing the options, Leith concluded there was no realistic alternative to an internationalist solution for the global minerals problems. First, he noted frequently how high-grade deposits of most minerals occurred in only a few localities, and he knew that in the interest of an efficient use of physical and human resources required to recover the ores, minerals should be obtained from their natural sources of supply, not from low-grade, high-cost deposits sheltered behind walls of government restrictions. Furthermore, he argued that if high-cost minerals producers like the United States attempted to rely on poor-quality domestic supplies of chromite and manganese, this would mean "early exhaustion of local supplies, lowered efficiency in use, and higher cost."[39]

In considering policy options, Leith exhibited keen interest in having an international organization control minerals and other resources, allocating supplies "to the advantage of the greater number of nations rather than to the advantage of the few that are strong enough to dominate the situation and which will in general prevent economic friction from endangering a league of nations based on political and policing considerations." Although an internationalist in outlook, Leith recognized the practical difficulties of referring natural resource issues to an untested world agency, including the concern that such an agency would apply political criteria for allocating resources to a process previously conducted in the economic marketplace subject to the pressures of supply and demand. Also,

Leith recognized the disadvantages of international mechanisms for the U.S., a nation sufficiently rich in resources and powerful political-ly to rely, if necessary, only on domestic resources and bilateral agree-ments with other nations. Finally, such an internationalist solution, however desirable on theoretical grounds, must pass the litmus test of political acceptability. "Whether the time has come to establish a league of nations with economic control can be determined only by our individual and collective answers to the question whether we are willing to make the necessary economic sacrifices, individually and nationally, in the interest of world harmony."[40]

Later Leith had some opportunity to help shape the new world order when he accompanied members of the Inquiry to Paris, serving as a minerals adviser. While he discussed minerals issues with foreign representatives on an informal basis, helped with studies of German reparations discussions, and considered plans for an economic com-mission under League of Nations auspices, the University of Wis-consin geologist, like other economic specialists, became disillusioned. He wrote his wife in the United States: "This is certainly a gay life if one's ideal is nothing to do. We come down to the office in the morning wondering what we will do with ourselves all day. Nearly every one else seems to be in the same boat. There seem to be plenty of problems which will soon absorb our attention but the uncertainty and lack of organization prevent us getting started. In the meantime we read, visit, sleep long hours and eat three large meals a day."[41]

Part of the problem stemmed from the fact that President Wood-row Wilson exhibited no interest in substantive economic or natural resource issues, preoccupied as the president was with his grand de-sign for a League of Nations, a political security association among nations. Leith attributed part of the friction between Clemenceau, the French premier, and Wilson to "the President's failure, or lack of desire, to consider the [economic] situation concretely."[42]

At the center of realistic efforts to devise a durable peace, Leith thought, was the success of a British and French proposal to estab-lish an international economic commission. "I left Paris with a pro-found conviction that the economic commission will be the real League of Nations; that without it the League of Nations will amount to little." Unlike discussion of political and security mecha-nisms, the economic commission was "not a plan looking forward to a hypothetical future situation, but a step taken in absolute self-defense, because of the great economic and commercial problems that are fairly swamping the Paris conference."[43]

Leith left Paris in February disillusioned by "the relative futility of the efforts of what might be supposed to be on the whole the world's strongest group of men to meet the present world-shaking developments." He said, "One gets the impression that individually and collectively they are being tossed about by great elemental forces which they cannot measure or direct. Only a very small proportion of the important problems which came up could receive any consideration whatever." Many important questions were treated casually by exhausted and overworked leaders, and as a result he forecast the deliberations would produce a "patched up peace, a crude plan for the future, which will be assailed from every quarter and which must be regarded only as the barest start, which will require many years to develop into anything like a systematic international machinery."[44]

Despite this frustrating experience Leith, ever idealistic about the ultimate triumph of some form of international cooperation, committed himself to the long-term task of educating "the world to an international viewpoint." Woodrow Wilson's visionary approach Leith distrusted, "but I feel that the stake is so large that such considerations should not prevent our whole hearted aid in the great purpose." He anticipated that "it will take generations to educate the world to an international viewpoint, and it requires an optimist to hope that this may be possible at all." These difficulties and obstacles as well as the "inadequacy of present personnel to meet them should not deter us from making the start." For without some such commitment "there seems to be nothing to prevent the world drifting rapidly into a state of economic chaos in which the germs of future wars will find congenial atmosphere for development."[45]

Out of efforts to wage World War I and create a stable postwar order emerged, among specialists like Charles Kenneth Leith, a conviction that policymakers must awaken to the implications of natural resource interreliance. Both the Allied embargo and German submarine attacks on shipping forced the belligerents to search for secure materials supplies and to experiment with substitutes for the critical imports required to sustain a style of warfare based on modern technology. Previously quantities of domestic coal and iron were sufficient to assure a strong military base for an industrial nation but

World War I demonstrated to all involved the dangers of resource exhaustion, from rapid depletion of iron, copper, and other minerals. It showed the critical importance of new materials, especially nickel, tungsten, and chromium, as well as manganese, the ferroalloys unavailable in adequate quantity and quality in another of the major belligerent nations.

Faced with unprecedented problems of supply and distribution, the industrial states intervened in peacetime market decisions to help obtain vital supplies and promote their distribution for military needs. This growing involvement of governments in private economic decisions marked a return to mercantilism—the philosophy of political economy dominant in the eighteenth century. In effect, as shifting technology widened the resource needs of industrial nations and as more rapid consumption depleted domestic supplies of energy and materials, the world faced a scramble for raw materials, a scramble involving governments as well as private enterprise.

Chapter Two
Dependent America and the Quest for Mineral Self-Sufficiency

IN FORMULATING public policy, "lessons" of previous experiences—especially the traumatic episodes—often influence government officials. Policymakers, like generals, tend to replay the last war, and sometimes these preoccupations with the past discourage the imaginative thinking required to adapt national policies to rapidly changing circumstances. Certainly for the generation in power during World War I, this first mechanized war caught governments unprepared for the acute problems of obtaining vital supplies from extended overseas suppliers. The submarine, ocean mine, and blockade all offered convincing evidence how major powers had become vulnerable to external economic sanctions. Their minds engraved with these lessons, officials of Germany, Britain, Japan, and the U.S. all searched in the 1920s for ways to advance national self-sufficiency and to assure their own country's freedom of action in a future war. The fear of exclusion from overseas supplies rather than the fear of mineral exhaustion (except for petroleum) prompted the world's leading powers to explore a number of divergent policy options. These ranged initially from a search for cooperative solutions within the League of Nations to more nationalistic expedients—including government backing for developing substitute materials and high-cost domestic reserves of scarce materials. Also, the major nations sought to safeguard preferential resource positions in overseas colonial areas.[1]

If policymakers initially worried about shortages and supply disruptions, the marketplace defined a different set of operational conditions—overproduction and depressed prices. Commodity prices began to fall as the war moved to its close. A sharp drop in copper prices, for instance, saw the cost of a pound of this red metal descend from 43 cents in 1918 to 26 cents in 1920, measured in constant dollars. Similarly, tin fell from 156 cents per pound to 72 cents in 1920, although both copper and tin would rally to approach their World War I highs before the Great Depression arrived. The drop in minerals prices reflected a predictable cutback in war-related orders, but it also resulted from an overexpansion of mining capacity and technological improvements. For instance, although the demand for copper climbed during the 1920s, capacity did too. Arrival of new low-cost supplies from mines in Chile, the Belgian Congo, Canada, and Rhodesia helps explain the glut. Technological developments contributed to the zinc industry's problem. A new electrolytic process expanded the opportunities for refining and permitted companies to exploit ore deposits once considered too distant for economical transportation. From a different perspective, depressed prices after World War I coincided with a trough in Kondratieff's long-wave theory. A new round of expansion would occur about twenty years after World War I, in the late 1930s, as industrial nations recuperated from the depression and as military spending began to rise again.[2]

One approach to raw-materials problems involved efforts under League of Nations auspices to regulate trade in raw materials and define terms of access. Convinced that the rivalry for natural resources contributed in an important way to the origins of international conflict, a number of participants at the Paris Peace Conference had offered proposals, ranging from suggestions to remove discriminatory trade barriers—and in one version *all* export and import duties on raw materials—to plans for a raw-materials embargo, which would deter future aggression. In particular, French and Italian delegates assiduously pushed schemes to remove trade barriers, while the British toyed with a joint Anglo-American raw-materials sanction employed at League of Nations direction. These initiatives, however compelling to their advocates, failed to attract the sympathetic support of President Woodrow Wilson, who resolutely concentrated on winning world support for his political association of nations without seeming to recognize how important parallel economic and financial arrangements were to the effectiveness of any international organization.

Postwar economic conditions also encouraged interest in international solutions to raw-materials problems. After World War I many European countries had inadequate supplies of domestic resources and insufficient means to purchase reconstruction materials abroad so as to rehabilitate their own industries and national economies. And a number of international conferences focused on the problems of inadequate supply and distribution. At the first International Labour Organization Conference, held in Washington late in 1919, Italian delegates unsuccessfully sponsored a resolution urging a permanent League of Nations Commission to promote the "just distribution" of raw materials among countries in accordance with their needs. Similarly, the International Congress of Miners unanimously approved a resolution in August 1920 calling for an international office for distribution of fuel, ores, and other raw materials. In June 1920 the International Chamber of Commerce debated raw-materials problems and passed another resolution calling for expanded production of raw materials, an agency to assemble output data, preferential treatment for Allied countries in the allocation of raw materials, and recognition of the dangers of international price discrimination and monopoly abuses as affecting materials prices. Ironically, these discussions and debates occurred as raw-materials shortages eased and as the world economy entered a sharp depression in 1921, an acute slowdown characterized by excessive production and inadequate consumption of raw materials. Like generals preparing for the last war, delegates to world conventions railed against the dangers of resource shortages, and neglected to prepare for the opposite conditions.[3]

At the Brussels Financial Conference in 1920 and the tenth session of the League of Nations Council in October 1920, Italian delegates again took the lead in pushing for international investigations of the problems of "have-not" nations in obtaining raw materials and purchasing them. Self-interest, as well as a commitment to international cooperation, shaped Italian perspectives, for this Mediterranean country lacked almost all minerals, except zinc, necessary for industrial life. Understandably, Italy railed against international trusts and monopolies, and it also objected to the notion that raw materials belonged to a nation having political control, insisting instead that minerals belonged to the whole world. These positions conflicted with British interests, and London's spokesman Arthur Balfour vigorously disputed the Italian claim. As he put it, somewhat bluntly, the capital equipment and skill to mine coal were "at least as great as those required for the growth of vines: and if it be said that only in certain parts of the world coal can be extracted, it is quite as true to say that only in certain parts of the world can vines or olives be grown."[4]

Despite differences separating raw-material producing and consuming nations, these discussions produced agreement that the League of Nations Economic and Financial Committee should sponsor an examination of the entire raw-materials question, including the sensitive issue of monopolies. The international agency selected Italian professor Corrado Gini to undertake the investigation, and his report, issued in August 1921 after the collapse of commodity prices, reached controversial conclusions. Because the League undertook its study largely to appease insistent groups of workers who wanted international supervision of monopolies and raw materials, observers might have anticipated Gini would offer suggestions calling for some form of international supervision. But the Italian professor did not. He considered, and dismissed, two broad options: one, the nationalist solution, which rested on achieving national self-sufficiency through territorial adjustments; and two, the so-called socialist, or statist, solution, which rested on creation of an international bureaucracy to acquire and distribute raw materials equitably. From Gini's perspective the former option threatened the sound economic principle of specialization according to comparative advantage in peacetime, while the latter rested on the false notion that international bureaucracies could effectively establish prices and distribute materials. While Gini doubted the world was then willing to adopt complete freedom of trade, a prescription which would allow market forces to adjust supply and demand, he nonetheless suggested specific steps to promote a free-trade regime. These recommendations included measures to discourage use of restrictive export duties, to eliminate monopolistic practices, and to assure equal opportunities for trade and commerce to all League members in every mandated territory.[5]

The Economic and Financial Committee lacked authority to implement these proposals, but it did approve the Gini report, even though the conditions of scarcity which prompted the original investigation no longer prevailed, except in a few areas where nations still lacked adequate credit and foreign exchange to purchase reconstruction materials. The League of Nations committee took a firm stand against export restrictions, warning material producing nations against allowing such measures of economic defense to "degenerate into measures of economic aggression." Conceding it had no information linking international monopolies to the problems of obtaining raw materials, the League study group nonetheless announced firm opposition to any controlled distribution of raw materials, in part because any regulatory scheme must necessarily involve "the international control of the whole internal economic life of the countries concerned."[6]

Gini's report did not defuse the commodity controversy; the issue resurfaced at the Genoa Economic Conference in 1922. There the Soviet delegates once again urged a socialist solution, namely "a systematic and organised distribution of these raw materials," so that reconstruction might proceed, but the Russian panacea failed to capture widespread support. Instead, the conference merely approved more resolutions condemning excessive export duties on raw materials and urging general adoption of the most-favored-nation principle in commercial relations, a device intended to reduce discriminatory trade.[7]

Predictably enough, discussions of the raw-material problems generated an avalanche of rhetoric and resolutions but little substantive achievement in the early 1920s. There was little international organization could do but discuss these matters. The problems of consuming countries, such as Italy, after World War I stemmed from currency maladjustments, and only after central bankers offered leadership for the task of achieving a general stabilization of currencies in 1924 and 1925, could conditions develop conducive to stable currency rates and international capital movements. And as international economic conditions improved, major commodity exporting nations could gradually relax their own duties and restrictions, at least briefly. Instead of shortages the 1920s saw acute commodity surpluses resulting from overextended production; and these conditions of distress, as well as political uncertainties, invited new forms of private and governmental controls on access to key deposits of vital materials.[8]

All attempts to achieve internationally-guaranteed access to vital raw materials foundered on the rocks of rival national interests, and, as a result, both the victorious Allies and the defeated Central Powers took independent steps to cope with raw-materials shortages and the dangers of overreliance on other nations. For Germany the situation was especially acute. This industrial nation, once the dominant steel producing nation on the European continent, lost 80 percent of its iron ore production, about 30 percent of its steel facilities, and 30 percent of its coal production in the peace settlement. Faced with French military occupation of the industrial Ruhr, Germany undertook a course of reconstruction that saw the emergence of strong industrial combinations, such as Vereinigte Stahlwerke A.G. in the steel industry and I.G. Farbenindustrie in chemicals. So as to reduce reliance on the iron ores of Lorraine, now under French political control, Germany negotiated long-term contracts to buy low-phosphorus iron ore from Sweden and Newfoundland. Meanwhile, German technology achieved successes in producing substitute and synthetic materials, including magnesium and aluminum—especially electron, a magnesium-aluminum alloy. Also, German scientists developed the Haber process for removing nitrogen from the air, and a process for producing synthetic oil by the hydrogenation of coal. Concerned too about supplies of copper, about 35 percent of which came from the United States before World War I, Germany developed its capacity to resmelt metals and the government provided financial aid to subsidize a high-cost domestic producer of copper, the Mansfelder Kupferchieferbergbau A.G. From these tentative efforts to cope with raw-material dependence would come more ambitious plans in the Nazi era to heighten rapidly Germany's self-sufficiency as preparation for war. In 1929, however, Germany needed to import 80 percent of its iron ore, the bulk from Sweden and Spain, and 85 percent of its oil (the remaining 15 percent came from domestic and synthetic sources). Also, Germany remained dependent on imports for all other ferroalloys, except for some low-quality manganese from domestic suppliers.[9]

Like its neighbor Germany, France also depended heavily on raw-material imports, including large quantities of copper, lead, zinc, and the ferroalloys, as well as nickel and chrome from its South Pacific colony of New Caledonia. And, like Germany, the lessons of World War I counselled French policymakers to make better provisions for a future war. Partly as a contingency plan against possible loss of Lorraine ores, the French government developed low-phosphorus iron deposits in Morocco and Algeria. Also, France began to stockpile copper, manganese, and certain other strategic metals during the mid-1920s, steps that caused considerable comment in mining circles. Sensitive, too, to the dangers of overreliance on the unpredictable United States for both crude petroleum and refined oil products, Paris at first contracted for U.S. petroleum companies to build refineries on the European continent, and then the French demanded that the new facilities refine Rumanian and Middle East crude oil, actions that helped lessen French reliance on North American crude oil.[10]

Competition for secure supplies to sustain the iron and steel industries of the major industrial powers temporarily benefited the new Soviet government in Russia. That regime, eager to undertake an ambitious development plan but lacking adequate technical and engineering personnel, granted a concession to American capital, as part of the so-called Harriman syndicate, to develop a manganese deposit in the Caucasus region east of the Black Sea. Before World War I the Krupp interests from Germany exploited this field, but the Soviets, apparently anxious to balance competing capitalist interests, arranged for American investors, including the banking house of W. A. Harriman and the Bethlehem Steel Company, to gain the preponderant interest in a manganese mining concession that would soon abort. The Soviet government imposed a $4 per ton tax on the ore, an amount which together with high labor costs made the concession financially unattractive to the American corporation. As a result, the Harrimans soon negotiated a new contract transferring the concession back to the Soviet government.[11]

The Far East was not a region of primary concern to the mineral importing nations of the North Atlantic during the 1920s. Except for tin and rubber, as well as tungsten and some other specialty items, this area was considered inferior to regions closer to industrial centers. Leith summarized a common view among geologists when he wrote that Far Eastern nations lacked "an adequate basis for independent industrial development." Such pessimistic forecasts did not discourage the development-minded Japanese, who inhabited an island conspicuously deficient in iron ore, high-grade coking coal, and petroleum. They continued to cast covetous eyes on the iron, timber, and petroleum deposits of Manchuria and Siberia.[12]

For Great Britain, center of the world's most extensive empire and hub of international finance and commerce, World War I was also a searing experience. On paper the British Empire contained enormous reserves of vital minerals—including Malayan tin, Australian lead and zinc, Canadian nickel and asbestos, Burmese tungsten, and Rhodesian copper and chromite. But London awoke to discover that enemies and potential rivals had penetrated its store of minerals. German business interests had contracts "covering nearly the whole of the Australian output of copper, lead, and zinc," reported the official Dominions Royal Commission in 1917. Tungsten, found in Burma, Australia, and New Zealand, all in the British Empire, flowed to Germany, where it was processed and then sold to the English steel industry. And the United Kingdom found that the Dominion of Canada's vital supplies of nickel and asbestos moved commercially to the United States where these materials were processed, and sometimes reexported to countries outside the English-speaking world, such as Germany. Britain also discovered the potential dangers of depending on areas outside its political bloc for vital materials—such as petroleum and cotton, both obtained primarily from the United States.[13]

How should London lock the imperial door? The Dominions Royal Commission suggested in 1917 the direction British policy would follow in the 1920s when it stated: "We regard it as vital that the Empire's supplies of raw materials and commodities essential to its safety and well-being should be, as far as possible, independent of outside control." Specifically, this panel urged a coordinated mineral survey of the empire to determine, in part, "whether workable deposits exist of such minerals as quicksilver, platinum, borax and potash, which are at present obtained almost solely from foreign sources." Petroleum and cotton received special attention. Asserting that the United States and Russia both withheld portions of their own oil reserves for naval purposes, the commission suggested taking steps to set aside some oil-bearing regions in the empire for possible defense needs. Noting "the dependence of the Empire, and indeed of the world, on the United States of America . . . for 70 percent of the cotton crop of the world" the commission recommended efforts to develop cotton in tropical parts of the empire, such as India, Egypt, Africa, and the West Indies, as well as Australia and the Union of South Africa. To encourage production of materials within the empire, the report suggested bounties, government purchases at a minimum price, preferential purchasing of imperial materials, and restrictions on foreign control. Noting how Canada and New Zealand restricted foreign investments in petroleum, the study commission suggested "these clauses might be applied more widely and by other Governments of the Empire, not only to petroleum but also to other minerals if there is reason to apprehend that effective control might pass into foreign hands." It recommended such clauses to safeguard the oil-bearing shales of New Brunswick and Crown forest lands.[14]

Britain also used export controls to strengthen its global resource position against potential rivals. Although the United States consumed about 50 percent of the world's tin, it produced almost none at home—depending on quality ore from Malaya and the Dutch Indies. As a result, Britain smelted the bulk of world tin production at home, in Australia or Malaya. To keep the United States from obtaining the high-grade East Asia tin necessary to develop an independent smelting capacity in North America, the British in 1903 imposed a heavy export tax on all ore exported from Malaya, to prevent the United States Steel Company from profitably operating a smelting plant in Bayonne, New Jersey. But World War I gave the Americans an opportunity to break the British stranglehold. A shortage of shipping facilities temporarily enabled the American Smelting and Refining Company to build a plant at Perth Amboy, New Jersey, and a few years later in 1918 a British firm joined with the National Lead Company to construct a smelter at Jamaica Bay, Long Island. These facilities rested on use of Bolivian ore, but after the war, when Britain no longer wanted competition from American-based smelters, the British smelters cut by half the price of smelting Bolivian ores, effectively making the Perth Amboy plant uncompetitive. To prevent the Americans from obtaining quality Nigerian ore, which was mixed with impure South American tin for smelting, London again threatened to impose a preferential export duty, as it had in Malaya. These moves effectively undercut efforts to establish an independent tin industry in North America. Similarly, the British took action during the 1920s to safeguard Canada's timber resources. Canadian provinces clamped embargoes on timber and pulpwood to prevent that dominion's raw materials from going to American saw mills and pulp mills until, at least, an intermediate stage of production occurred in Canada.[15]

After the war American policymakers also observed a perceptible erosion of Britain's longtime support for an open door policy in dependent areas. That policy, which emerged late in the nineteenth century when Britain and the United States sought to protect China against the designs of other imperial nations, provided equality of treatment—regarding import and export duties and similar commercial matters—for *all* nations, including the colonial power. While the

United States would vigorously assert this principle in the 1920s, Britain's own enthusiasm for free competition faded, as the empire abandoned its historic commitment to free trade, erected a commonwealth preferential system which discriminated against foreign commerce and encouraged closer ties between Britain and its dependencies, and ultimately abandoned the gold standard (in September 1931), a move marking in an important way London's decline as a financial center. Efforts to consolidate its imperial resources, to safeguard tin smelting in Southeast Asia, to protect Canadian forest lands, and to support rubber prices, created serious conflicts with the United States. But none of these conflicts aroused more attention than the joint Anglo-French move to exclude Standard Oil of New Jersey from Middle East mandates assigned to the two European countries by the League of Nations. Eager to reduce their own reliance on North American suppliers and realizing that the world war hastened depletion of North American oil reserves, some British oil experts forecast that soon the United States might turn to Britain for its oil requirements. "At $2 per bbl.—a low figure—that means an annual payment of $1,000,000,000 perannum, most if not all of which will find its way into British pockets," asserted Sir E. Mackay Edgar. After protracted and intense negotiations United States oil firms obtained a foothold in the rich Iraq fields in 1926, a share that would lead to even more extensive American involvements over succeeding decades.[16]

The State Department, naturally enough, interpreted the breakthrough, that is, "equitable participation of a group of American oil companies in the Turkish Petroleum Company," as a triumph for the open door principle, offering equality of treatment in mandated territories. In this episode Washington successfully invoked the principles of John Hay to keep British and French firms from jointly cornering petroleum supplies outside the Western Hemisphere on which the United States might become dependent in future years. Elsewhere, Washington also used diplomatic pressure to contain Britain's petroleum investments in the Western Hemisphere and to acquire leases for American-based oil firms in the petroleum-rich Dutch Indies, an initiative that remained controversial for many years. The Dutch government, although eager to reward Britain with oil leases in return for naval protection in the Asian region, preferred to maintain a double standard, fearful, the Hague claimed, that any American participation would establish precedent for also extending concessions to the petroleum-hungry Japanese in the extended overseas empire.[17]

Elsewhere, the open door principle was often honored in the breach, for during the postwar decade many governments, including the United States, imposed nationalistic restrictions to discourage investment in colonial areas, or portions of the national domain. The United States, for instance, restricted foreign access to resources held in the public domain, but continued to permit foreigners to invest in private land holdings. A number of foreign countries went further, nationalizing domestic resources or sharply regulating private investments in mineral resources. Mexico, for example, nationalized all oil concessions, declaring subsurface resources the property of the state. And, in the most extreme act of nationalization, the new Soviet government dispossessed private owners and imposed complete state control over all Russian mineral resources.[18]

Around the world, this growth of government involvement in minerals industries represented a new closed door, a euphemism for measures restricting foreign participation in domestic minerals industries. In Canada and the United States such state encroachment seemed relatively mild in the 1920s, but in France, Russia, and Japan "any alien activity in mineral resources" was the exception, involving a special deal with the government. To overcome closed door restrictions, British and American companies, especially in the sensitive energy area, increasingly resorted to government pressure for their own advantage.[19]

While the continental countries looked to self-sufficiency and substitution as the principal instruments for guarding against future materials shortages, and the island seagoing empires, namely Japan and Britain, turned to imperial self-sufficiency, the United States responded differently. The leading producer and consumer of raw materials in the world, the United States, blessed with its own bountiful resources, was unaccustomed to depending on outside materials suppliers in peacetime, and the American public remained relatively insensitive to how changing technological and political conditions dictated a new concern for secure foreign supplies. One prominent citizen who sought to educate the large popular audience was William C. Redfield, formerly secretary of commerce in the Wilson administration, who published a book in 1926 with the arresting title, *De-*

pendent America. Determined to show the average citizen how nations had become mutually dependent, Redfield warned against becoming so "auto-intoxicated with an illusive vision of our country's self-sufficient status, that we are reluctant to face realities." There were thirty materials, he said, including such items as antimony, chromium, manganese, mica, nickel, rubber, tin, and tungsten, in which the United States produced insufficient quantities to meet even its own peacetime requirements.[20]

Among trained minerals specialists—such as Leith, Smith, and Spurr—a different approach emerged, for these experts sought to influence not the general public but rather key domestic interests, such as the mining industry, and the policy-oriented elite. In articles for *Foreign Relations*, a new journal devoted to international affairs, in meetings held under the auspices of the recently-founded Council on Foreign Relations, and in summer seminars such as the Williamstown Institute of Politics (which brought together a constituency each summer in the Berkshire hills of Massachusetts to discuss critical issues), Leith and others sought to alert influential citizens to the mineral necessities of international relations. Convinced, too, that the United States government and minerals industry needed a comprehensive minerals plan, based on a thorough inventory of domestic resources and on official support for United States firms operating abroad, the small group of specialists organized a blue-ribbon panel to prepare a set of principles that might guide United States policymakers. At the invitation of Spurr, now president of the Mining and Metallurgical Society of America, Leith organized the panel, including both government and private mining engineers and geologists. Among them were H. Foster Bain, director of the U.S. Bureau of Mines, and George Otis Smith, director of the U.S. Geological Survey.[21]

In November 1921, this prestigious study group released a statement of the fundamental principles to which nations should subscribe if the world was to use resources efficiently and avoid international conflicts. These principles, incidentally, were the very ones Leith emphasized repeatedly in his public and private comments—and contained the points Leith and his disciples sought to engrave in the public memory. First, the specialists noted, mineral resources were "wasting assets fixed geographically by nature." Because the distribution of ore deposits varied widely—for instance, aluminum and iron appeared commonly in the earth's crust, while copper and the ferroalloys occurred in only a few widely dispersed high-grade deposits—no country could rely exclusively on its own resources. Consequently, "international exchange of minerals cannot be avoided if all parts of the world are to be supplied with needed materials." Second, national restrictions, such as legislative enactments, duties, embargoes, and the like, could not divert or close channels of international exchange without provoking unnecessary friction among nations. Third, minerals should be concentrated, smelted, or fabricated near sources of supply in order to reduce bulk and to benefit mineral suppliers, except in instances of excessive local costs.[22]

Other recommendations concerned mineral exploration and overseas development of primary materials in backward areas. As a fourth point, the group favored "freedom of exploration" so that the private mineral industry might replenish ore reserves depleted by production, thus meeting the growing needs for higher per capita consumption in years ahead. Except in time of war, governments should not restrict equal mining opportunities and discriminate against foreign producers. Fifth, convinced mineral demand would translate into political pressure on backward nations, the specialists proposed joint action to assure equal access not only to the government applying pressure but also to all nationals. "Disregard of this principle has been the cause of much international friction," Leith and his colleagues declared.[23]

Finally, to achieve these principles the experts favored more active United States government action to secure equal access for American mining firms as well as to protect United States firms in their operations abroad. Here, they said, the United States should follow the example of other governments in protecting their own corporate citizens. The report recommended against general use of import restrictions to curb foreign mineral sales in the American market, for these obstacles seemed likely to accelerate depletion of domestic mineral resources as well as to impose an unnecessary cost in efficiency and money on American consumers. In tone the minerals report was clearly internationalist. The United States should actively pursue equal opportunity abroad—the open door principle—so as to conserve its own low-grade resources. Because they were sensitive to wasting assets and the limited distribution of quality ore deposits, the specialists opposed subsidizing high-cost domestic mining except where clear evidence pointed to the conclusion that protection would help develop a strong and efficient domestic industry. The report mentioned flake graphite as one example of a mineral meriting protection, but it mentioned no others—not copper, manganese, chromium, or tungsten, the industries lobbying strenuously for political assistance. The specialists clearly believed that these metals, especially the latter three, must come from high-grade foreign deposits.

In defense of these free-trade-like conclusions, the minerals committee later emphasized that "a wise national policy should in general favor the free use of foreign sources of supply of minerals which we do not have in adequate quantities, in order to conserve our own resources; that if we long continue on our present policy of exploiting our resources to the utmost, regardless of their limitations, some of them will be soon exhausted, making the United States entirely dependent upon other countries for these minerals in times of peace—and dangerously dependent in times of war." [24]

At a time when domestic mining interests bombarded Congress for tariff protection, the scientists also sought to shape national policy in the metals area, and thus their investigations extended beyond glowing statements of principle to concrete recommendations, which ordinarily conformed closely to internationalist ideas. Subcommittee reports on antimony, chromium, and manganese urged stockpiling, not protection, to guard the United States against the dangers of dependence on foreign suppliers. Concerned that supplies of antimony (a lustrous silver white metal used in antifriction bearings and shrapnel lead) could be cut off if a belligerent—perhaps Japan or Great Britain—shut off shipments from China, then the world's principal supplier, the specialists urged using proceeds of a domestic tariff to purchase a stockpile of 4,000 tons. This quantity would meet United States needs for six months, and would cost about $750,000. Another report on chromium concluded that while this country had ore reserves sufficient for about twelve years normal supply—and it anticipated further exploration might increase these reserves materially—the federal government should not resort to import protection. A duty on chromium would "only result in the speedy exhaustion of the better grade and more readily accessible ore bodies and leave this country in time of war dependent upon those ore bodies which even with a high import duty cannot compete in peace time and upon such overseas importations as could be made during a war." [25]

In view of intense lobbying in behalf of a tariff shelter for American manganese producers, the subcommittee report on this mineral aroused controversy. The scientists, concerned about apparently inadequate domestic supplies of high-quality ferromanganese, containing 78 to 82 percent manganese and employed as a deoxidizer in steel production, recommended building a war emergency stockpile of 600,000 tons over a period of six to nine years, a supply thought likely to meet steel production demands for about two years at World War I levels. Also, Leith's experts favored further investigation of substituting spiegel and high-manganese pig-iron for ferro in order to economize on manganese supply requirements. Government, while encouraging technological advances, should maintain a perpetual inventory of domestic manganese resources, and it should discourage artificial stimuli in peacetime which, in effect, would "simply tend to deplete an already extremely limited reserve of ferro grade and chemical ore." [26]

This comprehensive minerals report served a useful purpose, forcing industry and government to consider systematically the implications of resource depletion in an interdependent world where all nations seeking a higher standard of living inevitably exchanged products—both manufactured goods and raw materials—with other countries. The report failed to achieve Leith's immediate goal—the development of a national minerals policy. Part of this failure stemmed from irreconcilable differences among mining companies themselves and among consumers of mineral products. For instance, at this time copper, lead, and zinc producers generally put protection high on their list of priorities in order to block serious foreign competition, but producers of sulfur and coal, who competed easily in world markets, generally favored national policies likely to bring about removal of foreign barriers to U.S. mineral exports. American mining companies, eager to protect existing investments, understandably viewed the Leith report as an idealistic, free-trade document, one insufficiently receptive to the advantages of encouraging a strong domestic industry, even though the quality of American ores might prove inferior to external supplies. Some producers, especially the powerful manganese lobby, even insisted protection would lead to a self-supporting domestic industry, but scientists said such claims lacked credible evidence which would justify infant-industry protection.[27]

Pressure for protection reached a peak in 1922 when a Republican president and Congress approved the Fordney-McCumber Tariff, a measure imposing stiff duties on many materials previously on the free list. The measure clamped a $1 per ton duty on imported bauxite, partly to protect Arkansas producers. Even so, imports of bauxite continued upward and in 1925, for the first time, exceeded domestic production. Exhaustion of domestic ores and the opening of new ore deposits in Surinam and British Guiana would demonstrate that protection failed to achieve a self-sustaining industry. Manganese producers also won a temporary victory in 1922, and the new tariff provided a 1¢ per pound duty, an amount equivalent to 100 percent protection. Despite assurances that this protection would create a thriving domestic industry, the results proved disappointing, as the experts anticipated. At first the protection sheltered domestic industry and it revived enough to capture 10 percent of the American market, but the more rapid depletion of domestic ores at higher prices did not lead to discovery of new reserves. On the eve of World War II, one minerals expert wrote: "The experience of the past 10 years has pretty definitely shown that a tariff of approximately 100 percent has not and can not promote the development of the domestic industry to anything like the extent that its advocates predicted."[28]

But tungsten offered a different story, and a high level of protection here probably maintained a volatile industry, so that the United States had some domestic base to meet its gargantuan appetite during World War II. Although tungsten remained on the free list from 1913 to 1922, political pressure led to a 45¢ per pound duty on ore in 1922, an amount equivalent to 476 percent duty. This move sheltered domestic industry from the cheap Chinese supply, and although the tariff imposed a heavy burden on U.S. consumers it may have served a long-run national interest, since there were no other major supplies available within the Western Hemisphere, except for isolated Bolivia.[29]

Where Leith and the other metallurgical engineers exerted influence during the interwar period, in addition to their public educational efforts, was with military planners. As a result of Bernard Baruch's recommendation that a group of officials engage in peacetime studies making plans for obtaining raw materials and distributing these during war, the National Defense Act of June 4, 1920 placed responsibility for planning industrial mobilization in the office of the Assistant Secretary of War. In this office the planning branch, directed by Col. H. B. Ferguson, established fifty-four commodity committees composed of supply officials, but with advice from the Bureau of Mines. Out of this work emerged early lists of strategic materials, defined in the early 1920s as "raw materials essential to the prosecution of a war, which cannot be procured in sufficient quantities from domestic sources, and for which no satisfactory domestic substitute has been found." Later, in 1932, a new category would emerge for "critical materials," which would be less difficult to secure than strategic materials because they were either less essential or more obtainable in adequate quantities from domestic sources.[30]

Military materials planning moved slowly, partly because of personnel shifts, and in March 1928, Assistant Secretary C. B. Robbins invited Leith, Col. Arthur Dwight, and Dr. J. E. Spurr, the latter two affiliated with the major engineering associations, to join a Mineral Advisory Commission intended to discuss changes in world movements of minerals, changes in domestic supplies of minerals, and other topics related to mobilization requirements. Exposed to the military commodity reports, which incidentally drew heavily from the work of Leith and other minerals specialists in the early 1920s, the University of Wisconsin geologist was "impressed by their general excellence," but he noted how the minerals plans failed to correspond to the color plans, which the military planners devised to prepare for different contingencies. For example, War Plan ORANGE envisioned a Japanese-American war in the Pacific. The commodity work, however, all began with the "assumption of early elimination of imports, whereas there seems to me a high degree of probability that for almost every commodity imports in some part will continue." But procurement planning continued to lack the flexible assumptions demonstrated in the rainbow war plans. In August 1933, Lt. Col. C. T. Harris, Jr. pointed out "the only time that all sea lanes would be closed effectively would be in a war against a combination of nations having naval supremacy," that is, in all likelihood an Anglo-Japanese coalition. Even under these conditions, Harris argued, "coffee from Brazil, wood from South America, manganese from Cuba, tin from Bolivia, and leather from South America, would unquestionably seep into this country in appreciable quantities." Until the early 1930s materials assumptions rested on the circumstances envisaged shortly after World War I, a hostile Anglo-Japanese coalition. Although the dissolution of this alliance at the Washington Conference in 1921–1922 helped to puncture the idea of a war against Great Britain and Japan, the RED-ORANGE Plans, based on this premise, remained the foundation for commodity planning.[31]

While defense officials contemplated future mobilization requirements and imagined ways to achieve self-sufficiency in wartime, peacetime economic conditions in the 1920s offered further evidence of how mineral interdependence subjected industrial nations to outside political and economic pressure. Overexpansion of minerals industries during World War I climaxed in the early 1920s with slumping commodity prices. The recession as well as a reopening of established shipping patterns exposed high-cost domestic producers to intense foreign competition, and many, experiencing economic difficulties, turned to their governments for assistance. As a League of Nations study showed, "surplus productive capacity and often huge excess stocks were . . . the direct legacy of the war." And these, in turn, spawned a number of private and governmental restrictions on the flow of raw materials, a trend reminiscent of the mercantilistic intervention characterizing eighteenth century commerce. In the 1920s, as in earlier times, governments appreciated the short-run advantages of imposing controls. Not only would restrictions cushion economic adjustments at home, it was thought, but also they might strengthen the national resource position at the expense of rivals. But for a country exposed to such mercantilistic restrictions there were unilateral techniques for defense, as the American experience during this decade illustrated.[32]

A variety of government restrictions flourished after the war to protect producers experiencing the frustrations of acute supply and demand fluctuations, and many of these affected the United States directly. While some nations clamped export taxes on minerals, the United States Constitution forbade export duties. Consequently, some American firms turned to other instruments of government protection to stabilize their industry and artificially boost prices of exported products. In 1918 Congress passed the Webb-Pomerene Act which exempted export trade associations from prohibitions of the existing antitrust laws so long as the export combinations did not seek to restrict competition at home. This law, passed primarily to aid small businesses to compete with large foreign combinations, provided an opportunity for copper firms to organize the world market. American firms organized a copper-export association at first to liquidate excess World War I stocks, and then they combined again in October 1926. This time the American firms brought in foreign firms as nonvoting associates, effectively controlling 95 percent of the world's output of refined copper in order to fix prices. At that time copper hovered about 15 cents per pound and rose as high as 24 cents per pound before the depression. A League of Nations study later concluded that the high prices stimulated overexpansion, especially in Chile and Africa, "so that the industry entered the depression in a state of hopeless over-expansion." United States government officials tolerated the copper combine, in part because American capital controlled about 75 percent of world mine production, but the copper monopoly disintegrated early in the depression before a Federal Trade Commission investigation considering its effect on domestic prices was completed.[33]

A number of commodity-control schemes flourished in the 1920s, but the three most bothersome for American consumers of industrial raw materials were in potash, nitrates, and rubber. For years the principal world supply of potash, a fertilizer popularly known to make starches and sugars, came from Germany and France, where a syndicate ruthlessly utilized national political power to control supplies reaching the world market. The syndicate controlled 95 percent of the world's potash, and the United States took about 30 percent of this supply, making America dependent on the monopoly in times of peace and war. Cut off from the European supplies during World War I, potash prices rocketed upward from $35 a ton in prewar times to over $400 a ton in 1917 and 1918. Frantic efforts to produce a domestic industry in war years led to extensive exploration of the West and to the use of salines in Nebraska, Utah, and California. What resulted was discovery of the vast subterranean potash beds of Texas and New Mexico, which soon began to supply American needs and permit the United States to export potash in competition with the German cartel.[34]

Similarly, nitrogen, another fertilizer, was controlled by a national monopoly—made possible because Chile had the world's largest supply of agricultural nitrogen. The Chilean government took an active role in activities of the Chilean Nitrate Producers' Association, and it collected an export tax, which constituted nearly 40 percent of Chilean governmental revenues and was passed along to the ultimate consumers in foreign nations. World War I disrupted the Atlantic supply route to continental Europe, and Germany, hard pressed for agricultural nitrates, developed the Haber process to remove nitrogen from the air. After the conflict modifications in the process suitable to commercial use effectively destroyed the natural monopoly Chile employed for national advantage.[35]

For the average American what dramatized the pernicious impact of foreign commodity restrictions was the rising price of rubber, resulting from a British government plan to restrict output in Malaysia in order to reduce excessive stockpiles accumulated at the end of World War I. Using prohibitive export duties, shipments were limited to a prescribed percentage of production, and alterations in the percentage reflected quarterly changes in the price of rubber. With rising demand for rubber tires rubber prices shot upward, as the United States automobile industry expanded rapidly through the successful efforts of Henry Ford to mass merchandise the Model T. Prices rose from 45 cents per pound in May 1925 to $1.21 per pound in July, arousing protests in the United States, the world's principal consumer of rubber.[36]

What these restrictions, and others, did was to place consuming nations temporarily at the mercy of outside economic monopolies, often sanctioned, or at least tolerated, by governments. How could world consuming nations cope with foreign cartels and government export restrictions? This question occupied the headlines and invited a congressional investigation. Recognizing the opportunities of reaping the political benefits, or alternatively bearing the onus for inaction, Secretary of Commerce Herbert Hoover launched a crusade against foreign cartels. He told the House Committee on Interstate and Foreign Commerce in January 1926 that nine governmentally controlled combinations—including Egyptian cotton, camphor, coffee, iodine, mercury, nitrates, potash, rubber, and sisal—had boosted prices so that American consumers would probably pay $1.2 billion for imports in 1926. This amount, he estimated, would cost Americans $500 to $800 million above reasonable prices. And, if the United States failed to counteract the monopolistic combinations then in existence, Hoover anticipated other such restrictive agreements would emerge. "There are some 20 or 30 other commodities in the world which could likewise be controlled by action of one government or by agreement between two governments," he stated.[37]

A number of weapons were available for attacking the cartels, and these included loss of diplomatic representation, reprisals against other governments, denial of loans, antitrust prosecutions, efforts to promote conservation at home, substitution of other products for the controlled item, and production in new areas outside foreign control. The United States government employed all of these techniques, and Hoover later claimed his efforts succeeded, stimulating production in other countries and the use of substitutes at home, so that in "five years' time all controlled materials except one were overproduced and sold at a loss by the producer." Specifically, the Commerce Department encouraged rubber conservation at home and production of rubber in non-British territory, thus helping to drive the price of rubber from $1.21 per pound to under 20¢ per pound. Similarly, Hoover indicated that his efforts to secure appropriations for drilling potential potash deposits in Texas and New Mexico ultimately relieved American consumers from the oppression of the German potash cartels and soon this country was actually exporting that fertilizer to the cartel's former markets. To undercut the Brazilian coffee cartel, Hoover and the State Department jointly took steps to discourage credits to the Brazilian coffee valorization program from the New York financial market, although the Brazilians ultimately managed to borrow in London. Higher nitrate prices stimulated synthetic production in the United States, while, after efforts to prosecute the Mexican sisal combination, the federal government sought to undercut the Mexican control scheme by developing alternative sources of supply in Cuba. These and other defensive measures, Hoover claimed, helped the United States cope with restrictive schemes—and they provide excellent case studies of how a powerful nation can exert pressure on a commodity-control scheme incompatible with its own interest.[38]

As champion of consumer interests the ambitious Hoover delighted in trumpeting his successes, but some businessmen and newspapers questioned the propriety and effectiveness of his actions. New York bankers doubted the benefit derived from denying American private loans to the German potash cartel and the Brazilian coffee valorization plan, because in closing the New York loan windows to Brazilian and German borrowers, the government instead made business for British private bankers. Hoover replied to these charges with the statement that "government owes some considerable responsibility to safeguard the interests of the general consuming public." A respected international economist also publicly questioned the results of Hoover's crusade against the cartels. Jacob Viner, a University of Chicago economist, suggested Hoover's public campaign against the Stevenson rubber-control scheme simply nourished a public panic and produced a sharp rise in rubber prices after Hoover attacked the rubber cartel publicly. Then, claimed Viner, when the effects of official publicity wore off, and the public took a clearer view of the situation, "it soon became apparent that the power of the export control over prices had been overestimated."[39]

Whatever the merit of Hoover's claims, it seems in retrospect that unilateral American action had only temporary effect on producers' combinations, and these restrictive schemes would survive, despite serious losses in the depression years. There was a resurgence of control schemes in the late 1930s as producers again sought to drive up raw-material prices. In the last analysis probably only effective international action, through the League of Nations, offered a permanent solution to restrictive practices, but during the interwar period the United States remained outside the collective international framework. And even with American membership it is speculative how successful efforts to devise acceptable international arrangements would have been, given doubts about the efficacy of commodity agreements.

The League of Nations, nonetheless, remained a forum for systematic consideration of commercial restrictions, and in 1927 the World Economic Conference, held in Geneva, enabled the world organization to contemplate economic remedies. Again, in keeping with the preoccupation of the 1920s with tariff barriers, delegates focused on problems relating to tariff liberalization, and initially it seemed they might concentrate on raw-materials controls, for in opening statements American and British delegates exchanged sharp comments on rubber restrictions. Any prospect for coordinated international action in this area died in committee, however, for a key working group opted first to consider difficult and controversial import tariffs. After laborious negotiations and considerable bickering on this item, the delegates were too exhausted, and they chose simply to draft hastily some provisions dealing with export duties. Reflecting no detailed consideration, these statements simply reiterated the principle of nondiscrimination and favored low duties, if states felt obligated to invoke any restrictions. The language also cautioned against international control agreements, indicating that they could check technical progress, endanger important sections of society, and harm particular countries. Also, these obstacles to commerce could encourage monopolistic tendencies and the application of unsound business methods. They should not "lead to an artificial rise in prices, which would injure consumers."[40]

Historians sometimes interpret the 1920s as a transitional decade, in which United States diplomacy exhibited conflicting patterns. On one level, the Senate rejected membership in the League of Nations and the voices of isolationism successfully thwarted other efforts to collaborate with the League of Nations. But, if George Washington's recommendations to avoid entanglement in European affairs gained a new life after the agony of intervention in World War I, other integrative forces compelled American diplomats and financial leaders to forge new bonds of cooperation with foreign powers. These extended from limited attempts to regulate the naval arms race to central-bank collaboration for the purposes of stabilizing major currencies and coping with the vexing war debt and reparations problems.

Similarly, for the United States the 1920s marked an important transition in natural resource policies, as this industrial power became more reliant on foreign suppliers. Previously, the U.S. had relied primarily on its own natural resources for development. Indeed, for the period 1900 to 1929 this nation produced at home 96 percent of all the minerals it consumed, and traded on an equal basis for the rest. While the complexity of modern industry created new demands for materials like manganese, chromite, tungsten, nickel, asbestos and other materials unavailable in adequate quantity and quality within the United States, growing industrialization and interdependence in the global economy enabled the United States to export large quantities of its own minerals, including copper, lead, zinc, petroleum, phosphate, and sulfur. Despite the strong materials position, disturbing trends were emerging. For instance, during the decade of the 1920s imports of iron and ferroalloy ores began to surpass exports, and the same pattern prevailed for other metal ores. Whereas America exported over 2 percent of its domestic consumption of iron and ferroalloy ores during the preceding decade, and nearly 10 percent of other metal ores, the figures changed dramatically during the postwar decade. Now the U.S. imported 4 percent of domestic consumption for ferroalloy ores and iron and 11 percent of other metal ores. It was an ominous trend, reflecting the gradual transition of the United States from its role as a global supplier to its emerging position as a dependent consumer of world primary products. Incidentally, these figures offer persuasive evidence to counter the claim that the United States achieved industrial dominance by consuming mineral resources from the rest of the world. This pattern did not apply to the United States, for the North American economic giant became a net importer of raw materials only after reaching a dominant economic position. And, in the process of promoting domestic economic development, this country exported large quantities of industrial raw materials, including petroleum, copper, and other minerals.[41]

Along with growing United States reliance on international trade to meet raw-material needs, there were other important trends shaping this country's vital interests and, ultimately, its diplomacy. For one thing, the postwar economic recovery revived consumption of established materials, such as iron and copper, as well as a range of new materials. Economic geologist Charles Leith noted in 1931 how the United States mined and consumed more minerals in the last twenty years than in its preceding history. Per capita consumption, he observed, multiplied fifteen times in only forty years. "A single Lake Superior iron mine now produces every two weeks a volume of ore equivalent to the Great Pyramid of Egypt, which required the toil of vast hordes for several decades and has been long regarded as one of the most stupendous works of man." Not only had the production and consumption of iron, copper, and zinc, to name a few metals, exceeded levels reached in the entire nineteenth century, but also introduction of new energy fuels—oil and gas—along with such established power sources as coal and water had substantially increased industry's capacity to complete work. Improved technology, allowing more efficient use of fuels, permitted U.S. production to rise 70 percent from 1913 to 1928 while energy consumed increased only 38 percent.[42]

During the 1920s expanded demand for established materials tended to converge on a few high-quality accessible sources of supply in the North Atlantic region. Iron, an element abundant in the earth's crust and available on all continents, came principally from deposits in the industrialized world—Lake Superior and Alabama in the United States, Scandinavia, the region near Luxembourg, as well as portions of England and northern Spain. In these regions two-thirds of the world's coking coal was also recovered, and the co-existence of iron and coal, together with a favorable industrial cli-mate, encouraged growth of the iron and steel industry. As Leith noted, 90 percent of the world's steel-making capacity was confined to three regions—the United States, Britain, and the Ruhr.[43]

Similar patterns of concentration appeared in other sections of the mining industry. Among fossil fuels, for instance, the United States retained its premiere position in 1929, producing 68 percent of the world's petroleum supply, more than the 65 percent produced in 1913 even though world production had quadrupled. In coal the United States held approximately the same position in 1929 (35 per-cent) as it did in 1913 (39 percent). And as a producer of copper the United States continued to provide 48 percent of the world's sup-ply, compared to 56 percent in 1913, even though new ore deposits in Rhodesia and the Congo threatened to challenge a dominant Ameri-can position in world copper mining. Mounting demand for ferro-alloys also converged on a few key suppliers outside the home territories of any major world power. For instance, the global steel in-dustry relied on a few limited districts in India, southern Russia, the Gold Coast of Africa, and Brazil for high quality ore. Chromite came primarily from Rhodesia, India, and New Caledonia. Nickel was mined almost entirely in Canada. Peru supplied the bulk of the world's vanadium supply, and China produced most of the tungsten. What this commercial pattern displayed, Leith observed, was that "about thirty of the principal mineral districts account for over three-fourths of the value of the world's mineral production."[44]

In the 1920s a new pattern of commercial interdependence bound nations, for nearly a third of the world's mineral tonnage moved across international boundaries—much of this material iron, coal, and petroleum. For consuming nations, especially those lacking abundant reserves of natural resources, these trends had ominous political and security implications. The United States and Great Brit-ain controlled access, commercially and militarily, to the world's richest mineral reserves. The two dominant English-speaking coun-tries controlled 53 percent of the world's coal reserves, 48 percent of iron, 76 percent of petroleum, 79 percent of copper, 81 percent of lead, and 74 percent of zinc. Among the major strategic materials, Germany dominated only the potash industry, a monopoly which proved short-lived as the United States government encouraged efforts to develop major deposits around Carlsbad, New Mexico. Anglo-American ownership, as well as these countries' dominant sea position, meant that in a future political confrontation the two North Atlantic seafaring nations could deprive landlocked continental belligerents of critical supplies.[45]

Despite the apparent Anglo-American shared dominance of world mining, the United States, not Great Britain, was emerging as the principal source of capital and managerial talent to develop new mineral reserves. Between 1919 and 1929, America's direct foreign investments nearly doubled, growing from $4,880 million to $7,553 million. And, while direct investments in manufacturing and petroleum displayed the greatest increases, the book value of mining investments climbed from $876 million to $1,227 million—much of this sum in Canada ($318 million) and South America ($528 million).[46]

Along with a concentration of mineral resources under Anglo-American political control, the 1920s also witnessed a parallel trend toward private concentration and monopoly over the production and processing of natural resources. A variety of factors shaped this pattern, including technological advances as well as the desire of producers to control prices and production in order to stabilize markets. Potash and nitrate monopolies preceded World War I, and soon these arrangements extended to many of the newer materials as well. In 1929 commercial monopolies dominated production of nickel, vanadium, aluminum, potash, asbestos, mercury, diamonds, bismuth, sulphur, and natural nitrates. Concentration also occurred in copper, iron, lead, petroleum, tin, and manganese. Leith discovered that two companies—Anaconda and Kennecott—controlled 34 percent of the world's copper production, while five major oil companies, led by Standard Oil of New Jersey and its British-backed rival, Royal Dutch–Shell, supplied 35 percent of the world's petroleum. These monopolies and cartels, often operating independently of national political power, established the prices and terms of trade for key industries vital to the prosperity and defense of independent states, raising serious problems about the coexistence of private and public power. In the minerals industry there was a growing trend to horizontal integration, as the large vertically integrated companies, which had previously unified both mining and processing under one corporate management, increasingly sought to diversify their own sources of supply. These moves offered a hedge against exhausting a single major deposit and against the danger of exclusion from other world reserves. The competition for manganese provided a good example of these maneuvers, for that material, critical in steel production, existed far from major steel-producing centers in North America and Western Europe. Concerned about future supply availabilities, corporations from the major industrial areas converged on a few known sources of supply—the English in India and the Gold Coast, the Germans in Nikopol, and the Americans in Soviet Georgia, India, the Gold Coast, and Brazil. While the Americans reached a business arrangement with British firms to mine manganese deposits within the British Empire, a similar struggle for copper reserves involved a national test of wills, since London feared the strength of a U.S.-dominated copper-export association. In general, although some British and American observers viewed this competition as one for national survival and global dominance, the two English-speaking nations and their nationals operated more as competitors than as mortal rivals. Leith observed that commercial firms of other countries were "hopelessly outdistanced" in this intense quest for ore.[47]

As the 1920s moved to a close, the world minerals industry, like the international economy, confronted a series of problems involving complicated political and security matters as well as economics. To minerals specialists like Leith and other geologists in the United States and Great Britain, the situation warranted a comprehensive study to evaluate the world's mineral resources and suggest a United States mineral policy. After consulting with a representative of the British Empire Mining and Metallurgical Council, Leith organized the study in conjunction with the prestigious American Institute of Mining and Metallurgical Engineers and other associated groups, including the Council on Foreign Relations. And in a revealing move Leith, the Wilsonian-internationalist, designated the group the Mineral Inquiry. If Leith hoped to formulate the basic principles for resolving minerals problems, he soon discovered that circumstances were unfavorable for policy initiatives in this area. For one thing, as he wrote later, any solution to mineral problems depends "in the last analysis on eliminating fear." He conceded "the problem of minerals in international relations is so complex that progress is likely to be slow."[48]

The Mineral Inquiry did not reach definite conclusions, but Leith presented a set of tentative conclusions that would hopefully guide future discussions, and perhaps influence national policies. These included revisions of established internationalist proposals, encouraging "wider adoption of the open-door policy" and "reciprocity arrangements through readjustments of tariff, exchange, and other restrictive measures." Also, the Mineral Inquiry recommended a practical solution for the vexing war debts–transfer problem. The United States should accept critical raw materials, such as manganese, chromium, mercury, mica, tin, nickel, rubber, tungsten, cobalt, radium, and coconut shells. This stockpile would serve as a form of "national insurance," allowing the U.S. to "convert part of the debt into materials and lay them aside." These and other principles, Leith emphasized, would give this country no "unfair advantages over other nations," because the suggestions afforded a "reasonable basis for any international understandings that may become necessary in the minerals field."[49]

Rising demand and the increasing supply interdependence of industrial areas tended to integrate national economies into a single world market, but science and technology again strengthened the hands of mineral consumers, especially in Western Europe and North America. What technology offered was more efficient utilization of scarce minerals and a variety of substitutes which, together, eased the pressure on finite mineral resources and limited, to a degree, the monopolistic power of cartels and other restrictive measures. During the postwar decade, for example, increasing use of scrap metal, especially copper and iron, helped hold down the demand for ore. In 1922 a glut of copper scrap forced primary producers to shut down for ten months, so that over the period 1920–1923 more than 60 percent of copper sold came from scrap. Also, development of ferrous alloys permitted more economical use of iron in steel production as the quality of steel improved. These alloys also helped prolong the useful life of minerals, and other improvements in engineering designs made possible significant weight reductions in structural materials without sacrificing strength.[50]

A parallel search for mineral substitutes also pushed more than thirty-four new materials beyond the experimental stage during the interwar period—and many of these also came primarily from foreign suppliers. Among the new minerals found only in a few rich deposits around the world were beryllium, an alloy with copper, obtained from beryl ore located in Argentina and Brazil, and industrial diamonds found in Africa and Brazil. New light metals, such as lithium and magnesium, made their appearance. Quartz crystal, important for radio and telephones, came from Brazil; and radium, located in Canada and the Belgian Congo, gained new use for medicinal and luminous purposes. What these new materials did was both to offer industrial economies greater flexibility, for aluminum and other light metals could substitute for steel in some uses, and also greater dependence. Previously the web of global trade was confined largely to steel-making alloys, plus a few other bulky metals, like copper, lead, zinc, and tin. Improved technology conserved older established metals, but it did so, in part, by expanding reliance on substitute materials. But since many of these were imported, the quest for substitutes paradoxically left the U.S. more reliant on foreign suppliers.[51]

From a different perspective the 1920s witnessed all of the problems and issues that would complicate international politics in the future. Sensitive to the dangers of excessive reliance on foreign materials supply, the major powers looked for ways to strengthen their own economic and military positions. In particular, Britain and the United States competed openly for scarce quantities of petroleum, and their minerals producers battled to establish secure supply positions in other metals. At the same time the 1920s witnessed an awakening of nationalism as Mexico and the Soviet Union took drastic action to restrict outside investments, and other states experimented with taxes and controls. Beneath the competition of governments and cartels was changing technology, making the world community even more dependent on foreign materials but also giving modern industrial states, like Britain, Germany, and the U.S., greater economic flexibility to substitute for foreign materials. These conflicting patterns undoubtedly puzzled average citizens, but Herbert Hoover's public crusade against the cartels emphasized—although briefly—how national interdependence and individual prosperity offered both opportunities and perils.

Chapter Three
Minerals and the
Origins of World War II

IN EXPLAINING the outbreak of the Second World War, modern historians emphasize such underlying factors as militarism, nationalism, imperialism, and racism. Each contributed importantly to the combustible world climate of 1937–1939. Scholarly accounts show convincingly how Prussian and Japanese militarism generated an expansionist mentality, and how the other basic forces made their own contributions to a bellicose mood. The German nation, its ambitions frustrated repeatedly, set out again to dominate the continent, assure primacy of the Teutonic race, and achieve world empire. Under Nazi leadership the quest for racial purity led both to territorial expansionism and to the blatant persecution of Jews, whom Adolph Hitler blamed repeatedly for Germany's defeat in 1918. Similar themes influenced the Asian political scene where Japan, another latecomer to industrialization, turned to force as the instrument for establishing its regional primacy. And even Italy's Benito Mussolini amused and aroused the world with similar nationalistic and racial pronouncements, couched in terms that appealed emotionally to his followers.[1]

What standard explanations of the war's origins often neglect, however, is how underlying material difficulties contributed to German, Italian, and Japanese expansionism, and a resulting global war. To a degree the problems these countries faced were cyclical, the production of a severe world depression and the resulting contraction of multilateral trade. Certainly for Japan and Germany this trade discrimination disrupted traditional export markets and encouraged a quest for economic autonomy, as, in fact, it did in other industrial countries, including the U.S., where leaders sought to insulate the domestic economy from a global contraction. Had the open international economy, which reemerged in the late 1920s, not disintegrated, Germany, Italy, and Japan might have recovered their national esteem gradually and satisfied national ambitions through peaceful commercial competition and sustained prosperity. This happened after World War II, but not in the early 1930s.[2]

But there was also an important underlying structural problem—the uneven global distribution of raw materials among industrial states—that contributed directly to a collapse of world peace. In earlier times the size of a nation's territory and population, its military forces, and treasury wealth largely determined its comparative power and prestige. But in the twentieth century secure access to a vast quantity and variety of natural resources also became a key determinant of power. Coal, petroleum, iron, and copper, in particular, became the four indispensable materials for defense production and war-making. Smaller quantities of other materials—especially mica, tin, chrome, manganese, nickel, and tungsten—were also vital to national security.[3]

But in the interwar period, leaders of Germany, Italy, and Japan complained vigorously and repeatedly that the uneven distribution of these key materials was both inequitable and intolerable. As late as 1939, Britain and the U.S. did control over three-fourths of all mineral resources, while the three dissatisfied powers held only 11 percent. Except for Germany's ample coal deposits, the Axis lacked adequate energy, especially petroleum. They also had serious deficiencies of other critical materials—copper, the backbone of electrical manufacture, and ferroalloys, essential to steel production.[4]

It is at least arguable that the three industrial latecomers had no actual need to control foreign raw materials—they could easily export industrial products and purchase needed raw materials. This was undoubtedly true, but the notion rested on several premises unacceptable to leaders in Berlin, Rome, and Tokyo. They questioned whether the international economy could avoid periodic depressions, and they saw economic autonomy, or autarky, as a device to isolate the home economy from global disruptions. Furthermore, the international trade option required the three "have-not" countries to accept Anglo-American leadership. Without their own sources for industrial materials, the dissatisfied powers could not hope to challenge effectively the existing world order. They were destined, under this option, to remain in the shadows of Britain and America as second-rate powers. Another option offered a dangerous alternative way to cope with an inadequate domestic resource base and rapid population growth; it was war.

The link between mineral deficiencies and World War II is complicated. Without colonies or rich domestic resources, and facing the serious domestic problem of achieving higher living standards with high population growth, the three concluded independently that war was an acceptable way to achieve a permanent economic solution based on territorial expansion and self-sufficiency. Thus, to succeed in war, Germany and Japan began in the mid-1930s to stockpile vital materials. From their perspective, then, materials were both the vital precondition for successfully waging war and the goal of conquest— sufficient materials to assure long-term self-reliance.

The lack of a diversified domestic minerals base was an important determinant of Italy's interwar foreign policy. Far more than its European neighbors, Germany and France, Italy was a "have-not" nation, reliant on external suppliers of industrial raw materials and vulnerable to outside pressure and sanctions. Italians who aspired to a significant role in world politics chafed at their dependent condition and blamed President Woodrow Wilson and other peacemakers of 1919 for frustrating Italian desires to obtain a dependent colonial empire in Africa. Italian leaders continued to think the acquisition of an empire would realize a burst of glory for Italy comparable to that of the onetime Roman Empire.[5]

In Benito Mussolini Italians had a forceful leader determined to recapture his country's dignity and prestige—through territorial expansion even if it meant war. In numerous public speeches the Fascist leader openly discussed his solution and the considerations behind it. With a population of about 40 million and a narrow, mineral-poor peninsula to inhabit, the land of Julius Caesar faced critical economic adjustments in the 1930s when the pressure of population closed on scarce resources. "We are forty millions," said Mussolini, "squeezed into our narrow but adorable peninsula, with its too many mountains and its soil which cannot nourish so many. There are around Italy countries that have a population smaller than ours and a territory double the size of ours." What were the implications of this position? "It is obvious that the problem of Italian expansion in the world is a problem of life and death for the Italian race," Mussolini argued. "I say expansion: expansion in every sense: moral, political, economic, demographical." In brief, as the Fascist boss stated elsewhere, Italy could only expand or explode—and either option augured difficulties for Italy's foreign neighbors.[6]

More than a materialistic quest for land and raw materials occupied Italian foreign policy. Mussolini also sought to glorify Italian fascism and to attain great power recognition. One vehicle for achieving these goals was his quest for a "New Roman Empire"— one that offered the average Italian a return to glories this southern European nation experienced last under the great Roman rulers. The acquisition of empire elsewhere, perhaps in Africa, would reawaken Italian pride and compel the dominant European powers to accord Italy the consideration deserving to a great power.[7]

The Great Depression offered the daring Mussolini an irresistible opportunity to achieve this dream. On the one hand, Japan's thrust into Manchuria late in 1931 proved how ineffectual the League of Nations was as a collective security mechanism, and the successes of this Asian maritime nation offered an object lesson to dissatisfied nations elsewhere. And, on the other hand, the international economic crisis, disrupting trade and domestic employment in the market economies as it did, generated public discontent and protest, something that Mussolini shrewdly, in the tradition of dictators elsewhere, sought to divert with foreign policy maneuvers. Historian George Baer observed in his *The Coming of the Italian-Ethiopian War*, that Mussolini "repeated the classic maneuver of dictators, to try for success abroad to take people's minds off troubles at home." What Mussolini also calculated was that neither France nor Great Britain had the strength of commitment to League of Nations principles to impose sanctions on Italy. And to discourage further any resort to effective sanctions (such as withholding oil and denying Italy use of the Suez Canal, the vital transportation route between the Mediterranean and the Red Sea), the boastful Italian leader warned loudly of reprisals against southern France and against British fleet dispersions in the Mediterranean.[8]

Italy was vulnerable to tough raw-materials sanctions, dependent as it was on foreign supplies of coal and oil as well as cotton and wool, the nonferrous metals, iron, steel, and copper. How should the League respond to Italy's blatant act of aggression? Members of the League debated this issue at length, and after Mussolini launched his full-scale assault on Ethiopia in late 1935, the Geneva-based world organization finally agreed on sanctions. They would include an embargo on imports of Italian goods, restrictions on war material exported to Italy, and a ban on sales of rubber, bauxite, aluminum, iron, and certain other minerals. From one perspective, it seemed to be a comprehensive set of restrictions, but there was a vital omission—petroleum. Had the great powers, including the United States, agreed to undertake a ban on petroleum sales, the petroleum sanction alone might have achieved the goal—that is, deterrence of aggression. Mussolini told Hitler that an oil sanction would have compelled him to withdraw from Ethiopia within a week. What discouraged effective League of Nations action more than anything else, however, was the concern that petroleum sanctions against Italy would only serve to push the Italian Fascist government closer to Germany, and the objective of Britain and France during 1935 was to isolate Hitler, not strengthen his coalition.[9]

The Italian crisis of 1935 displayed the League of Nations at its weakest, and raised critical questions about the disposition of major powers to apply minerals sanctions, when the prospects for discouraging aggression seemed high. This episode damaged the League of Nations in two respects. First, the League failed to honor the spirit of its charter and take effective action to deter or punish aggression. Second, members of the League displayed an unseemly lack of unity in discussing how the international association should respond to a clear breach of the peace. Like the Manchurian episode, the attack on Ethiopia served mostly to strengthen existing public doubts about the efficacy of the present international organization. Irresolution and division among the major European powers in a position to thwart Mussolini's designs stemmed from the hard-nosed calculation that territorial conquests in Ethiopia would appease Italy's hunger for empire and resources, thus discouraging the Italian Fascists from joining forces with Nazi Germany and supporting a general redistribution of colonies or further territorial conquest. Unfortunately for this scheme, in attempting to drive a wedge between the European dictators, the Anglo-French strategy succeeded only in driving a stake through the heart of the League of Nations collective security mechanism.[10]

Failure of League of Nations sanctions discouraged some advocates of sanctions, but not minerals specialist Charles K. Leith. Leith and Thomas Holland, a British advocate of minerals sanctions, remained convinced that "there seems to exist in mineral raw materials the power for the collective maintenance of law and order." This opinion held, despite the failure of League sanctions in the Ethiopian episode, because the League sanctions were not carefully designed or executed. What Holland and Leith realized was that the United States and the United Kingdom controlled about 75 percent of the world's mineral resources. Consequently, Washington and London had the means to deny potential aggressors access to vital materials regardless of League of Nations opinion.[11]

Ironically, while Mussolini rationalized his expansionist moves in Africa as necessary to secure territory for Italy's surplus population and raw materials for Italian industry, the New Roman Empire failed to fulfill these goals. For one thing, contrary to Mussolini's propaganda, Italy's birthrate was declining, not rising, and emigrating Italians preferred to take new residence in the United States or other developed countries, not participate in a colonial experiment in remote Africa. Secondly, while Mussolini spoke of his colonial riches, and a troop of traveling journalists dutifully reported mountains of iron ore waiting to be developed with Italian technology, this Mediterranean nation lacked enough mining engineers to develop its own limited domestic resources, let alone exploit a self-sufficient mineral empire in Africa. Indeed, throughout the period Italy remained dependent on either the Western Hemisphere or Rumania for oil when petroleum engineers knew of rich oil deposits in another Italian colony, Libya. When foreign oil companies proposed to explore Libya, Fascist officials turned down the offer. Having created an illusion of technological "primacy," Mussolini's regime risked a loss of face if it turned to foreign oil companies for assistance in developing domestic or colonial reserves.[12]

To Germans the frustrations of an inferior position in world politics remained an intolerable burden. Locked geographically between two powerful rivals, France and Soviet Russia, Germans could not escape believing adverse circumstances had thwarted only temporarily their destined emergence as a world power. Their memories of the World War I defeat, the Allied economic blockade, and the French occupation, all rankled in the German consciousness and stiffened a resolve to gain vindication. The German people particularly resented the way the World War I allies insistently pressed their demands for heavy reparations payments while they simultaneously impeded German efforts to boost exports, and thus earn the foreign currencies required to meet international obligations. In such a climate of economic malaise and psychological agitation, it is no wonder the doctrines of a University of Munich geopolitician, Karl Haushofer, received a sympathetic hearing. Haushofer taught a version of environmental determinism, concluding that geographical extension of the German state was necessary to acquire material resources and achieve a dominant global position.[13]

Among those influenced by geopolitics was Adolph Hitler, a single-minded Austrian sign painter-turned-politician, whom Haushofer visited in prison. Hitler, a bright individual with an untrained mind and a gift for oratory, would devise and initiate a burst of territorial aggrandizement intended to remedy permanently Germany's dependent position and achieve both growing space and material resources to satisfy the needs of Germany's increasing population. Hitler also sought to implement his own absurd racial theories glorifying ethnic Germans and discriminating against Jews. His exposure to racial theories in pre–World War I Vienna persuaded Hitler that the German race was engaged in a struggle for survival which the Aryans were destined to win. They would eventually destroy all lesser races, especially the Jews. Territorial expansion, then, was also a device to help purify the European races and gain additional living space for the Aryans. This fanatical preoccupation with racial purification emerges clearly in Goebel's diary: "One must not be sentimental in these matters. If we did not fight the Jews, they would destroy us. It's a life and death struggle between the Aryan race and the Jewish bacillus."[14]

Unlike many politicians who adroitly adapt their own plans to changing circumstances, Hitler resolutely pursued his final solution regardless of obstacles. He was a fanatic. Hitler's early writings and later conversations display a startling continuity of thought regarding his bold plan to extend Germany's territory eastward at the expense of Soviet Russia. Anticipating that Bolshevism, which he identified with international Jewry, would expand westward overwhelming Germany, Hitler resolved to strike first, creating a German empire in the east. This expansion, he believed, would necessarily require the ruthless annihilation of captive peoples who resisted Nazi expansion. Along with his peculiar racial theories, at the core of Hitler's thinking was the conviction that only the Soviet Union had sufficient living space as well as food and raw materials to satisfy Germany's ravenous appetite. To the Nazi leader, war against Russia was an essential, indeed logical, element in the long struggle to establish German hegemony on the continent and reduce reliance on potentially unreliable foreign sources of raw-material supply. It would also benefit the Aryan race.

Repeatedly in public statements Hitler spelled out his vision of German dominance in Eastern Europe and its meaning for the German people. In September 1936, he reportedly told journalists: "If we had at our disposal the Urals, with their incalculable wealth of raw materials, and the forests of Siberia, and if the unending wheat fields of the Ukraine lay within Germany, our country would swim in plenty." During World War II itself he alluded again to this powerful vision. "A fault we must never again commit is to forget, once the war is over, the advantages of the autarkic economy." He continued: "There is no country that can be to a larger extent autarkic than Europe will be. Where is there a region capable of supplying iron of the quality of Ukrainian iron? Where can one find more nickel, more coal, more manganese, more molybdenum?" With the addition of this area, Hitler said: "We shall be the most self-supporting State, in every respect, including cotton, in the world. Timber we shall have in abundance, iron in limitless quantity, the greatest manganese-ore mines in the world, oil—we shall swim in it."[15]

However brutal and diabolical a later generation might consider Hitler's means, few could deny the Nazi leader had a consistent plan with specific objectives. And, had Nazi Germany actually annexed the Ukraine and other designated areas, Hitler's foreign policy might have permanently and decisively improved Germany's geopolitical and resources position in ways that would have enabled the Nazi leader and his chosen successors to play a dominant role in global politics.

During the 1930s many German and foreign officials misinterpreted Hitler's determination to seek a military solution for his country's economic problems. For instance, Hjalmar Schacht, the liberal economist aligned with industrialists, apparently never believed Hitler seriously intended to resort to war in order to break Germany out of its interdependent position in the world economy. On the one hand, Schacht lobbied vigorously for the Nazis to pursue an export-oriented solution to economic prosperity, one based on conservative economic policies at home and acquisition of colonies abroad. And, on the other hand, Schacht urged foreign nations to restore German colonies as a conciliatory gesture. For instance, in a January 1937 article in *Foreign Affairs*, Schacht warned that peace "cannot be preserved without drastic territorial readjustments," and he urged the Allies to provide Germany with colonies, including a return of Tanganyika. In other conversations he hinted Germany wanted access from Belgium to the mineral-rich Congo.[16]

Singlehandedly the liberal economist rebutted claims from Britain and others that Germany did not need colonies because it could easily purchase raw materials on world markets. Schacht retorted: "Germany does not possess the means of paying for them in foreign currencies; and she does not possess the means because foreign countries do not consume enough of her wares." Rejecting, too, any call for national self-sufficiency as an alternative solution, the financial expert claimed it "is opposed to the general principles of civilization" and it "will necessarily lead to a lowering of the standard of life of the German people." But he warned that German leaders had no choice, because "no great nation willingly allows its standard of life and culture to be lowered and no great nation accepts the risk that it will go hungry."[17]

What Schacht sought were territorial readjustments as a peace palliative. He bluntly warned American readers of his article that unless the United States joined in promoting a colonial empire for Germany—not simply the return of lost colonies—Nazi leaders would most certainly embark on their own nationalistic solutions. "There will be no peace in Europe until this problem is solved." To maintain peace, Schacht seemed to say, the Western nations should appease Hitler with colonial territory, but the liberal economist could not guarantee that Hitler would accept territorial adjustments in lieu of a military solution.[18]

Committed to the idea of colonial restitution, Schacht approached representatives of France, the United States, and Great Britain with his peace proposal. French authorities expressed some interest in the idea during a visit to Paris in summer 1936. The Americans turned a deaf ear to Schacht's suggestion that President Roosevelt exercise global leadership and summon another Washington conference to solve, this time, Germany's raw-material needs. But from the British there was greater interest in territorial restitution as part of an overall settlement also involving German and Soviet guarantees for independent nations of Eastern Europe, and a German commitment to participate again in League of Nations activities. There were several obstacles. For one, Neville Chamberlain's British government, like the French government, had questions about the authenticity of Schacht's suggestions, for it was known the little economist differed frequently with more aggressive Nazi officials. Also, London had difficulty devising appropriate territorial compensation, but eventually decided to return certain West African mandates, specifically British and French Togoland and the Cameroons. This proposal, which was delayed by emergence of other important business, eventually lapsed after Hitler himself told Lord Halifax, late in 1937, that he saw no connection between colonial adjustments and European affairs. Chamberlain, however, persisted in efforts to devise a general plan for appeasing Berlin. At one point he considered a new colonial administration in Central Africa, to be established on a demilitarized and international basis from British, French, Belgian, and Portuguese possessions. But the German government declined to spell out specific proposals for stabilizing Central Europe, and after the annexation of Austria early in 1938 colonial adjustments took a back seat to other problems directly affecting European peace. Throughout this phase, while London toyed with offering colonial concessions for continental commitments, Hitler looked for detente with Britain; he proposed abandoning colonial claims if London conceded Berlin a free hand in Europe.[19]

While Hjalmar Schacht assiduously promoted colonial readjustments, perhaps realizing more clearly than Hitler that guaranteed access to raw materials lay at the center of Germany's economic and political malaise, Hitler himself sought a free hand to launch a war against the Soviet Union. Believing, in the last analysis, that Britain and France would jointly block German efforts to acquire colonies and develop healthy and reliable international trade, Hitler concentrated on a military solution. As he put it, "The sword had to stand before the plough and an army before economics."[20]

That Germany must pursue a path toward self-sufficiency in order to reduce its economic vulnerability and prepare for the eventual war against Russia emerged in Hitler's 1936 memorandum outlining a four-year economic program. In this statement the Nazi leader spelled out his conviction that the war would be a series of short hard blows, not a war of attrition like World War I, for Hitler doubted his enemies would allow Germany to prepare adequately for an extended war within his own lifetime. Determined to prepare the German economy and military for a conflict within four years, Hitler proposed a major armaments buildup and use of existing foreign exchange for obtaining whatever materials were required to facilitate the arms preparations. He opposed Schacht's favorite panacea, export expansion, because it would simply delay completion of the arms program. "In four years," said Hitler, "Germany must be completely independent of foreign countries so far as concerns those materials which by any means through German skill, through our chemical and machine industry or through our mining industry we can ourselves produce."[21]

This document was no directive for autarky, or self-sufficiency. Rather Hitler sought to conserve German resources while accumulating vital raw materials from abroad in order to improve prospects for a successful war. "The definitive solution," Hitler said, "lies in an extension of our living space, that is, an extension of the raw materials and food basis of our nation."[22]

How should Germany prepare for the impending conflict? The führer wanted a rapid development of synthetics materials—especially petroleum, synthetic rubber, and other materials. He also favored heavy domestic investment to develop low-grade iron ores, so as to reduce dependence on Scandinavia at whatever cost. Dominating Hitler's approach to economic warfare was his conviction that Germany must develop at home its capabilities to meet wartime needs regardless of the cost. In many ways this program brought stunning successes. Aluminum production increased rapidly, doubling in only three years. Germany also doubled its synthetic oil production capacity and established reserve stockpiles good for perhaps six months. Synthetic rubber technical advances enabled the Third Reich to meet 20 percent of its rubber requirements from synthetic processes. Steel production, a more conventional indicator of industrial might, also revealed the impact of Hitler's plan, as it increased more than 20 percent in three years after 1936. Oddly, although Germany launched a war against Poland with only enough munitions to last six weeks, the industrial economy had sufficient resources to last for a war extending nine to twelve months.[23]

Hitler's military advisers knew better than he that Germany had inadequate military and industrial resources to endure a protracted war of attrition, like World War I. For, despite much talk of insulating the German economy from outside economic pressure, the Third Reich continued to rely heavily on outside suppliers for critical materials. Ten to 20 percent of German foodstuffs came from abroad, two-thirds of its oil, and 80 percent of its rubber. Among the critical ferroalloys used in steel production, Germany had potentially fatal shortcomings. Two-thirds of its critical iron ores came from foreign sources, as did 25 percent of Germany's zinc, 50 percent of its lead, 95 percent of its nickel, and 99 percent of the bauxite used in producing aluminum. Unless Hitler's armies quickly acquired and secured new sources of supply, Germany's prospects for victory—and insulation from the unstable world economy—would falter.[24]

Mineral deficiencies and economic insecurity also contributed in an important way to the expansionist designs of a third nation—Japan. From the late nineteenth century this emerging industrial power aspired to dominate and lead East Asia, but despite rapid economic growth and advancing military capabilities Japan was vulnerable to exogenous disruptions. This ambitious nation lacked a rich and varied domestic minerals base. In particular, Japan had insufficient iron and coking coal for a self-reliant iron and steel industry. Also, Japan lacked adequate petroleum and most other metals with important military applications. According to Thomas Holland, a leading British minerals expert, "The mineral resources of Japan itself are wholly insufficient to meet her industrial plans and apparent military ambitions." Inevitably, Japan must look elsewhere for vital raw materials. Geologist H. Foster Bain noted accurately, "If Japan is to realize her destiny as a leader in modernizing the East, it will necessarily be as an importer of raw materials and exporter of finished products."[25]

How would Japan obtain reliable access to raw materials? This was the crucial question that troubled Japanese policymakers and lay behind the island nation's foreign policy during the interwar period. Essentially, there were two options open to Tokyo: either secure colonies or economic dependencies in Asia, or alternatively rely on international trade. During World War I, when the European conflict diverted other world powers from Asian affairs, Japan had pursued the first option, by imposing twenty-one demands on neighboring China. These provisions, designed to achieve strategic and economic dominance in Manchuria among other goals, mentioned specific mineral deposits, such as iron mines in central China. However, at the close of World War I the two leading naval powers, Great Britain and the U.S., cooperated at the Washington Conference to restore an Asiatic balance of power, one based solidly in treaty structures; and this multinational initiative temporarily harnessed the Japanese bid for unilateral advantages in China. During the 1920s these arrangements obliged Japan to cooperate with the major Western powers and expand international trade. And Japan prospered. Its trade volume doubled as it specialized in textile exports. In 1913, raw silk made up 30 percent of Japan's exports; by 1929 this type of trade amounted to 37 percent. Commerce with the U.S. expanded and increased in importance, for in 1929 America took 43 percent of Japan's exports.[26]

A convergence of unfavorable political and economic factors pushed Tokyo leaders to abandon their international cooperation in the 1930s and to pursue a unilateral solution based on expansion and war. On the political level renewed Soviet interest in Asia, particularly in Manchuria, coupled with a revival of Chinese nationalism, posed new external dangers to Japanese interests on the Asian mainland. Japan worried about the possible spread of Communist ideology into China, something that posed a new threat to Japanese interests. At home officials also awoke to a Malthus-like concern about exploding population and limited resources. The 1925 Japanese census showed that the island nation's population was increasing rapidly—doubling in only two generations to 60 million in 1925. With only about 29 percent of its land cultivable, Japan faced difficult decisions about how to support and feed a burgeoning population and how to promote higher living standards.[27]

This dilemma invited comparison with Britain's nineteenth century situation. With its population rising similarly, Great Britain had pushed industrialization to create factory jobs for workers. In this effort the English exploited domestic coal, iron, and tin reserves, and exported manufactured goods, as well as coal, to dependent overseas areas. These trading partners, in turn, supplied Britain with foodstuffs and necessary industrial raw materials, such as cotton, copper, and petroleum. There were two other major advantages Britain enjoyed in the earlier age. The country possessed an industrial-technological lead over commercial rivals, thus ensuring export markets for its products; and it successfully exported large numbers of people to overseas colonial areas—thus relieving the homeland of over-crowding and reducing the pressure of population on limited resources, a problem that worried economist Thomas Malthus. Japan faced a much different situation, for it began to industrialize rapidly after Britain, France, Germany, and the U.S., and so lacked Britain's technological lead. Furthermore, Japan had few overseas investments, and faced discrimination against its manufactured exports and settlers in areas concerned about cheap imports and sensitive about heavy Japanese immigration. Significantly, Japan, unlike nineteenth century Britain, needed reliable foreign supplies of coking coal, iron, petroleum, and ferroalloys.[28]

While Japanese leaders pondered their domestic dilemma and external security concerns, the world economy collapsed. This emphasized for Tokyo policymakers the fragile nature of international trade and the advantages of a self-sufficient empire, an objective that also had its political appeal to a nation desirous of attaining world power status. Between 1929 and 1931 Japan's exports dropped 50 percent. Collapse of the market for silk in the U.S. produced agrarian unrest in Japan, and, incidentally, this internal dissatisfaction helped bring a transfer of political power to military expansionists. Increasingly, the appeal of a self-contained empire, absorbing Japanese manufactured goods and supplying necessary raw-material imports, gained broad public backing. The quest for an autonomous empire would underlie Japanese foreign policy until its defeat in 1945.[29]

Japan's pursuit of a unilateral solution emerged clearly in September 1931, when the army intervened in Manchuria, the region of north China long considered vital to Tokyo's interests. Within a few weeks the Japanese had created a client state called Manchukuo. At the League of Nations, where diplomats condemned Japanese aggression, the officials from Tokyo patiently explained the considerations that prompted a resort to military expansion. In these and other public presentations, the Japanese expressed anxiety about access to raw materials—specifically, coal, iron, and petroleum—in a multilateral international economy. Manchukuo, like Korea and Formosa, was considered an integral component of an autonomous empire centered in Tokyo. Nor was this new direction a surprise to American officials. U.S. ambassador to Japan Joseph Grew recognized that this quest for economic security had become a fundamental objective of Japanese policy, and enjoyed mass support.[30]

That basic raw-materials issues were a major cause of German and Japanese expansionism in the 1930s is an interpretation that Germany's ambassador to Japan, Herbert von Dirksen, emphasized in his memoir. Both countries, he noted, wanted "to create economic spheres of influence in which they could purchase raw materials and sell their finished products unhampered." Unable to reach an accommodation with the Western powers who controlled global resources, and unwilling to tolerate further economic uncertainty and political inferiority, the two dissatisfied nations chose the "dangerous Lebensraum philosophy" which "led to the catastrophe" of World War II.[31]

Frustrated and embittered with existing relationships, the "have-not" nations used the cover of the global depression to violate League of Nations security guarantees and grab territory, but this pattern does not mean war was inevitable with the great powers. America, France, Great Britain, the Soviet Union, and others collectively held a preponderance of military power—although not sufficient political resolve to uphold the Versailles order. Their deliberations focused on two basic options—use of a minerals sanction to deter aggression and punish lawbreakers; and diplomatic initiatives to mollify the aggrieved. The first option, sanctions, appealed to those alert to the implications of mineral interdependence in the modern world. Indeed a French geologist, L. De Launay, proposed the idea of a mineral sanction in 1917 as a device for restraining Germany. This idea also appealed to the distinguished British geologist, Thomas Holland, and to C. K. Leith, both of whom recognized Britain and America had the resources to make a minerals sanction effective with or without support from other League of Nations members. But the geologists had some difficulty communicating the notion of a mineral sanction to economists, who preferred to appease the dissatisfied powers with devices for reducing trade barriers, and by promoting equal access to critical materials. Leith, for instance, had difficulty at a 1937 international studies conference in Paris winning support for his Anglo-American mineral sanction proposal. His message that the control of the world happens to lie in the possession of raw materials appeared to fall on deaf ears. And then there was the domestic political problem. Reliance on a trade embargo as a means for deterring war would antagonize affected U.S. materials suppliers, many of whom had political clout in Washington. This was particularly true for the producers of petroleum, coal, steel, and copper, all items essential for the conduct of war.[32]

As the imperial power with the most extensive empire, Great Britain had much to lose from the breakdown of collective security and from the resort to force. Consequently England pushed in September 1935 for a League of Nations enquiry into the whole problem of access to raw materials. In his call for an international study, Britain's representative, Sir Samuel Hoare, asserted "the problem is economic rather than political or territorial. It is the fear of monopoly—of the withholding of essential raw materials—that is causing alarm." After some delay, resulting in part from the Ethiopian war, the General Assembly of the League of Nations approved a resolution calling on its Council to set up a committee of enquiry to evaluate equality of commercial access to raw materials for all nations. The terms of the enquiry focused on problems of "commercial access" and by implication this phrase excluded consideration of the territorial adjustments that Hjalmar Schacht wanted.[33]

Despite its nonmembership in the League of Nations, the United States received an invitation in the autumn of 1936 to participate. Middle-echelon officials in the State Department and foreign service correctly diagnosed the British-initiated study as a sham. Prentiss Gilbert, the American observer in Geneva, reported the investigation was intended to demonstrate that difficulties in obtaining access to raw materials lay entirely in the economic realm and could be removed through normal economic adjustments, especially measures to revive international trade and limit commercial restrictions. "Such a result," he stated, "would thus greatly diminish the force of the argument of non-colonial powers that the possession of colonies is essential to ensure an adequate supply of raw materials." And another State Department official dismissed the proposed conference as "nothing but an empty gesture" for the real problem concerned not "commercial access in time of peace" but access to materials in time of war. Consideration of these interrelated matters rested inevitably on a thorough evaluation of European political problems, not simply on an evaluation of colonial raw materials. Nevertheless Secretary of State Cordell Hull, always ready to strike a blow for tariff liberalization, authorized American participation, and soon other nonmembers of the League of Nations, including Brazil and Japan (but not Germany and Italy), consented to participate. In retrospect the German decision, which was interpreted then as a protest against the terms of the League study, revealed Hitler's priorities. The Nazi leader was more concerned with preparing for war than he was with achieving token diplomatic concessions.[34]

While the absence of Germany and Italy was a signal that these two alienated nations looked to unilateral solutions, the Japanese delegates sought a diplomatic solution short of force. During debate the Tokyo delegates argued vigorously for extension of the open door principle, elaborated initially in the 1884 Congo-Basin Treaty, to all colonial possessions. They also urged freedom of trade in raw materials and manufactured articles as well as freedom of movement for labor and technology necessary to exploit colonial raw materials. While conceding that discrimination, such as the barriers to Japanese exports, contributed to the global problem, a Japanese representative claimed that much of the present international instability stemmed from an unequal distribution of natural resources. "To be quite frank," said Mr. Shudo, "the raw material question can never be settled satisfactorily without an equitable redistribution of the territories." By espousing high principles and equal access to raw materials the Japanese ploy impressed many diplomats. It was conciliatory and yet insistent. U.S. ambassador Joseph Grew in Tokyo noted that the Japanese demand for equal access to territories "is motivated by the Japanese government's present desire to secure the availability of necessary raw materials through diplomatic means if possible."[35]

In 1937 the League of Nations Raw Materials Committee issued its report, and it identified two problems. First, some nations had protested they were unable to purchase raw materials, and second, some claimed that they could not obtain the foreign exchange required to pay for raw materials. Payments problems, the report said, "vastly transcend in importance those in regard to supply." Taking the approach that commodity problems resulted from economic maladjustments, not lack of access to supplies as Germany believed, the report recommended a series of measures, including relaxation of restrictions to promote freer trade and capital movements. Also it favored extending the open door principle, a controversial point which saw the Japanese and American representatives take a common stand against the European imperial powers. The latter, especially Great Britain, France, Portugal, and the Netherlands, resisted any statement that might appear to extend the open door principle to their own colonial areas. Although they asserted their own territories were open to foreign trade and investments, the British, French, and Dutch delegates claimed the development of these colonies must occur for the benefit of natives and without an abnormal influx of capital from abroad.[36]

On these issues the United States took a more conciliatory line than did the major European powers, who believed that they had too much to lose from opening colonial areas and removing discrimination. The conference recommendations themselves reflected these deep divisions, and so they contained qualifications that limited general application. Nonetheless, at Japan's insistence the League study group agreed to present these recommendations to an international conference, but in 1938, as the political storms gathered, few diplomats cared to press the open door principle.[37]

Within the United States the administration of President Franklin D. Roosevelt contemplated several courses of action against the rise of economic nationalism and the challenge of Italy, Germany, and Japan. The deep-seated appeal of isolationism, which revived in the aftermath of World War I, seriously constricted the president's policy options, discouraging any desire the White House might have to pursue a strong-armed diplomatic approach in concert with the League of Nations or Great Britain to punish aggression. Among knowledgeable minerals specialists a consensus developed behind an emergency stockpile program to help insulate the United States from the economic disruption of another world war. This approach gained support in September 1934, for instance, when a Planning Committee for Mineral Policy, which incidentally included the ubiquitous Professor Leith, suggested the government accumulate supplementary supplies of manganese, chromium, tungsten, nickel, and tin, as well as perhaps mica and mercury, to guard against an emergency even though the United States more nearly approached "self-sufficiency . . . for national defense . . . than any other country."[38]

Brooks Emeny, a young Harvard University political scientist, reached a similar conclusion in a much-discussed book, *The Strategy of Raw Materials*, which War Department officials enthusiastically assisted and recommended for publication. In this important study, based in part on Emeny's access to planning branch officials and memoranda, the author compared seven major world powers—the United States, United Kingdom, Soviet Union, France, Germany, Japan, and Italy, and reached the familiar conclusion that only three powers—the United States, the United Kingdom, and the Soviet Union—had a large measure of raw-material self-sufficiency. Except for one mineral, antimony, the two English-speaking nations had perfect unity in supply, providing they retained control of the seas, said Emeny. "These two national groups, which account for over 60 per cent of the world's industrial output and exercise financial or sovereign control over 75 per cent of the mineral resources, hold the balance of power in so far as the essential commodities of peace and war are concerned." To prevent temporary shortages and cushion the inevitable adjustments in time of national emergency, the author suggested the United States accumulate inventories of several materials—including manganese and chromium, which were available in nearby Cuba, and tin.[39]

Meanwhile, the military services themselves pushed quietly within the administration for a strategic stockpiling program. In May 1934, for instance, they suggested the United States might settle outstanding war debts with European powers by accepting payments in strategic materials—including manganese, chromite, tin, tungsten, optical glass, nickel, mica, antimony, and coconut charcoal. Another scheme discussed in the bureaucracy involved a possible bartering of surplus American agricultural crops, such as cotton, for minerals. What both proposals had in common was a way of circumventing the need for Congress to authorize a minerals purchase program at the expense of more pressing domestic priorities.[40]

In 1935 as the Italian invasion of Ethiopia increased the danger of war and prompted discussion of international sanctions, State Department economic adviser Herbert Feis developed a plan for establishing an interdepartmental committee to purchase $25 million annually in strategic materials at home or abroad, or, indeed, from direct barter of surplus agricultural products; but this proposal seemed premature. In 1936 Congressman Charles Faddis introduced his own plan to acquire strategic materials, barter farm products, and cancel war debts in exchange for appropriate materials. Despite interest in both executive agencies and the Congress, the United States did not establish a comprehensive stockpiling program, although the national legislature did authorize the Navy to purchase small quantities of strategic and critical materials—including tin, manganese, tungsten, optical glass, and manila fiber—for its own potential needs.[41]

More than anyone else President Franklin Roosevelt was responsible for blocking a materials-purchase program at this time. Locked in a political struggle with his congressional opponents over plans to reshape the Supreme Court, the embattled chief executive displayed little personal enthusiasm for mobilization preparations. Like his countrymen, the president hoped the United States could avoid another world war, and he saw no urgent need for undertaking costly preparations. Until Nazi Germany turned against France in the spring of 1940, President Roosevelt was the chief barrier to an effective stockpiling program, and in this opposition he displayed a foolish shortsightedness. Repeatedly, when proposals for a stockpile program came to the White House, Roosevelt told his powerful budget director, Daniel Bell, to block them on the grounds that "the proposed legislation would not be in accord with the program of the President."[42]

In fairness, while Roosevelt did nothing to construct a program, proponents of stockpiling disagreed among themselves about the contents of any legislation. On Capitol Hill, for example, some legislators wanted to obtain foreign minerals and raw materials from barter deals involving the disposal of surplus farm products. Others simply wanted to persuade foreign nations to repay World War I debts in raw materials. But the most powerful bloc, the Western mining lobby, which displayed its political muscle earlier with successful lobbying for a silver-purchase program, had a different goal in writing stockpile legislation. Instead of enabling the government to purchase high-quality foreign materials, the mining lobby insisted that any federal program subsidize domestic minerals-producing areas. To those unfamiliar with mining and with the skewed distribution of high-quality mineral resources, this proposal for a nationalistic subsidy program to assure raw materials self-sufficiency had emotional appeal.[43]

Officials in the executive agencies disagreed about how a stockpile program should be administered, thus complicating any White House initiative had Roosevelt desired it, but the bureaucracy agreed on one thing: any program to purchase domestic materials for a raw materials inventory contradicted the nation's larger military and industrial interests. Not only would exploitation of high-cost domestic supplies create serious technical problems of adapting domestic industry to low-grade ores, but it would also deplete further the emergency reserve available in the United States should foreign aggressors succeed in closing vital merchant shipping lanes. As State Department economic adviser Herbert Feis told his boss, Secretary of State Hull, "The Army and Navy are strongly of the view that foreign sources of supply should be used, and that the limited domestic resources should be reserved for possible emergency."[44]

Late in 1938, after the fateful Munich Conference, new pressure developed within the executive branch and Congress for Roosevelt to back a stockpile program. An interagency committee, chaired by Feis, recommended $25 million for direct purchase of strategic materials and $500,000 for exploration of domestic deposits as "the irreducible minimum program" best designed to acquire strategic materials and develop domestic supplements. The committee, which contained representatives of the military agencies as well as the State Department, urged administration support for this proposal, which was introduced in Congress by Senator Elbert Thomas (D., Utah). The president agreed his subordinates could propose constructive modifications to the Thomas bill, as the Utah Democrat requested, but Roosevelt once again refused to back the necessary appropriations to establish an effective stockpile. He told Undersecretary of State Sumner Welles that this step "would upset his entire budget arrangements." In March 1939, however, the chief executive shifted his position slightly; now he would not oppose a congressional initiative even though he personally had no intention of asking for stockpile funds. However the president's thinking extended only to a $10 million request, not the $25 million annually that executive agencies desired. To Herbert Feis the Roosevelt figure was "clearly insufficient even for a good start."[45]

During 1939 national leaders explored several approaches. Southern Democrats, including Georgia Congressman Carl Vinson, chairman of the House Naval Affairs Committee, and Senator James Byrnes of South Carolina, both backed a direct-barter scheme which would have had the federal government purchase $100 million of surplus agricultural commodities and exchange these for tin, manganese, chromium, and other materials. The plan, appealing primarily to farm interests, looked silly to *The American Metal Market*, a minerals-industry newspaper. "It certainly is a sad commentary on our present economics that we contemplate reverting to the same trade methods of John Smith and the Pilgrim Fathers with the Indians in the seventeenth century." And neither Britain nor the Netherlands, the two countries with supplies of tin and rubber, were interested in the scheme.[46]

Eventually Congress took more constructive action, passing a bill authorizing the appropriation of $100 million over the next four fiscal years for strategic stockpiling. But this was a pyrrhic victory for advocates of an ambitious purchasing program, for when the appropriations committees completed their action, in consultation with the White House, Congress appropriated only $10 million, the amount Roosevelt had agreed to accept. Faced with insufficient funds the Army-Navy Munitions Board recommended purchases of tin, manganese, tungsten, chromium, quinine, manila fiber, optical glass, and quartz crystal—but 40 percent of the entire appropriation was to be for buying tin. Most of the available funds were obligated before January 1940, and not until June, after the Nazi armies turned against Scandinavia and France, did Roosevelt yield to the recommendations of his advisers and request additional appropriations. Altogether Congress appropriated $70 million of the authorized $100 million for government inventories. The remaining $30 million was never appropriated, for the Roosevelt administration soon resorted to more efficient procurement procedures, involving extensive use of the Reconstruction Finance Corporation.[47]

In essence Roosevelt's dilatory approach to stockpiling cost the nation dearly, for after the United States entered the war this country had to launch an expensive crash program to obtain strategic and critical materials at home and abroad. Within the context of prewar maneuvers the president's inaction in stockpiling, like his quixotic and vacillating efforts to discourage German and Japanese aggression, only served to embolden the "have-not" nations who were determined to effect a redistribution of global resources by force, if necessary.

If Germany's raw material deficiencies offer an environmental explanation for Hitler's expansionism, the Nazi need to secure continental deposits of high-quality materials helped shape Hitler's specific challenge to the European order. During the mid-1930s German commercial interests had maneuvered to obtain safe supplies of iron, tying up the important ores of northern and central Sweden and employing pressure to shut the British out of Spain, as Hitler's support for fascist leader Francisco Franco gained Germany the almost exclusive use of Spanish Morocco's iron deposits. Austria and Czechoslovakia, the first prizes in Hitler's string of conquests, contained some deposits of iron ore, magnesite, lignite, and timber, but more importantly their inclusion in the Third Reich gave Hitler geographical propinquity to the rich resources of southeastern Europe, which were vital to his overall strategy. Compelled to cope first with the combined threat of France, Soviet Russia, and Great Britain to Germany's industrial and material interests in the north, the Nazi chancellor entrusted Mussolini, his Italian surrogate, with the key responsibility of consolidating control in Rumania and southeastern Europe, a decision Hitler would later have cause to regret. Because over half of Germany's inadequate oil supplies came from Rumania, control of this nation was crucial to German military ambitions. Also, once Britain resorted to economic warfare in order to shut off Germany from South American and Asian sources of supply, control of southeastern Europe gained added importance to the Nazis. Germany itself produced little bauxite for aluminum, but Hungary and Yugoslavia provided an estimated 23 percent of the world's supply in 1939. Also, while Germany lacked chrome, Turkey produced 20 percent of the global supply. And Yugoslavia promised to provide vital quantities of antimony, copper, and lead. Not only as a supplier of war materials, but also as a producer of foodstuffs, this region of southeastern Europe loomed large to Hitler's success strategy; but unfortunately for his ambitions, Mussolini proved unable to stabilize the region. Guerrilla resistance as well as Allied diplomatic initiatives in the area would eventually cripple the German war machine.[48]

Hitler's northern offensive against Denmark and Norway in April 1940 had specific minerals objectives. Concerned that Britain might seize Narvik, the Norwegian port through which much Swedish iron ore passed on its way to Germany, the Nazis launched a successful campaign intended to safeguard access to 51 percent of Germany's iron ore requirements.[49]

More ominous was the prospect that Stalin's Red Army might shut off Berlin's access to a variety of strategic materials in an eastern arc extending from Finland to Rumania. Not only was the Soviet Union in a position to control German access to the Petsamo nickel mines in Finland, but also the Red Army stood within one hundred miles of the vital oil fields of southeastern Europe. This concern hung over Hitler's military moves, and he confided to generals in January 1941 that "Russia can turn the Rumanian oil fields into an expanse of smoking debris . . . and the life of the Axis depends on those oil fields."[50]

Initially, an underprepared Stalin sought to appease Hitler's materials appetite by agreeing to a nonaggression pact and to trade arrangements that, temporarily at least, turned the Soviet Union into a German storehouse. These trade arrangements helped compensate Germany for losses sustained when British economic controls isolated the Third Reich from Western Hemisphere supplies. For instance, Russia exported more grain to Germany than Germany previously purchased from Argentina. And the 900,000 tons of oil the Kremlin pledged Hitler amounted to nearly 25 percent of Germany's war requirements. The Soviets also agreed to provide iron ore, phosphates, scrap and pig iron, 100,000 tons of chrome ore, as well as platinum, manganese, and timber. Finally, the Soviet Union served as an indispensable conduit for South Asia supplies, as soy beans, rubber, and tin flowed through Communist hands to reach the German economy. Stalin exacted a price for his benevolent policies, for he requested, and obtained, German war materials that Hitler and his generals realized would be employed ultimately against German armies when the Nazi dictator ordered his forces to attack in the East. While trade temporarily gave Stalin some leverage over Hitler's actions, it failed to divert Germany from the long-planned assault on Russia. Hitler remained convinced, despite Stalin's trade concessions, that a victory over the Soviet Union, which the Germans viewed with contempt, offered the only certain route to ultimate victory and national self-sufficiency.[51]

In Tokyo the Japanese expansionists had watched as Germany defeated France, Belgium, and the Netherlands in 1940, and now they faced an irresistible temptation. With the major European powers preoccupied closer to home and unable to guard their colonies, Japan contemplated a southward sweep to seize raw materials lacking in Japan, Manchuria, and Korea, and to consolidate the East Asian sphere of influence that expansionists also wanted for reasons of national prestige and security. Fearful that the United States and Great Britain might embargo raw material shipments, including aviation fuel, unless Japan in turn abandoned its war with China, the Tokyo leaders coveted the Netherlands East Indies as a more reliable petroleum source. War Minister Tojo put his government's designs bluntly: "The Government has a policy: it desires to obtain materials peacefully from the Netherlands East Indies, but depending on the circumstances, it could use force."[52]

The United States also awakened to the strategic importance of Southeast Asia as a supplier of tin, rubber, and other industrial raw materials. Erle Dickover, the American consul general in Batavia, repeatedly cabled Washington that Japanese totalitarianism posed a genuine danger to United States interests in Malaysia. He pointed out that 92 percent of America's natural rubber supply, 71 percent of its palm oil, 75 percent of gutta percha, 98 percent of tin requirements, and 93 percent of kapok requirements came from Malaysia. Practically all of the quinine supply came from the Netherlands East Indies. "Should Japan obtain control of our essential raw materials from Malaysia, we would lose the principal club which we are now holding over their heads, namely, economic sanctions." If Japan captured Southeast Asia, Dickover asserted, it could impose sanctions on trade with the United States, threatening to cut off our supplies of rubber, tin, gutta percha, and other items unless the Roosevelt administration acquiesced in Tokyo's designs.[53]

These warnings gained meaning to policymakers when Stanley K. Hornbeck, the State Department's expert on Asian affairs, circulated an article, "American Raw Material Deficiencies and Regional Dependence," which University of Michigan geographer Robert B. Hall prepared for the *Geographical Review*. In this scholarly analysis Hall concluded that the lands west of the Pacific could completely supply the demands of the United States in ten of seventeen strategic commodities—and only two strategic materials, quartz crystal and quicksilver, were unavailable in that region. Challenging the older view held among geologists that Asian mineral resources lacked significance for the Atlantic region, Hall concluded: "No other part of the world bears so vital a relationship to the United States in case of emergency." And he argued that "the United States would be compelled, for its existence as a major industrial state, to wage war against any power or powers that might threaten to sever our trade lines with this part of the world." To Hornbeck these arguments provided additional justification for a firm policy toward Japan, one that employed materials sanctions to discourage further aggression.[54]

In the summer of 1941 Hornbeck's tough approach prevailed

and President Roosevelt froze Japanese assets, a move interpreted as closing all trade between the United States and Japan. For the Tokyo expansionists the American embargo posed a fatal danger to efforts to achieve a coprosperity sphere, since Japan lacked the technological skill to achieve self-sufficiency in fuels quickly, through rapid development of synthetic energy. The Japanese planning chief, Suzuki, concluded: "If we go forward with our national policy depending solely on synthetic petroleum, there will be a very serious defect in our national defense picture within a certain period of time. This is very dangerous, given a world torn by wars and a situation in which we are trying to conclude the China Incident." Realizing that the Soviet Union no longer could block a Japanese move in Asia, for Hitler's armies were moving on Moscow, Japanese leaders toyed with a dangerous option—one intended to achieve imperial self-sufficiency through the use of force. As the American embargo began reducing energy imports, Suzuki noted how "our Empire's national power is declining day by day." He had a plan. "I believe it is vitally important for the survival of our Empire that we make up our minds to establish and stabilize a firm economic base." From its southern area, a region formerly under the control of Britain and the Netherlands, Japan could obtain in about six months sufficient supplies of oil, bauxite, nickel, crude rubber, and tin. Except for high-grade asbestos and cobalt, Japan would have achieved the necessary degree of self-sufficiency to assure regional preponderance in Asia.[55]

This plan rested on the assumption that Japan could control shipping and sea lanes. To maintain three million tons of shipping, the figure required to meet import needs, Japan would need to expand its own shipbuilding capacity and limit its own shipping losses, an assumption later shown to involve a misplaced act of confidence. For in 1942 and 1943 the American submarine force, not the Japanese navy, dominated the shipping lanes, and the Allied attack on shipping soon reduced the importation of raw materials and, in this manner, shattered the foundations of basic industry.[56]

Privately Japanese leaders seem to have recognized, but declined to articulate, that their country's success in attacking the United States Navy and seizing Southeast Asian island colonies rested on circumstances beyond their own control, especially the outcome of Hitler's attack on the Soviet Union. Asked about the chances for success in a war against the United States, Great Britain, and the Netherlands, the Japanese Navy declared in October 1941: "We will be all right at the beginning; but if the war is prolonged, our chances will depend on the international situation and the determination of the people." Approaching their decision somewhat fatalistically, the Tokyo war leadership appears to have believed intermediaries might persuade the Americans to concede Japan an autonomous empire even after Japan resorted to force in December 1941.[57]

In thirty months, from September 1939 to March 1942, an aggressive Axis coalition stunned the western democracies and the Soviet Union with blitzkrieg, lightning moves the dissatisfied powers employed to seize the raw materials vital for their economic self-sufficiency and political independence. After its startling successes in Scandinavia and against France, Germany advanced into the Soviet Union, reaching the outskirts of Moscow late in 1941. In the Pacific, Japan administered a mortal wound to American air and naval forces in Hawaii and then proceeded against other British, Dutch, and American positions in Malaya, the Dutch East Indies, and the Philippines. After the collapse of Britain's important naval base at Singapore early in 1942, Japan was in position to advance against India, perhaps ultimately cutting through the petroleum-rich Middle East to join German forces. In an unbelievable string of successes, the "have-not" powers of 1939 broke out of their deficit position and by early 1942 seemed on the verge of consolidating a new global empire that would leave the United States surrounded by hostile neighbors in the Western Hemisphere.

Specialists in the U.S. Bureau of Mines quickly grasped the serious implications of these Axis successes and sought to awaken a perception of these issues among policymakers and the general public alike. Elmer Pehrson, the bureau's chief economist, said the Axis moves were "influenced to a considerable extent by mineral objectives." The attacks "strike at rich and strategic mineral areas that heretofore have contributed much to the industrial strength of the United Nations." For the United States and its allies, these military initiatives were devastating. "The shutting off of supplies of tungsten and antimony from China, and of tin, manganese, and chromite, as well as rubber, manila fiber, and other non-mineral commodities from Southeastern Asia, already constitutes a serious loss to the United

Nations, and if the anticipated pincer movement on the Indian Ocean isolates the Asiatic Continent, we face the loss of more important sources of manganese and chromite, strategic mica and flake graphite," Pehrson said. Russia's military power had been crippled with the loss of its manganese, iron, and coal industries of the Ukraine, he noted. And the Japanese occupation of Malaya and the Netherlands East Indies partially alleviated the Axis petroleum deficit.[58]

According to the Bureau of Mines analysis, what had happened in the last two years was "unbelievable." While in 1939 the Axis powers occupied only 3 percent of the world's land area, accounting for only 10 percent of total population and not more than 5 percent of mineral resources, they now dominated 13 percent of the land area, 35 percent of the population, and about a third of the mineral wealth. Precise comparisons became difficult because some facilities were destroyed, but Pehrson calculated that the Axis controlled only 6 percent of global iron ore production in 1939. However in early 1942 they dominated 46 percent and soon might hold 55 percent, if the drive into the Indian Ocean achieved its material objectives. Similarly, while the Axis produced less than 1 percent of global petroleum in 1939, production of synthetics and control of southeastern Europe increased that figure to 7 percent. If the Axis completed a drive toward the rich oil fields of Asia Minor and Russia, it would command 22 percent of these energy resources. In another area critical to war mobilization the Axis had overcome serious deficiencies, too. In ferroalloys the three Axis countries increased their control of world manganese production from 2 percent to 30 percent, of chrome from 3 percent to 30 percent, and of tungsten from 6 percent to 60 percent. "If the move toward the Indian Ocean is successful, the Axis will control or isolate more than two-thirds of the world's supply of these materials."[59]

From the mass media the American public learned that the underlying contest for resources was a principal theme of World War II, since further Axis successes in the Middle East and south Asia could cripple the British Empire and handicap American supply efforts. *Newsweek* business editor Milton Van Slyck described the conflict as "essentially one of minerals," as the "have-not" nations desperately sought to become the "haves." In the autumn of 1942 he concluded the Axis were achieving their ambitions. "The grim, inescapable conclusion is that the United Nations have been losing the war."[60]

Fortune, Nation's Business and *Business Week*, determined to keep their readers apprised of supply developments, also published grim interpretations of the military situation. As *Fortune* put it, "The overrunning of the Philippines knocked out at one murderous blow a quarter of the U.S. supplies of chromite." Without chromite this country could not make armor plate for military uses. And the Japanese capture of Singapore and Malaya "cut off three-fourths of the U.S. imports of tin. Without tin the U.S. cannot make certain vital solders and alloys, or keep its military commissariat moving smoothly. War on all fronts has crippled the flow of three-fourths of the U.S. supplies of manganese. Without manganese the U.S. cannot make a ton of steel." A crisis had arrived, *Fortune* concluded, for "war and losses in the Far East have dangerously upset the geopolitical balance of the U.S. economy." *Business Week* bluntly warned readers that 1942 was the "year to win or lose" now that the Axis had captured Singapore, for if Japan captured India and Hitler's troops reached the Middle East, then Hitler might "swap with Japan the things that will strengthen his war machine for a long showdown with London and Washington." In essence, if the Axis could hold what they had already seized, and add other territories while the Allies prepared for the counteroffensive, "they may become too strongly entrenched to be dislodged from the distant bases left to us." The key campaign from this perspective seemed to be the emerging German offensive in the Middle East, for if Hitler attempted a pincer attack on this oil-abundant region from his positions in Turkey and Libya and succeeded in capturing British garrisons along the Suez Canal, Hitler would dominate the Eurasian mainland.[61]

Germany and Japan entered 1942 on the verge of a tremendous geopolitical victory. From a threadbare resource position the "have-not" powers successfully combined diplomatic bluster and military force to improve their materials inventory while weakening the Anglo-American materials monopoly. Although still short of petroleum and copper, as well as certain ferroalloys like chromium and tungsten, the Axis achieved miracles. Their problem in late 1941, as the disparate United Nations coalition slowly mobilized to halt the expansionist challenge, was to protect effectively a far-flung, hastily acquired empire and to use the spoils of aggression in a global war of attrition.

How had natural resources contributed to a global war and international discord during the late 1930s? Briefly, for Germany and Japan, the two significant aggressors, the absence of a diversified domestic materials base and assured overseas sources of supply was a constant source of frustration. Both had growing populations and unfulfilled aspirations to dominate in world councils. The status quo powers firmly rejected calls for a redistribution of global resources, claiming that self-sufficient empires made sense only if a nation aspired to war. But the Germans and Japanese found little solace in the recommended alternative—participation in nondiscriminatory trade and multilateral payments. They encountered some discrimination against the exports needed to generate foreign exchange for servicing international obligations and for financing raw-materials purchases. Finally, the Great Depression disrupted the effective use of world trade to promote an efficient distribution of labor among nations. Politically, adherence to an open world economy, one maximizing the economic benefits of international exchange, rested on global prosperity, something vitally lacking in the 1930s until economists learned better how to use fiscal and monetary policies to stimulate demand.

In seeking security through self-sufficiency Nazi Germany and militarist Japan both pursued an ultimate objective and an immediate need. To Hitler long-term national salvation depended on military conquest of a rich agricultural and mineral region in western Russia. For the Japanese expansionists the ultimate goal required domination of an East Asian Co-prosperity Sphere—a bloc including Manchuria, Korea, and Taiwan, as well as Indochina and the Dutch Indies. In pursuit of long-range goals, both made short-term preparations. To prepare for the war he considered necessary and inevitable, Hitler sought to seize vital materials—Swedish iron ore, Finnish nickel, Soviet manganese and oil—and these short-range calculations shaped his overall military strategy. Japan, however, made fewer preparations for war with the great Western powers, expecting that strife in Europe would cloak its advance in Asia. But this strategy underestimated America's moral and legal commitment to China—and when President Roosevelt clamped financial and economic sanctions on trade in 1941, the Japanese high command made the fateful decision. They would attack U.S. military positions in order to obtain more time to consolidate an Asian empire. Ironically, the U.S. resort to sanctions—including scrap iron and petroleum—precipitated the Japanese decision for war with America, although Tokyo's unremitting quest for an autonomous Asian empire, rich in materials and living space, lay behind the Pacific conflict.

Chapter Four
Resources for Victory

STRATEGIC resources shaped the conduct and outcome of World War II in ways that political and military historians often neglect. Internationally the global conflict involved a concerted Axis effort to capture foreign territory and secure minerals and other resources vital to national economic aspirations. For Germany and Japan the vital territorial objectives were areas of southern and western Russia, the petroleum-rich Middle East, and former British and Dutch colonies in Southeast Asia. Britain and America, the two underwriters of the old order, sought to block this challenge to their own preponderant global position, and they worked together to devise an economic and military plan likely to contain the Axis. Militarily, the United Nations coalition first employed their superior naval forces to lock Hitler on the Eurasian land mass away from the material riches of the Middle East, Africa, and South America, while other naval forces strove to check the Japanese drive in East Asia against European and American colonial possessions—especially India, Burma, and English-speaking portions of the British Commonwealth. The English-speaking allies also recognized the importance of economic warfare to their overall strategy, for disruption of Axis exports, imports, and access to the resources of peripheral European countries could weaken, perhaps disable, the German and Japanese war economies.

Domestic resource mobilization was also crucial to the conduct and outcome of World War II. Rich in most important mineral resources, except the ferroalloys, and isolated effectively from the immediate war zones, the U.S. had to develop its own domestic resources as well as obtain materials from elsewhere in the Western Hemisphere in sufficient quantity to satisfy military and civilian requirements. In mobilization, as in economic warfare, domestic politics and administrative competition both imposed their own constraints, but in the last analysis, the sheer quantity of American resources would overwhelm such obstacles, and eventually would overwhelm the Axis, who also had political and organizational problems. Hitler and his allies lacked sufficient human and material resources to win a war of attrition against Great Britain, the United States, and the Soviet Union combined.

From the outbreak of war in Europe on September 1, 1939, the major powers scrambled for resources, and sought to deprive their adversaries of crucial supplies. Like Germany, Britain depended on other countries for vast quantities of industrial raw materials, and the conflict produced severe dislocations of existing supplies, compelling the English-speaking nation to look across the Atlantic to Canada, the United States, and other nations for replacement materials. Heavy blows fell on Britain's economy in 1940 when Hitler's move against Scandinavia shut off one-third of iron ore imports as well as timber and other minerals. Then the Nazi triumph over France and the Low Countries and the Italian campaign against Greece disrupted access to traditional sources of bauxite, iron, and ferroalloys.[1]

While London maneuvered to obtain replacement supplies, it moved to create scarcities in Germany, despite that country's efforts during the 1930s to bolster domestic production and limit reliance on foreign sources of supply. British planners at first expected that a systematic program of economic warfare designed to deprive Germany of foreign markets and access to outside supplies, together with bombing attacks on German industrial facilities, would contribute to an eventual Nazi defeat. If Germany "be no Achilles with a single vital spot, she is vulnerable and can be bled to death if dealt sufficient wounds," the planners concluded. Among the techniques developed in the British Ministry of Economic Warfare was a system of navicerts, or naval certificates, designed to restrict shipments at the source rather than rely on the successful interceptions of naval vessels. London also sought diplomatically to sign trade agreements with neutrals, especially continental neutrals like Sweden and Switzerland, among others, pledging that they would not reexport to Germany goods which had passed through the British blockade. In essence, then, the British program for economic warfare differed from earlier experiences because it relied less on a conventional naval interdiction of shipping lanes than it did on restricting supply at the source, before vital materials could be loaded on neutral ships or airplanes.[2]

While London did succeed in disrupting Germany's direct trade —Berlin's export statistics showed an 80 percent decline within a few months—the system contained important loopholes. Eager to avoid antagonizing friendly neutral nations, especially the United States, and even hostile neutral nations, like the Soviet Union which served as an important conduit for Asian supplies before June 1941, the king's government declined to adopt the tough measures required to shut off neutral commerce totally, and thus give a swift economic blow to the German economy. Only after Germany invaded the Soviet Union, the U.S. entered the global war, and the United Nations allies began to take the offensive in November 1942, did the navicert system of trade controls become an effective tool of economic warfare.[3]

Successful economic sanctions against the Axis depended in 1940 and 1941 on the willingness of President Franklin Roosevelt to pursue a policy of benign neutrality, sympathetic to the goals of Britain and her allies. Late in 1939 Roosevelt persuaded Congress to modify the neutrality laws so that belligerents might obtain arms on a cash-and-carry basis, but the President declined at that time to restrict sales to the aggressor nations. Despite an understandable reluctance to move ahead of domestic opinion, Roosevelt did take several partial steps late in 1939 which effectively supported London's program of sanctions. In December the White House urged a "moral embargo" against nations guilty of bombing and machine-gunning civilian populations from the air. Outraged at reports of Soviet air attacks on Helsinki, Finland, Roosevelt used this episode to justify a "moral embargo" on airplane components, including aluminum, molybdenum, nickel, and tungsten, and these restrictions had some impact. Although not mandatory, because the State Department considered a formal embargo an unneutral act, the "moral embargo" served to discourage American trade with the belligerents at a time when the administration declined for domestic political reasons to join with the British in a general program of economic warfare.[4]

A significant shift in the American position emerged during the spring and summer of 1940 when Germany moved against Scandinavia and Western Europe. As domestic opposition to isolation eroded and support for assisting Britain waxed, the national government moved to control critical exports, improve planning for economic warfare, and procure foreign supplies required to supplement U.S. deficiencies. Congress passed the Defense Act in July 1940, authorizing the president to prohibit or curtail exports of military equipment and supplies, including a range of basic materials: aluminum, antimony, chromium, industrial diamonds, manganese, magnesium, mercury, molybdenum, platinum metals, quartz crystals, quinine, tin, tungsten, and vanadium among others. Although part of an effort to restrict exports, this program was not primarily an economic warfare program. Roosevelt imposed controls to prevent shortages in the U.S., not to promote shortages in totalitarian nations like Germany and Japan. Much to Britain's regret, the American restricted list did not contain a number of commodities vital to warfare, such as copper, nickel, lead, zinc, cobalt, scrap iron, cotton, and all petroleum products, for in these the U.S. generally anticipated adequate supplies.[5]

The German military moves also compelled Washington to consider defense mobilization requirements in the United States and to devise administrative arrangements for procuring emergency supplies of materials vulnerable to German or Japanese attacks, such as tin and rubber. In May 1940, the President announced creation of an Advisory Commission to the Council of National Defense (NDAC). This seven-member advisory commission, which reported directly to the president himself, included Edward R. Stettinius, a former steel executive, who handled industrial materials problems. A planning agency, NDAC lacked operational responsibilities or specific authority, and soon found itself at odds with the Army-Navy Munitions Board, which was authorized to handle stockpile purchases, even though the Treasury Department executed the actual procurements. It was perhaps understandable that differences of perspective should emerge between the two divergent agencies, one with a general planning function and the other responsible for military planning and procurement.[6]

Concerned primarily with military needs, the Munitions Board tended to think primarily in terms of acquiring strategic materials, "those essential to national defense, for the supply of which in war dependence must be placed in whole, or in substantial part, on sources outside the continental limits of the United States and for which strict conservation measures will be necessary." Among the most urgent foreign materials deserving purchase, it concluded, were these: abrasives, antimony, chromium, manganese, mercury, mica, nickel, quartz crystals, tin, and tungsten. These items could be supplemented by purchases of other critical materials—that is, materials less essential or obtainable from domestic sources. The Munitions Board placed these items on the critical list: aluminum, asbestos, graphite, platinum, and vanadium, but not, interestingly enough, either copper or zinc. Ironically, as it turned out, both the NDAC civilian planners, who took a more pessimistic view, and the Munitions Board woefully underestimated the number of commodities needed as well as the quantities required for American defense requirements to combat the Axis.[7]

Collapse of France and the smaller European nations in 1940, together with the disruption of their overseas colonial empires, left a major economic and political vacuum in world politics. In particular, the loss of European markets was a blow to Latin American nations, who previously counted on continental markets for 25 percent of export sales. Hit now with the full impact of Britain's economic blockade, designed to shut off German-dominated areas from Western Hemisphere supplies, the Latins faced desperate circumstances. In Washington officials feared that these commercial dislocations might prompt some hemisphere nations to forge bilateral commercial agreements with the Axis, or that circumstances might entice German or Japanese colonists in Brazil, Uruguay, Argentina, and several other countries to overthrow existing governments. The U.S. government also worried increasingly that an expansionist Japan might seize overseas colonies of Britain and the Netherlands, and such a military move could shut off Western Hemisphere access to vital supplies of tin and rubber. In May 1940, for instance, the U.S. had only a five-months' supply of tin and a three-months' supply of rubber. This supply deficiency seemed so serious that economic warfare expert William Y. Elliott advocated drastic measures. The United States should "pay through the nose if necessary, exert diplomatic pressure when necessary and get the materials in that we can't substitute for or for which there is not available domestic ore at higher prices."[8]

A number of schemes surfaced in official Washington to treat aspects of the global supply problem. State Department Under Secretary Sumner Welles promoted a proposal for a hemisphere cartel to pool surplus production and market these items jointly to other non-hemisphere countries. And the ambitious Secretary of Agriculture, Henry Wallace, lobbied for his proposal to finance the purchase of strategic materials with either gold or barter of agricultural products. But neither scheme gathered sufficient support, and the administration resorted, instead, to a simpler expedient for aiding the Latin Americans and for building up domestic stockpiles. It sponsored special legislation allowing the Reconstruction Finance Corporation to create satellite corporations for purchasing strategic materials. Previously, the RFC had engaged primarily in domestic financing, but now in June 1940 it obtained a new mandate for providing loans to corporations for the purposes of "producing, acquiring, and carrying strategic and critical materials as defined by the President." The financial agency could also create corporations of its own to produce, acquire, and carry such materials and to make payments against the purchase price. Under this authority four satellite corporations were established—the Rubber Reserve Company, the Metals Reserve Company, Defense Plants Corporation, and Defense Supplies Corporation. Of these, the Metals Reserve Corporation, assigned an authorized capitalization of $5 million, would take principal responsibility for purchasing and storing reserve supplies of tin and manganese, the two strategic materials American planners believed this country must obtain from foreign suppliers no matter what happened in Asia and Europe.[9]

During the 1940 presidential election, administration officials sought to assure a troubled public that the government had already made giant strides in preparing for any disruption of international trade routes. Donald Nelson, coordinator of purchasing, for instance, stated on a radio program in September that "to date, we have acquired more than half of the strategic and raw materials needed for our stock pile." Several days later the *Washington Post* reported that NDAC arrangements for purchasing strategic materials had succeeded in obtaining "a major part of the strategic raw materials needed for the defense program."[10]

In point of fact, this country was woefully underprepared for a military emergency, and officials at the technical level knew the facts. Charles K. Leith, a consultant to both NDAC and the Army-Navy Munitions Board, concluded the U.S. had less than 15 percent of the raw materials needed for a two-year emergency. Along with these items already delivered or in transit, America had ordered another 15 percent of anticipated needs, but some of these deliveries were not scheduled until 1944. This situation was hardly compatible with the demands of efficient military mobilization or a flexible preparedness program. A year before Pearl Harbor the American stockpile had serious deficiencies. There was *no* inventory of asbestos, industrial diamonds, mercury, mica, or wool—all materials identified as critical to American defenses. The stockpile did have several strengths. It contained 92 percent of the quinine goal, 53 percent of requirements for tungsten, 40 percent for rubber, 35 percent for antimony, but only 25 percent or less of requirements for the remaining items.[11]

A number of diverse factors contributed to this unsatisfactory situation. Administrative delays had impeded purchases of antimony and asbestos when the Munitions Board failed to approve stockpile recommendations. And war conditions prevented some deliveries; for instance, shipping bottlenecks interrupted the flow of chromite from Turkey, while a British blockade of Madagascar disrupted the graphite purchase effort. Closure of the Burma Road into China hurt tungsten acquisitions. Shipping problems also slowed the purchase of manganese, while negotiating delays complicated the acquisition of mica and wool from the British Empire. Perhaps the largest individual obstacle was Jesse Jones, the dollar-conscious Texan who served as federal loan coordinator and as head of the Reconstruction Finance Corporation. Considering some commodity prices excessive, Jones delayed purchases, believing prices might decline, thus enabling the RFC to make a better bargain with the taxpayer's dollars.[12]

Not only did the government have trouble purchasing the critical and strategic materials it identified, but also Washington, inexperienced as it was in preparing for a general mobilization, under-estimated minerals requirements, especially of items the U.S. produced in large quantity, such as copper, lead, and zinc. Although these materials had a myriad of uses in wartime, officials failed to anticipate the extent of U.S. military needs. Private industry offered little guidance, for it anticipated gluts, not shortages, a perspective shaped in the oversupply conditions of the 1930s. As an example, the copper situation is instructive. In April 1939, the Army-Navy Munitions Board evaluated materials needs and confidently stated: "No contemplated national emergency would call for supplies of copper in excess of those readily available from present mines and plants."

During the summer of 1940 it reiterated this conclusion, saying: "It can be seen that with only the United States to consider, our ability to produce copper in war is sufficient for all foreseen requirements." Later that year new forecasts developed, and by December President Roosevelt wanted the Metals Reserve Company to buy up to 100,-000 tons of copper from Latin America, principally from Chile. Over the next year before Pearl Harbor the RFC would obtain 500,000 tons of foreign copper as military demands for this metal, used in shell casings, increased rapidly. In short, the optimistic assessments of 1939 underwent dramatic revision in 1940, and from this point onward copper, as well as lead and zinc, became a material of strategic concern. Chile, long a dominant supplier of copper, became a vital strategic supply source for the U.S. within the Western Hemisphere.[13]

During 1939 and 1940 the American political system adapted slowly to the implications of global warfare, and this procrastination frustrated some nonpoliticians less sensitive to the elected officials' need to consult and build a consensus behind a program of action. For example Major William S. Culbertson, previously a member of the U.S. Tariff Commission and Herbert Hoover's ambassador to Chile, bluntly told the Army Industrial College in November, 1940: "We are engaged at the present time in economic warfare with the totalitarian powers. Publicly, our politicians don't state it quite as bluntly as that but it is a fact. Since we are participating in this war on the side of Great Britain and on the side of China, in an economic sense, it seems to me that we should put aside pretense and go to it with our full strength."[14]

After President Roosevelt's reelection, the U.S. moved gradually but deliberately toward involvement as it expanded defense production facilities, steadily increased overseas purchases of strategic materials, and began to lend-lease large quantities of military resources to Great Britain and the Soviet Union. As with other major shifts in national policy, such as intervention in World War I, events moved slowly, and sometimes policies seemed contradictory. While wary congressmen delayed budgetary requests for military needs, a nervous public searched in vain for expedients short of full-scale U.S. involvement. In this climate it is understandable that domestic producers of minerals, as well as of other production goods, avoided a headlong rush into war production, for fear of overexpanding facilities as had occurred during the previous war. Less understandable was the administrative mess in Washington. President Roosevelt seemed to thrive on competition among his subordinates, and he avoided appointing a domestic mobilization czar comparable in personal strength and stature to South Carolina industrialist Bernard Baruch on whom President Woodrow Wilson relied.[15]

The case for accelerating economic warfare preparations gained a boost on November 27, 1940, when the president received a comprehensive proposal from the Advisory Commission to the Council of National Defense, recommending "affirmative economic actions to strengthen and integrate the defense program." Suggested actions ranged from accelerated stockpiling and closer supervision of exports to preclusive purchasing designed to deny the Axis bloc vital raw materials. In justifying a vigorous economic defense program at this juncture, the Board warned that Germany and Japan flagrantly used the neutral U.S. as an entrepôt to bypass British trade controls, that Japan and Germany themselves obtained war supplies in the Western Hemisphere, and that diffusion of administrative responsibility for economic-defense programs among a number of official agencies complicated an efficient and effective national policy in this area.[16]

As an example of Axis purchases in the United States intended to evade British Empire trade controls, the report cited the shipment of 530,000 pounds of cobalt from the Belgian Congo to America, then on to Japan. This quantity, incidentally, represented an estimated full year's consumption for Japan in normal times. Similarly, Japan sought Colombian platinum, Canadian cobalt oxide, and other items, in the U.S. President Roosevelt also learned how Germany took advantage of this nation's neutrality to purchase 74 tons of rutile (titanium oxide) from Brazil; this was then shipped from the United States across the Pacific to Vladivostok, and across the Soviet Union by rail to its final destination, Nazi Germany. The longer President Roosevelt refrained from imposing tight export controls, the longer Axis powers would use such loopholes to buy the strategic materials required to cover their own resource deficiencies.[17]

Another key recommendation concerned preclusive purchasing of materials "so as to preempt the market for materials needed by other countries." This clause alluded to the serious problem of German and Japanese purchasing in other Western Hemisphere nations. By late 1940 officials in Washington not only recognized this problem, but now proposed to deal with it by having the U.S. openly engage in preclusive buying, not simply purchases to meet American mobilization needs. In future loan and purchasing agreements with other Western Hemisphere nations, the U.S. should seek pledges to control the export of certain commodities to the Nazis, Japanese, and their allies.[18]

During 1941 Washington moved to curtail this neutral trade, but not swiftly enough to please the beleaguered British who were eager to tighten the economic noose around the Third Reich. In the late spring British officials complained that the U.S. had undertaken "no effective action" to halt the dangerous flow of strategic commodities to Japan and Germany. But soon the American efforts began to bear fruit. Jesse Jones and the Reconstruction Finance Corporation, in cooperation with the State Department, negotiated a series of agreements with Latin American governments designed to disrupt this flow. In return for accepting export controls restricting shipments of materials to the Western Hemisphere, and in a few instances to Great Britain, the U.S. offered Latin Americans stable export prices at relatively high levels for periods of one to five years. This initiative had mixed results. First successes came in accords negotiated with Brazil and Mexico in May and July 1941. Brazil and the U.S. signed a two-year purchasing contract calling for the Portuguese-speaking nation to restrict exports of twelve key products, including bauxite, chromite, industrial diamonds, manganese, mica, nickel, quartz crystals and several others. While helpful in restricting open trade, the agreement encouraged the minerals-hungry Axis to enter smuggling, and from this point onward the illicit traffic presented a real problem, especially for small items like industrial diamonds. Along with these bilateral agreements, the State Department successfully persuaded U.S. businessmen in Latin America to break contracts or withhold shipments to the Axis. And through indirect pressure on private firms, Washington moved to shut off Japan from Chilean copper, Colombian platinum, and Mexican lead and zinc, among other commodities. But it was more difficult for the U.S. to control small independent producers, such as many of the Colombian platinum suppliers. These efforts to isolate the Axis from Western Hemisphere strategic materials would continue throughout the war, requiring vigilant efforts from agents of the Federal Bureau of Investigation (FBI) who combed the area south of the Rio Grande for subversives and worked hard to guard vital industrial raw-materials facilities from foreign sabotage.[19]

Meanwhile, the imminence of war sparked recommendations for a crash import program. In 1940, the NDAC had adopted a two-year stockpile goal as the basis of mobilization planning, largely because it seemed suited to existing budgetary circumstances. But in 1941 William Y. Elliott, now serving as stockpiling expert in the newly-created Office of Production Management, called for a more intensive program more suited to deteriorating international conditions. It was no longer reasonable to assume the United States could not be cut off from critical materials for longer than two years. If the British fleet were destroyed, as now seemed possible in 1941, the U.S. Navy might have the impossible task of trying to assure access to overseas supplies of long-flake graphite from Madagascar and mica from India, as well as chromium from Turkey, India, and South Africa. To assure access to vital supplies of tungsten, needed in shells and projectiles, Washington would need to control the west coast of South America, and to assure supplies of manganese and bauxite this country must safeguard the east coast of South America. Rather than stake the national existence on survival of Britain's fleet, Elliott urged intensified stockpiling, especially purchases of mica and graphite, mercury, industrial diamonds, and chromite. With ample inventories of these items the U.S. would have some protection against the consequences "if England went down." Partly as a result of these criticisms the OPM officially altered its stockpiling priorities in May 1941 to establish a three-year domestic supply.[20]

These efforts to expand the emergency stockpile conflicted with the practical problems of additional procurement. In revising the basic stockpile priority in 1941 OPM added several new materials, including kapok, quebracho, and cadmium, as well as hides, drugs, and chemicals. The planning authority also substantially increased the goals for copper, quartz crystals, graphite, lead, and certain other materials. To Jesse Jones and his aides in the RFC who actually purchased the items, these new objectives seemed impracticable. In some instances the new goals exceeded annual world production and presented difficulties given the "shortage of shipping space." Concerned, too, about using tax dollars prudently so as to avoid what might later be termed wasteful spending, Jones operated under the presumption that "unless we proceed in a prudent and business-like manner, our effort could easily cause more harm than good." He added: "Obviously in making purchases, we must take into account the wise policy of the administration to avoid price inflation." Avoiding inflation remained a priority for Jones, but the planning agency (OPM) held a different philosophy, believing that buying "all the available world production at this time . . . is justified as an immediate insurance against being cut off from very remote sources of supply before substitutes or domestic production have been definitely established." In the short run Jones, the cautious former Texas banker, prevailed with his homespun philosophy that "haste makes waste," but not without criticism.[21]

Attacks on Jones, which reached a peak in 1942 when Vice-President Henry Wallace lashed out at his political rival, became intense during the spring of 1941. Writer Eliot Janeway was one of the first to make Jones a scapegoat for the lagging stockpile program. He accused the federal loan administrator of having asserted that America needed rubber, tin, and other materials to achieve security, but "he did little more than talk." Jones had proceeded too cautiously in negotiating for rubber supplies, fearful the emergency might end and the U.S. would face another monumental problem disposing of surplus stocks. Nor, according to Janeway, did Jones anticipate or understand the shipping shortage caused when German submarine attacks in the Atlantic diverted merchant vessels from the Pacific to the more lucrative and dangerous North Atlantic convoy route. Indeed, Jones was so eager to save the taxpayers a single dollar that he at first refused to permit ships to land cargoes of rubber on the Pacific Coast for rail shipment to rubber fabricators in Akron, because rail shipping rates added to basic costs. According to Janeway, Jones ordered merchant ships carrying rubber to go through the Panama Canal, thus adding more than sixty days to the length of a single voyage. Other criticisms concentrated on Jones' alleged failure to arrange for swift merchant shipping to carry vital supplies of tin, tungsten, and other strategic metals out of the war zone to safety.[22]

An impartial view of the stockpile program in December 1941 confirms the popular criticisms of government preparedness. After Pearl Harbor presidential assistant Harry Hopkins learned from an assistant that "we are so far below our objective for most commodities as to justify the general statement that the stockpile program for most materials has been a failure." Government reserves contained *no* beryllium ore, *no* cobalt, *no* iridium, and only *1* percent of both cadmium and graphite requirements. The inventory was sufficient only for 16 percent of both chromium and manganese supplies; 20 percent, mica and cork; 24 percent, tin; 25 percent, mercury; 28 percent, tungsten; 30 percent, rubber. Only in zinc concentrates did the U.S. have as much as 59 percent of three-year requirements.[23]

Nor was the Roosevelt government geared up administratively to undertake a comprehensive economic defense program, although the president had taken some initiatives before this country formally entered the war. In July 1941, before freezing all Axis assets in an effort to prevent Germany and Japan from using the U.S. as an entrepôt, Roosevelt finally created an Economic Defense Board, and placed it under the overall supervision of Vice-President Wallace. Like its British counterpart, this new agency was expected to coordinate export controls, supervise import procurement, and take other economic action against the Axis. Established primarily as a policy-making authority, the Economic Defense Board began life with two serious handicaps. First, it lacked funds to undertake procurement and other operations, depending instead on the RFC, and Jesse Jones, to implement policy. Second, lacking a clearly defined mandate and an established division of authority with existing agencies, the new group faced competition from two older administrative power centers—the State Department and the RFC. The former, although an inefficient policymaking body while Cordell Hull served as secretary, traditionally handled intergovernmental negotiations, and it jealously sought to protect these prerogatives characteristic of a foreign ministry. The latter also emerged as a bitter competitor, for Jesse Jones, like Secretary of State Hull, detested the idealistic, liberal Wallace, and no amount of vice-presidential prestige could overcome this conflict of personalities and ideologies so long as President Roosevelt himself tolerated the situation. The Wallace-Jones feud gradually gained intensity, and notoriety, so that in 1943 the President opted to reorganize the economic warfare program again. This time he placed policymaking and procurement under the jurisdiction of a new agency, the Foreign Economic Administration, beyond the administrative reach of either Jones or Wallace. Not only did this ugly dispute underscore Roosevelt's own limitations as an administrator of civilian government, but also it embarrassed the chief executive and amused his Republican critics. From a different perspective the feud did nothing to facilitate cooperation with the British or other allies, and it complicated efforts to harness natural resources to the nation's wartime needs.[24]

Before Pearl Harbor, attempts to develop domestic minerals reserves and substitute materials also lagged, even though technicians recognized that North American mines might have to supply unprecedented quantities of materials until the U.S. and British navies could clear Nazi submarine packs from the oceanic transportation routes, thus reestablishing prewar supply patterns. Policymaking officials discounted the need for an emergency domestic materials program in public statements. For instance, Edward R. Stettinius, procurement chief of the Defense Advisory Commission, confidently predicted in July 1940 that America faced "no shortages" except perhaps in tin and rubber. *Business Week*, an important medium for communicating perspectives to the private sector, adopted the optimistic view that, except for the obvious shortages of rubber, tin, and chromium, the U.S. could either supply its own needs from existing domestic mines or find acceptable substitutes for items on the strategic and critical materials list. There seemed to be ample substitutes or supplies of the critical ferroalloys. Antimony, an alloy with a number of important military applications, including the hardening of lead used in shrapnel shells, was available in adequate supply from domestic and Mexican sources, if Japan should sever the China supply route. Similarly, the magazine claimed that chromium, an alloying ingredient used in armor plate and stainless steel, could be obtained from private inventories and domestic sources in adequate quantities to satisfy military needs if the Axis cut shipments from Africa, the Soviet Union, and Turkey. Cuba and the U.S. had sources scarcely "scratched," it asserted. And, to replace manganese from the Eastern Hemisphere, *Business Week* indicated that the "Bureau of Mines has developed a new process for extracting manganese from low-grade ore, of which we have unlimited quantities." Mica, previously obtained from Madagascar, might come from either domestic or Canadian mines in an emergency; also, substitutes like synthetic plastics could serve these purposes. Nor did Japanese dominance of Southeast Asia jeopardize America's war economy, for synthetics like Buna could serve for rubber. In place of tin, once obtained primarily from the Dutch East Indies and Bolivia, the U.S. could in a pinch curtail civilian usage, forcing the substitution of glass containers and cellulose wrappings for tin cans. In essence, the popular press conveyed the message that Uncle Sam, like Adolph Hitler, had adequate ersatz materials to meet the requirements of any likely emergency.[25]

While media accounts encouraged confidence in miracle materials, minerals specialists in the U.S. Bureau of Mines and the Geological Survey took a less sanguine view. Experts recognized the difficulties of suddenly adapting the large American economy to use of expensive ersatz formulas; inevitably, this type of emergency substitution would disrupt price stability and the rational allocation of economic resources, at least in the short term. So with a small quantity of funds appropriated in the 1939 stockpiling act the Interior Department began to explore intensively for new high-grade deposits of domestic ores, especially for materials on the strategic and critical materials list. They explored nearly 700 deposits, and sent more than 22,000 samples to laboratories for analysis. What the roving geologists sought was evidence the U.S. had quantities of nine key strategic materials—mica, quartz crystals, antimony, chromite, manganese, mercury, tungsten, nickel, and tin. Privately, the Interior Department reported that most of these investigations uncovered little material with much promise for production under normal conditions, although some low-grade deposits might supply strategic materials in an acute shortage.[26]

Conservation and substitution of materials offered interesting possibilities for reducing American dependence on external supplies, and before Pearl Harbor U.S. scientists considered some of these options. Engineers began to substitute lead for tin in some uses, and this avenue of research led to the inclusion of lead on the strategic materials list. To conserve nickel, a vital material available in Canada and New Caledonia but unavailable in adequate supply to meet all possible war requirements, scientists substituted other alloys, reducing the amount of nickel used in plating. Another promising way to conserve tin, devised in scientific laboratories, was to reduce sharply the thickness of tin coatings, and substitute collapsible tubes of other materials. These methods, together, promised to save 10,000 tons of tin annually—a substantial proportion of domestic consumption which approached 70,000 tons in 1939. And to conserve tungsten, scientists urged substitution of molybdenum, another alloy used to toughen steel, but one of which the U.S. possessed the principal world supply. Last, to cope with prospective zinc shortages growing out of an extended demand for brass to meet armed forces' needs, scientists suggested cutting the average amount of zinc in automobiles from 50 to 16 pounds.[27]

Importation, substitution, and conservation were all ways to cope with war-related materials shortages, but official Washington deliberately discouraged another possible option until this country actually entered the global conflict. Domestic mining of high-cost materials could generate emergency materials, but it was the consensus among officials in Washington "that a general appeal for increased production of strategic minerals should be avoided," a War Production Board historian wrote later. There were several important reasons for the slow evolution of a domestic minerals policy. First, experiences during and after World War I served as a recent reminder how federal policy had overexpanded the domestic mining sector, creating deep-seated adjustment problems that inevitably brought political pressure for relief and tariff protection in the 1920s. More recently the 1939 Strategic Materials Act established an explicit one-year limitation "for production and delivery from domestic sources," and thus the law prevented executive branch agencies from using available funds to encourage producers in the U.S. to explore and develop new mines, because such projects ordinarily required far more than a single year to gestate and produce additional materials. Finally, not until September 16, 1940, when revisions in the Federal Reserve Act allowed the RFC to make loans for development of strategic and critical minerals, did the federal government have authority to undertake either long-term purchase contracts, or other financial incentives, so as to stimulate domestic minerals production along lines of national need. In essence, the Roosevelt economic defense and minerals programs concentrated until quite late in 1940 on spot purchase of raw materials, and here with mixed results. Preoccupied with immediate purchases, the procurement agencies refrained from underwriting a far-reaching mining subsidy program, for the latter would undoubtedly bring residual problems of overexpansion and contraction.[28]

The winter of 1941–1942 marked an important transition in the protracted struggle against Axis expansionism. On the one hand, Nazi Germany and militarist Japan reached the crest of their global influence, while on the other hand the U.S. at last joined a be-leaguered United Kingdom as an active participant, an event important to harnessing an effective United Nations coalition destined to achieve ultimate victory in 1945.

Until the autumn of 1942, when the United Nations finally took the military offensive in North Africa, the English-speaking powers and their Soviet allies battled desperately to block an Axis strike aimed at mineral and petroleum deposits in southwestern Russia and the East Indies. All of the belligerents realized how critical it was to Hitler's design to obtain additional resources and a link through the Middle East to Japan before the United Nations took the offensive. In fact, in February 1942, military intelligence sources correctly anticipated a renewed Nazi thrust to obtain resources. Having depleted oil stores in the costly invasion of the Soviet Union in 1941, "Germany must secure, at the earliest opportunity, possible substantial supplies of oil. She can only obtain fabric oil in Caucasia or Iraq."[29]

Neither President Roosevelt nor his principal military advisers devoted enough attention to natural resource aspects of military strategy, although they did worry at length over Hitler's designs on the petroleum-rich Middle East. But middle-echelon officials in a variety of agencies understood clearly the resource implications of Axis initiatives in Asia, Africa, the Middle East, and Latin America, and their analyses percolated upward through their respective lines of command. In March 1942, a naval intelligence report warned: "If Japan can exploit the resources of the areas she has recently occupied (Thailand, Indo-China, Malaysia, Netherlands Indies, Borneo, Philippines) and maintain lines of communication, she is on the verge of achieving a degree of self-sufficiency in war materials which rivals (and in some items far surpasses) that attained by any other power in history, including the United States."[30]

Experts in the U.S. Board of Economic Warfare worried about the consequences of a successful German thrust across neutral Spain into western Africa. They concluded that loss of copper, asbestos, chrome, and cobalt resources in the Belgian Congo, British South Africa, and the Union of South Africa would have serious implications for the United Nations war effort. Western Hemisphere copper production would have to expand greatly if African production was unavailable—and this meant the U.S. must guard against Axis subversion and sabotage in Chile. Also, it seemed the Western Hemisphere could not replace Africa as a supplier of long fiber grades of asbestos and metallurgical grade chrome to meet 1942 military requirements. Most of all, cobalt from the Belgian Congo was vital. Said one BEW official, "If African cobalt is cut off, we would have to depend on our stockpile for relief. With economy and quick shipment of everything available in Africa, we would have approximately 18 months' supply." In essence, there were overriding natural resource requirements dictating that the U.S. and Great Britain block Germany and its Axis allies from successfully consolidating control in Eurasia and areas along the littoral.[31]

To Roosevelt and Churchill the Axis moves presented a distinct geopolitical threat, and in this area the leaders exhibited keen interest in the strategic thinking of geographers, in part because geopoliticians reportedly had great influence on the evolution of German strategy. Perhaps the clearest exposition of the consequences of an Axis victory appeared in the seminal 1942 writings of Yale University political scientist, Nicholas J. Spykman. In an account read widely in policymaking circles, Spykman raised the danger of America isolated in a hostile world. If Eurasia, Australia, and Africa were "brought under the control of a few states and so organized that large unbalanced forces are available for pressure across the ocean fronts, the Americas will be politically and strategically encircled." He even suggested that Germany and Japan, the prewar "have-not" powers, might employ an embargo of their own to deprive the Western Hemisphere of vital resources. Germany could withhold aluminum, manganese, mercury, and tin from Europe; chrome and manganese from Africa; and chrome, manganese, mica, and tungsten from the Indian Ocean area. Her partner Japan could embargo such strategic materials as chrome, Manila fiber, quinine, rubber, silk, tin, and tungsten through its control of the Far East. A Japanese conquest of Australia and surrounding areas would deprive the Western Hemisphere of important sources of wool and nickel. According to the Yale academician, "This situation is a clear indication that encirclement and blockade of the Western Hemisphere would make it exceedingly difficult for the United States to maintain a war industry adequate for defense."[32]

But the single most dangerous threat to American military requirements, Spykman stated, was not German dominance of Europe, the Near East, and Africa, although this region obviously had great significance, but rather Japanese control of Southeast Asia. "The Asiatic Mediterranean is perhaps the most important single source of strategic raw materials for the United States, and its control by a single power would endanger the basis of our military strength." Interestingly enough, Professor Spykman claimed the U.S. lacked a monopoly over any commodity of sufficient importance to influence German or Japanese behavior. But, ironically, Germany and Japan, the two "have-not" expansionist powers, had achieved sufficient resources from military aggrandizement to dominate Eurasia and deprive the North Americans of vital materials.[33]

Spykman seemed overly pessimistic about Western Hemisphere vulnerabilities, but in 1942 a number of policymakers shared his concerns, and for good reason. As a pack of German submarines attacked merchant shipping in the Western Hemisphere, Americans learned the high costs of failing to prepare. U-boats concentrated on disrupting the flow of bauxite from the Guianas. During 1942 these shipping losses endangered the aluminum expansion program, compelling the War Production Board to abandon its reliance on imported raw materials and resort, instead, to an "all-out" program designed "to make us domestically self-sufficient by eliminating all bauxite imports and utilizing greater tonnages of domestic low-grade, high-silica ores." During one three-week period in September and October, submarines sank fifteen bauxite carriers, reducing these deliveries at least 75,000 tons. Axis expansionism produced other American shortages as well. Tin imports ceased, and with Japanese victories in the Philippines, Malaya, and the Dutch East Indies, the Allies lost major sources of chrome, manganese, and tin. An acute shortage of shipping delayed imports of nitrates and copper from Chile.[34]

Shut off from nonhemispheric supplies and facing possible Axis dominance of the Middle East, South Asia, and Africa, American officials worried in 1942 about the next probable enemy objective—an attack on the Western Hemisphere or subversion of it. On February 17 William Donovan, the coordinator of information soon to take charge of covert activities as director of the Office of Strategic Services, warned the president that the "next move of the Nazis will be a frontal attack on New York, synchronized with the general Nazi organized revolution in all South American countries, timed to follow closely the fall of Singapore." In March FBI Director J. Edgar

Hoover also circulated warnings of dangerous Axis activity in Latin America. In particular, he feared German sabotage against petroleum facilities in Venezuela, bauxite shipping in Dutch Guiana, vanadium mines in Peru, and disruption of tin production in Bolivia, now the only secure source of that vital metal outside Japanese-occupied Southeast Asia. "It is known that the Axis powers have endeavored to create internal disorder in an effort to gain control of the Government and thus deter delivery of tin to the Allies," Hoover reported. The FBI director, whose agency had taken control of Western Hemisphere security operations as the OSS concentrated on activities in Europe, Africa, and Asia, reported other rumors the Germans and Japanese intended to use Colombia as a staging ground for assaults on American defenses in the Panama Canal Zone. "The strength of the Axis in this country is a serious threat to the defense of the Panama Canal," he concluded. Finally, Hoover reported information that Brazil's Japanese community, numbering over 280,000, had hand grenades, guns and antitank weapons and waited only for orders from Tokyo to seize an important seaport. "Even the larger city of Sao Paulo, frequently called the 'Pittsburgh of South America,' might not be able to withstand a surprise attack," the FBI official speculated.[35]

According to FBI analysis the Axis aspirations in South America remained similar to those revealed in the Zimmermann telegram of 1917. That is, Germany and other Axis powers "would use South America, or a part thereof as a base from which to attack our country." Unable to win control of a Western Hemisphere nation through diplomatic initiatives, "the enemy continues . . . to work in South America." Axis agents concentrated more on "the interruption of the flow of strategic raw materials to the Allies than on the effort to obtain the materials for its own use," the FBI asserted. What especially bothered U.S. intelligence officials was not the prospect of overt Axis activity but covert efforts to penetrate the ethnic communities, especially the Germans and Japanese, living in Latin America. Hoover recalled a 1939 comment attributed to Hitler: "We have no intention of proceeding with the conquest of Brazil by landing troops for the taking of the country. *Our armies are invisible.*"[36] (Italics added)

Against this background of Axis interest in disrupting Western Hemisphere trading patterns, Washington naturally watched events

south of the Rio Grande closely, especially in Bolivia. This moun-
tainous, landlocked Indian nation, situated between Chile and Argentina, where German agents were active, had a tradition of political instability as well as enormous mineral resources vital to the
U.S. during World War II. In 1939, the U.S. imported only $804,-
000 of products from Bolivia, but by 1942 outlays for Bolivian
tin, tungsten, antimony, and cinchona exceeded $41,000,000. As a re-
sult of long-term mineral contracts designed for both materials purchase and minerals development, Bolivia had become by 1943 the
most important supplier of tin and tungsten. America obtained 50
percent of its tin imports from Bolivia as well as one-third of its tungsten imports. And along with Mexico, Bolivia supplied United States
markets with large quantities of antimony. The small Andean nation
also supplied important quantities of cinchona bark, used in preparing quinine, after the U. S. lost access to primary supplies in Southeast Asia.[37]

In 1942 strikes in the tin mines and political unrest convinced
some Washington officials, including Coordinator of Inter-American
Affairs Nelson Rockefeller, that foreign elements sought to disrupt
the Bolivian political process and deprive this country of much-
needed tin. Vice-President Henry Wallace soon found himself at the
center of controversy in Washington for reportedly encouraging the
"electoral overthrow" of the Bolivian government "in order that it
might be succeeded by one of more liberal tendencies." Wallace
vigorously denied these charges, claiming he did not know President
Enrique Penaranda "was a reactionary" until some U.S. officials told
the vice-president that the Bolivian leader "looked on education of
the Indians of Bolivia as Communistic."[38]

This complicated internal situation simmered until December
1943 when a revolutionary government, headed by Alberto Villar-
roel, pulled a successful coup d'etat. Director Hoover informed the
White House that members of the new government had "Nazi con-
nections," and he noted also how closely linked some leaders of the
new government were with military leaders of Argentina who also
expressed pro-German sympathies. Eager to keep open the Bolivian
supply lines, although by December 1943 the American tin situation
was no longer acute, Washington refrained from offering the new
regime diplomatic recognition until Bolivia removed cabinet mini-
sters with Nazi associations. Later Víctor Andrade, minister of labor

in the revolutionary government, asserted that America's position as "the sole purchaser of our minerals" had enabled it to force a governmental change in La Paz.[39]

On the home front in 1942 industrial mobilization accelerated, creating additional demand for materials previously identified as strategic and critical but also boosting requirements for other materials as well. There were three principal options open to policymakers —foreign procurement, domestic production, and measures to conserve materials. Two days after Pearl Harbor the Supply Priorities and Allocations Board moved in desperation to expand foreign purchases, as it directed maritime authorities to "increase in every possible way the importation of scarce materials by utilizing all available cargo space." Unfortunately, despite the surprise attack and the obvious urgency, the Reconstruction Finance Corporation and its purchasing affiliates continued to dawdle in purchasing foreign supplies. In some instances, legitimate supply obstacles prevented these emergency purchases. The RFC said it was unable to contract for beryllium, as directed in December 1941, because "until June 1942 the principal supply source of beryllium was under private contract, and therefore no purchases were made by RFC until that time." Similarly, the purchasing agency was able to contract for only 318,000 pounds of cobalt, despite a 5,000,000 pound purchase order, because this country had limited facilities to treat Canadian ore and because, after April 1942, this nation lost maritime contact with Burma, the other principal supplier. Later America did obtain additional supplies of this vital metal from the Belgian Congo and French North Africa. In essence, then, although the Washington policymaking community sought to establish a three-year supply of strategic and critical metals, in many instances the actual supplies never reached a one-year level of consumption. Given the strategic situation and the administrative delays in implementing procurement directives, the serious stockpile deficiencies reflected the errors of purchasing "too little, too late."[40]

Within the hemisphere the U.S. did pursue successful policies to obtain additional foreign supplies. Metals experts concluded that, since Canadian production was heavily earmarked for the industrial requirements of Great Britain, this country must turn to Mexico as the "quickest source for increased quantities of lead, zinc, copper, mercury, antimony, and other minerals, which could be supplied by railroad transportation without submarine hazard." Consequently, in the spring of 1942 Yale University geologist Alan M. Bateman led a mission to Mexico that negotiated an important agreement opening the way for immediate production and purchase of war minerals. This soon resulted in a "flow of minerals . . . that glutted Mexican railways." Especially important to the U.S. were Mexican supplies of antimony, lead, zinc, and mercury, along with other materials. During the war years from 1941 to 1945 imports from neighboring countries increased rapidly. Despite labor unrest and inadequate rail transportation, purchases from Mexico climbed 236 percent, from $98 million to $231 million. From Cuba imports increased from $181 million to $337 million, up 185 percent, and Canadian imports jumped from $554 million to $1,125 million, up 203 percent.[41]

In developing foreign minerals for war use, Washington moved beyond techniques used for spot purchases, since an overriding objective was to expand production. In some instances, Washington offered straight term purchase contracts calling for purchases of stated quantities over a period as long as a year. This technique was used to obtain almost all of the foreign lead and 80 percent of imported copper. For hazardous mining operations too risky for private investments or where technical knowledge was lacking, the U.S. government actually undertook exploration development, road building and mining at its own expense or with repayment contracts for producers. This approach served to develop quartz, mica, and tantalite mining in Brazil. A different set of provisions were employed to secure submarginal copper and nickel in Canada, Chile, and Mexico. Washington devised a marginal-cost-plus-royalty contract, which provided incentives for holding down production costs, but nonetheless offered adequate incentives for developing submarginal ores. Finally, in some other episodes the government operated even more directly. The RFC financed government nickel production facilities in Cuba, when it seemed the United Nations allies faced a real shortage of that alloy early in 1942, particularly as the Japanese threatened New Caledonia.[42]

The Cuban nickel project stemmed from the planners' perception that physical limits on the expansion of Canadian nickel deposits and the Japanese advance in the South Pacific threatened to create a serious supply deficiency as war demand shot up from 150 million pounds annually to 250 million. Eager to bring into production Cuban laterite ores never produced successfully before on a commercial basis, Washington worked out an agreement with the Nicaro Nickel Company, a subsidiary of Freeport Sulphur Company, to construct and operate a plant in Cuba. To speed this project the Defense Plants Corporation actually financed the nickel plant, and the Metals Reserve Company, another RFC affiliate, financed operations and supervised the project. One of the important lessons from this successful experiment was that low-grade Cuban lateritic nickel deposits could be developed for industrial use, and as a result "the world is not dependent upon Canadian supply alone." In 1945, Cuban nickel production exceeded that of New Caledonia, the second leading producer (after Canada) until World War II. During the last half of 1945 this source produced at a rate equal to 30 percent of prewar U.S. nickel consumption, a remarkable feat, indeed, since Cuba had no production before the war.[43]

After the Japanese attack and America's formal entrance into the war, Washington also pushed a "crash" program to develop domestic supplies of ores and other scarce materials. Rocketing requirements for copper prompted the Supply Priorities and Allocations Board to subordinate "complicated checks on costs and profits" in order to concentrate on a single objective—producing "the *most copper in the quickest time*." As part of the effort to boost supplies of copper, as well as lead and zinc, from marginal domestic mines, the federal government devised the controversial "premium price policy," intended to promote maximum production for war purposes without increasing consumer prices, and exacerbating inflationary conditions. The scheme worked this way: the Metals Reserve Company agreed to pay premiums above ceiling prices of 2¾ cents per pound for lead and zinc and 5 cents per pound for copper for "over-quota" production during a two and one-half year period. This decision established an incentive for expanded production, and it helped generate new supplies of these vital materials for emergency needs. But the premium price approach also encouraged the type of domestic overexpansion that government officials had sought to avoid, and once again war-induced expansion of domestic mines would lead to severe, politically troublesome cutbacks. It is arguable that the lead and zinc industry did not recover from the World War II overexpansion until the 1960s when another war, this one in Indochina, pushed up the demand for these commodities.[44]

Pooling and conservation also helped the United Nations allies survive the first difficult year of global warfare. In January 1942, Britain and the U.S. established a Combined Materials Board, and it promptly recommended vigorous expansion of American domestic production of metals and minerals. This group urged increased production of nickel, vanadium, tungsten, and tin plate, as well as chromite, mica, and copper. The combined board soon encountered administrative and personnel difficulties but gradually it asserted a tight rein over the use of materials. Also, on December 9, 1941, the Supply Priorities and Allocations Board acted to curtail nonessential uses of scarce imported articles so as to conserve shipping space, and later that month it imposed a sweeping set of controls over civilian production and consumption. These restrictions extended so far as to forbid the use of copper for shoes, jewelry, and plumbing, among other things.[45]

Unfortunately these efforts did not proceed smoothly, and by late 1942 the whole War Production Board program for minerals was under fire in Congress and from the sometimes irascible Interior Secretary Harold Ickes. In testimony to a Senate Special Committee to Study and Survey Problems of Small Business Enterprise, chaired by James Murray (D.-Montana), Ickes complained that WPB officials opposed a coordinated minerals program. "It would be very helpful if the whole War Production Board organization saw more clearly the need for increased domestic production of minerals and metals." Also, the outspoken Interior Secretary grumbled that red tape and bureaucracy were thwarting efforts of his technologists to devise new competitive processes. "It may be that if we freed technology from the restrictions of interlocking corporate control and the ideology of monopoly, we would reap a harvest of new, highly efficient and self-contained medium- and small-sized operations," he said.[46]

How much should the government encourage the production of domestic materials, when by 1943 merchant ships could bring back high-grade foreign ores as ballast? That question again troubled Washington policymakers, as it had during American involvement in World War I. This time Secretary Ickes, whose department had a natural interest in promoting domestic mining interests, and Senator Murray argued vigorously for encouraging domestic minerals production, while the War Production Board took the opposite view. Yielding to domestic pressure, President Roosevelt told Senator Murray in April 1943, that "it is national policy to get the maximum possible output domestically and also to bring in as much as we can from overseas." Politically, it was impossible to defend the view that this country should purchase high-quality ores first, and use them as ballast on returning supply ships, no matter how logical this position in terms of efficient war production. Donald Nelson rationalized the administration's compromise—obtain as much as possible from all suppliers—in this fashion: "I size up the risks involved in seeking all we can get versus something short of that, the risks are much less serious under a policy of seeking all we can get." In effect, then, the WPB had no choice but to adopt the national policy of making "fullest possible use of small and marginal ore deposits," and this goal dovetailed with another objective, building up stockpiles of strategic and critical minerals in order to insure the U.S. against unforeseen developments. However necessary politically to appease an influential constituency (and it was), these decisions had the disadvantage of increasing domestic production of high-cost, low-quality ores. And from this government-sponsored expansion of domestic mining, it was only a small jump to the conclusion that postwar stockpiles should provide a peacetime market for the U.S. minerals industry so as to cushion the conversion problems.[47]

Other wartime government policies had more beneficial long-term results for the nation. Domestic exploration and technology programs achieved important gains. For instance, Geological Survey and Bureau of Mines data led to the exploration of the important San Manuel copper deposits north of Tucson, Arizona, where the Magma Company blocked out 425 million tons of 0.8 percent copper ore, containing some gold, silver, and molybdenum. And near Salmon, Oregon, the Bureau of Mines found a substantial body of cobalt-copper ore. In central Idaho private operators developed the nation's principal supply of tungsten and its largest source of antimony based on initial studies done in the Department of Interior. There were many other similar examples.[48]

In the War Production Board an office of production research and development, directed by the indefatigable Charles K. Leith, coordinated technological work on metals and minerals, and this work led to important results in devising substitutes and finding ways to conserve uses of scarce materials. Concerned about the overdependence on South American bauxite, which was vulnerable to

Nazi submarine attacks, scientists developed a lime-soda sintering process, enabling Bayer plants to use high silica bauxite deposits in Arkansas. Thus, while 54 percent of bauxite came from foreign suppliers in 1941, in 1943 more than 80 percent emerged from domestic mines. Technology had dramatically reduced, at least temporarily, this country's bauxite vulnerability. There were other important technological developments as well. Pilot plants showed how to remove alumina from clay and alunite, thus expanding domestic supplies for the aluminum industry. And, knowing how production of magnesium from brines and sea water involved a heavy consumption of electric power, technologists developed an inexpensive way to remove magnesium from dolomite, a very abundant rock. To save copper the WPB technology committee recommended using coated steel in place of cartridge brass, and this key substitution brought enormous savings in copper requirements.[49]

In addition to using a blockade and system of navicerts to isolate the Axis powers from outside supplies and to compel them to plunder occupied nations, Washington and London devised other imaginative tactics. Preclusive purchasing, which involved buying materials that might become available to Nazi Germany in neutral countries, enabled the English-speaking allies to take control of resources at the source rather than relying exclusively on intercepting vital materials in transit. Although Britain and France briefly dabbled in preclusive purchasing at the start of the European war, this policy only gained momentum and achieved major success after the U.S. formally entered the war, and earmarked dollars for these economic warfare operations.[50]

Before Pearl Harbor the RFC had purchased commodities in Latin American countries both to build up this country's materials inventory and to handicap Axis purchasing efforts, but these operations were ad hoc moves, not manifestations of a systematic preclusive buying program. That came in February 1942, when Jesse Jones, the federal loan administrator, wrote Roosevelt indicating that "on urgent recommendation of the State Department, WPB [War Production Board], and BEW [Board of Economic Warfare], we have agreed to undertake preclusive buying of strategic and critical materials on a highly non-commercial price basis, to prevent such materials reaching Axis countries." These agencies wanted to start the preclusive campaign in Portugal and Spain, buying tungsten, tin, wool, sheepskins, and perhaps mercury. "Some of these products, notably tungsten, have been driven to price levels far beyond world market prices, reflecting urgent need of Germany for such materials," he said.[51]

With President Roosevelt's approval, the RFC created the U.S. Commercial Company, modeled after its British counterpart, and gave it a broad mandate "to produce, acquire, carry, sell or otherwise deal in strategic and critical materials as defined by the President." For the most part, these undertakings took place in neutral European countries, like Spain, Portugal, and Turkey, adjacent to Nazi Germany, although a few secondary operations did take place in Africa and Latin America. For instance, the U.S. bought 4,000 tons of electrolytic copper of Katanga origin in Angola, small quantities of platinum in Argentina, and major supplies of the same material in Colombia, as well as industrial diamonds in Brazil and Venezuela at more than 50 percent above market price. At the periphery the preclusive program sought to discourage the shipment of small items, easily smuggled aboard an airplane or a merchant ship bound for a Spanish port.[52]

On the Iberian Peninsula and in Turkey, Allied preclusive operations made a major contribution to the Axis defeat, slowly depriving Germany of two vital ferroalloys required for modern warfare: tungsten and chromium. Substantially all of Germany's tungsten came from the Iberian Peninsula, although Germany ran great risks in efforts to supplement this with submarine shipments from the Far East. Late in 1943 Germany made other important strides to conserve tungsten by use of carbide cores in armor-piercing projectiles. British and American purchasing operations were so successful in Spain and Portugal during the summer of 1943 that Nazi Armaments Minister Albert Speer reported to Chancellor Hitler in November that the Third Reich had only a 10.6 month reserve of wolframite, the ore containing tungsten, and a 5.6 month reserve of chromium. The latter shortage was more dangerous, Speer thought, because without chromium "the manufacture of planes, tanks, motor vehicles, tank shells, U-boats, and almost the entire gamut of artillery would have to cease from one to three months after this deadline, since by then the reserves in the distribution channel would be used up." But Adolph Hitler displayed surprisingly little interest in the desperate materials situation; instead he was far more excited about new tank programs, which ironically depended on the availability of chromium and tungsten for their production.[53]

Political circumstances in Portugal, Spain, and Turkey varied, and these conditioned Allied economic warfare operations. In Portugal the government regulated tungsten sales strictly, despite smuggling operations and a thriving black market, and as Germany's military fortunes waned the Salazar government slowly exhibited support for the United Nations, pragmatically choosing to identify with the likely victors. Finally, in June 1944, the Portuguese government clamped an embargo on all tungsten exports to the Axis, a move that helped seal Hitler's doom. Between 1942 and 1944, however, the two English-speaking powers bought sizable quantities of Portuguese materials—5,649 metric tons of tungsten ores and concentrates, costing $53,460,000. It is estimated that another 5,555 metric tons slipped out through Spain to Germany.[54]

Far more than Portugal, which after all was vulnerable to United Nations military pressure against its possessions in the Azores, Africa, and Asia, the Spanish dared display overt sympathies for the Axis cause, although General Francisco Franco's government would also read the winds shrewdly. Perhaps as repayment for Nazi aid during the Spanish civil war, Franco maintained a Spanish military division on the eastern front fighting the Soviet Union. But the Madrid government was vulnerable to American political pressure, because it needed Western Hemisphere petroleum. The U.S. government adjusted the price of this oil upward to compensate for prices paid the Spanish government for raw materials purchased. In Spain the wolfram operations were complicated by the fact that tungsten lay close to the earth's surface, enabling farmers to exploit deposits. When the wolfram ore reached market it often cost ten times the world price. But recognizing that Spanish wolfram was absolutely essential to German military production, the British and Americans determined to shut off the flow, and in pursuing this objective they resorted to all the tricks of covert warfare. They created a Spanish cover operation, owned by Spanish nationals, to conduct extralegal operations such as smuggling or stealing ore from Axis-controlled mines. Also, Western agents sabotaged power and transportation facilities used to produce and transport tungsten. Altogether the two English-speaking nations acquired 5,418 metric tons of tungsten ores and concentrates, spending $136 million.[55]

To the German armaments industry, Turkish chrome was absolutely essential, and the Nazi regime used all the resources and diplomatic cunning at its disposal to keep open this source of supply. Realizing how important Turkish chrome was, Britain and France sought to tie up the source in January 1940, when they agreed to purchase the entire production for two years. This agreement expired late in 1942 and Germany successfully pressured this Balkan nation for an agreement calling for delivery of 90,000 tons of chromium annually. However Britain and the U.S. also leaned on the Turks from a different direction, and that government wavered, gradually exhibiting a pro–Allied sympathy after United Nations forces launched the North African campaign. In this ever-changing political situation British and American commercial companies engaged in active preclusive buying, and they procured over 800,000 tons of chromium at a cost in excess of $33 million. The commercial corporations engaged, as they did in Spain, in covert operations to disrupt Turkish supply shipments to Germany. On one occasion, for instance, over two hundred railroad cars bound for the Third Reich with vital chromium mysteriously disappeared, and on another occasion operatives mixed the precious chrome with other low-grade materials to reduce its effectiveness. As a result, the chromium supplies lagged or failed to meet German specifications. In 1943 the Axis received only 47,000 long tons out of 90,000 obligated, and in 1944, only 26,000 long tons arrived before the Turks suspended all deliveries in April.[56]

British and American economic warfare measures proved an important component in the overall United Nations strategy. If these measures did not bring the Nazi regime to its knees quickly, as proponents of the minerals sanction optimistically anticipated, the array of measures did isolate the Nazi economy, forcing it to pursue even harsher policies in occupied areas (which in turn encouraged resistance to the Nazis), and, most of all, denying the German economy the raw material cushion necessary to victory in 1941 and 1942. When the full impact fell on the German economy in 1943 and 1944, American and British bombers were effectively employing airpower to disrupt Nazi fuel supplies, especially in attacking the Rumanian oil fields. The successful ferroalloy campaign probably came too late to have major bearing on the outcome of the war, as W. N. Medlicott notes, but had other factors not intervened these shortages of tungsten, chromium, and other materials almost certainly would have led to the collapse of Germany's war production.[57]

From a different perspective, it is evident that the competition for raw materials contributed in a significant way to the onset and outcome of World War II. Had Germany and Japan sufficient energy materials and other industrial raw materials to meet growing national requirements, it is doubtful that territorial expansionism would have had such appeal to their respective leaders and elite groups. It is evident, too, that the need for specific materials shaped World War II military strategy directly. Access to the iron and ferroalloys of Scandinavia and the petroleum and manganese of Russia were major considerations in the fateful Nazi decisions to strike northward in 1940 and eastward in 1941 and 1942. Similarly, the need for secure petroleum supplies, and other raw materials, drove the Japanese to swing southward in late 1941, attacking U.S. installations and moving against remnants of the Dutch and British empires.

Western Hemisphere resources and United Nations dominance of maritime routes, sustaining the flow of African and South American materials to U.S. industrial facilities, also made a critical contribution to the outcome of World War II. Despite her own increasing dependence on foreign suppliers of ferroalloys, tin, rubber, and certain other materials, the U.S. remained relatively impregnable to serious supply dislocations. Arkansas bauxite and technological improvements aided the U.S. to survive the U-boat attacks on South American shipments, and the American economy also proved sufficiently flexible to find substitutes for other materials in temporary short supply. Ultimately, the overwhelming combination of physical, human, and industrial resources from North America brought about the Axis collapse. If Germany had had the good fortune to have acquired a resource base as bountiful as America's, World War II would certainly have lasted longer with more devastating destruction. The asymmetry of natural resources not only hastened the Axis defeat, it avoided the necessity of terminating a global war of attrition with the widespread use of atomic weapons, perhaps in 1947 or 1948.

Chapter Five
"Have-Not" America
and the Debate
over Postwar Minerals Policy

WORLD WAR II imposed a heavy burden on the American domestic minerals industry, and to many observers this rapid depletion of ore reserves had ominous implications. The U.S., it seemed, was becoming a "have-not" power, like Germany, Italy, and Japan, the three aggressive nations who sparked the global conflict.

Metals industry statistics offered ample evidence to support this grim forecast. During five years of mobilization and combat, domestic mines and wells produced in excess of 3 billion tons of coal, a billion tons of petroleum, 500 million tons of iron ore, 2¼ million tons of lead, 3½ million tons of zinc, 5 million tons of copper, 14 million tons of bauxite, 17 million tons of sulphur, 68 million tons of salt, and 3 million tons of potash. Production of ores reached unprecedented levels, substantially higher than in the prosperous 1920s. For instance, energy production climbed 25 percent above its peak in the 1920s, and for iron and copper mining the figures were 43 percent more and 13 percent more, respectively. Altogether, reported the Army-Navy Munitions Board, "the quantity of minerals produced in 1943 was 57 percent greater than the output in 1918 and 23 percent above that in the boom year, 1929."[1]

The extraordinary demand for raw materials did not boost prices precipitously, as happened in World War I. This time government employed a variety of techniques, including premium price plans and purchasing agreements, to hold down inflationary price increases. In constant dollars, the price of a barrel of petroleum fell during World War II about 12 percent, while it rose 61 percent during the First World War. Nor did the constant dollar prices of copper, lead, petroleum, tin, and zinc reach World War I peaks. Except for zinc, each of these commodities cost more in constant dollars before the war in 1937 than in 1944. Government simply did not allow the price mechanism to signal shortages or to invite intensive exploration and development of new reserves until after the war ended.[2]

Meanwhile, not only did military and civilian needs drain domestic reserves but soaring demand for metals boosted imports sharply. During the interwar period the U.S. had been a leading exporter of copper, lead, and zinc, but during the war this country became a heavy purchaser of these items—importing, in 1943, 23 percent of copper, 35 percent of lead, and 35 percent of zinc consumed.

And, as the Defense Department's list of vital war materials multiplied from one dozen to five dozen, the U.S. also looked to foreign nations for previously unimagined quantities of rare materials, such as tantalum (used for electronics and synthetic rubber), beryllium (often used as an alloy to harden copper), and bismuth (employed as an alloy which melts at low temperatures in, for example, fire sprinklers). Also developments in military technology, such as radio and radar, created greater need for minerals previously valued "mainly as adornments of museum collections rather than as pressing industrial materials." On this list of scarce materials were steatite talc, quartz crystals, optical calcite, and some other items.[3]

From the national perspective what these shifting supply patterns and materials requirements meant was that the U.S. had outgrown its domestic resource base and become far more reliant on a number of less-developed, raw-material exporting nations, or colonies, who, because of the chance distribution of mineral resources, happened to possess materials vital to the Allies—and the Axis. During the war the United States imported about sixty varieties of minerals—and twenty-seven of these came *only* from foreign sources. "Except for coal, iron, and salt," said minerals expert Alan Bateman, "some quantity of every mineral needed for our war effort had to be imported." These materials the United States imported from fifty-three different countries extending from Canada and eleven Latin American nations, to Australia, New Caledonia, China, and India in the Pacific. Also wartime supplies arrived from Spain, Portugal, Cyprus, Turkey, and fourteen African countries.[4]

Before the United Nations coalition hammered out its permanent plan for international organization and nailed shut the Axis coffin, the White House had begun to consider postwar natural resource policy. In response to repeated urgings from Gifford Pinchot, the old progressive-forester, President Roosevelt ordered the State

Department to consider a world conservation conference. "Conservation is a basis of permanent peace. Many different kinds of natural resources are being wasted," the chief executive told Secretary of State Hull. While it appears President Roosevelt was planning to summon a conservation conference similar to the one organized by his cousin Theodore Roosevelt as president, State Department opposition, based largely on the belief that such a conference would undercut functions of the new United Nations and its affiliates, doomed the plan after Roosevelt's death.[5]

Pinchot, always a zealous and persistent advocate of conservation, then persuaded Secretary of the Interior Harold Ickes, another old-line progressive, to champion the idea, and in May 1945, he urged President Truman to convene a world conference. Sessions would consider such matters as a national inventory of natural resources, depletion of irreplaceable mineral resources, and a program of international cooperation to conserve natural resources, and thus contribute to world peace. Ickes explained that "the war drain on the natural wealth of the world has been terrific. The war has taken a heavy toll of the forests, the oil, the coal, and the iron and other metals, and has added to the already heavy depletion of soil resources." Anticipating further drains on limited resources as rebuilding of devastated areas began, Ickes asserted that "ample supplies of raw materials widely distributed throughout the world are necessary to provide the economic well-being without which world peace cannot long be preserved." He saw, in brief, the need for a comprehensive campaign to prevent unnecessary depletion and to provide equal access for all nations to world resources.[6]

Unable to generate serious interest at the White House in support of a dramatic move on the conservation front, Ickes turned to a popular audience. In an article designed both to inform and alert readers of a mass-circulation magazine, the Interior Secretary exhibited Cassandra's pessimism. "The plain fact is that we cannot afford another prolonged war in 20 or 30 years. . . . The prodigal harvest of minerals that we have reaped to win this war has bankrupted some of our most vital mineral resources," he said. "We no longer deserve to be listed with Russia and the British Empire as one of the 'Have' nations of the world. We should be listed with the 'Have Nots,' such as Germany and Japan."[7]

From Ickes' perspective depletion of America's natural resource

base had serious implications. Only nine of the major minerals required to support industrialization were available in sufficient quantity to last one hundred years, and more importantly the known usable
reserves of twenty-one key minerals would last only thirty-five years
or less. While the famous Mesabi Range in Minnesota, which once
produced high-grade iron ores and served as the principal source for
the large domestic steel industry, would soon be "only a rusty memory," the secretary conceded the U.S. held enough iron from other
deposits to last a century. Similarly, America faced no imminent
shortages of nitrogen, magnesium, salt, bituminous coal and lignite,
phosphate rock, molybdenum, anthracite, and potash.[8]

Where the immediate problem occurred, said Ickes, was in alloys and key nonferrous metals. For instance, the U.S. had only a
two-year supply of usable manganese ore in its proven domestic reserves, a seven-year supply of vanadium, and a four-year supply of
tungsten. Other important minerals with less than a thirty-five-year
supply included petroleum, copper, lead, tin, zinc, nickel, bauxite,
chromite, and cadmium. And while the U.S. previously had an
abundance of petroleum, except briefly after World War I, the Interior Department forecast growing dependence on sources of supply
outside the Western Hemisphere, including Saudi Arabia and Bah-
rein. In stating these unpleasant trends, Ickes sought to provoke
public awareness and to shape a consensus behind vigorous government efforts to develop mineral stockpiles, explore for new reserves,
concentrate scientific efforts on improving mining technology so as
to recover better low-grade ores, and, finally, stimulate awareness of
this nation's mounting resource dependence on other nations.

President Truman's Interior Secretary was not the first prominent
government official to make headlines on the "have-not" theme. Two
years earlier an outspoken War Production Board administrator,
William L. Batt, who like Ickes had a Republican political background, warned that Americans must cease thinking of their country
as a land possessing unlimited quantities of natural resources. Instead he saw this nation "passing from a country of plenty to a
country of scarcity in the field of metals and minerals and other essential supplies," despite improved prospects for recovering many
low-grade materials at somewhat higher costs. Batt compared America's resource position to Great Britain's, for that nation also at one
time utilized domestic coal and iron to gain a preeminent position in

world industry, but now Britain relied on heavy imports of minerals and foodstuffs to support its standard of living. "It may hurt our pride, but harden our decision, to ask ourselves if the remarkable combination of assets which enabled this country to develop its fantastic strength is not gone for ever."[9]

Another early proponent of the "have-not" thesis was Elmer Pehrson, chief of the economics and statistics branch of the Bureau of Mines, and a civil servant involved actively in all wartime mobilization issues. In a series of articles and addresses beginning in April 1945, Pehrson communicated to the mining and engineering community as well as to the foreign policy elite his view that while the U.S. was far from exhausting the basic resources for our industrial economy—such as coal and iron—"exhaustion is well advanced in a number of important subsidiary minerals so that we can no longer drift along with the easy-going philosophy that the earth will provide." His analyses suggested this country had exhausted nearly 60 percent of its original petroleum reserves, an estimated 60 percent of copper reserves, about 75 percent of original zinc reserves, and approximately 80 percent of lead reserves. Compounding the dangers of declining reserves, according to Pehrson, was the fact that "the rate of discovery of metalliferous deposits has been declining at an alarming rate for half a century." He considered it significant that no major metal-producing district had been brought into production since 1916. What declining rates of discovery foreshadowed was not simply long-term exhaustion but increasing reliance, over the intermediate term, on applying improved technology to known deposits so as to recover low-quality ores not presently economical to mine, and also reliance on discovery of subsurface reserves.[10]

These bleak projections, representing as they did an official view of America's changing natural resource position, disturbed many minerals experts outside government, and criticisms of the government's one-sided interpretation appeared in the specialized mining and engineering journals. While conceding that forecasts of a "have-not" mineral position served to focus public attention on the vital importance of minerals, the *Mining Congress Journal* said that such statements left "an oversimplified, a distorted picture in the mind of the ordinary reader." *Mining and Metallurgy*, the monthly journal of the American Institute of Metallurgical Engineers, editorialized against the "have-not" thesis, saying: "Those who worry about the exhaustion of minerals are either uninformed or they underrate the ingenuity and resourcefulness of the researcher and the engineer." What the pessimists ignored in their sensationalized accounts was that there were no imminent or long-term shortages of iron, aluminum, or magnesium; nor was there any shortage of coal, an indispensable energy source. With ample supplies of these materials scientists and engineers could utilize low-grade ores, such as manganese, which was "almost inexhaustible" in quantity, and they could interchange various scarce alloys. Moreover, while technology improved prospects for substituting abundant materials for scarce items, metallurgists expanded the list of ferroalloys, introducing beryllium, columbium, titanium, boron, tellurium, indium, selenium, lithium, zirconium, and tantalum, each widely used in war materials.[11]

Chiding Secretary Ickes' gloomy prognosis, the *Mining Congress Journal*, voice of the domestic mining industry, advanced its own bullish view of the future. "We deny the implied inability to improve or at least maintain the current status. The greatest 'know how' ever available to the industry is constantly improving our exploration techniques and utilization of lower-grade ore materials." The mineral shortage myth, claimed the experienced miners, was perpetrated by international economists more familiar with trade theory than with the special characteristics of mining. According to the mining industry, there were good reasons why production had outdistanced exploration in recent years, because war demand for minerals exceeded the industry's capacity to develop new reserves in the short-run. Declining exploration reflected temporary bottlenecks, not an inherent gap between depleting resources and rising consumer demand. For the future there were several developments favorable to more intensive exploitation of U.S. mineral reserves. Improved research techniques, resulting from advances in geophysics and geological interpretation, promised successful prospecting at greater depths in the near future. Also, improving methods of ore production and beneficiation would soon make lower-grade materials merchantable. For these reasons, the *Mining Congress Journal* boasted: "Our miners, technologists and executives possess the 'know how' to perpetuate American metal mining for many decades to come." What the domestic miners wanted was not a series of official dissertations announcing the demise of American mining, for these forebodings discouraged the investment capital needed to develop new reserves, and thus helped fulfill the prophecies. Rather the American miners needed and wanted, "relief . . . from many existing curbs, like overly limited S.E.C. [Securities and Exchange Commission] rulings, heavy taxation, low ceiling prices on metals *and constant land-grabbing threats by the Interior Department.*"[12]

Outside the official bureaucracy those concerned with mining were generally optimistic, not pessimistic. Essentially the private sector expected market forces to correct temporary shortages. Higher demand would boost minerals prices and over the intermediate term stimulate exploration and exploitation of new reserves. Improved technology would continue to increase the use of lower-quality ores and encourage substitution for scarce or costly materials. What government should do was to strengthen automatic marketplace forces through tax relief to the minerals industry, and to support United States–based mining companies abroad in their search for new ore deposits. Evan Just, the influential editor of *Engineering and Mining Journal*, called for a national mineral policy to promote "active cooperation" between Washington and the minerals industry. Among the provisions of a national policy, Just suggested adoption of tax policies designed to encourage exploration and development, including continuation of the mineral depletion allowance, a downward revision of the capital-gains tax, and a three-and-one-half year exemption from income taxation for all new mining ventures, such as Canada offered. These incentives, he asserted, would stimulate exploration.[13]

Within the large government and private research institutions, including the U.S. Geological Survey, scientists exuded confidence about the possibility of finding ample quantities of raw materials from domestic ore deposits. For instance William E. Wrather, director of the geological survey, looked in part to important developments in subsurface geology, and in this area similarities existed between the petroleum industry after World War I and the mining industry in 1945. Twenty-five years ago demand for petroleum jumped upward but domestic discovery levelled off, causing doomsayers to forecast exhaustion of American oil resources. In seeking solutions some petroleum experts pursued the time-tested approach of random drilling along the fringes of established oil-bearing fields, but some larger oil companies urged geologists to concentrate on subsurface geology—and that, claimed Wrather, is where the payoff came, rejuvenating the domestic oil industry in time to meet expanded oil requirements for the automobile age. "Faith in the ability of American scientists, scientific methods, and in a bounteous nature leads me to predict that great mineral resources remain to be developed," Wrather said.[14]

The same faith in technology and science existed at Battelle Memorial Institute, the large Columbus, Ohio research organization engaged in metallurgical work. Clyde Williams, the director, predicted that "scientific research and its practical application by industry" would expand America's resource base, just as research helped the Allies mobilize the world's largest industrial and raw-material resource base for combat against the Axis in World War II. Research, encouraged and supported partly from government funds, would develop high-grade subsurface deposits, improve metallurgical techniques for exploiting low-grade resources, and encourage substitution.[15]

If Secretary Ickes' warning exaggerated the consequences of minerals depletion, causing many to believe the United States was literally running out of ores, his public relations campaign awakened interest in Congress and helped crystallize support for a comprehensive minerals program, designed both to develop domestic resources and to prepare for disruption to overseas supplies. Within a year after the close of World War II the Interior Department began lobbying aggressively for a variety of minerals programs, including a national inventory of resources. Less than 10 percent of the U.S. was mapped on scales adequate for exploratory mining, said Julius Krug, who succeeded Ickes. "In this respect, the United States ranks with the less industrialized nations of the world." Utilizing the latest geophysical techniques applicable to metals, it was now possible to find significant mineral deposits under land. In this area of research the wartime use of the airborne magnetometer for locating U-boats under water had opened the way to a new type of geological prospecting. Recognizing that a good national inventory might cost $1 billion, the Interior Department urged Congress to support an exhaustive accounting, which would indicate clearly the degree of American dependence on foreign sources, the possibilities for sustaining domestic mining, and the opportunities for substituting one mineral for another and, indeed, plastics for certain metals.[16]

A second proposal concerned constructing a Saint Lawrence Seaway. This project would strengthen the domestic metals industry, since it would allow firms formerly dependent on Mesabi iron ore to obtain foreign imports at competitive prices. Without a seaway, "the tendency will be for metal fabricating to move out of the lake area, particularly toward the east coast, to gain the advantage of the lowest costs," Interior anticipated.[17]

More federal support for Bureau of Mines pilot plants and research oriented to use of low-grade materials was a third way the Interior Department proposed to counter depletion of existing resources. During World War II the Bureau of Mines pursued a number of projects to economize on imports of manganese, chromium, cobalt, magnesium, alumina, titanium, zirconium, as well as iron and steel. One of the Bureau's greatest successes lay in developing and employing a pilot plant to extract manganese electrolytically from low-grade ores. The product served as a substitute for nickel in stainless steels. In May 1947, the Bureau of Mines urged congressional support for seventeen similar projects, which would devise new methods for treating and using low-grade ore reserves and develop substitutes for essential ores and mineral products.[18]

Finally, Interior wanted Congress to continue subsidy payments to high-cost domestic mineral producers and stockpile minerals for future war needs. The mineral subsidy program, involving a continuation of wartime premium prices for production of copper, lead, and zinc, was extended in 1945 and 1946 for a total of $188 million in subsidies. But when manganese producers also pushed for subsidies in 1947, President Truman vetoed the entire premium price program, thus cutting off lead, zinc, and copper producers as well. Truman explained in his veto message that subsidies would only encourage excess production, creating additional minerals surpluses.[19]

A long-range postwar minerals policy rested on the conviction that science could, with federal support, counteract the steady depletion of America's mineral resources, and perhaps even expand this resource base both qualitatively and quantitatively. While technology could make the U.S. more self-reliant in another conventional war of attrition, some policymakers questioned whether ersatz materials could compete with high-quality natural resources in peacetime, and they recognized that some materials would undoubtedly continue to come primarily from foreign supplies. These considerations meant the U.S. must continue to trade, and the objective of national policy must be to promote the most efficient utilization of both global and domestic resources compatible with emergency security needs. It was evident that only an effective peacetime stockpiling program could serve as a cushion against disruptions to these global supply lines. Consequently, as early as 1943, officials in the War Production Board, the Army-Navy Munitions Board, and several other agencies worked to devise a politically acceptable program intended to continue stockpiling permanently and, if possible, to hold high-grade foreign materials in the emergency stockpile. Broad-based support for permanent minerals cushions reflected, incidentally, another example of government officials reading the lessons of past experiences and taking action to avoid similar errors in the future. Convinced now that minerals constituted a basic foundation for military might, experts believed, according to Alan Bateman, that "mineral stockpiles are more basic than battleships and bombers; their very existence might help avert future attack and guarantee the safety of our nation in years to come."[20]

No minerals expert was more sensitive to lessons of the past than Charles K. Leith, who during World War II served variously as an adviser to the War Production Board and the State Department. In a memorandum on postwar minerals policy prepared at the request of Assistant Secretary of State Dean Acheson in 1945, Leith emphasized how stockpiling was required to avoid the mistakes of two prior wars. On both occasions, despite adequate warnings, the U.S. failed to insulate its domestic economy from vulnerable foreign supplies until too late. Because the strategic materials list now contained sixty-five minerals, far more than the nine listed in 1940, the U.S. would require a greater volume and variety of foreign materials than in any previous conflict. This trend, as well as depletion of high-grade domestic ores, bothered Leith for he feared the consequences of repeating "our earlier mistakes. . . . The problem will be worse next time." What he advocated was a permanent strategic stockpile designed to hold high-quality foreign materials, not to subsidize high-cost domestic producers. An ancillary advantage, Leith noted, was that a stockpile could stabilize commodity prices and, as a consequence, the stockpile would help provide foreign nations with dollars needed for international trade.[21]

Other powerful arguments for permanent stockpiling came from William Y. "Wild Bill" Elliott, a Harvard government professor, expert on economic warfare, and later teacher of Henry Kissinger. Stockpiles would avoid the possibility that, in a future war, delays in expanding mining facilities would slow war mobilization. Also, only the federal government could be expected to maintain stockpiles, because it was exorbitantly expensive for private industry to hold inventories with even a year's supply. "No private corporation could afford to make the costly investment in materials like quartz crystals, industrial diamonds, strategic grades of mica, and graphite which were absolutely essential if we were to be relatively well protected against the loss of sources of these supplies." A third compelling reason for mobilizing resources beforehand, Elliott said, was the need to reduce pressure on wartime shipping. Not only did convoy procedures delay shipments but also heavy losses to submarine attackers inevitably endangered key domestic programs. For example, during one period in 1942, he said, the United States lost about one hundred ships in the short-haul bauxite trade between this country and the Caribbean Guianas. This heavy toll took place at a time when shortages of bauxite, needed for aluminum, threatened to delay the wartime aviation production program. On another occasion, Elliott indicated, the loss of a single slow freighter carrying strategic mica and graphite from Madagascar "would have had . . . crippling effects upon some of our most important aviation programs."[22]

Stockpiling would also guard against another danger: the U.S. might lose access to vital supplies in a future conflict. There were two serious possibilities. A future adversary might seize strategic materials, as Japan did in Southeast Asia. Or a potential enemy might wage an effective form of economic warfare, engaging in preclusive buying in Africa and perhaps the Western Hemisphere to deprive the U.S. of critical supplies in the same way this country and Great Britain functioned in neutral countries—Spain, Turkey, and Portugal—when the outcome of World War II hinged in large part on Germany's ability to obtain armor-piercing tungsten and chromium.[23]

Discussion of a postwar raw-materials stockpile as a type of war insurance intensified in 1943 as government agencies concerned with mobilization and reconversion weighed a series of critical decisions. As indicated earlier, the 1939 stockpiling authorization (PL 117) took a back seat during World War II to purchases of the Reconstruction Finance Corporation and its satellite agencies for immediate wartime use. Now in 1943, after the United Nations coalition reestablished control of vital maritime arteries, and as crash ship-building programs multiplied the maritime cargo fleet, the government had to decide whether to dispose of all surplus materials at the close of hostilities, or seek amendments to the 1939 law permitting consolidation of RFC materials into a single strategic stockpile with other government mineral holdings.

On this issue the minerals industry had a vital interest, and individual firms sought to influence an official decision. After World War I the government disposed of its surplus materials and these sales depressed the prices for current production, throwing the mining industry into a deep recession. To guard against a repetition, some industry spokesmen initially favored consolidating existing supplies into a national strategic stockpile, so as to insulate the market from government surplus disposals. Some members of the mining community also feared that government stockpiles might overhang the market, having a long-term potential for disrupting the domestic mining industry. Fearing another depression, the mining industry generally favored a stockpile plan. The *Mining Congress Journal* warned in January 1944 that the effect of "unregulated disposal of metal and mineral stocks at the war's end on employment in mining communities can be realized from the many months of unemployment and acute distress experienced after the last war." It urged: "For the safety of the nation and for the protection of our mining populations, a stockpiling bill should be enacted immediately."[24]

Among the bureaucracies most concerned with minerals problems and mobilization a consensus existed in behalf of a consolidated peacetime stockpile. Admiral William Leahy, President Roosevelt's Chief of Staff, wrote Donald Nelson, chairman of the War Production Board, that "the Joint Chiefs of Staff are of the firm conviction that stockpiles of strategic materials should be maintained after the war in order that we may not again be confronted with embarrassing shortages." Elliott also argued against suggestions to cut raw-material holdings, because this might result in "withdrawing the margin of safety and insurance against unforeseeable new requirements or against interruptions of supply." A note of dissent came from George Ball, then a middle-level official in the Foreign Economic Administration, who wrote State Department aide Eugene V. Rostow that the "Elliott school of thought over-emphasizes the national defense consideration and largely ignores the economic consequences which would flow from a large government-held stockpile of materials hanging over the market."[25]

While the State Department lacked operational responsibility for materials procurement, it was naturally sensitive to the foreign policy implications of permanent stockpiles. For one thing the position of these stockpiles "will have a considerable effect upon the bargaining position of the United States at the peace conference and in the negotiation of subsequent agreements for raw materials controls or for free access to postwar requirements of industry," asserted one memorandum. Large stocks, it was thought, would increase the American freedom of action and improve its bargaining position in peace deliberations; however, large stocks might also discourage foreign countries from continuing to supply materials to the United States. Other nations might fear the release of official holdings, thus depressing the market.[26]

There were other pressures on the decision process as well. Western miners, predictably enough, wanted to ensure that any stockpiling measure contained a provision subsidizing purchases of domestic resources. Elsewhere in the official bureaucracy, including the Bureau of the Budget and the powerful Office of War Mobilization, there were individuals who believed the government should promptly liquidate its materials inventories. Mobilization director James Byrnes received one recommendation arguing that "sound public policy would commend, if it were safely attainable, a program which would mean that at the end of the war the Government would own no stockpiles of strategic materials."[27]

During 1943 and 1944 three different approaches to critical stockpiling issues emerged in Washington, and each reflected a different constellation of interests and perceptions of the national advantage. First, Senator James Scrugham, a Nevada mining engineer, introduced a "Minerals Stockpile Act" in the 77th and 78th Congresses (1941–1945). This proposal would stockpile only minerals, giving mandatory preference to domestic materials, through a version of the "Buy American" principle, enacted in 1933. The plan Scrugham introduced in December 1943, (S. 1582) proposed a Mineral Stock Pile Control Board composed of "five outstanding members of the mining industry," and directed that all material holdings be held exclusively for emergency use as Congress directed. An obvious move to shelter the Western mining industry, this measure would assure a government market to domestic producers, and it would establish a legislative shelter for the industry against any future executive-branch effort to dispose of government stockpile holdings, such as had depressed the American mining industry after World War I.[28]

The executive bureaucracy, naturally enough, disagreed with the Scrugham approach. For one thing, it failed to provide stockpiles for nonminerals which might also be strategic, and for critical materials, such as rubber. Also, in freezing existing supplies and forbidding foreign purchases, the act would deny the government an opportunity to buy high-quality, low-cost foreign ores. It would also keep the executive branch from using mineral purchases to remove "deflationary factors" in mineral markets, and thus from bolstering the economies of friendly nations, said Interior Department Undersecretary Abe Fortas. Another defect, in the estimation of some administration officials, was Scrugham's provision for continuing premium price payments to marginal domestic producers, for this policy represented a continuing subsidy to uncompetitive Western miners.[29]

Ironically, while Senator Scrugham considered his plan a boon to American miners, this industry supported his proposal only "halfheartedly." The bill would, at least, freeze existing government minerals inventories, but it had several possible disadvantages. Longterm foreign purchase commitments, used to obtain high-quality ore at the cheapest prices, might strengthen the foreign mining industry, and accumulation of large federal stockpiles raised the possibility that a future administration might dispose recklessly of metals and minerals.[30]

Two other plans emerged from the government bureaucracy. A State Department committee which economic adviser Herbert Feis headed devised a permanent stockpiling bill in consultation with other agencies. And the military drafted its own proposal, one aimed primarily at significant revisions in Public Law 117, the 1939 Stockpiling Act. These different suggestions had certain common features differentiating them from the Scrugham approach. Both envisaged stockpiling other critical materials in addition to minerals, which the Scrugham proposal, written primarily with Western mining interests in mind, did not. Also, both executive-branch proposals avoided a clear statement of the "Buy American" provision in order to secure quality materials from abroad without underwriting marginal producers at home. And finally, neither the civilian nor the military suggestion gave the domestic mining industry control of the stockpile through the controlling board and the legislative process as did Scrugham's scheme.[31]

Where the Feis and military proposals differed significantly was in administration. Generally, the military-sponsored amendments would retain operational control for the armed forces and concede the Interior Department some participation, while the Feis plan placed the Secretary of State on the controlling board and left some administrative functions unclear. After a bureaucratic battle in 1944, James Byrnes, director of the Office of War Mobilization, decided to scrap both of these proposals. As a result, the administration had no stockpiling plan ready for submission to Congress until late in 1945, and that plan would reflect a broader configuration of interests than these earlier drafts.[32]

Meanwhile Congress moved precipitously to ease industry fears that government-owned accumulations of strategic and critical materials would be sold on the private market, depressing prices and triggering a serious dislocation of the war-expanded minerals industry. In the Surplus Property Act of October 3, 1944, Congress stipulated that all government-owned strategic minerals and metals designated as surplus would be transferred to the Treasury procurement account and added to stockpile holdings. But the measure contained ambiguous language regarding disposal of strategic and critical materials as well as procedures for transferring surplus material to the permanent stockpile. The act did, at least, direct the Army-Navy Munitions Board to recommend stockpile quantities for each strategic and critical item within three months, and then, one year after submitting these recommendations, the board might arrange for pruning government inventories of these surplus materials, unless Congress provided otherwise.[33]

The final decisive round in the struggle for a permanent stockpile policy began in early 1945 after the Army-Navy Munitions Board presented its recommendations to Congress, as required. The report did more than recommend appropriate quantities of materials for a stockpile. It also presented a case for a long-term program and recommended specific changes in the little-used 1939 measure. Recent experiences, the Board asserted, "demonstrate conclusively that the maintenance of stocks of strategic and critical materials is an essential element of national security." The strength of the Axis early in the Second World War derived to a large extent from supplies of raw materials accumulated before the conflict. Similarly, the limited ability of the U.S. to meet mobilization requirements then stemmed directly from failure to stockpile in the 1930s. The Army-Navy Munitions Board also noted how accelerated depletion of domestic reserves threatened to make the U.S. "even more dependent upon foreign sources" and these circumstances dictated raising stockpile goals. What the Board suggested was relaxation of the statutory "Buy American" requirement to permit easier purchase of foreign materials. Also, a new act should contain provisions allowing periodic stockpile rotation to avoid obsolescence. Advising that acquisition of minimum quantities must occur gradually, to avoid dislocations in commodity markets, the Board urged beginning these purchases early. It also mentioned the related need for legislation supporting stand-by facilities, pilot-plant operations, continuous technological research, and development of more economical processes for utilizing marginal domestic reserves. What contrasted distinctly with Leith's and Emeny's suggestions for government purchasing during the 1920s and 1930s was the number and variety of items the Army-Navy Munitions Board recommended accumulating. This list contained more than fifty strategic and critical materials, including copper, lead, and zinc, but not iron ore or petroleum. Along with a number of ferroalloys on earlier stockpile lists, this minerals shopping guide mentioned columbite and zirconium.[34]

With its established responsibility for minerals activities the Department of Interior naturally looked cautiously at these proposals, and soon decided minor differences could be reconciled. Understandably enough, Interior favored greater future emphasis on measures to develop America's domestic resources and utilize the surplus-plant capacity, which might exist, for instance, in the postwar aluminum industry. Interior emphasized the need to stockpile metals as well as ores. While only high-quality products should be stockpiled, Ickes argued that recent "developments in mining and processing can provide many metals from our present marginal ores on a commercial basis." Thus by encouraging the accumulation of ores the new stockpile policy would indirectly stimulate the domestic minerals industry, which increasingly relied on beneficiating low-quality ores. Specifically, Ickes recommended that the Army-Navy Munitions Board purchase aluminum, not simply bauxite, and manganese and chromium metals, not merely manganese and chromium ores. This shift in established procedures would enable the domestic mining industry to take advantage of improved technology and compete with low-cost foreign ores.[35]

Other administration spokesmen joined with Secretary Ickes in warning Senator Scrugham that amendments to the 1939 stockpile law must relax domestic preferences under the "Buy American" restriction, because "our domestic resources are not replaceable." State Department officials, long active in efforts to shape a coherent policy harmonizing international-security and economic-efficiency considerations, emphasized how unwise it would be for the U.S. to exhaust already inadequate high-cost domestic reserves when abundant foreign supplies were available. What the foreign affairs officials neglected, as Ickes and Interior did not, was how changing technology promised the use of low-grade ores in economical metals processes.[36]

Also, the State Department had an institutional preference for minerals policies benefiting foreign producers and governments in ways that would promote international stability. Preoccupied in the aftermath of World War II with assisting former enemies and allies to recuperate their economies, the State Department tended to discount technical possibilities for substitution among materials, and to minimize the dangers of overdependence on unreliable and politically unstable foreign nations for supplies. Of course stockpiles would reduce short-term dangers of outside economic blackmail, a danger so long as the U.S. opted for global interdependence rather than minerals self-sufficiency. The diplomats did not emphasize the corollary—that a decision to rely on trade for raw materials would discourage the domestic mining industry from undertaking the type of exploration and technological innovation required to overcome the potential dangers of dependence. Eager as the State Department was for a postwar stockpiling policy, it nonetheless cautioned against either unduly large stockpiles or rapid accumulations of raw materials, for other nations might interpret such moves as the opening of a gigantic stockpile race. "The result might be a world struggle for raw materials that would encourage the maintenance of state trading in all countries and that might deprive civilian industry of the necessary raw materials for restoral of civilian economic life." The foreign affairs specialists also worried that a raw-materials arms race could endanger the success of the United Nations and imperil world peace soon after the defeat of the Axis threat.[37]

While bureaucratic and parliamentary delays impeded enactment of stockpile revisions, a bill finally passed into law in July 1946, after encountering little serious opposition on the floors of Congress. The House of Representatives approved it without a roll call and in the Senate this measure (S. 572) passed fifty-six to thirteen. All but one opponent were Republicans. While such prominent Republican Senators as Arthur Vandenberg, William Borah, and Henry Cabot Lodge cast negative votes, several, including Robert Taft, Styles Bridges, and Warren Austin approved the stockpiling measure. For the most part the Senate vote defied clear party and regional affiliations, though an unusually large number of mining-state Senators opted not to vote, perhaps sensing that an affirmative vote might later invite political criticism in their home states.[38]

The 1946 law contained several important changes in national policy. For one thing, the measure provided that the Secretaries of War, the Navy, and Interior, acting jointly through the Army-Navy Munitions Board, should determine what materials were strategic and critical. This group would also determine the total amounts and qualities of each item to be purchased—that is, defining so-called stockpile objectives. The Secretaries of State, Treasury, Agriculture, and Commerce were to designate representatives to "cooperate" in handling these functions. In general, the final bill adopted an administrative framework proposed in the House and favored originally by the War Department and Interior, but opposed by the State Department.[39]

To protect domestic mining against release of stockpile materials and at the same time to permit use of these materials in national emergencies, the new bill provided that the president could issue an order releasing materials "for the purpose of common defense," but not, for instance, to stabilize commodity prices. For reasons of technical obsolescence or deterioration, the government might authorize other sales, providing both the Senate and House received six months advance notice and announcement of the sale appeared in the *Federal Register*.[40]

On the surface the law gave domestic miners protection against cheap foreign competition. It contained provisions subjecting stockpile procurement to sections of the "Buy American" Act of 1933 and leaving these imports subject to tariff duties. Also, the Departments of Interior and Agriculture were authorized to undertake scientific investigations "in order to determine and develop domestic sources of supply." As often occurs in legislation, there was a loophole, leaving open to executive interpretation how much the administration purchased from foreign suppliers. The original "Buy American" Act contained a clause authorizing exceptions when domestic purchases were determined "to be inconsistent with the public interest, or the cost to be unreasonable." Stating that the national interest was to accumulate stockpiles rapidly and with minimum cost to the public, President Truman announced in signing the 1946 act his intention to avoid "subsidizing those domestic producers who otherwise could not compete successfully with other domestic or foreign producers." Truman also stated his administration's opposition to government policies "fostering autarchy, for itself as well as for others." Instead, the U.S. favored a "large volume of soundly based international trade . . . to achieve prosperity in the United States, build a durable structure of world economy, and attain our goal of world peace and security."[41]

That the White House intended to avoid unnecessary subsidies and preferences for American mining and promote, instead, global interdependence was the unpleasant message Secretary of the Interior Julius Krug delivered to the American Mining Congress. "We should not hesitate to purchase abroad ample supplies of any materials needed for our internal economy which cannot be produced from domestic deposits under reasonable protection," he said. "We should encourage American industry to extend its operations in foreign fields as a means of assuring the United States adequate supplies of materials in which we are deficient. Foreign expansion is one method by which the industry is strengthened."[42]

In short, the 1946 stockpiling law was a compromise measure, acceptable to the self-interest of American miners, and yet consistent with the larger national interest, as defined by the executive branch. It assured permanent stockpile cushions against foreign embargoes and war while promoting technological solutions to make the American domestic resource base more versatile. Most of all, the act revealed how all interested factions benefited from past mistakes. For the hard-pressed Western mining industry, the measure provided "ample protection against the dumping of materials onto the open markets," said one leading minerals consultant (an issue, incidentally, that hampered domestic firms after World War I). For the government, determined this time to prepare adequately for the next war, the measure permitted peacetime stockpiling under military supervision. It was understood the actual materials inventory would not be a token program, as was the prewar program. This time the total bill would range from $3.5 to $5 billion. This time the minerals industry would have no influence over the conduct of the materials program, except insofar as a future Congress should modify the basic legislation. Congress, too, had learned from past mistakes; before World War II it displayed too much concern for domestic mining and too little sensitivity to economic and security considerations. Representative Thomas Martin, a Republican from Iowa, reminded his colleagues that the legislation was designed to meet any future emergency "so that we shall never again, as a nation, come up to an emergency without some provision for our own national protection." He also noted, in remarks prepared for the record, that an earlier House committee admitted on the eve of World War II that Congress misplaced its priorities. The Faddis committee report in July 1941 stated: "Emphasis over the past few years has been made on social reform rather than national security. As a Nation, we seem to have forgotten that without national security social reform might well prove meaningless."[43]

While the 1946 law represented significant improvements, it contained at least one dangerous loophole. Section 6 exempted from transfer to the new stockpile such "material as is necessary to make up any deficiency of the supply of such material for the current requirements of industry." Effectively, this provision authorized sales of government minerals inventories to private enterprise during the period of commodity shortages after the war, and as a result the stockpile, which stood to inherit existing government inventories of strategic and critical materials, lost "four to five hundred million dollars worth of raw material," reported Rear Admiral Roger Paine, a member of the Munitions Board. Ironically, then, Congress in seeking to please domestic minerals users who faced temporary supply shortages authorized sale of the very stockpile Congress sought to augment through postwar purchases. And by May 1948 the stockpile had received approximately $316 million in materials from the War Assets Administration and other agencies.[44]

Passage of the 1946 act (PL 520) established legislative authorization for a national materials reserve, but it did not establish the reserve. Initially, the Munitions Board calculated it would take approximately five years and about $2.1 billion to attain minimum objectives, based on a five-year future war in which the U.S. maintained some imports from Africa, India, the Philippines and other supply sources, without disrupting markets. Since approximately $300 million worth of materials would come from accumulated World War II supplies purchased by the Reconstruction Finance Corporation and its satellites, $1.8 billion would be required for market purchases—and spread over the five-year buying period, this meant an annual installment of $360 million. Here the appropriations process complicated stockpiling. The administration, so as not to disrupt an inflation-prone domestic economy, requested only $270 million, and Congress appropriated only $100 million for fiscal 1947. The following year, the Munitions Board requested $360 million, the Bureau of the Budget approved $200 million, and Congress appropriated $175 million—for a two-year total of $275 million.[45]

Efforts to complete the five-year purchasing timetable ran up against the hard realities of the budgetary process—constant budget cutting in the White House and additional paring on Capitol Hill. Frustrated with this situation, the National Security Resources Board, an agency established along with the National Security Council in 1947, approved late in 1947 a statement to President Truman pointing out how the stockpiling program was "seriously lagging," although supplies of strategic and critical materials were an "essential element of national security." The board reported that of sixty-eight items on the strategic and critical list, only four were available in amounts sufficient to meet minimum stockpile objectives for a five-year emergency. In addition, the stockpile was seriously out of balance. Many materials most vital to effective national security were lacking. "At the present rate of procurement, the minimum stockpile objectives will not be fulfilled for about twenty years," concluded the board.[46]

There were three reasons for the phantom materials reserve program, Thomas J. Hargrave, chairman of the Munitions Board, told the House Appropriations Committee in March 1948. Along with inadequate appropriations, he mentioned the unavailability of materials and higher prices. He said the board constantly faced the problem of deciding whether to pay more than the market price for materials needed in the stockpile. For the first two years of its existence, Admiral Roger Paine testified, the government deliberately declined to pay more than the market price for raw materials, believing that reconversion and controlling inflation took precedence over completing a national stockpile. "If we deliberately went out and paid more than the market price, we would be running two dangers. We would be running the danger of stimulating inflation and we would certainly be depriving industry of its basic needs." Unable to obtain adequate materials in the spot market, the Munitions Board encountered congressional resistance to its proposal for entering long-term contracts with producers, including those in other Western Hemisphere countries.[47]

Other components of the government program to protect the United States against a disruption of imported raw materials also encountered budgetary difficulties. Under Section 7(a) of the 1946 law the Department of Interior was directed to find new deposits of minerals, determine feasible methods of mining and treating ores now considered noncommercial, and perfect substitutes from domestically available materials. But Interior Secretary Julius Krug complained to Senator Joseph O'Mahoney (D., Wyoming) that funds requested in fiscal 1948 "are approximately one-half that expended at the wartime peak or 35% above that spent for strategic minerals in 1941." Even so, the House of Representatives proposed to chop these expenditures downward 37 percent from 1947 levels. This belt-tightening endangered the secondary minerals development program, said Krug, for it would mean curtailing essential portions of the marginal underground stockpile program and it would curtail additional exploratory work. And, he said, further budgetary reductions would lay off scientists and engineers with valuable resource knowledge and experience. In 1947, for example, the Bureau of Mines reported to Congress that its program for investigating and developing domestic mineral deposits cost $1.7 million and involved 223 employees, down from a peak of $8.4 million and 630 employees in 1944.[48]

Despite the pressures for budgetary retrenchment the Geological Survey and Bureau of Mines lobbied intensively for more funds to continue research work, claiming that previous studies had developed new techniques for using low-grade and off-quality reserves and for finding materials in short supply. In his 1948 annual report Krug reported how the Bureau of Mines and Geological Survey had tested thousands of domestic mineral deposits, yielding valuable information and disclosing substantial reserves previously unknown. One success was a low-grade copper deposit in Arizona, which originally seemed too poor to be of economic significance. Continued drilling, however, disclosed the presence of 500,000,000 tons of low-grade ore, or porphyry-type deposits. Similar research brought comparable disclosures of new manganese and iron-ore deposits, he reported.[49]

The Geological Survey continued its aggressive mapping program, Krug noted, designed to increase understanding of mineral deposits. Nevertheless, less than 10 percent of the nation had been mapped on adequate scale maps—and in this area the U.S. ranked with the world's backward nations. "We are a little behind Algeria, but we are ahead of Poland." There was also progress in Bureau of Mines laboratories in efforts to utilize low-grade ores and devise substitutes for scarce minerals. "The Bureau's metallurgists have proved that many of the leaner ores of iron, copper, lead, and zinc can be economically upgraded, thus making possible the use of formerly uneconomic reserves." And in the critical search for substitutes the Secretary reported the Bureau of Mines had developed replacements for Indian kyanite and for nickel, chromium, and tantalum, for some uses. The bureau "now is studying methods of manufacturing synthetic products to replace sheet mica and spinnable asbestos, and to develop substitutes for diamonds in industrial production."[50]

Despite limited successes in mapping resources and using new technology to develop metals from low-grade ores, the national minerals program lagged in the late 1940s. Both the executive and Congress supported the principle of stockpiling to cushion against embargoes and a war like World War II, but no sense of urgency motivated policymakers to alter budget priorities—which, incidentally, also crimped the national defense establishment during the same period. At the direction of the NSRB, Secretary of the Interior Julius Krug and his mineral agencies completed an exhaustive two-part confidential study of America's emerging mineral dependency early in 1948. After studying sixteen vital minerals—asbestos, bauxite, bismuth, cadmium, chromite, cobalt, copper, industrial diamonds, iron ore, lead, manganese, mica, nickel, tin, tungsten and zinc—the Interior study concluded that a dangerous raw-material situation existed. "Should an emergency arise in the near future in which access to foreign sources of supply were cut off or greatly curtailed, acute mineral shortages that would seriously impair industrial mobilization would develop within a few months." The United States had less than a six-month supply of asbestos, bauxite, copper, and nickel. It had only a six-to-twelve month supply of cadmium, cobalt, industrial diamonds, lead, and manganese. Bismuth, chromite, mica, and tin would last from one to two years, while tungsten and zinc could last two to four years. Iron ore would last over four years.[51]

In assessing strategic stockpiles of fifteen commodities, except iron ore, Krug concluded that stocks of only two of the fifteen being accumulated had reached or exceeded a quarter of their minimum objectives. Eleven of the stockpiles were at less than 10 percent of the maximum objective. These deficiencies required immediate action, especially to overcome serious deficits of manganese and chromite, for the U.S. depended on the Soviet Union for nearly half of its chromite consumption and a quarter of its manganese. This position, concluded the Krug Report, is "untenable from the viewpoint of security under any conditions we can foresee for some time." To cope with the precarious chromite situation, Krug's study again urged "vigorous action to increase imports," a domestic production program, and measures to promote conservation and long-term research. In emphasizing an imports program, Krug recommended "diplomatic action to obtain assurances as to the continued political availability of foreign sources of supply, provision of adequate bottoms for transporting the additional imports, and firm military plans to protect sea lanes." Along with chromite and manganese, the Secretary of the Interior urged priority programs to deal with potential shortages in asbestos, bauxite, aluminum, industrial diamonds (particularly bort), and tin. He noted particularly the short supply of crushing bort, a highly strategic material vital to many high-speed mass production mechanisms, for the U.S. had only a one-month supply and this material came exclusively from the Eastern Hemisphere.[52]

Along with this emphasis on imports and stockpiling, this comprehensive report called for increased domestic production of copper, lead, zinc, and iron ore. Recognizing that increased domestic output required "positive, aggressive governmental action," the Interior De-

partment secretary again called for a long-range program to help industry acquire capital and reinvest its own earnings, and requested
federal support for the Bureau of Mines and Geological Survey activities. Also critical to effective implementation of the Krug Plan
was the reemergence of the Interior Department as the agency supervising procurement and mineral development activities. As he stated:
"I recommend that the responsibility for developing and negotiating
long-range purchase contracts be delegated to the agencies familiar
with mineral resources and the business problems involved and having sufficient technical knowledge and staff to do the job." Krug
recommended also "that the National Security Resources Board suggest to the President that he designate a single agency with full authority for coordinating the various activities of the Government per-
taining to minerals." [53]

Another section of the Krug Report considered seventeen other
minerals, and reached similar conclusions about lagging stockpiles
and the United States' rising vulnerability to outside pressure. Especially dangerous, the report concluded, was mounting American dependence on Eastern Hemisphere sources of supply. "It would be
virtually impossible within a few years to develop in the Western
Hemisphere sufficient production to meet the most essential uses of
columbium, corundum, graphite, kyanite, steatite talc, and tantalum." [54]

Effectively, then, World War II and its aftermath focused official attention again on a problem that first emerged during World
War I—a problem of declining high-grade domestic resources and
mounting reliance on foreign sources of supply in a global war. And
while concern about America's emerging "have-not" status helped
convince Congress to authorize a permanent stockpile program,
neither the legislature nor the executive perceived an immediate danger warranting a crash purchasing program. Certainly the Interior
Department, eager to recapture control of the minerals program lost
to the hastily created wartime agencies who encroached on its established terrain, took the lead in trumpeting the need for a comprehensive national minerals program. These efforts would gain new
impetus as Washington policymakers appraised the implications of
deteriorating Soviet-American relations and the emerging prospects
for a military confrontation in the 1950s.

Chapter Six
Minerals and the Cold War

IN 1948 and 1949 a crisis atmosphere enveloped Washington. Another totalitarian challenge, Soviet Communism, ignited fear in U.S. policymaking circles. "Soviet efforts are now directed toward the domination of the Eurasian land mass," an important National Security Council (NSC) report concluded. The Kremlin had the military capability soon to dominate Eurasia, and then to utilize these vast resources for subjugating an isolated America. This external security threat coincided with and reinforced rising concern about this country's weakened natural resource inventory, a situation that geologist Alan Bateman termed a minerals "crisis."[1]

What undoubtedly helped generate anxiety about the future availability of industrial raw materials was the secular upswing in minerals prices and increased reliance on imports. From the mid-1930s to about 1951 commodity prices moved upward in a pattern that resembled a Kondratieff long wave. Since World War II government intervention temporarily suppressed price movements, decontrol brought a sharp surge in the late 1940s. Crude petroleum prices climbed 69 percent in deflated dollars, while copper rose about 20 percent, lead 60 percent, and tin 75 percent. Domestic supplies, heavily depleted from heavy wartime utilization, could not satisfy rising demand. Previously America had exported substantial quantities of copper, lead, and zinc, but now the U.S. began to import significant quantities of these metals. A similar shift from exporting to importing characterized iron and petroleum. In 1948, for instance, the U.S. imported 26 percent of the copper consumed domestically, and for the first time since soon after World War I it became a net importer of petroleum. It was evident to minerals specialists that the late 1940s marked a "crucial turning point in the long-range materials position of the United States." Said Bateman: "It is inevitable that the United States will have to depend upon foreign sources and minerals."[2]

While internal deficiencies compelled this country to look elsewhere for large quantities of industrial raw materials, the expansion of Soviet power appeared to jeopardize access to critical materials in Eurasia and its offshore islands. In 1948, a Soviet-encouraged coup in Czechoslovakia, coupled with Kremlin pressure on other Eastern European states and the strength of Communist political parties in France and Italy, alarmed Washington. More than anything else, a cable from General Lucius Clay, then in charge of the European Command, set off a brief war scare. He suggested that war might come "with dramatic suddenness," and the Berlin crisis in June 1948 seemed to confirm the dire forecast. These moves, together with Communist-led strikes in Latin America and disruption in Southeast Asia, all appeared to support the view that Joseph Stalin and his Kremlin colleagues sought what Adolph Hitler and his henchmen failed to acquire less than a decade earlier—mastery of Eurasia and global dominance.[3]

The National Security Council was disturbed about these international developments. After defeat of the Axis the Soviet Union now "engaged the United States in a struggle for power," the ultimate objective being "domination of the world." In a short period the Kremlin had established "satellite police states" across Eastern Europe, and threatened Italy, Greece, Finland, Korea, the Scandinavian countries, and others. "Today Stalin has come closer to achieving what Hitler attempted in vain." American officials believed Soviet leaders would not hesitate to use armed aggression as well as political subversion to achieve their strategic goal—dominating "the potential power of Eurasia."[4]

Despite the flurry of anxiety after the Czech coup, Washington policymakers generally did not expect an overt military assault on Western Europe or the Western Hemisphere. Indeed, in March 1950, Admiral R. H. Hillenkoetter, director of the Central Intelligence Agency, told the National Security Resources Board (NSRB) that "in present or comparable circumstances a deliberate, unprovoked Soviet attack on the United States is improbable, as is any Soviet military aggression deemed to incur serious risk of war with the United States." But sometime in the mid-1950s, once the Kremlin acquired an atomic bomb and effective delivery system, it might resort to conventional or atomic warfare.[5]

Political and ideological warfare seemed a greater threat. U.S. officials feared that "Soviet political warfare might seriously weaken the relative position of the United States, enhance Soviet strength and either lead to our ultimate defeat short of war, or force us into war under dangerously unfavorable conditions." These political measures "short of war" appeared aimed at the "political conquest of Western Europe" through use of subversion, infiltration, and capture of political power—techniques refined over the last half century. Communists sought to exploit the high degree of political and social instability prevailing in war-weakened Western Europe as well as in colonial areas, especially the ones on which the U.S. and Western Europe were dependent for raw-material supplies. In brief, the Soviet strategy of global conquest appeared to rest on promoting chaos and disruption which would permit the disciplined Communist leadership to emerge.[6]

This pattern a Harvard University professor Charles C. Abbott outlined for officers at the Naval War College in November 1948. He warned that Communist and nationalist forces might shut off the highly industrialized, raw-materials importing regions from supplies produced in former colonial areas. While the U.S. was "moderately vulnerable to this type of pressure," our Western European allies are "distinctly vulnerable." In brief, he believed the Soviet regime was waging a policy of disruption globally to weaken the highly integrated and mineral-deficient capitalist economies. "Russian policy is furthered by the spread of economic chaos, by civil disturbance, the diminution of production and trade, inflation of currency, dislocation of channels of trade, and the disappearance of plants and individual business concerns," Abbott concluded. The Russians were masters of "economic cannibalism," the process of absorbing or destroying economic activity outside the Soviet Union.[7]

The Soviet moves disturbed prominent minerals specialists like Bateman and Elmer Pehrson, a Bureau of Mines expert. To Pehrson the visible signals were discouraging: "We must again prepare for a showdown with the forces of totalitarianism and conquest." Like nonscientists in the State Department, he evaluated Kremlin actions in geopolitical terms. "Control of the Eurasian Continent would jeopardize United States access to the minerals of Africa, without which our industrial efficiency would be impaired dangerously. This must be prevented at all costs," he said. Africa and Southeast Asia had special importance. "We cannot risk the loss of access to these areas as we did the loss of the world's greatest resources of tungsten and antimony in China," he warned.[8]

Before the collapse of China and the Korean War, Communist-inspired disturbances in South America and Southeast Asia had begun to worry specialists. Copper-exporting Chile remained sensitive in the late 1940s. Communists had labor union influence there, and in 1946 they obtained three cabinet positions in the new government of President Gabriel Gonzalez Videla. A year later, after unrest in the coal mines produced a national political crisis, President Gonzalez Videla claimed the Communists sought to overthrow his government, in order to deprive the U.S. of copper and nitrates. Despite some skepticism among foreigners, U.S. Ambassador Claude G. Bowers, a liberal-minded historian, shared this view, and he informed Washington there was "no possible doubt that [the] strike is ordered from outside as a major effort of Communism to take over in Chile as first step toward the Continent." With American assistance the Chilean government finally crushed the strike, but Communist sentiment in labor unions remained a potential problem. After the outbreak of war in Korea, for instance, Ambassador Bowers again warned that "the communist plan is to await the word from Moscow to start strikes in the mines, to do all possible to prevent the export of war material to the United States, and to engage in sabotage."[9]

The Venezuelan situation also troubled U.S. policymakers, and efforts to protect this nation's rich reserves of petroleum and iron in 1948 and 1949, when Washington worried about Communist labor influences, established an important precedent for U.S. government aid to American mining companies in other underdeveloped nations. In August 1948, the National Security Council approved a plan for protecting strategically important industrial operations abroad. It noted that "many materials of strategic importance to the United States are produced in foreign countries where the existence of strong communist parties or communist-dominated labor unions, the probable presence of Soviet agents, and the lack of effective industrial security procedures combine to render the production and shipment of such materials vulnerable to sabotage or subversive activities." Convinced that "the Kremlin will take full advantage of these conditions and make every effort . . . to disrupt the supply of such materials to the United States and its allies," the NSC directed the Central Intelligence Agency to plan protection for strategic facilities abroad and "conduct continuous intelligence surveillance of industrial operations of vital importance and under special threat."[10]

During the Korean War and its aftermath Washington extended this mandate to other foreign industrial facilities. For instance, the Eisenhower administration directed the CIA, with State Department concurrence, to undertake "covert surveillance" to protect four foreign-owned facilities. These were: (1) Union Miniere du Haut Katanga's processing facilities for cobalt in the Belgian Congo; (2) International Nickel Company of Canada's smelter and refinery for nickel; (3) bauxite facilities in Surinam and Trinidad; and (4) a Shell Oil refinery in Curaçao, which processed Venezuelan crude oil. The NSC also authorized similar CIA protection for these U.S.-owned facilities: (1) Nicaro Nickel Company in Cuba, which supplied 14 percent of U.S. requirements; (2) U.S.-owned bauxite mines in Surinam; (3) U.S. oil-producing fields and refineries in Venezuela, including the Standard Oil of New Jersey refinery in Aruba; (4) a Standard Vacuum Company oil refinery in Indonesia; and (5) copper production, power, and transportation facilities in Chile.[11]

Several other foreign facilities also received U.S. protection during the Korean conflict. These included tin and tungsten facilities in Bolivia, manganese production and transportation operations in the Gold Coast, tin production in Indonesia, columbite production in Nigeria, as well as manganese and chromite complexes in the Union of South Africa, Rhodesia, and Mozambique.[12]

Soviet attempts to sabotage and deprive the West of vital industrial raw materials became a major concern to American policymakers by 1948, and this priority remained through the 1950s until a massive stockpile procurement program reduced the dangers of external economic pressure. Southeast Asia quickly became a central consideration. In December 1948, the CIA and National Security Resources Board both were anxious about a possible loss of tin and rubber from the Netherlands East Indies (Indonesia). Such an occurrence would "be a net loss in world production which probably could not be made up from other sources." And Bureau of Mines expert Pehrson was privately critical of State Department efforts to encourage Indonesian independence, considering it an "ill-advised action" that "could become a serious threat to the continued flow of vital raw materials to this country from Dutch areas."[13]

To key policymakers terrorist raids in Malaya, opposition to the French in Indochina, and pressure on Thailand all seemed part of Soviet strategy to consolidate its dominance of Eurasia and cannibalize the West. Said the NSC in July 1949, "In seeking to gain control of SEA [Southeast Asia], the Kremlin is, of course, motivated in part by a desire to acquire SEA's resources and communications lines, but its immediate and perhaps even greater desire is to deny them to us." Early in 1950 the State Department argued for providing military assistance to Thailand and French Indochina in order to keep Southeast Asia from falling under Communist domination. Minerals were an important reason why the U.S. could not abandon that region. If Thailand were lost, for instance, the State Department feared the U.S. "would be unable to secure such strategic materials as tungsten, tin, and rubber in their present quantities." In short, the struggle for Indochina was very much a contest to keep open former colonial areas to the transoceanic flow of primary products on which the industrial prosperity of America and Western Europe depended increasingly.[14]

As the collapse of Southeast Asia became more probable, and American access to foreign minerals more essential, U.S. government planners carefully evaluated strategic mobilization needs. It was expected in 1950 that if a major war broke out with the Soviet Union, the U.S. and its allies would temporarily lose access to Middle East oil, materials from continental Europe, and some items from Southeast Asia. But this country could win a protracted war of attrition if it maintained access to essential supplies in the Western Hemisphere, Africa, and South Asia. A list prepared in June 1950, shows how world-reliant the American war economy had become. From Canada, the U.S. expected to import aluminum, fluorspar, lead, newsprint, nickel, platinum, pulpwood, uranium, wood pulp, zinc, asbestos. Mexico would sell antimony, fluorspar, lead, and zinc. In the Caribbean this country must obtain manganese, molasses, and sugar from Cuba as well as bauxite from Jamaica. South America would supply the following items: from Colombia, coffee; from Venezuela, crude petroleum; Surinam, bauxite; Ecuador, balsa; Peru, vanadium; Bolivia, antimony, asbestos, tin, and tungsten; Brazil, baddeleyite, beryl, coffee, emetine, manganese, mica, monazite, quartz crystals, and tapioca. Similarly Peru would provide quebracho, while Chile supplied copper, iodine, and sodium nitrate.[15]

Outside the Western Hemisphere the U.S. looked to Africa for certain strategic materials—among them, cobalt, industrial diamonds, palm oil, tin, and uranium from the Belgian Congo; pyrethrum from British East Africa; rubber, Liberia; cocoa and manganese, the Gold Coast; columbite, Nigeria; asbestos and chromite from Southern Rhodesia and from South Africa. Madagascar remained important as a supplier of mica and graphite. Only a few items must come from the Pacific region—grease wool, rutile, and zircon from Australia; grease wool from New Zealand; and beryl, kyanite, manganese, mica, and tea from India. This mobilization plan rested on the assumption that the U.S. must do without materials from Southeast Asia, at least temporarily, as it had in World War II after Pearl Harbor.[16]

Cold war competition in Europe during 1948–1949 raised each of the basic minerals issues—rapid depletion of American domestic reserves; dangerous reliance on a potential enemy, the Soviet Union, for defense-related materials; and growing dependence on colonial and newly independent nations for supplies.

American policymakers organized a rescue effort for Western Europe in 1947 when it was evident that the exhausted continent, including the British Isles, faced imminent economic collapse and political decay. Without U.S. assistance, Washington feared local Communist parties stood ready to benefit from this situation, perhaps winning political control in Italy during 1948, perhaps taking control of a disillusioned France through parliamentary penetration. While eager to speed Western European rehabilitation and economic integration with the so-called Marshall Plan, the U.S. also sought to minimize the inflationary impact of a large aid program on its own citizens. One option which appealed to the Department of Commerce officials, the military, and State Department experts, involved regulating exports to Soviet-dominated Eastern Europe. These controls would not only ease the inflationary burden but would also serve a second purpose—denying the Kremlin access to U.S. machinery and industrial equipment likely to strengthen Soviet military potential.

With a more comprehensive system of licensing for all commodities, this country could manage East-West trade for its own advantage, the experts believed.[17]

In reaching the decision to license and control East-West trade, late in 1947 and early in 1948, the U.S. government underestimated America's own vulnerability to Soviet trade reprisals. George Kennan's planners in the State Department concluded, for instance, that "imports from the U.S.S.R. and its satellites are neither vital nor of great importance to this country," a conclusion surprisingly at variance with the mineral facts. During the first nine months of 1947, this country had obtained 31 percent of imported manganese, 47 percent of imported chromite, and 57 percent of imported platinum— all from the Soviet Union and all materials in which America had a critical dependence on foreign suppliers.[18]

The problem emerged in full focus during the spring of 1948 when evidence mounted that the Commerce Department's new export restrictions on defense-related materials had sharply reduced exports to the Soviet Union and when the Kremlin itself warned about retaliation, including an embargo on raw-materials shipments to America. Bureau of Mines specialists warned about the dire consequences of a Soviet embargo, for American stockpiles held only an eighteen-month supply of metallurgical chromite and an eight-month supply of manganese at current consumption rates. If the Soviets cut off supplies, the U.S. would be unable to meet consumption requirements, and out of necessity it would draw down the stockpiles that planners hoped to build up. Most of all, importers complained to Congress about the reckless export-control policy. Said H. S. Robertson, an official of the Harbison-Walker Refractories Company, to a House investigating committee: "Some people who are talking about cutting off Russia from everything better have in mind that maybe we better do something about manganese and chromite before we start slapping the old Russian bear in the nose too hard."[19]

The American dilemma was clear: Washington could control the flow of exports to the Soviet Union and accept probable retaliation, or it could tolerate sales of American machinery in order to continue accumulating stockpiles of manganese and chromite. In order to protect the American materials base from the disruptive consequences of an outside embargo, the Bureau of Mines recommended a comprehensive program to build up this country's mineral self-sufficiency and reliance on non-Soviet sources while permitting sales of "important commodities other than those of a direct military nature" to Russia. A chromite defense program should accord top priority to developing railroad and port facilities in Southern Rhodesia and Mozambique in order to increase shipments from this second most valuable deposit of high-grade chromite. And, to develop other alternative supplies, the U.S. should offer long-range contracts to companies in Cuba and the Philippines. Lastly, the government should offer long-term contracts to private industry in the U.S. in order to construct a chromite beneficiating plant and to rehabilitate a concentrating plant in the Stillwater area of Montana.[20]

To strengthen the manganese position, the government should increase short-term imports from the Gold Coast, negotiate with India to improve rail facilities, and evaluate South Africa's needs for improved transportation facilities. A long-range manganese policy would seek to build up alternative suppliers within the Western Hemisphere, such as Brazil, through use of long-term contracts. Domestically, the government should inaugurate a premium price program designed to guarantee long-term domestic production and especially to encourage development of manganese production at Butte, Montana, where the Anaconda Copper Company had deposits. Other federal assistance should bring the Three Kids Mine in Nevada into production of a high-grade manganese concentrate or electrolytic manganese, and should accelerate use of low-grade manganese ores, including deposits in Aroostook County, Maine, and along the Cuyuna Range in Minnesota.[21]

As often happens when different government agencies supervise aspects of a foreign policy program, discordant and contradictory results occur, and this was the situation when the NSRB met on June 10, 1948, to resolve the matter. Department of Commerce Secretary Charles Sawyer, who replaced Averell Harriman in May, sought to continue a tough export-control program, but other agencies disagreed, warning that the Soviet Union might retaliate. NSRB Chairman Arthur Hill urged participants to accept the guiding principle that U.S. trade policy should concentrate first on maintaining and increasing the strength of the U.S. and countries friendly to it, rather than subordinating this objective to the task of weakening potential enemies. Army representative Theodore Draper also argued against rigid export controls, saying that Soviet reprisals, such as withholding food from Western Europe and raw materials from the U.S., might be more harmful to American security interests than allowing the Soviet Union to obtain general-purpose machinery like diesel railroad engines.[22]

Secretary of State George Marshall, a formidable and powerful figure, agreed. While recognizing the "vital position of east and west trade," he stressed immediately "the great importance of continued receipt of manganese and chrome from Soviet sources." Marshall recommended treating the Soviet Union like other nations in the area, such as Finland, while eliminating shipments of items that would greatly improve Russian military strength. In brief, America's dependent mineral position compelled top policymakers to modify economic controls in 1948 so as not to precipitate a Soviet raw-materials embargo until the U.S. had established alternative supply lines outside the grip of Kremlin officials. Once again, cold war considerations compelled the United States to secure raw-material supplies in underdeveloped areas, especially the Gold Coast, Brazil, and India.[23]

Meanwhile, as the Berlin crisis heightened public awareness and interest in the cold war rift, Washington explored ways to delay a Kremlin raw-material embargo. Thinking the Soviet Union might resort to manganese and chromite export controls after it completed its own stockpiling of rubber, wool, and tin obtained from Southeast Asia, State Department officials suggested a preclusive buying program, intended to prevent Moscow from completing its own stockpile buying. But the NSRB vetoed that proposal, because, in part, a surplus of rubber existed on world markets.[24]

At last, in December 1948, the Soviets notified shippers of impending cutbacks in chromite and manganese sales, a move long anticipated. Even so, the U.S. was inadequately prepared, and an interagency task force forecast the loss of Soviet manganese would bring curtailments in domestic steel production or use of existing strategic stockpiles. But as it turned out, fortuitous circumstances combined with successful emergency preparations to avoid the expected materials crisis in 1949. For one thing, the 1948–1949 recession softened commodity prices and industrial demand, so that prices of both commodities changed only slightly. For another, preparations to remove supply bottlenecks abroad paid off as the Gold Coast, India, and South Africa boosted their exports of metallurgical manganese to the United States. Total manganese imports, of all grades, actually increased 23 percent over 1948. And in chromite, Turkey managed to increase its exports of metallurgical grade to replace supplies lost from the Soviet Union. These circumstances together defeated the Soviet power play, showing once again the difficulty of employing successfully a raw-materials sanction.[25]

Efforts to elaborate procedures for the European Recovery Program, which was to deliver a $13 billion transfusion of American resources to an insolvent Europe, also joined containment and mineral-resource considerations. At the working level, specialists quickly recognized that a program to rehabilitate Western Europe, and thus save it from Stalinism, involved not only the sacrifice of American tax dollars but also use of scarce American natural resources. Unless aid recipients contributed raw materials from their own colonies to the United States to offset the transfer of American goods to Europe, the Marshall Plan would inevitably hasten the already advanced depletion of United States resources. Some type of reverse assistance from aid recipients attracted members of Congress who nervously contemplated public reactions to a multi-billion dollar peacetime assistance program. It also appealed to mobilization experts in the executive branch who saw an opportunity to accelerate stockpile purchases from the colonies of Marshall Plan beneficiaries. They knew that a cautious Congress had appropriated only $275 million for procurement of strategic materials, and at this rate the government would have only about 20 percent of its minimum stockpile objectives at the end of 1948.[26]

Proposals to trade American goods for strategic materials had surfaced before in Washington. At the close of World War I some talked of taking strategic materials in delayed repayment of Allied war debts. Then again, late in the 1930s, Britain and the U.S. negotiated a barter arrangement, exchanging surplus agricultural products for rubber and tin. This time the principal promoter of a strategic-materials offset agreement was none other than the ubiquitous William Y. Elliott, sometime Harvard University professor of government and government materials specialist, and now a staff director of the House of Representatives Select Committee on Foreign Aid. In a report released in November 1947, Elliott's panel suggested that colonial governments agree to supply a stated tonnage of strategic materials annually for ten to twenty years. At market prices existing then, the U.S. might obtain $200 million annually. The State Department's Working Group on Strategic Materials issued a similar recommendation, estimating that Marshall Plan recipients could generate $300 million in additional annual production, surplus to their own import requirements and available to the American emergency stockpile.[27]

The idea of using European Recovery to build up domestic minerals resources gained momentum in the bureaucracy, not because the idea was a panacea for stockpiling shortages but because the proposal had political appeal—it would help sell the European Recovery Program to a reluctant Congress. Soon the NSRB examined the idea and recommended to President Truman that objectives be achieved without "seriously depleting our own natural resources." To prevent a loss of vital materials, this government should make every effort to maintain imports as well as to expand the production of materials under control of participants in the recovery program. "Expansion and development of foreign sources of supply would serve the interests of both world recovery and national security."[28]

Washington seized on the idea of encouraging American investments in foreign mining ventures, not because the domestic firms lacked profitable opportunities at home, but because government officials saw an opportunity to achieve an American presence in high-grade foreign deposits which would confer long-range advantage to the U.S. and provide some repayment for the costs of rehabilitating Europe. "Prompt development of these urgently needed sources of supply by the application and utilization of American private investment, management, technical skills, and equipment should be encouraged," the NSRB said. What were the opportunities for obtaining minerals in overseas colonial areas? When the idea gained appeal, the State Department began to show enthusiasm for obtaining 85,000 tons of copper from the Belgian Congo and Britain's colony of Northern Rhodesia. Also, 110,000 tons of lead were believed to be available in French Morocco and Tunisia as well as in British Burma. The Belgian Congo and Burma might supply 113,000 tons of zinc, while Dutch and British colonies in Southeast Asia could generate 84,000 tons of tin. Supplies of other critical materials, including rubber, industrial diamonds, cobalt, chromite, manganese, bauxite, and tungsten might also be obtained.[29]

In writing legislation Congress and the executive established a three-part strategic materials program. First, the law sought to facilitate transfer of strategic materials to the United States for stock-piling. Second, it required spending a portion of Economic Coopera-tion Administration (ECA) funds to expand production of materials abroad so as to meet materials deficiencies in the United States. Here the act also required recipients to set aside local currencies equivalent to at least 5 percent of aid received in United States dollars, for the American government to buy strategic materials. Optimists antici-pated this provision would make available some $180 million for purchases in European countries and dependencies. Finally the legis-lation called for American firms to receive open door treatment— that is, equal treatment in investing and repatriating funds—from recipient nations. This clause delighted the powerful *Engineering and Mining Journal,* and it editorialized: "The ECA will have accom-plished much if it can secure for our mining companies the open door to foreign mineral development that many of them have sought and been denied, whether by legal or surreptitious means." It concluded, "The only logical avenue to a peaceful world is to have universal open-door policies for colonial areas."[30]

Obtaining raw materials for a "have-not" America ranked among objectives of the Marshall Plan, but actual results in this area fell far short of expectations. Initially, some planners had thought the U.S. might obtain several hundred million dollars annually in local counterpart funds, which this country might then spend to pur-chase available supplies for its North American stockpile. However war-torn European nations needed materials for their own immediate reconstruction, which was after all the principal goal of the Marshall Plan. In fact, so little was available for the U.S. to purchase with its counterpart funds that by December 1951, this government had ob-tained only $82 million in strategic materials this way, and U.S. re-ports now rationalized the situation, saying it would "be short-sighted and contrary to the principle of mutual cooperation and se-curity" to buy up raw materials which the Europeans desperately needed. Instead, the U.S. did earmark some European Recovery Pro-gram dollars as well as 5-percent counterpart funds to explore and develop new raw-material supplies, and to enlarge the output of existing mines. By June 30, 1952, when the aid program officially ended, Washington had committed $33 million of its own funds and the equivalent of $105 million in foreign counterpart currencies for minerals development projects. As official reports explained, these development projects "are necessarily spread over a long period, and a level of production sufficient to allow repayment in kind takes time to achieve." Altogether initial repayments in aluminum, lead, and industrial diamonds reached a total value slightly more than $1 million, and other quantities were scheduled for later repayment. These figures show how little the Marshall Plan contributed immediately to strengthening the U.S. stockpile. Nor did the European Recovery Program stimulate a heavy flow of private capital into minerals development projects. According to minerals expert Charles Will Wright, "responsible mine owners" feared government interference, and for this reason they declined to borrow counterpart funds. In short, traditional barriers to private investment discouraged direct investments in mining projects—namely, market uncertainties, unpredictable government regulation, exchange and export controls, and high taxes. Also, "because of the apparent nationalistic tendencies of their governments, private mining companies have preferred to do little until the future outlook is better established."[31]

An interest in developing minerals resources also characterized the Point Four Program, the economic assistance proposal first mentioned in President Harry Truman's State of the Union message in 1949. Truman suggested "making the benefits of our scientific advances and industrial progress available for the improvement and growth of underdeveloped areas," and among the scientific advances Washington offered to underdeveloped nations was aid in mapping and evaluating mineral deposits as well as in determining their commercial potentialities. Altogether this assistance accounted for only 1 percent of technical assistance budgeted for the first year. The Point Four Program, like the Marshall Plan, joined American idealism and self-interest. On the one hand, this country genuinely aspired to assist the economic development of new nations, and, on the other hand, it recognized that security and economic interests warranted underwriting a technical assistance program. And, without evidence that the United States cared for non-European nations, Washington feared these governments might yield to outside political pressure or internal factions hostile to continued participation in the emerging world economy.[32]

In terms of American raw-material needs, the Point Four Program served a vital purpose. With assistance from the U.S. Geological Survey and Bureau of Mines other governments would identify new deposits; and this information might encourage American mining firms to invest, developing the reserves both to the benefit of the host country and the U.S. In a sense altruism and enlightened self-interest combined. In a world facing materials scarcity new resources would generate higher export earnings for some needy nations, and in strengthening both the local economy and diversifying the foreign base for U.S. mineral imports, the program also strengthened the Western bloc against the Soviet Union. But Point Four rested on an untested premise. Washington supposed that demand for minerals and knowledge of lucrative deposits would generate private investments in minerals production, and consequently, the role of government was simply to encourage public exploration and development, but not publicly-owned recovery of mineral reserves. And, from a different angle, the Point Four Plan represented a simple extension of these principles applied in the Marshall Plan, to less-developed, non-European nations who also faced the twin dangers of Communism and economic deprivation.

How could the U.S. government encourage American firms to move abroad and exploit high-quality mineral deposits? This policy question troubled Truman administration officials in the late 1940s as domestic and international conditions reinforced the conviction that the U.S. must look elsewhere for resources to augment declining domestic reserves and meet soaring consumer demands. Not only did economic growth at home increase America's raw-material requirements but, simultaneously, the Soviet penetration of poor countries with untapped mineral riches heightened the risks of government intervention, nationalization, and political instability.

In some resource sectors, such as petroleum, a close pattern of industry-government cooperation existed. Energy-seeking firms moved abroad before World War I, investing heavily in adjacent Mexico. During the subsequent energy shortage, U.S. foreign policy supported American oil men, especially in obtaining concessions in the Middle East and Dutch Indies. Similarly, during World War II Washington supported its important resource-seeking corporations, especially encouraging the copper companies to expand production in Chile and the steel firms to search for manganese and iron ore in Brazil, Venezuela, and Newfoundland. Primarily the large integrated mining corporations involved in basic industries, such as energy and steel, led the way abroad, and the process of expansion served both the firm's interest—diversified sources of supply—and the national interest in obtaining access to foreign ore deposits. In other mining industries, lead and zinc for example, American firms exhibited more caution. In the most extreme examples, the U.S. relied almost entirely on foreign-controlled suppliers of chrome, nickel, and tin.[33]

Increasingly, nationalization and expropriation emerged as major impediments to private investments in less-developed countries. The growing tide of nationalization and creeping taxation, which began against British- and American-owned utilities in Latin America, soon extended to the oil industry, which faced threats of nationalization in Venezuela and a takeover in Iran. Eager to encourage the private sector, the Truman administration first sought to negotiate multilateral treaties, but two such efforts, the Charter for the International Trade Organization and a multilateral agreement negotiated in 1948 with Latin American nations, foundered. Subsequently, President Truman's advisers pursued the bilateral path—but with mixed results. Efforts to negotiate modernized Treaties of Friendship, Commerce, and Navigation faltered, though they contained such beneficial provisions to investors as nondiscriminatory treatment, convertibility of earnings and capital, and prompt, adequate compensation for expropriated properties. Only eight nations ratified these treaties. Among them were Ethiopia, Greece, Iran, Israel, Korea, Muscat and Oman, Nicaragua, and Pakistan by 1963. Essentially, this approach sought to formulate a code of conduct when contending parties themselves disagreed sharply about the rules of the game. Also the Truman administration set out to negotiate tax treaties which would relieve direct investors of burdens from double taxation, another serious impediment to investments.[34]

Another approach pursued inauspiciously in the Marshall Plan and later programs for less-developed areas involved investment guarantees for specific private investments. They would provide security against the inconvertibility of earnings, guarantees against seizure without prompt and adequate compensation, protection against physical destruction, and other guarantees for capital. President Truman sought in June 1949, to extend this program to underdeveloped areas and to place its administration under the Export-Import Bank, moves that initially encountered serious opposition in

Congress. While proponents of the program considered these efforts experimental and inconclusive, opponents claimed that the program did too little to stimulate overseas investments.[35]

Despite these initiatives, the Truman administration was unable to improve significantly the external climate for mining investments, and American firms remained hesitant about moving outside of Canada, Venezuela, and Chile—countries where the large energy and mining companies had operated comfortably for years. In 1949, there was a net direct investment capital flow of $54 million into foreign mining and smelting, and the bulk of this went to those three countries: Chile, $21 million; Canada, $15 million; and Venezuela, $15 million. *Mining Engineering* blamed lagging investments on "the rise of nationalism" in underdeveloped countries. Where young governments consider "mineral exploitation a usurpation of the people's natural heritage," mining capital "understandably has shunned these nations as being poor investment risks."[36]

Ironically, the State Department, which many revisionist historians consider too eager to promote private economic interests, received heavy criticism from the minerals industry for its inadequate and ineffective support. For instance, the *Engineering and Mining Journal* complained that the foreign affairs agency, and coordinate independent agencies, lacked a coherent purpose and a consistent minerals policy. To remedy its deficiencies the State Department must appoint experienced minerals experts to responsible posts so as to avoid future "squandering money, unrealistic planning, and expensive failure." Also, the State Department should accept greater responsibility for representing U.S. interests, not the desires of foreign nations. "The State Department must recognize that, although its activities lie abroad, its allegiance is to the people of the United States —all of them." The mining journal concluded that the State Department "ought to have an eye and an ear for the interests and complaints of those domestic producers and consumers who are inevitably affected by whatever the department does."[37]

Until June 1950, when North Korean troops armed with Soviet equipment moved southward across the 38th parallel, U.S. planners expected a Soviet-American military collision sometime in the mid-1950s, but probably not before. This target date offered American planners an adequate interval to build up stockpile holdings gradually. There was no urgent need to battle with Congress for emergency appropriations or to request economic control measures that would enable government officials to divert materials from the consumer economy. The NSRB, it is true, had argued for elevating defense-related priorities, and as a concession to this point of view the White House and Congress did slowly increase stockpile funding to a level of $600 million annually. But this was insufficient to prepare for a global war earlier than the mid-1950s. And in June 1950, the U.S. stockpile was woefully undersupplied. Government had about $1.4 billion in materials on hand and another $700 million on order. At existing rates of purchase officials estimated it would take 5½ years to complete the resource procurement program, and would cost about $6 billion. There were serious shortages of many key materials. The administration had achieved only 17 percent of its aluminum objective; 65 percent for bauxite; 51 percent for cadmium; 44 percent for chromite; 18 percent, cobalt; 51 percent, coconut oil; 31 percent, copper; 23 percent, cordage; 22 percent, diamonds; 57 percent, lead; and 35 percent, manganese. Also, 73 percent for muscovite-splittings mica; 14 percent for block-and-film mica; 10 percent, molybdenum; 12 percent, nickel; 68 percent, quartz; 53 percent, quebracho; 45 percent, rubber; 33 percent, tin; 32 percent, zinc; and 32 percent, tungsten.[38]

The tungsten shortage was especially serious, because Korea provided 25 percent of the American supply. This metal, critical for jet engines, once came primarily from China—and Asia supplied over 80 percent of the world's tungsten. Had the Soviet Union, and its Asian clients, acquired all the tungsten resources of Asia, including Malaya and Burma, as some intelligence sources believed the Soviets desired, then the Kremlin would have achieved "an economic strength far exceeding anything the western nations have." While American foreign policymakers did not send troops to Korea simply to protect tungsten supplies, the mineral deficiency was a consideration to Washington officials concerned with strategic supply issues. What especially disturbed White House level policymakers was the prospect that a Soviet consolidation of South Korea, like the Communist triumph in China, would signal the end of Western influence on the Asian mainland, and contribute to further Communist triumphs in Southeast Asia imperiling America's geopolitical and resources position.[39]

For Stuart Symington, the former Air Force Secretary now head of the NSRB, the Korean War materials crisis offered a personal challenge and an opportunity to achieve a long-time administration objective—a full stockpile. In staff discussions his aides urged Symington to push for a quick acceleration in stockpiling, beginning with a supplemental appropriation for another $500 million in fiscal 1951 and $1 billion in the fiscal-year 1952 budget. They also recommended increased production at existing mines, reactivation of stand-by plants, and construction of new mining facilities. Along with expanded production, the government needed to curtail unnecessary use, and in this area Spencer Shannon of the NSRB Materials Office favored both conservation measures and voluntary allocation agreements for industry, and mandatory controls to secure the necessary materials for armaments production and stockpiling.[40]

There were other ways, Symington learned, that the government could improve its short-term materials position. It might purchase and stockpile every available ton of Far Eastern natural rubber and reactivate synthetic rubber plants at home. To meet emergency aluminum needs the U.S. should reactivate aluminum plants, purchase and stockpile all Canadian supplies, and move every available ton of foreign bauxite to the United States for inclusion in the official stockpile. To meet low inventories of iron ore, materials experts urged purchases of foreign iron ore and strenuous efforts to move the iron through the Great Lakes to steel mills. Because copper had important war uses but was in short supply, the experts favored accelerating purchases and stockpiling as well as improvements to African shipping facilities, particularly the port of Beira, used to load copper from Northern Rhodesia. To meet other strategic materials requirements, the U.S. should buy all available Far Eastern tin; obtain manganese ore and expand Brazilian production; reactivate nickel facilities at Nicaro in Cuba; and bring pressure on the International Nickel Company to expand its own production so increases could be stockpiled. To meet zinc requirements, the U.S. should purchase foreign supplies. To satisfy molybdenum requirements, Washington should purchase and stockpile the Climax inventory and provide long-term contracts to invite expanded production. Finally, to deal with the critical shortage of chromite in official stockpiles the government should "maximize imports from major producing areas in the Near East and Southwest Pacific."[41]

And soon the Truman administration began to put together an emergency materials program. After Symington told the NSRB that "the existing stockpile situation" was "very serious," and emphasized how further procurement hinged on Congress' decision to appropriate more funds, President Truman recommended Congress reexamine the stockpile program as well as take other steps to meet military procurement needs. The chief executive recommended a massive federal program, providing loans and incentives for expansion of existing mining capacity, for technological developments, and for production of essential supplies. After some debate Congress did approve an emergency program—boosting stockpile procurements so that total obligations in 1951 exceeded purchases over the preceding 4½ years. Most important, Congress also approved the Defense Production Act in September 1950, and this omnibus measure provided the type of mandate for expanding minerals production that the experts wanted.[42]

Unlike World War II which occurred during a period of industrial underutilization and acute unemployment, the Korean War broke out as the American economy recovered from the 1948–1949 recession. An unexpectedly large demand for housing, automobiles, electrical appliances, and other civilian goods boosted the economy and tightened materials prices for copper and zinc. After the North Korean military began its southward thrust, prices surged upward because consumers anticipated military orders would bring government regulations and shortages. Altogether the index of commodity prices shot up 35 percent between June and December 1950, before Washington did issue restrictions to curb civilian demand for materials and before foreign supplies arrived in increased volume to satisfy mobilization requirements. Interestingly, the rise in commodity prices took place *before* government procurement for the stockpile heightened the demand for raw materials.[43]

For the Truman administration the Korean War offered an unexpected opportunity to overcome legislative resistance to higher federal spending for military and stockpiling purposes and to implement the defense mobilization and materials accumulations programs favored in the executive branch. The National Security Council and companion National Security Resources Board both had approved papers urging substantial budgetary commitments in their respective areas, but public apathy and congressional insistence that stockpile procurement not interfere with private consumption blocked serious achievements. As the chairman of the National Security Resources Board told President Truman after the Korean War began: "Very few people realize how grave is the growing shortage of raw materials available to the economy of this country—in time of war, in a period of mobilization or even in time of peace." Forty-five of the seventy-three essential materials on the stockpile list "are obtained entirely or almost entirely outside the boundaries of the United States and its possessions."[44]

To cope with the economic situation, the federal government belatedly took steps to curb domestic demand. The Federal Reserve acted to reduce consumer credit and discourage business expansion as well as halt housing starts. The government hiked income taxes, thereby reducing the purchasing power of corporations and individuals. In addition to these monetary and fiscal tools, the Truman administration also resorted to economic controls, including Defense Production Administration restrictions on production for certain civilian uses and government allocation of basic materials, like steel, aluminum, and copper. For other materials, such as rubber, tin, and tungsten, which the United States obtained extensively from foreign suppliers, the government itself took charge of importing, and in this way controlled the allocation of scarce materials for internal use. These measures, curbing civilian purchases and the private-enterprise sector, were necessary, the government believed, to permit a rapid expansion of military requirements without igniting a disruptive inflation. In essence, the national authorities sought to double the percentage of America's gross national production going to national defense (from about 8 to approximately 15 percent) without severe sacrifices from consumers. If Americans had to postpone some consumer purchases, work longer hours, and defer any expansion of federal welfare or health programs, this was the cost of containing the Soviet threat and assisting potential allies in Western Europe and Japan.[45]

Perhaps the most controversial Korean War experiment with controls involved cooperative efforts to allocate raw materials among the Western nations. During World War II, of course, two major powers, the United States and the United Kingdom, jointly allocated raw materials based on their own dominant position in world shipping. This procedure probably simplified the conduct of military operations, but it neglected commercial interests of smaller powers to the advantage of British and American firms. Seeking to avoid similar problems, the U.S., U.K., and France, especially the last, took the initiative now in organizing an International Materials Conference, a type of world machinery involving twenty-eight nations and several international organizations. Basically this mechanism involved a central group responsible for initiating action where its members favored cooperative action, and seven commodity committees, composed of nations producing and consuming 80 to 90 percent of the materials selected for review. Among the commodities considered were: copper, lead, zinc, manganese, nickel, cobalt, tungsten, molybdenum, cotton, cotton linters, cotton pulp, sulphur, pulp paper, and wool, all considered essential either to defense production or the economic stability of trading nations.[46]

The working committees devised allocation plans for copper, zinc, nickel, cobalt, tungsten, molybdenum, sulphur, and newsprint, a complicated procedure invariably raising difficult issues of national security and prestige. Among the delicate political issues were these: what percentage of production should be earmarked for defense uses? what percentage stockpiled for future emergencies? what percentage assigned to essential civilian consumption? Some producing countries feared that an international allocation system would interfere with normal trade patterns, reducing the amount available to their domestic customers. Others expressed concern that the U.S. might utilize the allocation mechanism for securing a trade advantage at the expense of other participants. Finally, there were disagreements about establishing a single world price for each commodity in short supply. Here consumer countries generally favored international agreements, while producing countries wanted to postpone action, hoping thereby to bargain for higher prices or more favorable marketing positions. Finally, there were other problems involving efforts to increase production. While consumers wanted more goods to hold down commodity prices, some producing nations exhibited reluctance, realizing that increased production could leave a glut when defense requirements eased.[47]

To many Americans the International Materials Conference was a collective discussion mechanism antithetical to U.S. interests. While considering the unifying principle—that is, "favoring the widest degree of fair sharing" involving distribution on the basis of "demonstrated needs" and on the basis of "equality of sacrifice"—the United States effectively refrained from using its strong dollar position to buy up scarce resources. Instead, nationalists complained, the State Department consciously adopted a policy of international cooperation among "countries opposing Soviet aggression" for political reasons not directly related to American needs for larger quantities of scarce materials. Thus, during late 1951, the United States limited its own imports of strategic materials—copper, zinc, nickel, cobalt, and tungsten—in order to assure other participating nations a portion of the global supply. As economist H. H. Liebhafsky concluded in one evaluation, "International control was made effective largely because of the restraint exercised by the United States."[48]

Conservative critics had an opportunity for public criticism when Nevada Republican Senator George Malone chaired a Senate subcommittee investigation in 1953 and 1954. This report, which reflected Malone's own belief that the United States should develop Western Hemisphere resources, concluded: "International control of production and consumption allocations may have depleted and retarded fulfillment of stockpile objectives." And Malone's report contained a warning against participation in permanent international organizations for controlling distribution and production. These "could inhibit our own going-concern industries."[49]

More important than international allocations to overcoming U.S. supply deficiencies during the Korean War was the major federal effort to expand materials production in the U.S. and other countries. Recognizing from World War II experiences that materials shortages often handicapped production schedules and that the United States had inadequate stockpiles for defense needs, the Truman administration and Congress drafted and approved the Defense Production Act, containing authority for a number of financial incentives, such as granting materials producers rapid amortization of new facilities for tax purposes, providing government loans and guarantees, and authorizing government materials purchases, through a variety of tested methods—exclusive purchasing contracts, commitments to purchase stated quantities at fixed or floor prices, and open purchase offers. As of March 1953, the government's financial exposure exceeded $3.5 billion, most of this on contracts to generate new supplies of copper, manganese, aluminum, nickel, and titanium. Senator George Malone learned that from July 1, 1950, to March 31, 1953, the federal government spent $527.9 million to expand domestic mineral production, most of this ($306 million) for expansion and procurement contracts to boost American production of chromite, copper, manganese, magnesium, molybdenum, and titanium. But another $594.1 million went for minerals expansion projects abroad, most of this sum for manganese and nickel development. The results were mixed. Inevitably, it is difficult to expand mining production quickly, although the government claimed, in particular, that its domestic tungsten purchase program facilitated stockpile purchases. Later criticisms would show that Washington diluted quality standards to satisfy the domestic producers, a decision that prompted criticism a decade later from then-Senator Stuart Symington.[50]

In terms of long-range American foreign policy, the Truman administration made a far-reaching decision. Eager to boost total resources available for the Korean emergency, then of unknown duration, the executive branch and Congress turned outward, encouraging foreign suppliers and increasing U.S. reliance on other nations. This decision, understandably enough, reflected the internationalist thinking that shaped American foreign policy in the decade since Hitler's armies moved westward against France in 1940.

An important lesson emerged from experiences in the 1948–1952 period. Confronted with Soviet-bloc initiatives to separate colonial regions of Asia from the Western bloc, and fearful Communist successes in Asia would invite similar thrusts elsewhere in Africa, the Middle East, and Latin America, the U.S. defined its security globally. This basic decision to contain expansive Communism along the periphery of the Sino-Soviet area rested on a number of considerations. These included the essential idealism of the American people and their belief in human rights; a geopolitical concern that Soviet successes in harnessing the human and industrial resources of Eurasia posed a serious threat to Western civilization; and a conviction that the success of efforts to organize a stable world depended on the determination of major nations to punish aggression wherever it emerged. Another factor contributing to Washington's emerging global security frontier was the recognition that the prosperity and political stability of the U.S. and her potential allies hinged on access to vital resources available in peripheral regions vulnerable to Communist aggression.

In the spring of 1952 the Central Intelligence Agency circulated national intelligence estimates evaluating the economic importance of these outlying regions to the U.S. The loss of South Asia, an area comprising India, Pakistan, and Ceylon, "would have a serious effect on the industries of the United States and the rest of the free world if such loss should occur before 1954, particularly as consumption of these materials is expected to increase sharply in that period" resulting, in part, from war-related demands. The most serious Western losses would be manganese, mica, and graphite.[51]

After the Soviet Union embargoed manganese shipments in 1948, India gained importance as a principal supplier of high quality material, providing about 20 percent of free-world manganese production. Alternate supplies existed, but it would take several years to develop these deposits. Meanwhile, the U.S. stockpile, 45 percent complete, was sufficient only to offset India's production for a period of 2½ years. In addition, 67 percent of free-world mica production came from India, and loss of these materials would impose severe hardships on the U.S. and its allies. The United States stockpile, only 20 percent complete for block-and-film mica, would offset the loss of Indian supplies for only about one year. Similarly, Ceylon produced amorphous graphite, essential for electric brushes in aircraft. If this source were lost, the U.S. and its allies would have grave difficulties, for Ceylon supplied the world, and the U.S. stockpile represented about one-fourth of Ceylon's annual exports.[52]

The CIA estimate also claimed other areas in the Far East had vital supply importance to the United States and allies. Loss of a region, including Japan, South Korea, Taiwan, the Philippines, mainland Southeast Asia, Indonesia, Australia, and New Zealand, would be a "severe one to the rest of the Free World," especially because this region had important deposits of tin, tungsten, chromite, rutile, rubber, abaca, coconut oil, and wool. "The loss of the Far East would mean . . . a loss of 60 percent of the Free World's output of tin; 70 percent of its rutile, and roughly 30 percent of its chromite and tungsten."[53]

But Asia was not so immediately important as Latin America, Africa, and the Middle East. Loss of South America, the CIA report concluded, would be a "serious" blow to the U.S. in the 1952–1954 period, because it would be unlikely this country could obtain Eastern Hemisphere resources in the event South America were cut off. South America possesses "rich resources of various minerals which are ex-

ploited predominantly for export, chiefly to the United States."
Among the important items were bauxite, copper, manganese, rare
earths (monazite sands), beryl, mica, tin, tungsten, columbite, and
tantalite. "It contains the only resources of manganese ore that are
large enough to supply the requirements of the Western Hemisphere,
a factor of great significance from the longer range viewpoint. South
America is the only important source of tin and beryl in the Western
Hemisphere." [54]

During the Korean War the U.S. realized the vast strategic importance of mineral-rich Africa, perhaps the world's richest single
area. The Gold Coast, for instance, emerged as an important supplier
of battery and metallurgical-grade manganese, while Nigerian columbite was of "highest importance as an alloy for jet engines and certain steel products." But nations in Southern Africa deserved the
closest attention. The Belgian Congo had immense natural-resource
inventories, including cobalt used in jet engines. The Union of South
Africa, Southern Rhodesia, and Mozambique together supplied a
variety of critical items—manganese, chromite, asbestos, copper, corundum, platinum, and uranium. Concluded a NSRB official, "While
our loss of the supply of individual items would not be of the most
critical nature, in combination they would represent a serious impact
if denied to us." [55]

To American analysts the Middle East also held great significance, especially as a supplier of much-needed chromite and petroleum. Turkish chromite ore represented 35 percent of the free world's
production and its loss would necessitate "large withdrawal from the
U.S. stockpile" as well as "development of expanded production in
Southern Rhodesia," a move requiring both time and heavy investments to develop replacement mineral deposits. Loss of the Middle
East would necessitate severe rationing of petroleum, "more severe
than World War II rationing in the United States," for that region
was the "world's most promising region for future oil development." [56]

Taken together the mineral deposits of Asia, South America,
Africa, and the Middle East—a region of underdeveloped nations—
were vital to both the long- and short-range security of the U.S.,
Western Europe, and Japan. American security planners recognized
clearly how the Soviet threat to these regions jeopardized the military
and economic foundations of the Atlantic region. In an October 1953

statement of basic national security policy, the National Security Council said: "Although largely undeveloped, their vast manpower, their essential raw materials and their potential for growth are such that their absorption within the Soviet system would greatly, perhaps decisively, alter the world balance of power to our detriment." It anticipated the "Soviets will continue to seek to divide and weaken the free world coalition to absorb or win the allegiance of the presently uncommitted areas of the world, and to isolate the United States, using cold war tactics and the communist apparatus."[57]

During this first phase of the cold war struggle American policymakers did not view U.S. global interests solely, or even primarily, in terms of access to foreign strategic and critical materials. Since nonscientists made top policy, technical issues often were ignored, or cloaked in different language, during White House discussions. But resource considerations were an important element in American policy decisions. Often materials issues were addressed only in sweeping geopolitical terms. There is no question that Secretary of State Acheson and his colleagues had a geopolitical world view, and believed that the dominance of the Eurasian land mass by a single power or totalitarian coalition endangered American security.

Support for an open-world economy, an underpinning of recent U.S. policy, rested in part on the belief that trade was vital to supplement inadequate domestic resources if the U.S., Japan, and Western Europe were to maintain high standards of living. Policymakers believed that the Soviet threat, like the Axis challenge, endangered this efficient allocation of global resources, and dictated that America abandon hemispheric isolationism in favor of collective security mechanisms. This recognition marked a significant break with prewar thinking. Before World War II the U.S. could easily neglect the raw-material basis of diplomacy because the Western Hemisphere was self-sufficient in energy, iron, and copper, the prerequisites for industrialization. America's mineral deficiencies dictated an internationalist foreign policy during the Truman presidency.

Chapter Seven
The Paley Report:
A Mid-Century Minerals Survey

THE KOREAN War not only aroused concern about how the United States would meet immediate defense needs in a world threatened by Soviet communism but also imparted a note of urgency to considerations of long-term materials supply. "There is nothing more important to the future security of the United States than obtaining, now and in the future, an adequate supply of those raw materials necessary to build up our defenses and maintain our economy," said Stuart Symington, chairman of the National Security Resources Board. Recognizing that the political climate was ripe for a full-scale investigation, he persuaded President Truman to establish a five-member Presidential Commission in order to consider the broad and long-range implications of materials policy and then report recommendations to the president and Congress.[1]

Truman created the President's Materials Policy Commission (PMPC) in January 1951, and at Symington's suggestion selected William S. Paley, president of the Columbia Broadcasting System to chair the panel. Other members of the commission included George R. Brown of Houston, Texas, a prominent construction engineer who was president of the Brown Engineering Corporation, and also chairman of the board of Texas Eastern Transmission Corporation, a major transporter of energy. From the mining industry Truman appointed Arthur H. Bunker, president of the Climax Molybdenum Company, who was also a director of Lehman Brothers, the private New York bank. The other two commissioners came from two different constituencies. Eric Hodgins was a writer and editor for *Fortune* magazine, a Henry Luce publication. Finally, Edward S. Mason, a prominent economist, had a string of impressive credentials: he had served as a principal adviser to Will Clayton, the undersecretary of state for economic affairs, was dean of the Harvard University School of Public Administration, and president of the American Economic Association. This panel had balance, both in terms of its members' political affiliations and career experiences, although the minerals industry believed the commissioners and their supporting staff had too little direct experience with day-to-day problems of the metals industry. Certainly the group did include a large number of specialists with academic credentials as well as some holdovers from New Deal investigations. Grumbled the *Mining World*: "Sticking out like a sore thumb is the ubiquitous Samuel Lipkowitz [a staff member] of horrendous memory from WPB [War Production Board] days. . . . One never knows who may have crawled under the tent."[2]

Paley's instructions established definite boundaries for the materials investigation, expected to last six to nine months. "The task of the Commission," said President Truman, "will be to make an objective inquiry into all major aspects of the problem of assuring an adequate supply of production materials for our long-range needs and to make recommendations which will assist me in formulating a comprehensive policy on such materials." The commission was expected to study the following issues: long-range requirements, long-range supply outlook, anticipated materials shortages, and consistency and adequacy of existing government programs as well as private industry practices. In evaluating these items, it is significant that the commission was also instructed to consider "the needs and resources of the nations with which the United States is cooperating closely on military security and economic matters," for this instruction ruled out a nationalistic report insensitive to the general benefit of all America's allies.[3]

Most important in shaping final recommendations dealing with international aspects of minerals policy was Paley's decision to have economist Edward Mason take principal responsibility for guiding staff work in this area. Mason had definite ideas about how this presidential commission might contribute to the evolution of government policy. For one thing, a "forceful statement" that "the country is running into materials problems" would prepare the government and informed citizens for appropriate legislative action. The commission's important contribution, he said, would be in "presenting proposals in respect to public policy and government machinery. Tax policy, public domains, and better machinery to secure supplies from foreign sources were . . . the kind of areas in which the Commission's most constructive work could be done."[4]

Mason, and other commissioners, made certain implicit assumptions as a starting point for their own research and analysis—and these premises defined the investigation and shaped the final recommendations to Truman and Congress. There were three important guidelines. First, the commission anticipated a continuation of economic growth for the next quarter century at the rate of 2.5 to 3 percent annually. Second, while asserting that private enterprise was "the most efficacious way of performing industrial tasks in the United States," the panel favored continuing the existing "mixture of private and public influences on the functioning of our economy." Finally, Paley's group adopted an internationalist outlook consonant with the broad outlines of President Truman's global foreign policy. "We believe that the destinies of the United States and the rest of the free non-Communist world are inextricably bound together." What this meant in more specific terms, the commission said, was that the United States "must return in other forms strength for strength to match what it receives" in order to provide the enduring basis for increasing raw-material imports. "If we fail to work for a rise in the standard of living of the rest of the free world, we thereby hamper and impede the further rise of our own, and equally lessen the chances of democracy to prosper and peace to reign the world over."[5]

Materials strength was a prime ingredient for national security and economic growth in the future, the panel believed. With a strong materials position the United States would grow and remain strong, "which in turn is the foundation of rising living standards in peace and of military strength in war." Convinced that the United States and other non-Communist nations must coordinate their materials strength, the Paley Commission specifically rejected national self-sufficiency, a clear alternative to interdependence, and advocated instead that the United States pursue the policy of lowest-cost materials acquisition from whatever source. "Self-sufficiently [*sic*], when closely viewed, amounts to a self-imposed blockade and nothing more."[6]

The Paley Report, released in June 1952, made an important contribution, especially in offering the concerned public a thorough historical survey of the American materials position at mid-century. It underscored how consumer demand had expanded geometrically while "our spendthrift use of our rich heritage of natural resources" had depleted the nation's natural stockpile of vital industrial materials. Unlike some earlier government interpretations, such as Secretary of the Interior Harold Ickes' hyperbolic warnings, the report avoided exaggerating claims of America's "have-not" position; instead it asserted only that the United States had less. "The time had clearly passed when we can afford the luxury of viewing our resources as unlimited and hence taking them for granted," the panel stated. "In the United States the supplies of the evident, the cheap, and the accessible (chemically and geologically) are running out." What this meant was that "we have skimmed the cream of our resources as we now understand them; there must not be, at this decisive point in history, too long a pause before our understanding catches up with our needs."[7]

In specific terms, "the United States appetite for materials is Gargantuan—and so far, insatiable." Two and a half billion tons of materials were being consumed annually to keep the United States functioning and to support its standard of living. Each person, out of a total population of 151 million, used up eighteen tons of materials annually on the average. Fourteen thousand pounds went for energy materials to heat homes and offices, operate automobiles and trains, and run the boilers of industry. The average citizen used another ten thousand pounds of building material—items such as lumber, stone, sand, and gravel—as well as eight hundred pounds of metals. "Such a level of consumption, climaxing 50 years of phenomenal economic progress, has levied a severe drain upon the United States endowment of natural resources." During the first half of the twentieth century the American population doubled, per capita income rose from about $325 in 1900 to $864 in 1950 (measured in 1939 dollars), but "our consumption of minerals, including fuels, rose to six times 1900 totals. By 1950—in comparison with the year 1900—we were taking from the earth

Two and one-half times more bituminous coal.
Three times more copper.
Three and one-half times more iron ore.
Four times more zinc.
Twenty-six times more natural gas.
Thirty times more crude oil."

The President's Materials Policy Commission concluded that in almost every metal or mineral-fuel category, American consumption since the outbreak of World War I had exceeded the entire quantity of that material used anywhere in the world since the beginning of time.[8]

With demand for raw materials multiplying in the fifty years after 1900, a new relationship had emerged between America's material needs and its available resources. "Our national economy had not merely grown up to its resource base, but in many important respects had outgrown it. We had completed our slow transition from a raw materials surplus Nation to a raw materials deficit Nation." The study noted evidence to confirm this emerging deficit pattern. At one time America was a major exporter of copper, lead, and zinc, but now it had become the world's largest single importer of the same materials. Also, the United States had begun to obtain from foreign sources of supply substantial quantities of petroleum and iron-ore requirements, "which long were hallmarks of United States self-sufficiency." Other evidence that the United States had outgrown its resource base emerged from figures comparing domestic production and consumption of materials other than food and gold. In 1900, this country *produced* 15 percent more than it consumed; in 1950 the country *consumed* 9 percent more than it produced. In 1975 Paley's panel anticipated a possible 20 percent production deficit, which, in fact, proved low. By 1973 domestic minerals consumption exceeded production by 27 percent.[9]

Based on its own projections the Paley Commission foresaw a sharp rise in demand for raw materials—perhaps a 60 percent jump—between 1950 and the 1970s, sufficient to bring a doubling of the gross national production in real terms. Among materials most in demand would be aluminum (up 291%), fluorspar (187%), tungsten (150%), petroleum (109%), and nickel (100%). However, the demand for other important materials would climb more slowly—rubber (up 89%), iron ore (54%), copper (43%), zinc (39%), and tin (18%).[10]

Commodity consumption varies considerably from year to year depending on economic circumstances, but in general the Paley forecasts did prove remarkably accurate, except for tin, which experienced declining demand because of growing use of substitutes.[11]

Mushrooming demand for primary materials posed serious adjustment problems, Paley's commission concluded. To some extent, expanded supplies would come from additional exploration and discovery, especially of subsurface deposits. Also, advances in technology would undoubtedly bring about a fuller and more efficient use of known reserves, and would permit greater use of known low-quality ores. Perhaps, too, such unemployable materials as silicon would find new applications. In particular, the report emphasized how synthetics, like plastics, could supply future needs. "Synthetics can be expected to play an expanding role in our materials stream and hopefully can relieve some of our most serious difficulties." Nevertheless consumption was likely to outstrip added supply from these diverse sources, and the commission predicted rising costs for raw materials as better quality ores were used up and as it became necessary to produce additional quantities from less accessible and lower-cost resources. On this controversial conclusion, incidentally, the commission offered little evidence to support its thesis, except the fact that prices of certain key commodities, like lead and zinc, rose more rapidly than the wholesale price index from 1940 to 1950. The commission suspected that presently high prices "show that the pressure against limited resources is boosting real costs." As it turned out, however, the prices of lead and zinc fell sharply during the late 1950s and did not rise back to Korean War levels, measured in constant dollars, until the early 1970s.[12]

Rising costs, the David Ricardo type of resource scarcity, differed from Malthusian predictions of resource exhaustion heard a few years earlier when the Interior Department trumpeted warnings of a "have-not" America. In fact, the Paley Commission found no evidence to warrant concern about resource exhaustion, and it rebutted that thesis sharply. "The problem is not that we will suddenly wake up to find the last barrel of oil exhausted or the last pound of lead gone, and that economic activity has suddenly collapsed." Instead, "we face . . . the threat of having to devote constantly increasing efforts to win each pound of materials from resources which are dwindling both in quantity and quality."[13]

To counteract the inexorable push of higher costs, the President's Materials Policy Commission recommended that the United States pursue a policy based on the least-cost principle—that is, the nation should obtain materials at the least cost possible for equivalent values. In practice, this meant the White House study group rejected the protectionist pleas of domestic mining interests who asserted that cheap foreign labor costs threatened the jobs of American miners. Even in situations where vital defense materials were concerned, the Paley Commission spurned the notion government should protect high-cost domestic mining in peacetime with tariffs and subsidies. "The fallacy of self-sufficiency as a basic guide to sound materials policy is, in short, that it costs too much." Not only would protection add to the bills of American consumers but also it would handicap other non-Communist countries to sell their exports in the large American market. "Interference with these normal channels of trade would inevitably check economic growth at home and abroad. The political consequences of self-sufficiency, with its accompanying damage to carefully established security arrangements, would prove even more serious." In essence, the materials study rejected the self-sufficiency option, not only for reasons of economic efficiency but also because it contradicted the broad outlines of President Truman's political and security policies, which were based on rehabilitating and integrating the Atlantic bloc and Japan under the American defense and economic umbrella. In recommending the mineral interdependence option the commission did not evaluate carefully the trade-off between high-cost efforts to achieve national self-sufficiency and greater political independence versus economic benefits and political costs of relying on foreign suppliers extensively.[14]

While advancing the least-cost principle and recommending purchases of less expensive foreign materials, the Paley Commission also recognized the United States would still "look to its own reserves for most of its minerals supply." In the past intensified use of the vast North American continent enabled the United States, with 9.5 percent of the world's population, to produce almost half of the world's industrial materials. This pattern would continue, and geologists would likely discover new deposits of basic materials—for instance, copper, lead, zinc, uranium, vanadium, tungsten, antimony, petroleum, natural gas, and sulfur. Beneficiation of subcommercial grades of ore would make domestic iron, aluminum, titanium, beryllium, thorium, shale oil, fluorine, and graphite all merchantable. Beneficiation might also ease manganese supply problems, too. Development of synthetics was expected to ease the supply of industrial diamonds, sheet mica, quartz crystals, and asbestos. But for six materials the United States would remain heavily dependent on imports without the benefit of significant new discoveries, beneficiation, or synthesis. These were chromium, nickel, tin, cobalt, platinum, and mercury—all materials for which the United States remains reliant on foreign nations in the late 1970s. However for another group of materials the United States had supplies adequate for the next twenty-five years: magnesium, molybdenum, coal, phosphate, potash, lime, salt, sand, clay, gypsum, borax, barite, and feldspar.[15]

Facing greater minerals consumption and higher costs for some materials, the Paley Commission considered it important for the national government to reform and extend existing minerals programs. On one level, Congress needed to strengthen the Department of the Interior's capabilities, especially in collecting and analyzing facts on materials reserves and the process of exploration and development. The report also suggested the Department of Interior give more attention to the analysis of professionally trained economists, a recommendation reflecting the Paley Commission's own obeisance to practitioners of the once "dismal science." And it recommended a complete census of mineral industries, something already authorized by Congress, be taken in 1954 and every five years afterward.[16]

Central to the domestic minerals recommendations was support for subsurface geology and extensive mapping. Recognizing that prospectors already had thoroughly combed the continental U.S. and Alaska for outcroppings, the commission suggested: "From now on, the search for these minerals must be directed toward deposits hidden in the earth." Believing that an effective national minerals policy should concentrate on obtaining critically needed materials, the panel favored emphasizing development of better equipment and exploration methods as well as modifications in federal policies to "stimulate the efforts to make new discoveries, and promote the effective development of the deposits that are found." Among specific recommendations was support for an accelerated program of topographic and geologic mapping, because at the present rate of work it would take 150 to 200 years to complete, despite the fact that mapping had continued for nearly 100 years. "Only 25 percent of the United States and Alaska are covered by topographic maps good enough for today's needs. Only 11 percent of the United States is covered by geologic maps of sufficient scale."[17]

Consistent with the Paley Commission's penchant for expanding government activities, it urged that the federal authorities take a more active role in exploration, where the national interest appeared to dictate and where the prospect of reward was simply too small to entice private exploration. Here some precedent existed. After World War I, for example, the Department of Interior launched an intensive effort to discover potash, so as to release this country from the grips of a German-dominated cartel; and this program uncovered vast new deposits in New Mexico and Texas which ultimately made the United States a leading exporter, too. Other federally sponsored exploration during World War II led to discovery of important tungsten deposits in Idaho and copper sources in Arizona. The report suggested that the U.S. Geological Survey reemphasize finding emergency solutions to materials shortages, not concentrate exclusively on expanding general geologic knowledge for long-range benefit.[18]

The commission also urged important modifications in federal laws governing mineral resources on public lands. Previously, most production of metals, and a few nonmetals, involved the location system in which the government transferred a small tract, usually about twenty acres, to an individual prospector as a reward for discovery. Since future mineral discoveries were likely to require subsurface geology techniques, the commission believed the old location system inadequate. Not only was it difficult to search and file a claim under this system, but also subsurface operations often required larger claims to be economical. Paley's group recommended that the government extend the concession-leasing system, already used extensively for oil, natural gas, coal, and several other materials, to metallic ores. Such an approach, which provided large exclusive exploration rights over an extended area, would allow use of advanced exploration techniques and bring about a higher rate of discovery for subsurface materials, it was thought.[19]

More than better mapping and mining law reforms was necessary to stimulate exploration and extraction on federal and private lands. The commission identified a clear need for federally sponsored mining incentives, ranging from tax-depletion allowances to a series of subsidies, loans, premium payments, and long-term purchase contracts. Because minerals exploration involved heavy risks, private capital might not develop domestic reserves in a way best suited to serve national policy, it was argued; and as a result the United States could become unduly reliant on lower-cost foreign suppliers. Also financial incentives to promote long-term mineral development could cushion deleterious fluctuations in short-run commodity prices, and thus help protect a mining industry important to defense efforts. Traditionally, the United States government relied on tariff protection to guard domestic miners, an approach favored in the American industry because it avoided direct administrative intervention from Washington. In 1952 however, the Paley Commission rejected further tariff protection, claiming that "overriding national interest points clearly to the desirability of eliminating the obsolete tariff barriers." These border duties increased costs to domestic consumers, limited the inflow of materials from friendly foreign nations, and often bore no direct relation to this country's need for a foreign material. In particular, tariffs often discouraged importation of processed materials, such as aluminum, and according to Paley this pattern increased costs to consumers. It was more expensive, for instance, to ship bulky ores frequently. Persuaded that a national minerals policy for the cold war era should not damage efforts to promote a reciprocal reduction of tariffs, the commission concentrated, instead, on promoting tax incentives and federal subsidies for the home mining industry.[20]

One recommendation involved the minerals depletion allowance—an incentive first placed in the 1913 federal income tax. Essentially it was a deduction from taxable income permitted in recognition of the gradual exhaustion of a depletable property. In a sense the minerals depletion allowance was analogous to the depreciation allowed a business to recover cost of plant and equipment without paying taxes. For the minerals industry, depletion allowances, ranging at that time from $27\frac{1}{2}$ percent for oil and gas to 15 percent for most metals, were a time-tested device for enticing exploration and development. While it did not conduct a lengthy investigation on this point, the Paley Commission concluded that "percentage depletion should be retained because of its strong inducement to risk capital to enter the mineral industries," but that present rates need not be raised.[21]

Finally, the commission considered the gamut of loans, subsidies, and long-term purchasing agreements. These techniques first gained favor during World War II, and Congress revived them during the Korean War when it passed the Defense Production Act. Basically, the report reaffirmed the importance of long-term contracts and standing purchase offers to maintain a domestic minerals industry ready for emergency expansion. But the commission did observe that premium price plans, which allowed the government to pay more than the market price to stimulate production, were "ill-fitted for use as part of a long-range price policy," despite their obvious utility in an emergency. In another area the Paley Report favored advancing federal government funds to small mining concerns and prospectors in order to encourage exploitation of small deposits and because small prospectors and firms offer "an important pool of trained manpower available for expansion of minerals output in the event of an emergency." Except in minor details, the Paley resources review accepted the need for government to employ a versatile array of incentives to boost domestic minerals production.[22]

More interesting questions emerged with reference to less-developed nations. Many of these countries, located mostly outside the North Atlantic region, had the vital resources needed to supplement American and European domestic deposits—thus assuring continued growth in the United States and Western Europe. For the industrial countries to achieve a 67 to 75 percent increase in raw-materials consumption over the next twenty-five years, they would need greater quantities of mineral imports—and the commission forecast the United States might import 20 percent of its material requirements in the mid-1970s. For high tonnage items such as oil, iron ore, zinc, manganese, bauxite, and possibly copper, "there is little doubt that the less developed areas have high-grade reserves which after satisfying their own expanding requirements, are able to supply the import needs of the rest of the free world for the next quarter century and beyond."[23]

The real policy question in 1952 seemed to be whether private capital, another outside source of development assistance, would flow into underdeveloped countries at a rate sufficient to develop the low-cost deposits required to satisfy the expanding demand of industrialized nations. Recent United States experience offered some reasons for doubt. In late 1950 the United States private direct investment abroad amounted to $13.5 billion, and of this sum $4 billion was in petroleum and another $1.3 billion in mining and smelting. Eighty-three percent of the amount invested in mining and smelting was concentrated in the Western Hemisphere, but this was only $100 million more than twenty years earlier. To meet spiraling materials requirements, the Paley Commission estimated that private capital outflows must increase rapidly beyond the $50 million annual average for new foreign mining investments after World War II. Copper alone would need $100 million annually for each of the next twenty-five years. "The Commission is by no means convinced that the new investment will take place with sufficient speed and in adequate volume to provide for free world needs or to help build the economic strength of the less developed nations to desirable levels in the next few decades."[24]

What were the principal impediments to foreign investments in minerals development? The commission surveyed officers in about fifty materials-seeking firms and learned that they often encountered greater foreign government interference with their operations than did investors in commercial and industrial firms. Uncertainty about local political conditions, unfamiliarity with local traditions and procedures for conducting business, limitations on outside direct ownership, government restrictions on management decisions, irregular and inconsistent tax procedures, restrictions on currency convertibility and unpredictable exchange rates—all these served as barriers to foreign minerals development. Beneath these irritants was latent concern that host countries might dispossess the foreign investor of his property through arbitrary action. Expropriation, or creeping expropriation, involving various techniques to squeeze the foreign investor, helped poison the atmosphere for international investments. Basically at issue was the always delicate problem of reconciling the social and economic aspirations of the host country with the foreign investor's interest in earnings and security for his capital—and these issues called for the highest form of economic statesmanship to reconcile differences.[25]

How could the United States government promote a more favorable climate for foreign minerals investments? The commission endorsed, first, the current practice of negotiating treaties of friendship, commerce, and navigation (FCN treaties), designed, insofar as possible, to give American investors national treatment in foreign resource development. Such a provision was included in treaties with Colombia, Uruguay, and Israel, although others, such as treaties with Denmark and Ireland, reserved natural resources in a preferential way to their own nationals. According to the Paley Report, these long-term agreements had the virtue of offering a framework of law governing economic relations, and in this way discouraged expropriation without prompt and just compensation. For shorter periods of time and for specific situations, not the general investment climate, Paley's group recommended negotiation of special resource agreements involving executive authority. The panel also spoke favorably of the new disposition in Washington to guarantee private investors not only against currency inconvertibility but also against expropriation. As Washington gained experience with these experimental guarantees, the commission suggested ways "may be devised to increase the effectiveness of the guaranty for material enterprises."[26]

Changes in United States tax laws could also encourage minerals investments abroad, the commission observed. It "heartily" endorsed changes in the Revenue Act of 1951 that liberalized the foreign tax credit system, making it easier for United States investors to operate in other countries. These procedures, while exceedingly technical in nature, were intended to end double taxation of income earned abroad and to provide special inducements for future foreign investments.[27]

While asserting that private investment "must be the major instrument for increasing production of materials abroad," the Paley Commission thought government agencies must provide assistance to assure the development of materials needed in the free world. Here the study group challenged the widespread belief that a less-developed country should seek diversified economic development rather than relying on exports of raw materials. Paley's report noted that "materials production for world markets makes possible a more rapid expansion of industry, agriculture, and public utilities by providing foreign exchange that can be used to buy equipment for industries and farms, and to construct irrigation, hydroelectric, and transportation systems." From this perspective United States technical assistance could contribute both to national development and to greater production of world resources if it concentrated heavily on undertaking geological surveys and preliminary exploration and providing advice on mining technology. Two other agencies—the Export-Import Bank and the International Bank for Reconstruction and Development, the former a U.S. government agency and the latter a United Nations affiliate—could play important roles in providing public development loans to facilitate foreign materials expansion. In South Africa, for instance, an IBRD loan helped improve railway and shipping facilities needed to facilitate transportation of that country's enormous reserves of chrome and manganese. Certainly the American interest extended beyond limited assistance to raw-materials development, and the Paley Commission suggested that a host country's willingness to support and undertake natural resource production "might be an important factor in assessing the country's ability to service additional loans for economic development."[28]

Very often study commissions recommend creation of a new public agency to continue a function permanently, and the Paley Commission did just that. A new permanent agency could finance foreign materials production, it suggested, where security considerations warranted and private investment declined to assume risks. This agency would have authority to make long-term purchase arrangements including price guarantees, enter management contracts, and provide loans for risky investments which the Export-Import Bank could not properly undertake. During World War II emergency agencies had performed many of these tasks, as the government employed management contracts widely to construct emergency defense production facilities. Abroad the U.S. government developed the Nicaro Nickel plant in Cuba, copper production in Mexico and Chile, and vanadium in Peru. In this area, then, the Paley Commission resurrected older panaceas from wartime experience. Together with an accelerated stockpile program, these solutions would presumably provide the extra materials needed both for expanded peacetime consumption and for emergencies.[29]

Perhaps the most controversial single recommendation to emerge in this blue-ribbon investigation concerned international agreements to regulate commodity prices. Sharp fluctuations in commodity prices during the interwar period had dislocated markets, upset anticipated export earnings, and generally encouraged producing firms to devise private production and marketing arrangements known as cartels. To economists on the 1952 study commission the report offered an irresistible opportunity to speak out in behalf of intergovernmental commodity agreements to restrict production and prices, both in the interests of consumers and producing nations. Such a recommendation, if adopted, involved additional limitations on free-market forces; but it was consonant with the proposals on international commodity agreements included in the earlier Havana Charter for an International Trade Organization, which incidentally the United States Senate failed to approve. Arguments for international buffer stock agreements in the 1950s rested on the Paley Commission's expectation that the world faced a scarcity, not a glut, of commodities. Internationally negotiated cushions would provide some benefit to consuming nations and entice expanded production. In the past volatile mineral prices frequently discouraged additional capital investments to expand capacity, a factor likely to handicap economic growth again in the 1950s and 1960s if, as the commission forecast, a shortage of vital raw materials slowed growth. In a statement congruent with the State Department's efforts to structure the economic sphere with international mechanisms and agreements, Paley's report asserted that "failure to work toward stability would continue a major source of economic strain in the free world, and would leave the door open for reappearance of the prewar cartels and restrictive agreements with consequent limitations on production, consumption, and trade."[30]

What procedures did the Paley Commission propose in order to cope with dangers of overdependence on unreliable foreign sources of supply during periods of conflict? Assuming, as did U.S. strategic plans, that a future conflict would be a war of attrition between the Soviet Union and the United States in which this country might rely temporarily on its own low-grade domestic supplies and available stockpiles, the study group noted two remedies. First, it urged continuation of a permanent stockpiling program and concluded that in general the present stockpiling program "is well conceived and . . . its statistical goals have been kept up to date in the light of current trends and possibilities." Concerned, too, about the military vulnerability of Western Hemisphere production and supplies, the report proposed to establish secondary stockpiles in the ground and in technology banks. Here the thinking ran to intermediate-term development of domestic copper, low-grade manganese, bauxite, and other materials where the government could beneficially mark out low-grade ore reserves for emergency use. Also, the report suggested "moth-ball" production facilities and "stand-by technology" stockpiles to prepare in an emergency for extracting oil from shale and aluminum from clays. Emergency preparations might permit utilizing synthetics or some substitutes for high-grade mica, quartz crystals, industrial diamonds, asbestos, tin, and lead, all imported in substantial quantities.[31]

In preparing and rewriting this report the President's Materials

Policy Commission consulted both representatives of government agencies and outside specialists from the minerals and academic communities. Among these participants were Evan Just, influential editor of the *Engineering and Mining Journal*, himself once the director of a strategic materials division in the Economic Cooperation Administration, and Charles K. Leith, minerals adviser to government agencies for more than fifty years. One such discussion with outside specialists considered the fundamental policy issue—should the United States look outward for needed raw materials and encourage global cooperation, or should the government seek to limit outside dependence and develop domestic resources? Arguing for global interdependence, geologist Alan Bateman emphasized that certain geographic regions held minerals richer than those materials remaining in the United States. He listed Northern Canada, the African plateau, Siberia, and the Brazilian shield as all offering potentialities "for ore discoveries which are greater than in our own country because they have hardly yet been explored and many parts haven't been scientifically explored."[32]

To such arguments that the country should look elsewhere for oil, bauxite, antimony, chromite, copper, and other scarce materials, Ira Joralemon, a conservative minerals specialist, had serious objections. "Is it right for us, because we are a rich country," he asked, "to grab 10 times our share of all these foreign natural resources in order to maintain our standard of living at an enormously higher standard of living than all of our friends?" This same issue, he indicated, emerged in nineteenth-century Britain, and that country also opted to become dependent on an overseas empire for the mineral bases of prosperity. Joralemon asked: "Are we doing something that is decent and . . . in the interest of long-range welfare and peace to go out and grab the resources of other countries when we already have more than our share at home?"[33]

Philip Coombs, director of the commission staff, responded that President Truman's directive did not ask how "the U.S. can reap the world's resources." Rather the commission was directed to look at foreign needs as well as America's own requirements. "It is a question," he said, "of getting workable conditions of labor among the countries so you get a cross flow of materials and a reasonable cutting up of the pie." Many industry representatives participating in commission work also shared the basic premise that America lacked sufficient resources at home and inevitably must work out with private corporations and foreign governments ways to obtain rich ores from non-American sources.[34]

For seventy-seven-year-old Charles Kenneth Leith these internationalist conclusions represented the culmination of a crusade he and other minerals specialists had waged unsuccessfully since World War I to alert the public and its political leaders to the realities of minerals interdependence. In one discussion Leith admitted that he and his contemporaries had failed to communicate their message to the larger public audience, but now the Paley Commission had another chance to "dramatize it and make somebody else, but ourselves, understand it." The retired University of Wisconsin geologist repeated his basic analysis of how mounting demand for minerals and the concentration of supply on a few key ore deposits shaped international relations in the 1950s, as it had since World War I. "There is no country, no continent, no hemisphere that by any possibility can get enough of everything for both its economy and war purposes within their own borders," Leith stated. "In other words, nature has made one world out of us as far as this minerals' supply is concerned, and we just have to shoot hard for the one-world target."[35]

If a consensus generally existed among commission members that the United States must import greater quantities of foreign materials, government officials and industry spokesmen did not agree among themselves on how the public and private sectors should cooperate effectively to advance the national interest and secure supplies of vital resources. In particular, industry criticized the State Department's ineffective support for American enterprise abroad, a view in conflict with the common view that U.S. embassies act as the advance agent of private enterprise. Complaining that the State Department often refused to protect American mining firms, Leith recalled one incident involving the Kennecott Copper Company. It sought diplomatic assistance to help resolve problems in Chile, but Secretary of State Cordell Hull declined, saying according to Leith, "That's a sad story and there isn't anything I can do with it." Leith told members of the Paley Commission: "I saw a copy of the letter. I take that as official notice from the American Government to stay out of the foreign mineral investment, and that's getting right to the heart of minerals policy."[36]

But Hull's economic adviser, Herbert Feis, told the commission a different story. Diplomatic influence could and did stimulate minerals investments, benefiting other countries as well as U.S.-based corporations. "It can help to create and maintain a workable basis for American participation in the development of foreign raw material resources; and provide guidance, and protection for such enterprises." Diplomacy, he added, could appeal to common national political and economic interests, using these bonds to overcome obstacles and secure cooperation. "In short it can, and must, encourage, lead, instruct, appeal, induce, urge, and in case of special need, shove other countries along the course."[37]

In general American industry had little confidence in the State Department representing private interests effectively, and it depreciated the importance of both investment treaties and guarantees in stimulating the export of American capital to underdeveloped regions. Confronted with a variety of unpredictable circumstances abroad, ranging from currency-convertibility restrictions to discriminatory taxation and political interference, the private sector suggested two possible devices. One involved government exemption from antitrust prosecution so that private minerals firms could negotiate three-to-five-year commodity contracts with foreign concerns and governments. These commodity contracts, which would provide a floor price for minerals production, could provide foreign suppliers with the necessary predictability to encourage minerals production. In essence, a three-to-five-year contract offered a short-term solution, for it provided insurance against unexpected price fluctuations; but any long-term solution rested on persuading the private sector to undertake a long-term commitment to foreign minerals development and exploitation.[38]

Second, a State Department business advisory council recommended another device to strengthen the American position in foreign minerals production: creation of a single government agency having clear and undisputed authority to assist private enterprise and to allocate equipment and consumer goods to the raw-material exporting nations. While the State Department would retain policy-making authority, the new procurement agency would represent the coordinated bargaining power of the United States and conclude bilateral agreements with foreign governments. The gun behind the door in negotiations with foreign governments was United States willingness to "withhold our aid or support from those foreign powers who do not join in and contribute equitably to the common defense effort." This idea, while included in the report, was never implemented.[39]

After completing their work, Paley and his fellow commissioners trooped to the White House to present a copy of their recommendations to President Harry Truman. Knowing the chief executive's penchant for blunt speech, Paley said simply: "You asked for it. Here it is." The broadcasting executive told his friend Stuart Symington: "The baby is being born. . . . I must admit that during the past fifteen months I have more than once regretted the day you talked me into this project. Now that it is almost over I feel that I wouldn't have missed it for the world. . . . It taught me a hell of a lot and I have hopes that it may do some good." He commended Symington for "having the foresight and imagination to know a long time ago that this job needed doing."[40]

Truman in turn praised Paley and his colleagues for "a very constructive job." He added, "The document should serve for years to come as a basic guide in providing adequate supplies of the materials we and other friendly nations of the world must have if we are to expand our economy and at the same time remain secure from threats of aggression." Although politically the president was a lame duck, not seeking reelection, he nonetheless commended the materials report to members of Congress and directed executive agencies to prepare a thorough analysis within sixty days containing suggestions for implementing the recommendations.[41]

This decision to seek other official opinion revealed Truman's own sense of caution. It purchased time for concerned groups, both inside and outside government, to review the findings and air their own interpretations and conclusions as the retiring administration calculated the political advantages and ascertained what specific recommendations the national interest required. The sixty-day delay meant, too, that the Truman administration itself would have to make no recommendations to Congress, because the legislature traditionally recessed to permit its members to campaign for reelection.

Initially, the report was obscured by the competition for Republican and Democratic presidential nominations, and the Paley Report received limited attention in the national media. Since one Luce editor, Eric Hodgins, served on the materials commission and supervised writing the final product, it was understandable that *Time*, another of Henry Luce's publications, should adopt a friendly stance to this "comprehensive report." Accepting the premise that "the U.S., which has long been considered a bottomless store of natural resources, is fast running through its wealth," *Time* said the Paley Commission had offered a "levelheaded, thoughtful glance at the material needs in the next quarter century." Conceding that Congress might turn a deaf ear to these suggestions, it concluded: "The fat years of the U.S. have ended; even Congress will have to shape its legislation to the possible lean years ahead." The *New Republic* asserted that the Paley Commission "confirmed the well-known fact that the United States is running seriously short of raw materials." While noting some conflict between lofty statements of principle and practical recommendations, this liberal journal of opinion suggested, "If only as a new publicity weapon, the Commission's handsomely made-up, well illustrated set of reports dramatizing these problems may be worth the money they cost."[42]

Negative reviews appeared in the *New York Times* and the *Wall Street Journal*, two newspapers important in shaping elite opinion then as now. The former questioned projections of rising costs for raw materials and asserted "the problem of materials—at least under a free enterprise system—is essentially a problem of technology. And no mathematical formula has yet been devised for plotting in advance the direction on the time-table of technological advance." The latter, a financial newspaper wedded to principles of laissez-faire liberalism, blasted Paley's dire predictions, pointing out that none of the earlier forecasts about exhaustion of coal and petroleum supplies had come true. Rather, recommendations for "long-range planning" were most likely to bring about the shortages forecast. "If there is one thing that could bring the dire predictions to actuality it is Government control. Let a government begin to allocate something and there immediately develops a shortage where none existed before."[43]

Conservative economics writer Henry Hazlitt, a regular *Newsweek* columnist, considered the report a sham. "It begins by fearing an alleged 'crisis'; it ends by concluding that only more government power, more government controls, more government bureaucrats, can save us from it." For Hazlitt, and indeed for some mining industry critics of the government study, the national commission displayed an interventionist bias in favor of controls and against the free market.

"All these schemes can only end by further 'politicalizing' every economic transaction—by socializing, regimenting, and eventually totalitarianizing our economy at home and throughout the so-called 'free' world."[44]

Members of Congress, concentrating their guns on the autumn political campaigns, devoted little attention to discussing the results seriously, as President Truman suggested, but in fairness to the legislators, few constituents studied the recommendations either. In the Senate Texas Democrat Lyndon Johnson, a first-term member who investigated tin and nickel procurement problems during the Korean War, expressed some doubts about specific recommendations but he praised the report as a "thorough, painstaking, yet bold and daring study of a complicated and vast field." That was not the opinion of his Republican colleague Senator George Malone, a former mining engineer from Nevada. He branded the Paley Report "one of the most dangerous reports ever made to the American people." It "misrepresents the potentials of our economy. Through fear of a shortage of raw materials, it is an attempt to convince the American people to turn their backs on our American system and enter into a program of exploiting the world for a source of cheap raw materials." Not only was Malone concerned about opening the American market to cheap-labor produced foreign materials, thus undermining the domestic economy, but he said that hemispheric self-sufficiency offered a reasonable alternative. "The Western Hemisphere can be made self-sufficient in the production of the strategic and critical materials we need, and the lines of communications can be protected in case of emergency, although the lines of communication for the rest of the world cannot be protected in that event."[45]

The mining industry evaluated the study from different perspectives. Two leading publications, *Mining Engineering* and the *Engineering and Mining Journal*, offered generally approving commentaries. The first noted that the report confirmed the much-discussed "crisis in raw materials" and it concluded that if "the U.S. is to continue on a course of progress, it must procure raw materials wherever it can at the lowest possible cost. Natural resources are clearly an area in which the broadest cooperation between industry and government must exist to achieve efficient exploitation, economic consumption, and expansion of sources of supply." And it advised: "The message of the Paley report requires action comparable to that of the North

Atlantic Pact. . . . Don't let it die!" Evan Just's periodical, the *Engineering and Mining Journal*, disliked some specific proposals but said the report offered the minerals industry "an excellent idea of the way the trend of the times is headed." For instance the study emphasized how changing technology promises new opportunities for discovering ore bodies and promoting cooperative exploration with government.[46]

Vociferous opposition appeared publicly in vigorous debates sponsored at mining conventions, such as the meetings of the American Mining Congress. Critics from the domestic mining industry assailed the "have-not" thesis, which if true offered a persuasive rationale for developing new foreign mineral resources. "The 'Have Not' argument rests upon half truths," wrote John Kelly, a Washington-based natural resources consultant critical of the Paley forecast. An uninformed public was being "panicked into supporting overseas ventures while writing off domestic mines as empty holes useful merely for raising mushrooms or storing documents against atomic raids." To develop domestic reserves, Kelly said, miners needed only incentives to prospect and develop deposits. He also criticized the official study for encouraging increased dependence on potentially unreliable foreign nations where "the rising spirit of nationalism threatens to cut off shipments from an increasing area of the world—outside of the Soviet bloc." This trend, he predicted, would lead to "nationalization of the mines" and to "loss of Uncle Sam's investment." Noting reports that the Soviet Union was developing a large submarine fleet capable of disrupting major shipping routes, Kelly called the Paley conclusions "as much nonsense as betting our wartime salvation on untried mines located beyond the submarine curtain."[47]

Criticisms of the report's generally internationalist conclusions focused, in part, on the State Department imprint. According to S. H. Williston, an official of the Cordero Mining Company, the Paley Commission staff included "those who have been held responsible for the State Department's policy of keeping the American minerals in the ground, and pseudo-economists, who have long advocated an American 'have not' policy and a desire to become entirely dependent on foreign sources of our raw materials." Another mining industry critic considered the internationalist recommendations harmful to America's long-term interests, for they encouraged this country in the immediate future to consume other people's minerals with "reckless prodigality." This, he said, "would inevitably cause increasing hatred against us by all the peoples that are falling further behind us in the race for greater comfort and material security. It is real isolationism. It can result only in an eventual war in which we will be the lonely fat boy with a big stick of candy, surrounded by hungry toughs." The critic, Ira Joralemon, who incidentally served as an outside evaluator of the report before its release, believed that national self-sufficiency remained a viable alternative to dependence on low-cost foreign supplies. He asserted: "In all save a few materials such as nickel and tin we would be far better off than the rest of the world even if we had to depend on domestic sources alone." He reasoned that continued technological progress, enabling the United States to make use of lower grades of ores than those mined abroad, would continue to reduce our dependence on foreign countries.[48]

Other comment concentrated on the commission's questionable conclusion that the world faced rising costs for materials, and especially on the recommendation of developing international buffer stocks to encourage foreign production of strategic materials. Simon Strauss, a vice-president of the American Smelting and Refining Company, and a prominent industry spokesman on minerals trends for a generation after World War II, noted that proposals for buffer stocks were essentially designed to extend government control over the network of private cartels that failed to regulate commodity prices in the past. "The substitution of politicians for industrialists does not make the cartel theory any more palatable," he said. For the private firms the least desirable feature of international organizations supervising buffer stocks would be the potential for political pressure disrupting the market. "Investors would be bound to look with a jaundiced eye at the existence of huge inventories of metals in the hands of a group of government officials subject to political pressures: Elections in Chile, revolutions in Bolivia, confiscation in Iran. One can't forecast what the nature of that political pressure would be." Essentially, the private firms disliked the possibility that governments, responding not to rational market forces but to political pressures, might jeopardize the orderly function of private markets. As Andrew Fletcher, president of the St. Joseph Lead Company, said pointedly: "There is no reason to believe that governments which cannot stabilize their own affairs, or balance their budgets, can collectively stabilize metals and minerals sold in international trade."[49]

The report attracted little foreign comment, although the *Econ-*

omist, a London periodical which was then troubled about the shortage of dollars to facilitate the rehabilitation of world trade, noted that the Paley Commission's forecast of rising world demand promised to benefit the export earnings of America's immediate neighbors, namely Canada and Latin America, more than others. For the British Commonwealth the report had ominous implications. Eight industrial materials (wool, rubber, tin, manganese, copper, lead, chrome, and bauxite) had generated $620 million—or nearly 40 percent of the sterling area's total dollar earnings—in 1950. But lagging demand for natural rubber and certain other materials, like tin, would sharply reduce Commonwealth material exports, so that the $620 million in 1950 dollars promised to generate only $515 million in demand during 1975.[50]

Everything considered, the Paley Report represented an important undertaking—a comprehensive, independent, yet official study of the nation's resource base and potential. As such it was the first sweeping study since Theodore Roosevelt's administration and a model for a series of different resource commission studies in the 1970s. The report embodied prevailing assumptions about America's need to assume a global role, and in this regard the 1952 Paley study marks a significant shift in national materials policy. Stockpiling acts in 1939 and 1946 both stated that the policy was designed to "decrease and prevent wherever possible a dangerous and costly dependence of the United States upon foreign nations for supplies of these materials in times of national emergency." In 1952 United States policy no longer aimed to limit reliance on foreign suppliers; instead it wished "to insure an adequate and dependable flow of materials at the lowest cost consistent with national security and with the welfare of friendly nations." Policymakers now assigned priority to interdependence so long as this goal was consistent with national security and the welfare of other non-Communist nations. While the general public missed the far-reaching implications of this conclusion and other commission recommendations, and Congress itself chose not to act on the specific proposals, the thorough study remained a responsible appraisal of this country's resource position at mid-century.[51]

Chapter Eight
From Scarcity to Plenty–
President Eisenhower and Cold War
Minerals Policy, 1953–1963

WHEN President Dwight Eisenhower took office in January 1953, there were two contradictory interpretations of America's resource position, and proponents of each sought to shape administration policies. On the one hand, William Paley and some policy-oriented officials in federal agencies sought to alert the new president to the policy implications of a weakened resource base. Eager to win administration support for his committee's recommendations, Paley wrote President-elect Eisenhower that "our country has moved into a new era in its economic history, an era in which we can no longer produce enough of many materials at a cost basis to satisfy our expanding economy or security needs. I believe that this trend will continue and increase." Others of this persuasion, including officials of the newly formed Resources for the Future, a research group funded in part by the Ford Foundation, urged the new chief executive to dramatize the difficult materials issues with a national conservation conference much like the one President Theodore Roosevelt sponsored. And during the presidential campaign Eisenhower did seem to endorse the conference ideal, saying, "It is high time that the Conservation Conference of 1908 should be re-born in a mid-century setting!"[1]

Within the Washington bureaucracy a number of officials responsible for mobilization preparations worried not so much about long-term minerals exhaustion or rising costs as about the immediate problems of shortages, which could jeopardize U.S. defenses should another major war occur within the next few years. Supplies of the principal ferroalloys, cobalt, nickel, columbite, tantalite, tungsten, and beryllium, remained "inadequate to meet the indispensable minimum requirements for full-scale war even under strenuous wartime efforts to expand production, curtail consumption and effect substitutions." In another war supply insufficiencies might cut back production of jet engines, vital to modern air power. Consequently, military and civilian planners favored accelerated supply programs both in the U.S. and abroad to expand the production of nickel and cobalt in Cuba, boost cobalt supplies from Africa and South America, increase production of South Korean tungsten, and obtain new supplies of columbite and tantalite as well as beryl from foreign suppliers. Both in the short-run and in the long-run the U.S. appeared more reliant on foreign suppliers to meet its own resource deficiencies.[2]

Ironically, a different picture of the future existed in the American mining industry and among some private sector minerals specialists. It was a vision of surplus production and advancing technology, not the pessimism of resource depletion and rising costs. Domestic mining faced "a time of crisis," asserted the *Engineering and Mining Journal* in February 1953. The Korean War boom, which brought "expansion on the grandest scale in the industry's history," had ended, leaving an industry with surplus capacity in lead and zinc. Domestic mining, which had expanded rapidly at government insistence to meet emergency supply needs, now faced sharp readjustments, resulting from overexpansion, government-regulated prices, and an uncertain future demand for materials. And American miners feared a flood of cheap foreign minerals, ironically the result of a Korean War crash government program to stimulate overseas minerals production.[3]

The scarcity thesis, with its dire long-term projections of rising costs, had little appeal to private minerals specialists. They attributed recent price fluctuations, in part, to artificial conditions resulting from emergency government purchases, and to quixotic regulatory policies intended to control demand, regulate supplies, and allocate production internationally. These official actions, extending over more than a decade since the outbreak of World War II, had distorted underlying supply-and-demand conditions and produced unrealistically pessimistic forecasts, such as the Paley Commission's prediction of higher costs.[4]

In fact, the cornucopians were right, for the next major survey of materials requirements and availabilities conveyed a more sanguine tone. A Resources for the Future study, published a decade after the Paley Report, debunked the scarcity thesis, saying that "many industries see the problems of the immediate future as those of glut rather than of scarcity." Technological progress had held the threat of scarcity in check, opening previously neglected geographical regions and removing potential shortages that emerged soon after World War II. For example, not only had the airborne magnetometer facilitated exploration of difficult terrain, locating subsurface ore deposits such as nickel in Manitoba as well as lead and zinc in New Brunswick, but also similar advances in geochemical exploration, which relied on chemical analysis of rocks and soils, produced other major discoveries in the U.S. and abroad. Other important developments in extractive metallurgy, including concentration and beneficiation, as well as the prospect of exploiting sea nodules containing manganese, nickel, copper, and cobalt, all worked to counteract any trend to rising materials prices. Abundance, not scarcity, had become the watchword.[5]

From a different perspective, the long upswing in commodity prices, which began in the mid-1930s, had ended, and for the next twenty years minerals prices remained relatively stable. Among the materials used in large volume, lead and zinc declined in constant-dollar terms, remaining beneath Korean War levels into the 1970s. Generally the period from 1953 to the middle 1960s was characterized by a surplus productive capacity in basic industries, including mining. Several factors undoubtedly contributed to this pattern, reversing the upward price trend. For one thing, new supplies appeared in areas of the world like Africa, the Middle East and Australia, that produced few minerals before World War II. New exploration techniques like the airborne magnetometer and geochemical methods achieved new discoveries in North America. Also, demand for some materials, like copper, lead, and zinc, simply did not expand as rapidly in the 1950s as during the preceding period. Politically, the reversal in commodity price trends had major impact. It eased pressure on leaders to implement such far-reaching recommendations as the Paley Commission proposed, for circumstances had changed.[6]

In addition to the conflicting themes of scarcity and plenty, the cold war shaped Eisenhower's approach to minerals issues. Like his predecessor, President Eisenhower accepted the reality of the Communist world challenge and concluded the U.S. must collaborate with foreign allies to contain Kremlin influence. Personally familiar with the writings of Vladimir Lenin, author of the Soviet revolution, Eisenhower disputed the alleged inevitability of capitalism's collapse.

Instead, he believed moderation and pursuit of mutual benefit and advancement could overcome conflicts between labor and capital, as had occurred in the U.S. The same principles could close the gap between rich industrial nations and backward areas. Convinced that Communism was "aggressive," reaching out to "absorb every area in which can be detected the slightest discontent or other form of weakness," the president believed American leadership could establish a world system that "will allow backward people to make a decent living," thus undercutting the appeal of Communism. World trade and international cooperation for mutual benefit Eisenhower deemed a vital bulwark of a durable global system, for successes in these areas would make the world "so secure against the Communist menace that it would gradually dry up and wither away."[7]

Defense of Western Europe and Japan was vital to Eisenhower's diplomatic strategy, and so was continued access to world resources. More than any president since Herbert Hoover, he understood the dangers of excessive reliance on foreign suppliers. As a military commander confronted with countless supply problems, he had learned first-hand the importance of strategic materials in wartime, and Eisenhower recognized how dependent his country had become on foreign lands for vital materials—tin, cobalt, uranium, manganese, natural rubber, and crude oil. Soviet dominance of regions producing these materials posed a distinct threat to American security. "Unless the areas in which these materials are found are under the control of people who are friendly to us and who want to trade with us, then again we are bound in the long-run to suffer the most disastrous and doleful consequences."

While the new leader himself favored cooperation with other nations for mutual benefit, he entered office at a moment of national self-doubt. An inconclusive and costly land war in Asia taxed public backing for international undertakings, and a search for Communists at home raised serious questions about the integrity and judgment of many public officials. Eisenhower's own supporters were divided, and many had isolationist leanings. Some Republican leaders such as Senator Robert Taft of Ohio seemed to favor more limited international commitments, hearkening back to the "fortress America" policy advocated by ex-President Herbert Hoover in the 1930s as a device for isolating the Western Hemisphere from global turmoil. In economic and materials discussions other wide differences also emerged. Traditionally Republicans, more than Democrats, favored protective tariffs, and some anticipated the Eisenhower administration would reverse the reciprocal-trade program for tariff liberalization. Domestic mining interests from Republican strongholds such as Colorado also pressured for a protectionist minerals policy to guard American miners against cheap foreign competition. Consequently, it was possible Eisenhower might disregard the controversial Paley Report with its recommendation that the U.S. apply the least-cost principle, purchasing cheaper foreign metals and energy. Instead the new regime might pursue policies designed to insulate the Western Hemisphere from overreliance on potentially unstable foreign suppliers. At stake, then, was the future of American foreign and economic policies.[8]

But Eisenhower and his principal advisers, who incidentally reflected the philosophical outlook of the powerful New York legal and banking community, had no disposition to revive Hooverism and isolationism. Instead, they sought to combat isolationism and protectionism among Republican conservatives. Gabriel Hauge, a young economist who later emerged as president of Manufacturers Hanover, one of New York's leading international banks, helped shape the administration's outlook as White House economic adviser. He observed the emotional appeal of pre–World War II policies and warned the president that "America, at the peak of her economic power, is showing increasing signs of turning inward again economically." Such a trend "stems either from egregious ignorance of how best to preserve our real self interest as a nation or from moral stupidity that suggests we can wallow in our own wealth and high standards of living and still be secure in the world." Hauge added: "Keeping the frightened Little Americans from turning America inward to her own destruction is one of the great tasks ahead." To prevent a revival of recidivistic policies, he told another friend, "There is no blinking the fact that we have a considerable job to do with respect to a certain group" of the Republican Party in Congress.[9]

In order to promote consensus on the administration's foreign policy initiatives, both among Republicans and Democrats and between different Republican factions, President Eisenhower had Congress establish a Hoover-type commission, including representatives from Congress. This bipartisan President's Commission on Foreign Economic Policy would "examine, study, and report on the subjects of

international trade and its enlargement consistent with a sound domestic economy, our foreign economic policy, and the trade aspects
of our national security and total foreign policy; and . . . recommend
appropriate policies, measures and practices." Eager to avoid weight-
ing down the panel with protectionists who might offer solutions in-
congruent with Eisenhower's own internationalist outlook, the chief
executive deliberated and then chose Clarence B. Randall, a Chicago
steel executive, and Lamar Fleming, Jr., a Houston businessman, as
chairman and vice-chairman, respectively. Other panel members included representatives of labor, business, and Congress as well as a
prominent international economist, John H. Williams, closely affiliated with the New York Federal Reserve Bank.[10]

The White House got what it desired. The Randall Report, sub-
mitted to Eisenhower in January 1954, supported expanding international trade, but not economic aid, to close the global dollar
shortage; and it urged increased U.S. government support for private
investments abroad. Believing that "private investment" must "undertake the job of assisting in economic development abroad," Randall's
group urged "full diplomatic support" for establishing an international "climate conducive to private foreign investment." To promote this pattern, Washington should provide tax breaks—including
a 14 percent reduction on corporate rates for foreign income, and
other tax revisions to offset foreign taxes paid against domestic taxes.
Also, the panel wanted a continuation of existing investment guarantee programs, including coverage for risks of war, revolution, and
insurrection, in order to stimulate additional capital flow.[11]

Where the new report diverged sharply from the Paley study
was in its approach to commodity-price fluctuations. The Randall
Commission "does not believe that extensive resort to commodity
agreements will solve the problem of price instability; and it believes
that such agreements introduce rigidities and restraints that impair
. . . economic adjustment and . . . individual initiative." Rejecting
commodity agreements, the report favored measures to reduce or remove trade barriers, promote diversification of export economies,
and pursue domestic economic and stockpiling policies likely to avoid
disruptive commodity-price fluctuations.[12]

Like the Paley Commission, Randall's panel anticipated mounting U.S. dependence on imported raw materials. The staff analyses
considered briefly and then rejected the self-sufficiency option, saying

"this transition of the United States from a position of relative self-sufficiency to one of increasing dependence upon foreign sources of supply constitutes one of the striking economic changes of our time." While America might obtain sufficient manganese from low-grade domestic ores, slag recovery, and more efficient steel-making technology, it lacked adequate lead and zinc to remain independent of outside suppliers for even a decade. Copper reserves might last for twenty more years. But for other metals, such as tin, nickel, platinum, and metallurgical grades of chromite, the United States remained reliant on imports. "Unless geophysical prospecting discloses deposits that are now unsuspected, it is reasonably certain that we shall never be able to meet our requirements for these metals from domestic sources." If the Randall study concluded that intensified development of foreign minerals was "a compelling necessity for the United States and free nations generally," it also considered minerals development a "promising means of enlarging wealth and productivity"—that is, promoting foreign economic development. The difficult trick was for the United States to encourage and support private investments and to persuade host governments that "investors in the development of sources of needed materials must be assured against frustration of their ventures by unpredictable or capricious levies on exports or production by the countries of origin."[13]

In making the case for international dependence, not minerals self-reliance, Randall offered little encouragement to the domestic minerals industry. The report flatly ruled out protective tariffs, except where economic conditions might justify them. And it suggested the Defense Department should subsidize vital domestic suppliers out of its own budget, not through tariff protection. One commission member, Republican Senator Eugene Millikin from the mining state of Colorado, appended a strong dissent. "Recommendations of this section . . . would dangerously increase our dependence on foreign sources for needed strategic and critical materials." Millikin understandably preferred to back policies that strengthened domestic mining, not policies likely to turn portions of his home state into ghost towns.[14]

The Randall Report represented a victory for internationalist Republicans, like Eisenhower, and a defeat for those who favored protection and hemispheric self-sufficiency. Its conclusions corresponded to the Defense Department's own best estimate of national interests. As Secretary of Defense Charles Wilson indicated, the United States needed allies in the struggle with communism; it needed strong allies tied closely, both militarily and economically, to the United States; and it needed to cement these ties through bonds of mutual economic interest. In brief, the strength of American defenses hinged "upon the maintenance of strength overseas." Along with protecting the economic and security interests of nations occupying key geographical positions in the United States defense system, such as Japan and Western Europe, "it is essential that foreign sources of scarce materials needed for defense remain in friendly hands." One mineral-exporting nation the Defense Department wanted to keep "out of the hands of potential enemies" was copper-rich Chile.[15]

In creating the bipartisan Randall Commission with conservative members of Congress as participants, Eisenhower and his aides shrewdly silenced isolationist critics, except for one key mining state senator. George ("Molly") Malone, a Republican maverick from Nevada who boasted he could still rope a calf, was a vigorous opponent of foreign trade and aid; he once stated "all these sons of bitches need is a referee in bankruptcy." In 1953 Malone persuaded the Senate Republican leadership to support his own investigation to determine what critical raw materials were accessible to the U.S. in wartime and in what way the government could encourage production of vital materials. For the next ten months Malone's subcommittee conducted hearings from coast to coast and then released conclusions critical of official policies. These recommendations deserve attention not so much because they influenced policy, for they did not directly, but because Malone's critique of interdependence represented an alternative to official policies.[16]

The report, which incidentally bore Malone's own imprint far more than the opinions of other subcommittee members, was shrill and biting in tone. "The vital security of this nation is in serious jeopardy," it asserted. "We are dependent for many of our essential raw materials on sources in far-off lands, many under the control of possible fickle allies or timid neutrals, some veritably under the guns of our potential enemies." The "have-not" thesis Malone dismissed as "one of the greatest frauds and hoaxes ever perpetrated on the American people." For errors of analysis and misguided policies the onetime mining engineer criticized specialists and State Department personnel. Various commissions of economists, "so-called experts, not experienced in problems of production," developed the scarcity thesis. Malone accused second- and third-echelon State Department officials, inexperienced in problems of business and mining, of pursuing minerals policies beneficial to foreign producers, and thus extending this country's reliance on outside sources of supply. "Through education, environment and background," he said, "they are trained to placate foreign powers and try to build up friendship with foreign powers. They hope to accomplish this by entering into trade agreements with foreign powers, giving them benefits and advantages through division of our markets." These officials encourage other nations to "build up their production of strategic and critical raw materials which work to a disadvantage and at the expense and destruction of our domestic industries and thus weaken the security of the Nation."[17]

Malone considered the policy of relying heavily on low-cost foreign suppliers a serious danger to American security in wartime. Existing policies of reliance on cheap imported materials, such as manganese from India, chrome from the Philippines, uranium from the Belgian Congo, tin and rubber from Indochina, and columbite and cobalt from Nigeria, "led us into a policy which compels us to underwrite their security and their present political and economic status quo. This situation requires that sea lanes to and from these areas be kept open for our sea transport in time of war." Soviet bombers, he warned, could strike foreign mines and transportation facilities everywhere, except in South Africa, South America, and Australia. A serious danger to American shipping came from the Soviet submarine fleet, already "several times as strong as was Hitler's in 1941." Moreover, he added, "the Communist doctrine has politically neutralized some of these areas so that in war we may be unable to buy strategic materials from them."[18]

What did the Nevada senator suggest? First, close cooperation among nations of the Western Hemisphere, which Malone considered "the only dependable source of the necessary critical materials in time of war. This area can be defended and can be made self-sufficient in the production of such materials." Second, he wanted increased depletion allowances for producers of critical minerals so as to encourage further production. Third, he recommended accelerated stockpiling to assure available supplies in time of war. Fourth, the government should undertake efforts to improve self-sufficiency through more extensive research in beneficiating low-quality ores and developing substitutes. Research would encourage new uses of coal and the development of oil-shale deposits. Also, Malone wanted increased production of titanium, "a new wonder metal," because this metal was heat resistant, noncorrosive, nonmagnetic, and had a high strength-to-weight ratio.[19]

Although an individual enterprise somewhat embarassing to his own party's leadership, Malone's report presented, intellectually, a fundamental challenge to the premises underlying post–World War II minerals policy. In once again asking whether self-sufficiency was possible, Senator Malone touched a position, which an earlier generation of leaders defended vigorously before Pearl Harbor. Former President Herbert Hoover, who once championed hemispheric solidarity himself and who also had credentials as a world renowned mining engineer, wrote Malone: "I believe that with the proper encouragement the Western Hemisphere could be so developed as to produce the following raw materials in sufficient quantities for our defense in a war without our going further overseas." He listed these: coal, iron, manganese, copper, lead, zinc, nickel, aluminum, silver, tungsten, uranium, chrome, titanium, vanadium, antimony, molybdenum, quartz crystals, and mica. "We could develop more tin in Latin America, and no doubt in war could use many substitutes," concluded the former president. For Hoover the Nevada senator's inquiry seemed relevant, because with additional stockpiling the U.S. could both stimulate Western Hemisphere production and achieve adequate defense supplies at home.[20]

Other support for Malone's conclusions came from General Albert Wedemeyer, a prominent military strategist, who incidentally favored a fortress-America position before World War II. In a future war, Wedemeyer speculated, the U.S. might lose its bases close to the Soviet heartland and be compelled to conduct offensive operations from Western Hemisphere air bases. Enemy action might deny the U.S. access to supplies outside the Western Hemisphere. "Realism," he indicated, "demands that the United States be prepared at all times for the worst contingency which, of course, would be that the initial operations of the enemy may compel us to operate militarily from the Western Hemisphere and to resort to our own sources of raw materials and industrial facilities." Other military witnesses, including General Bonner Fellers and Major Alexander de Seversky, also agreed that in wartime the U.S. might face what Malone called "the grim possibility that we will not be able to guarantee the safe movement of supply vessels between distant foreign ports and our own."[21]

Did the U.S. and other American nations compose a self-sufficient bloc? In testimony Bureau of Mines experts admitted the hemisphere lacked only seven vital materials—industrial diamonds, chromite, cobalt, columbium-tantalum, tin, tungsten, and asbestos. It was unlikely, said the experts, that these materials would become available in the future from discovery, beneficiation of submarginal resources, or through changed economic conditions. But within a decade developments in technology would suggest a different conclusion, harmonious with Malone's belief. The development of synthetic diamonds, discovery of new Canadian reserves of asbestos, and development of other materials in the Western Hemisphere would erode the established view that a "have-not" hemisphere remained vulnerable and incapable of achieving a level of self-reliance. Now self-sufficiency became technologically attainable, although at a high price.[22]

Privately, some government officials had political and security reservations about relying only on this hemisphere for strategic and critical materials, even if it were possible. One official in the Office of Defense Mobilization noted that adoption of Malone's prescriptions would "seem to reduce the prospects of keeping any allies outside this hemisphere. It might well encourage, therefore, the spread of the Communist orbit to other nations with whom we are currently attempting to develop and maintain joint defense." Also, in writing off non–Western Hemisphere supplies "it would seem that we are encouraging, at least to some degree, the development of those resources by the enemy." In brief, while the U.S. might proceed alone, hemispheric isolation meant this country must forego permanently a collective security policy, essentially writing off the importance of Western European allies and conceding the Soviet bloc control of the economic and political destiny of areas along the Eurasian periphery. This assumption contradicted the tenets of American foreign policy since intervention in World War I.[23]

Whipsawed in two directions—by domestic miners and some isolationists who wanted protection and national self-sufficiency, by conservationists and internationalists who favored implementing the Paley recommendations—President Eisenhower sought a moderate solution, and he established a blue-ribbon panel to review the national minerals position and recommend an administration policy. He announced on October 26, 1953, that Interior Secretary Douglas McKay would chair a Cabinet Committee on Minerals Policy, composed also of Secretary of State John Foster Dulles, Commerce Secretary Sinclair Weeks, and Director of Defense Mobilization Arthur Flemming, who represented the agency recently created to replace the National Security Resources Board and to coordinate stockpile policy. In ordering the review, Eisenhower emphasized that recommendations should take into account that "the prudent use and development of domestic mineral resources, as well as assured access to necessary sources abroad, are indispensable to the operation of an active economy and a sound defense." The president also mentioned the need to consider such recent problems as materials shortages, an uncertain supply situation, and mounting requirements for an expanding home economy, as well as the presently depressed conditions in domestic mining districts resulting from war-produced expansion. The chief executive advised that "every effort should be made to preserve this newly added economic strength through policies that would be consistent with our other national and international policies." In essence, the new president chose not to ignore the Paley recommendations; rather, he urged his own people to "draw on" this work and prepare their own recommendations within six months.[24]

The direction Eisenhower's mineral policies would take became clearer in March 1954, when the Cabinet Committee released its interim report. The most important recommendation involved an intensified stockpile program, a point, incidentally, with certain benefits for the ailing domestic lead and zinc industries. In justifying an expanded program of government minerals purchases, the report noted how the U.S. had gone to war three times in the last forty years. On each occasion the country lacked adequate stockpiles, then accumulated materials frantically during the military emergency, and soon faced the equally serious postwar problem of utilizing surplus productive facilities as peacetime demand subsided from mobilization-period peaks. "Our past mistakes caused us to divert scarce materials, manpower, military forces, as well as money, to produce at the most difficult time what we might have had on hand had we acted in advance." At present, the report noted, the U.S. government had about $4.2 billion in materials on hand, although wartime stockpile objectives were approximately $6.8 billion. This last amount would supplement materials obtained from foreign suppliers during the course of a five-year emergency period. Altogether the stockpile contained fifty-five metals and minerals.[25]

Justification for expanded stockpile purchasing as a mobilization measure rested on a new strategic assessment that the United States could no longer safely rely on foreign imports to provide large quantities of vital materials during a future war. The Cabinet Committee report said the long-term stockpile objectives were designed to "reduce dangerous and costly dependence on sources of materials outside of the United States and accessible areas as defined by the National Security Council, as well as to eliminate in wartime production programs the necessity for conservation measures so stringent as to jeopardize essential war-supporting activities." In particular, the report recommended increased purchasing of large-bulk items, like manganese, chrome, and bauxite. It also suggested that stockpile materials be upgraded to enhance their usability and to conserve electric power, transportation, manpower, facilities, and time—all likely to be scarce in a war emergency.[26]

An explicit objective of the new "safe-level" minerals stockpile program was to alleviate depressed conditions in the domestic minerals industry, which the Office of Defense Mobilization considered an important component of America's military mobilization base. The report directed that in stockpile purchasing "preference should be given to newly mined metals and minerals of domestic origin." But the government might continue to obtain strategic and critical metals in exchange for surplus agricultural commodities; and it might also continue transferring materials to the strategic stockpile obtained under provisions of other legislation, such as the Defense Production Act and the Surplus Property Act, among others. In essence, this set of recommendations, approved at the cabinet level, set out to strengthen a temporarily-depressed domestic mining industry because an operational domestic mining base could prove an integral part of a future war mobilization effort. This conclusion, that the government should stockpile domestic materials, involved a controversial line of analysis, one hardly compatible with the Paley Commission's recommendation that the U.S. procure materials according to "least-cost" considerations.[27]

While stockpile changes touched the heart of the administration's minerals program, the report also offered other initiatives designed to strengthen the domestic minerals base. These included efforts to modify the existing tax structure so as to stimulate discovery and production of minerals, and efforts to strengthen and expand financial assistance to private industry for exploration. Other proposals involved accelerating the Geological Survey's programs of topographic and geologic mapping, and intensifying the Bureau of Mines' program of mineral and metal research aimed "at the development of latent resources, new mineral raw materials, and improved utilization of existing raw materials."[28]

President Eisenhower approved the cabinet report and proceeded swiftly to implement the "safe-level" stockpile recommendations. In an April 14, 1954 letter to Arthur Flemming, who supervised the stockpile program, the president stipulated that in preparing wartime materials assessments, American planners should hereafter assume "no wartime reliance on sources of minerals located outside of the United States, Canada, Mexico, and comparably accessible nearby areas, as defined by the National Security Council." This executive decision reversed the premises of Truman-era planning, for previously the U.S. assumed limited supplies would arrive from nonhemispheric sources throughout an emergency. Later that year, in December, the National Security Council extended the definition of "comparably accessible areas" to embrace Central America, islands of the West Indies, and those South American countries bordering on the Caribbean. Nonetheless, the 1954 changes in materials assumptions were of major consequence. In stipulating that all nonhemispheric supplies, as well as material from portions of South America, could not be counted on as a source of supply in a future war, the new administration effectively raised the ceiling for stockpile purchases. This provided domestic lead and zinc miners, and others, a vast new market for their surplus production.[29]

Ironically, domestic mining interests protested the "safe-level" stockpiling policy because it seemed inadequate. Senator Eugene Millikin, the powerful and cerebral Colorado Republican leader, told Eisenhower the new program "wouldn't do a bit of good for domestic mines, that it would lose every mining state for the Republicans, that it didn't help in the problem of repeated opening and closing of mines, that there was not a word of hope in it anywhere." He also protested the program "would be a death blow to the mines, and that he would be run out of Colorado if he tried to take this back as the best the Administration could do!" The president listened patiently, and then offered to present the plan in the most favorable light. But he indicated the "Administration couldn't do everything wanted by every miner in Leadville."[30]

What domestic lead and zinc producers preferred was tariff protection against imports from Canada, Australia, and South America, and, incidentally, this option appealed both to Assistant Secretary of the Interior Felix Wormser and the U.S. Tariff Commission, who investigated the import situation and recommended protection to the White House. During the spring of 1954 President Eisenhower evaluated his options. An increase in lead and zinc tariffs would please domestic miners and powerful Republican supporters in the minerals industry, but at the same time it would contradict his own commitment to a liberal trading policy, such as the Randall Commission urged. Moreover, the State Department opposed lead and zinc duties, because higher import barriers would adversely affect allies like Canada, Mexico, Peru, Bolivia, and Australia. "The two countries most seriously affected are Canada and Mexico, with which we have long boundaries which expose us to many dangers unless we have the good will of our neighbors," John Foster Dulles warned. The Secretary of State offered a solution, one likely to satisfy domestic miners and also avoid antagonizing neighboring nations. It involved accelerated stockpiling of domestic lead and zinc and voluntary restrictions by countries that normally export these items to the U.S. market. "The State Department is prepared to urge foreign governments to assume a responsibility for creating healthy conditions in the lead and zinc industry." And, in August 1954, the President approved the State Department approach, announced a program to increase stockpile purchases and promote voluntary restrictions on lead and zinc imports, and assured legislators from mining states that stockpile purchases would be confined to newly mined domestic metal. Eisenhower, always moderate in his judgments and sensitive to foreign and domestic political interests, had finessed another explosive situation.[31]

Masterful as the lead and zinc program was in accommodating

divergent political interests, it was hardly justifiable in terms of economic efficiency or national security. During the course of the purchase program, which lasted from 1954 to 1958, the federal government bought 293,665 tons of lead and 457,718 tons of zinc—all from domestic sources which cost the government $204,040,395. Heavy purchases for government stockpiles provided a large market for American mines; in the last seven months of 1954, for example, the government bought 42 percent of all domestically-mined lead and 45 percent of all zinc. And, as these purchases buoyed prices, foreign imports of the same metals began to flood the huge American market, creating a new threat to the health of domestic lead and zinc mining. To benefit foreign subsidiaries of American producers and support world lead and zinc prices, Washington also resorted to bartering surplus agricultural commodities for the two metals. This program cost $147,122,449 in farm products and gained 221,245 short tons of lead and 323,168 tons of zinc. Together the domestic purchase and foreign barter programs inflated stockpile accumulations beyond all defensible limits. The military realized that no realistic assessment of direct military interests justified the subsidy program for lead and zinc. After all, in time of military emergency the U.S. could easily obtain all needed supplies of these two metals from neighboring Mexico and Canada.[32]

Not only did Eisenhower and his advisers purchase materials for the security stockpile to shore up sagging prices for materials in excess supply, but also they diverted minerals bound for the stockpile in order to depress prices and meet shortages. For instance, in 1955 the flood-ravaged Naugatuck Valley of Connecticut could not obtain quantities of copper to employ highly skilled workers in copper-finishing plants, and the administration worked closely with Republican Congressman James Patterson to see that deliveries of copper bound for the stockpile and Defense Production Act inventory were diverted to industrial consumers. "This is being done," the White House indicated, "even though the copper stockpile objective has not been reached." Altogether the administration diverted nearly 42,000 tons of copper from government inventories at a time when stockpile objectives for copper were only half complete.[33]

Similar problems emerged with nickel and aluminum where demand also outpaced supply. Despite a 13 percent increase in world nickel production, supply failed to satisfy civilian and stockpile needs in 1955, so the government diverted 24 million pounds to industry from scheduled shipments to the national stockpile. Some of the metal diverted to private consumers, incidentally, came from the U.S. government's nickel plant at Nicaro, Cuba, operated under a management contract with the General Services Administration. Eager to develop new sources of supply, and achieve greater independence from the International Nickel Company, a Canadian company dominating the world market, the United States government fostered the development of standby supplies in Cuba. In 1955 and 1956 the government also deferred more than 450,000 tons of aluminum scheduled for stockpile deliveries in order to satisfy heavy consumer demand, and this amount increased the supply of aluminum available for private users about 20 percent. In effect, the Eisenhower administration employed stockpile purchases to shore up depressed minerals prices, and it deferred acquisitions to hold down prices for items in short supply. Use of official raw-materials inventories for political and economic purposes had begun.[34]

Throughout the mid-1950s the Eisenhower administration pursued a systematic policy of building up materials stockpiles, and the explanation for this vigorous policy rests with Eisenhower himself. The old general believed raw materials were better than gold; "the materials in our stock piles represent insurance against disaster," he told friends at a White House stag dinner. In 1956, when other members of the National Security Council suggested the government economize and cut back on its mobilization stockpile, because raw-materials reserves caused uncertainty in the commodity markets and because these inventories seemed anachronistic in an age of atomic war, Eisenhower stood firm. He declined to cut back the program for two principal reasons. First, "the theory of the thirty to sixty day war has nothing whatsoever to back it up." While the Soviet Union and the U.S. might accomplish "mutual destruction of terrifying proportions, yet this would not in itself necessarily end the war," the president concluded. "Wars are conducted by the will of a population and that will can be at times a most stubborn and practically unconquerable element." The retired general, his perceptions locked to a future war of attrition, cited the siege of Carthage, the bombing of Britain in 1940, and the Allied offensive against Germany in 1943–1945 as evidence a population might still need reserve supplies despite nuclear warfare. Second, Eisenhower saw stockpiles as a cushion against depletion and shortages. "The material resources of the world are constantly being depleted, and at an accelerated pace. The time is bound to come when some of these items will begin to mount sharply in price. Some may even become almost completely exhausted," he anticipated. In these circumstances, "the nation that has supplies of presently used scarce materials will obviously have more time to work out this problem than will others." In short, reserve supplies involved short-term budgetary costs but they did not "constitute a drain upon the long term resources of the nation," Eisenhower thought.[35]

In February 1957, the cabinet debated whether to hold or dispose of excess inventories of twenty-three materials. While proponents of disposal argued this option would reduce "the Government's costs of investment, interest, storage, and, for some materials, such as rubber, rotation to prevent deterioration," opponents, including the president, argued that sale of these materials would represent government interference with commodities markets and that government needs occasionally change, so that it might become necessary in the future to reenter the market as a purchaser. The president approved a recommendation that, since stockpile materials were a long-term reserve, the government should announce its determination to retain all strategic and critical materials acquired. Despite this top-echelon decision, staff continued to lobby for disposal of excess inventories. The Bureau of the Budget, in particular, eager to cut federal spending and boost receipts, viewed minerals accumulations as potential federal revenues. At the staff level they argued vigorously that Eisenhower's general minerals program tended "toward a price support program. The National Stockpile and the Defense Production Act have both been used to justify purchases not considered essential to defense needs," said one official. Eisenhower himself remained firm in his conviction that the government should continue to acquire nonperishable resources. The chief executive told congressional leaders how he shocked Treasury Secretary George Humphrey with the comment that he preferred accumulating manganese, not gold, in Fort Knox, "on the basis that you can't make bullets out of gold."[36]

Lower-echelon defense planners considered Eisenhower's stockpile mentality recidivistic in an era of thermonuclear warfare. At the time the administration decided for political reasons to expand its material inventories in 1954 to relieve Western mining interests, these defense planners already had begun to question the propriety of a five-year mobilization program, on which the long-range stockpile objectives rested. No consensus emerged, however, for the three principal military services disagreed about defense ends. Air force planning, for instance, rested on the belief a future conflict would involve strategic nuclear weapons and terminate in thirty to sixty days. But the army and navy adjusted more slowly to the notion of a short atomic war spasm; they preferred to plan for another war of attrition, and in these circumstances a ready stockpile had critical value.[37]

What temporarily resolved this debate and precipitated major changes in stockpile objectives and disposal policies was the Soviet Union's dramatic space shot in October 1957, lifting a tiny Sputnik into earth orbit. Now the Kremlin's arsenal included not only hydrogen weapons but also a demonstrated capability to develop intercontinental ballistic missiles. In the post-Sputnik reassessment it was evident the Eisenhower administration must realign budgetary priorities, placing more dollars on education and technology and less on such marginal items as a materials stockpile. The Sputnik episode also strengthened the school of strategic thought that believed a future Soviet-American conflict would involve nuclear weapons and would not be an extended war of attrition. In a nuclear war raw materials would have little military value, either for prosecuting the conflict or for rehabilitating a war-stricken nation's economy. According to planners, the U.S. might better stockpile consumer goods and other machinery needed to recuperate an industrial nation after atomic war.[38]

These interrelated considerations prompted Gordon Gray, head of the Office of Defense Mobilization, to commission an outside Special Stockpile Advisory Committee, headed by Holmon D. Pettibone, a Chicago financier, to review current stockpiling policies and programs. In January 1958 the panel, which included Dean Earl Butz of Purdue University as well as Admiral Arthur Radford and General Walter Bedell Smith, proposed a series of major revisions. It suggested reducing the emergency procurement period from five to three years, a step likely to reduce stockpile requirements. It also urged giving the Director of Defense Mobilization more flexible authority to dispose of surplus materials, although all commercially usable metals and minerals should be retained. Also, the committee recommended that "in stockpiling, emphasis be shifted from raw materials to finished items and vital supplies for survival." This change in emphasis from accumulating raw materials to acquiring goods necessary for relief and rehabilitation "should be of great value" in the aftermath of a nuclear war because the U.S. would have stockpiled "power, man-hours, transportation and facilities."[39]

Faced with these sweeping revisions, President Eisenhower and the cabinet formally approved a reduction in stockpile assumptions in April 1958. Hereafter strategic planning assumed a three-year war, not a five-year conflict of attrition, and this compromise contained its own perils. It authorized inventories greater than necessary to cope with a nuclear conflict but inadequate to counteract a protracted war of attrition in which hostile submarines might isolate the United States from foreign supplies. More importantly, this adjustment made large quantities of government inventories surplus. At the 1961 market value, Washington now had nearly $350 million in surplus aluminum, $442 million in tin, $220 million in metallurgical chromite, and $214 million in rubber. Of seventy-five items held in strategic and critical stockpiles, fifty-seven exceeded long-term or maximum stockpile objectives for a three-year war. Several years later a Senate investigating committee estimated, using 1961 market values, that total inventories amounted to $7,397,541,600, and this shift in strategic values left a surplus inventory of $3,390,866,000—meaning, in essence, that nearly half the total government stockpiles were excess.[40]

The cabinet review also incorporated several other recommendations. It agreed to retain surplus strategic materials, so that disposals would not "cause serious economic disruption or adversely affect the international interests of the United States." It decided against seeking more flexible authority at the present time to dispose of excesses. It stressed "rapid mobilization in the event of an emergency," but not the upgrading of materials to a degree that would "impair flexibility of use."[41]

The Pettibone reforms, in effect, produced less than either the blue-ribbon panel of outsiders or some administration defense planners wanted. It is true that the administration for the first time agreed to cut back the stockpile—but the three-year period represented little more than a political compromise between air force types who anticipated a quick nuclear war and army planners who thought in terms of a conventional, protracted general war. Some of the new language drew attention to a need for preparing emergency materials for post-nuclear war relief and rehabilitation, but in fact another four years would pass before stockpile planners made any serious and systematic examination of this contingency.[42]

During this period the government maintained not one but three major stockpiles. First, pursuant to legislation approved in 1939 and 1946, the government had a national stockpile which at the close of 1961 had cost $6.4 billion. A second government inventory contained materials generated under provisions of the Defense Production Act, and at the close of 1961 it had involved total acquisitions of $3.6 billion. Conceived as part of a general mobilization plan this stockpile was designed "to raise our mobilization base by the rapid expansion of domestic production through the use of price incentives." In effect, the General Services Administration simply announced it stood ready to purchase quantities of asbestos, beryl, chromite, columbium-tantalum, acid grade fluorspar, manganese, mercury, mica, and tungsten.[43]

As it turned out, this approach had serious flaws. Not only did the purchase program prove unduly costly but also the government accumulated substantial inventories of substandard materials and failed to improve the mobilization base. In 1962 the Senate Armed Services Committee examined these shortcomings. According to its report, prepared under the direction of Senator Stuart Symington (D.-Missouri), federal officials bought manganese, a highly important strategic alloy, at a cost of $34.5 million for material with a December 1962 market value of only $4,730,000. Similarly, the government purchased mica at $14.97 a pound (this was four to five times the prevailing world price)—and 40 percent of the mica bought failed to meet stockpile specifications. In December 1962 the mica had a market value of $2.25 a pound, which the Senate committee considered a $29.8 million loss for the government. Also, the federal purchasing agents acquired both tungsten and chromite at prices double or treble the world price as part of their effort to stimulate domestic mining and establish a viable domestic production base. Unfortunately, despite sizable price incentives for such materials as manganese, tungsten, and chromite, the government buying failed to create a self-sustaining domestic industry, and when government purchasing ceased, production in these mines declined sharply. For instance, while at the height of government buying 715 mines operated in the U.S., only 3 remained at the time of tungsten hearings in 1962 after termination of the purchase program. Reported the Symington committee, "Enormous sums of money were spent by the Government in these domestic purchase programs to purchase material at several times the market price. But they all failed to establish a mobilization base." [44]

A third independent inventory of raw materials emerged under Agriculture Department jurisdiction. Eager to reduce accumulations of farm surpluses held under authority of the Commodity Credit Corporation, Congress passed the Agricultural Trade Development and Assistance Act of 1954. It authorized the government to barter surplus foodstuffs for strategic materials of which the U.S. was a net importer, where the cost of storage was less than the cost of holding the farm products bartered. Secretary of Agriculture Ezra Taft Benson, a booster of the program, saw this opportunity to reduce his storage costs and cut the politically-sensitive farm surpluses in exchange for needed materials. President Eisenhower also liked the idea, and he said the U.S. should "miss no opportunity to replace perishables with non-perishable resources which might some day be exhausted." And the domestic mining industry liked the idea, for it offered a convenient device to purchase and remove from the private market commodities in surplus supply which tended to depress world prices. In practice, however, a study for Clarence Randall's Council on Foreign Economic Policy showed that "rarely does the farm produce go to the same country the mineral comes from." Ordinarily private traders first obtained a cash order for grain and then sought a cash selling order in minerals from another country before approaching the federal government to approve this "barter" deal. Nonetheless the arrangement flourished, helping to slice Secretary Benson's discomforting farm surpluses. From the beginning of the program, the government had bartered goods valued at $1,151 million, and acquired materials valued at $947 million—including industrial diamonds ($174 million), ferrochrome ($179 million), ferromanganese ($123 million), lead ($66 million), and zinc ($86 million). [45]

During the 1950s these programs swelled in size so that by December 1961, total materials acquired had cost the government $8,910 million, while custodial and administrative expenses consumed another $361 million. At current rates of interest, calculated a critical Senate investigating committee, the programs cost the government

$293 million annually to retain only the present inventory of strategic and critical materials.[46]

But Eisenhower himself never wavered in the conviction that these stockpiles represented a good investment economically and militarily for the American people. He reminded Senator Clifford Case, a Republican member of the Senate committee, that in both the Second World War and the Korean conflict the United States lacked adequate materiel at the beginning, necessitating costly and disruptive materials expansion programs. "When I became President I was determined that we benefit from these mistakes of prior years," he said. "As a result today of this entire enterprise we have, for the first time in our history, stockpiles of strategic and critical materials." He defended the "Nation's investment in these stockpiles," as "comparable to the investment made in any insurance policy. If an emergency does not arise, there are always those who can consider the investment a waste," said the retired president. "If, however, the investment had not been made and the emergency did arise, these same persons would bemoan, and properly so, the lack of foresight on the part of those charged with the security of the United States." Contrasting his own approach to these matters, Eisenhower pointed out: "I firmly rejected the policy of too-little, too-late stockpiling. As a result when my administration left office in 1961, the Nation was strongly situated in this regard to deal with the forces of international communism." In looking forward, Eisenhower approved reviewing these programs periodically to keep them adjusted to changing conditions, but he expressed hope that members of Congress "will not permit anyone to dispose of any quantities of any of them until they have assured themselves, after listening to competent testimony that this disposal can proceed without injury to the national security." He concluded with the trenchant observation that "while in such matters hindsight is often desirable and even enjoyable, foresight is always a necessity." Clearly, maintaining adequate supplies of strategic and critical materials was an issue close to Eisenhower's heart, and in this area of public policy the retired general left an important legacy. His views represented the interplay of personal experiences as an army general and his own perceptions of how previous administrations seriously neglected materials preparations. It was a mistake Eisenhower determined not to repeat.[47]

While the changing technology of warfare and the Soviet Union's emergence as a nuclear power capable of delivering atomic warheads on American targets dictated a reassessment of U.S. materials programs, Eisenhower faced one more crisis in lead and zinc, one that defied easy resolution. Initially, the Republicans had sought to cushion adjustments from overexpansion during the Korean War with a minerals purchase program and with diplomatic initiatives to promote voluntary foreign curbs on lead and zinc exports to the United States. This program, which the administration launched in 1954, quickly boosted minerals prices, expanded the national stockpile, and, ironically enough, proved self-defeating. With higher prices for lead and zinc in the United States more, not less, of these metals arrived from abroad.[48]

In essence, the State Department's move to secure voluntary cutbacks achieved only limited success, despite vigorous steps to win cooperation from other governments. Certainly the president of Peru did urge mining companies not to increase exports above normal levels, and the Canadian government advised domestic producers that the "increased stockpiling program was for the benefit of United States producers." Also, Australia promised it would "cooperate in any feasible and equitable manner found necessary." But Washington had difficulties with some other producing countries. For instance, the State Department did not make representations to Bolivia, a small producer, for political reasons. "Its economic position is so critical that any reduction in exports would increase its need for grant aid." Washington also pursued a softer approach to the Mexican government, partly because two large mining companies with interests there, American Smelting and Refining Company and the American Metal Company, feared that "a strong approach would adversely affect their position through possible encroachment by the Mexican Government on their mining activities." Both mining companies, however, volunteered to participate in lead and zinc limitations, and the American Smelting and Refining Company told its shareholders how, in 1954, the proportion of Mexican lead "shipped to consumers in the United States was the smallest in any year since before entry of the United States into World War II."[49]

Lead and zinc entered a second trough in 1957 after the American economy began to slow from the 1955 and 1956 recovery. As a result, prices of lead and zinc sank to near 1954 levels. In addition, overexpansion abroad and the suspension of U.S. agricultural barter deals helped depress prices and increased import competition. The British government exacerbated the situation when it agreed to sell 20,000 tons of lead. And now the Western mining industry, employing about 15,000 miners, began to lobby for protection.[50]

Once again Eisenhower heard a chorus of distressed voices call for import restrictions. While domestic interests organized an intensive lobbying effort, Eisenhower also learned from the State Department how unilateral action could damage political relations. Domestic and foreign policy interests conflicted, and Eisenhower recognized this dilemma. He told assistant Sherman Adams that "there are no completely satisfactory answers to such problems as these." According to the president, "Any policy of ours that would completely divorce some of the mineral producing countries from the society of friendly nations we are trying so hard to build up could have eventual consequences of the gravest nature."[51]

Eager to mollify critics at home and abroad, as well as to alleviate distress, the administration first half-heartedly pushed a tariff proposal in 1957, and then a plan for subsidies to domestic lead and zinc miners in 1958. The latter recommendation, although its details evolved, involved a sliding scale of payments to minerals producers, and over a five-year period the program was expected to cost taxpayers $30 million annually for each mineral, or a total of $300 million.[52]

The subsidy idea encountered sharp opposition—even within Eisenhower's own cabinet. Secretary of Agriculture Ezra Taft Benson angered the president when he characterized the minerals plan as another "Brannan Plan," a reference to President Truman's Secretary of Agriculture who recommended a system of payments to farm producers to discourage chronic overproduction. The president responded that other solutions—tariffs or quotas—seemed likely to elicit bitter reactions from South American producers reliant on the large American market for their mineral exports. Public opposition came from the *Wall Street Journal*, concerned as usual that federal handouts would interfere with automatic supply and demand adjustments in the free market. And the domestic mining industry objected, too. Subsidies seemed certain to open the door to political interference while they provided only temporary relief. What the domestic lead and zinc industry wanted were import quotas, for these would restrict the inflow of cheap foreign production, while preserving the Western mining industry. Incidentally, the giant American Smelting and Refining Company, which imported the two metals, vigorously opposed quotas. "If protection for domestic producers is necessary," it said in 1959, "a modest increase in tariffs would be a more appropriate and less discriminatory method." [53]

Meanwhile, as Congress discussed a subsidy (and eventually opted not to underwrite it), the Tariff Commission reported to President Eisenhower that "domestic producers of lead and zinc were experiencing serious injury." Eisenhower had encouraged domestic producers to seek a determination from this bipartisan commission, in part to gain time for the administration and also to gather support for any executive action disrupting international trade. The Tariff Commission had authority to determine whether imports were excessive and to recommend appropriate relief, but only the president could act. This time, however, the Tariff Commission reached a divided judgment. Three Republican members urged both tariffs and quotas, while the three Democrats favored only a return to 1930 tariff levels on lead and zinc. [54]

Eager to avoid prolonged debate, especially in an election year when divisions could hamper Republican chances, the president announced on September 22 that he would limit imports, using quotas, to 80 percent of the average annual commercial imports during a five-year period extending from 1953 to 1957. Blaming Congress for its own inaction on the subsidy alternative, Eisenhower said: "There is no doubt that the domestic producers are in genuine distress. They have substantially curtailed their production, and large commercial stocks have accumulated within this country." The resort to quotas represented "an equitable approach to a difficult problem affecting many sources of supply." In fact the administration opted for quotas, not tariffs, not only because the quantitative restrictions would preserve a portion of the American market for all foreign producers, even high-cost Peru, but also because the State Department believed "a tariff increase would tend to be more permanent than the proposed quota." [55]

Nonetheless, the unilateral move ignited a wave of protests in producing nations. In Lima, Peru, *El Comercio* complained: "Quotas on lead and zinc constitute economic aggression on our country." Peru seemed likely to lose $20 million annually. The *Melbourne Herald* commented that Australia's "dollar-earning capacity faces a serious setback at a time when we need overseas funds to pay for capital goods and so maintain a high rate of national development." Both the *London Times* and *American Metal Market*, the newspaper of the United States metals industries, agreed that quotas offered only a temporary solution to America's domestic mining troubles. At least the quotas "may be made to serve as a breathing spell to enable us to formulate a more realistic policy than we have pursued in the past," the metals newspaper suggested.[56]

While taking unilateral action to benefit domestic miners, Eisenhower's aides proposed international discussions to consider more permanent solutions, and U.S. diplomatic representatives sat down with other delegates in Geneva late in 1958 to examine these options. U.S. delegates proposed that lead and zinc exporting nations agree to limit their sales on world markets, although Canada, a large and efficient exporter of these commodities, opposed a marketing agreement. The United States also voted in favor of establishing a United Nations study group to consider long-term solutions. In the short run, however, the Eisenhower administration had no intention of either increasing its imports of lead and zinc, a move benefiting the exporting nations, or joining a buffer stock arrangement, which might attempt to smooth out supply and demand for the two materials.[57]

Opposition to international control schemes for lead and zinc, incidentally, characterized the Eisenhower administration's approach to minerals, which was a significant modification of policy pursued in the Truman era. Shortly after World War II the United States helped draft the Havana Charter for an International Trade Organization, an accord accepting commodity controls as a necessary evil to protect small producers and wage-earners from disruptive price fluctuations. These principles, embodied in the General Agreement on Tariffs and Trade, established the foundation for negotiations in wheat, sugar, tin, and coffee. Tin negotiations began pursuant to the internationally agreed procedure in 1947, and the need for an agreement gained support as production surpassed consumption, a trend, however, that the Korean War reversed with spiraling tin prices. As prices for tin collapsed later in 1953 when the war ended, the U.S. concluded stockpile purchases, and the advance of technology halved the amount of tin required in making tinplate, producing nations feared the perils of overproduction and underconsumption. Major consuming nations, especially the U.S., worried that economic distress in Bolivia, Indonesia, and Malaya, the principal tin exporters, would lead to chaos and even Communist-style takeovers. General Thomas Wilson, chairman of a tin mission to Malaya, reported in November, 1951 that success by Communist-directed elements in that country could easily encompass "tin producing neighbors with the result that well over one-half of the world's production might, in a surprisingly short time, become unavailable, except on Communist terms."[58]

Faced with this dangerous international situation in Southeast Asia, as well as potential turbulence in Bolivia, Eisenhower's aides evaluated whether or not to back some type of buffer stock accord for tin. On these issues the Interior and State Departments locked in battle. Felix Wormser, the onetime lead industry executive now serving as the administration's top minerals policy specialist in the Interior Department, vigorously opposed further U.S. participation in the tin negotiations. The dispute was part of the continuing bureaucratic tug-of-war between different cabinet agencies as well as a clash of personalities. Presidential assistant Sherman Adams learned that "there is bad blood between State and Interior. Apparently Wormser feels State is trying to set minerals policy." But also there was a fundamental clash of economic philosophy and political interests. On the one hand, the State Department, mirroring interests of small producing nations as well as the export advantages of American agriculture, tended to support the principle of commodity agreements for wheat, sugar, and tin, a principle, incidentally, emerging unmistakably in the Paley Commission's report. United States political interests required some tolerance for internationally sanctioned price-fixing agreements, the foreign policy experts argued. "We cannot overlook the fact that among the countries which may have the most pressing need for some sort of price stabilization in tin are Malaya and Indonesia, and that these countries occupy highly strategic positions in the struggle against communism in Asia." Bolivia and the Belgian Congo also stood to benefit economically and politically from an agreement. Wormser, on the other hand, expressed a hard-line free-enterprise approach. "Commodity agreements involve an economic philosophy which I think is contrary to the open competitive market doctrine . . . under which our Nation has grown great. Am I to conclude that competition *must* be enforced domestically but not internationally?" If the Eisenhower administration agreed to support the international commodity agreement approach, Wormser told another minerals expert, Secretary of the Treasury George Humphrey, then "I ought to begin at once to make certain that the commodities under the wing of the Interior Department receive equal consideration with tin." Ultimately opposition from Wormser, as well as from domestic opponents of commodity agreements, prompted the executive branch to abstain from seeking U.S. participation in the international tin agreement, although Washington informally encouraged other nations to proceed with implementing the agreement. Instead of encouraging a variety of commodity agreements to benefit hard-pressed small countries suffering from fluctuating world commodity prices and market instability, the U.S. turned to other forms of direct assistance, including foreign aid. Late in the 1950s, for instance, Washington began to underwrite Bolivian budget deficits in order to promote political stability and economic development in that resource-rich Andean country. Out of this experience with tin discussions emerged an official policy cool to commodity pacts. "There are few situations where international commodity agreements may be appropriate or desirable and the United States would be prepared to participate in a particular commodity agreement only when such participation can be demonstrated to be clearly in the national interest," decided the Council on Foreign Economic Policy in October 1955. As a consequence, when the lead and zinc issue boiled over in June 1958, the National Security Council determined to uphold established policy, although the U.S. would encourage discussion and exploration of "possible approaches" with other concerned governments.[59]

Import quotas and voluntary agreements to cut back lead and zinc exports to the United States helped check a deteriorating situation for domestic miners. But the lagging market for these materials obliged small American producers to mount an active public relations campaign designed to obtain assistance for producers of several materials, including copper, iron ore, aluminum, lead, zinc, fluorspar, and petroleum. The political success of this lobbying effort became clear to the administration when Congress passed House Concurrent Resolution 177 in 1959, declaring it the sense of Congress that a sound and stable domestic mining industry is in the national interest; that further mineral reserves should be discovered at home and developed; and that greater research should be directed to promoting the use of domestic minerals and metals. The resolution also declared that a sound and stable industry cannot be achieved if "based upon the importation of foreign materials," and a "critical dependence upon foreign resources should be avoided." [60]

Clearly the legislative branch of government was in a protectionist mood, for one report asserted: "The *principal cause* of the depressed conditions that presently exist stems from excessive imports." This line of analysis ignored the principal reasons for extensive imports, including the availability of high-quality ores at lower cost than the products of American domestic mines. Even the Interior Department, long a sympathetic friend of home mining, recognized the imprudence of a self-sufficiency policy. "The concept of supporting maximum production of all metals and minerals, irrespective of cost, is unrealistic and cannot be reconciled with the free enterprise system." But it was clear that the resolution expressing the intent of Congress posed a serious problem to the Eisenhower administration. If it pursued the recommended course, the White House would undercut established foreign economic policies. If it ignored the resolution, "Members of Congress from mineral areas will utilize the statements . . . to belabor the Administration." [61]

Shrewdly assessing the government's dilemma, lead and zinc miners pressed again in 1960 for subsidies, anticipating that election year politics offered opportunities for gain. In particular, the White House lobbied to block legislation that would increase tariffs on lead and zinc, because the State Department felt this "would gravely impair our relations abroad, particularly in Latin America where our problems presently are critical." Mexico, Peru, Canada, and Australia especially feared Congress would pass tariffs, which posed an even greater threat to their lead and zinc exports than did the quotas of 1958. One of the strongest representations against tariff increases came from Mexican President Lopez Mateos who told Eisenhower that the Mexican public would resent additional protectionism "as an act inconsistent with the solid friendship existing between our two countries." [62]

But Congress passed a subsidy measure, not a bill mandating higher import duties, and Eisenhower faced a delicate political decision two months before the presidential election. On Capitol Hill legislators approved a subsidy scheme calling for federal payments to make up the difference between market prices and a benchmark price of 17 cents per pound for lead and 14½ cents per pound for zinc. Mines producing not more than 2,000 tons of ore annually would receive the federal stipends. After careful analysis Eisenhower opted to veto the proposal, despite its popularity in mining districts, because, he said, it "would negate the progress of recent years, increase the problems of lead-zinc producers, subject the market to instability, and burden our taxpayers with unsound subsidies." [63]

If Eisenhower successfully blunted the protectionist initiative, his successor President Kennedy succumbed, and on September 21, 1961, signed a subsidy program for 273 of the nation's 315 lead and zinc mines. This law, similar in basic outline to the bill Eisenhower vetoed a year earlier, placed a $16.5 million ceiling on payments over the next four years. Interestingly, of the $4.5 million appropriated for the first year, only $654,140 was actually disbursed. Until the Vietnam War, when demand for the two commodities soared again, prompting President Lyndon Johnson to repeal quotas on foreign imports, the domestic lead and zinc industry remained troubled with excess capacity and unemployment.[64]

This episode, involving two important base metals, illustrates well how the interplay of domestic politics and foreign policy shaped national materials policy in the post–World War II era. As a global power with extensive political and economic interests the U.S. could no longer yield easily to domestic political pressures to protect home producers at the expense of other nations. At each stage in the lead and zinc controversy Eisenhower and his aides had to balance foreign and domestic repercussions, for precipitous action threatened cordial and harmonious diplomatic relations with America's immediate neighbors—Canada and Mexico—as well as developing nations in Latin America. This delicate interplay of domestic and foreign policy considerations also shaped stockpiling policy in the 1950s. In 1954, for instance, when imported tungsten from Bolivia failed to meet minimum quality standards for America's strategic stockpile, some wished to cancel the purchase contract, but the State Department insisted it was better to procure inferior metal than to risk political instability high in the Andes. Washington feared cancellation of the contract could bring to power a revolutionary government "less favorably disposed toward the aims and objectives of the United States, and of the western world in general." An economic collapse and political chaos might accompany a change of government. "Such developments in Bolivia would be most undesirable from the standpoint of United States security." Political and security calculations also shaped a tungsten purchase agreement with South Korea, Senator Stuart Symington discovered. To shore up the war-weakened economy of that small Asian land the United States agreed to pay artificially high prices for tungsten in 1952. Similarly, when the Eisenhower administration decided to dispose of surplus stockpile materials so as to benefit the national budget, foreign governments protested that precipitous selling could depress commodity markets and create violence in small countries reliant on earnings from a single export crop or mineral. For instance, in 1959 and 1960 Chile worried that Washington might sell surplus copper, but President Eisenhower assured President Jorge Alessandri that the present administration had no intention of liquidating copper stockpiles, and would never employ these sales to depress world prices.[65]

As the 1950s drew to a close, the minerals picture contained both encouraging signs and portents of future distress. No longer did officials discuss seriously the dangers of resource exhaustion, or worry about the implications of rising materials costs, as they had in the decade immediately after World War II. Instead, partly in response to predictions of shortages and ambitious government-subsidized metals development programs, the world experienced overexpansion and underconsumption. In nickel, aluminum, copper, and iron, as well as lead and zinc, new supplies had outstripped demand. Also the metals industries faced increasing competition from other products such as plastic and fiberglass which cut into aluminum sales, and compelled the latter industry to devote large sums of money to develop new uses for the metal. While aluminum and uranium were the boom minerals of the 1950s, *Engineering and Mining Journal* predicted the momentum of the 1950s would carry over into the 1960s, perhaps with beryllium and tellurium acting as spearheads of a continuing metals boom.[66]

Another source of encouragement came from the international minerals balance. While the United States continued to import large quantities of materials from low-cost, high-grade foreign suppliers, the American trade balance for raw materials remained positive until 1964. Much of the resources imported to service needs of American industry came from the "captive mines" of United States–owned firms abroad. During the 1950s the book value of U.S. direct investments increased from $11.79 billion in 1950 to $31.82 billion in 1960, and of these amounts direct investments in mining jumped from $1.13 billion to $2.95 billion. During the decade American mining investments quadrupled in Canada, so that by the opening of the 1960s the U.S. had a greater stake in the minerals of Canada than in all Latin America. Minerals investments in English-speaking countries would continue in the 1960s with Australia and South Africa emerging as major mining centers. This trend derived from the confidence investors had in English-speaking countries with their distinctive political stability, familiar laws and customs, and favorable business climate. In emerging countries of the Third World hostile ideology often led to nationalization and expropriation without prompt and adequate compensation.[67]

What jeopardized the future in the estimation of Washington policymakers was a new intense round of cold war competition for control of key geopolitical areas. Alarm bells sounded in October 1957, when, according to Kennedy administration aide Theodore Sorensen, the Soviet Union "launched simultaneously the first space capsule to orbit the earth and a new cold war offensive to master the earth—an offensive relying on Western disunity in the face of nuclear blackmail and on anti-Western nationalism in the underdeveloped areas." Not only did Premier Nikita Khrushchev threaten Western Europe with Soviet medium-range missiles and diplomatic threats at Berlin, but increasingly the Russians also competed in underdeveloped countries, supplying economic and military assistance to further national revolutions and weaken the capitalist West. To some extent, the Soviet actions involved competition with Communist China for leadership of the international Communist movement, but to the generation of Americans in positions of leadership the challenge had dire implications. "If it succeeds in extending Communist rule throughout Africa and Asia, the Kremlin will have assured its victory in the battle for the world. . . . The Western World will be forced to surrender without the firing of a shot," said Vice-President Richard Nixon. "We ourselves may be starved for essential raw materials and crushed without a single warlike act." Central Intelligence Agency director Allen Dulles warned that "the fateful battles of the cold war will, in the foreseeable future, be fought in the economic and subversive arenas."[68]

The emergence of a Communist Cuba under Fidel Castro, more than any other single event, brought about a fundamental reconsideration of America's vulnerable economic position. To many

Americans Cuba was only a vacation pleasure land, but to minerals experts Cuba remained a crucial component of American mobilization plans. At other critical periods in the past this "pearl of the Antilles" had supplied the U.S. with vital manganese, nickel, and chromite, and in the future Washington looked to Cuba to supplement domestic resources. The communization of Cuba seemed to William Y. Elliott, the economic warfare expert, part of the Kremlin's "guided revolution" that previously produced the takeover of China and threats to Korea and Southeast Asia, all areas containing important deposits of strategic materials essential to the economic security of the Western-style market economies. In the immediate future, Elliott believed, the U.S. faced more than the continuing threat of nuclear war or a conventional struggle of attrition. There was a real danger that the West would lose mineral-rich territories for indefinite periods of time, as a result of successful Communist political maneuvers, such as in Cuba, or the expropriation of foreign investment and the breakdown of law and order in underdeveloped nations. "We cannot afford Cubas, or the sanctioning of nationalized theft called collectivization. The result is confiscation, not even compensated expropriation," he said. Successful bursts of expropriation would destroy a prosperous, efficient, and increasingly integrated international economy, leaving communism "as the residuary legatee of chaos—in accordance with one design shared by both Moscow and Peiping." To cope with this menace Elliott and others favored continued foreign and military assistance programs. "The price we pay in foreign aid and defense programs," said this veteran of cold war competition, "has had a great deal to do with our not losing" more of the underdeveloped nations. Interestingly, the most valuable single pawn in this Soviet-American struggle, in Elliott's opinion, was South Africa. "If we lost even the gold of South Africa's new production, without any alternative source of supply, the access to Soviet manipulable reserve strength might jeopardize the monetary stability of the whole Free World." [69]

Concern about the fate of the mineral-rich Belgian Congo, a newly independent nation supplying the U.S. with cobalt, industrial diamond bort, columbite, copper, tantalite, tin, tungsten, and zinc, prompted Presidents Eisenhower and John F. Kennedy to support a United Nations presence in order to maintain the union of Leopoldville and the breakaway province of Katanga, which, incidentally, contained the bulk of known mineral riches. Kennedy, according to Sorensen, did not want the Congo "to become another Cuba, providing Communism with a strategically located military base, vast natural resources and a fertile breeding ground of subversives and guerrillas."[70]

While a Kremlin success in this central African nation posed a long-term threat to the stability of white-supremacist regimes in Rhodesia and South Africa (which also had vast reserves of strategic and critical materials), the Congo turbulence did not jeopardize American industry or defenses in 1960. For one thing, of all the materials imported from the Congo, only cobalt and industrial diamonds were purchased primarily from that nation. Without any further supplies from the Congo the U.S. had stockpiles sufficient to meet cobalt needs for five years. Also, government inventories had excess diamond bort, used primarily as an abrasive in grinding, and this quantity would suffice until synthetic bort production could be expanded. More than anything loss of the Congo threatened the stability of Western Europe, for Europe lacked strategic stockpiles, and any cutoff augured acute problems for these users of industrial diamonds and cobalt.[71]

Evaluations of the Soviet politico-economic offensive varied, and the Central Intelligence Agency, for instance, believed Elliott exaggerated reality with his conclusion that all Soviet actions in the Western world were designed primarily to inflict economic damage on the industrial nations, particularly the United States. Nonetheless, this perception of an intensive cold war struggle for control of strategic materials resembled the analysis senior-level American policymakers voiced late in the 1940s when Communist moves threatened the tin, rubber, and tungsten supplies of Asia. Previously policymakers believed stockpiles could cushion supply interruptions until the U.S. developed emergency reserves at home and recaptured control of sea lanes. Now as the Soviet Union developed its own strategic warfare capabilities (which incidentally Premier Khrushchev erroneously claimed were superior to those of the U.S. in the late 1950s and early 1960s), American policymakers wondered *if* the U.S. could recover lost territories before supply interruptions exhausted stockpile inventories. The State Department learned from stockpile sources that where loss of territory to unfriendly hands might involve loss of access to scarce resources for long periods, "even large stockpiles might not be a sufficient answer."[72]

The best way to correct supply deficiencies of indispensable materials, concluded one government expert, was through technology, not a stockpile. Certainly the latter served a useful and necessary purpose, for diversified materials inventories gave the U.S. necessary flexibility in its national posture with which to buy time, provide a rough and ready reserve for hot war, and serve the tactical economic and political needs of the U.S. in a cold war. But technology offered a more extensive and more permanent corrective than did temporary stockpiles. By the early 1960s it was possible to claim that "available or foreseeable technology enables us to supersede most uses of stockpiled materials."[73]

Ironically, advancing technology promised to reduce American reliance on foreign suppliers *and* to increase the economic disruption abroad that produced Communist-style takeovers and nationalization of mineral investments. It seemed by 1962 that the most vulnerable areas to Communist penetration were places where the "United States has withdrawn its economic interest—places whose products are not needed in quantity commensurate with existing production." Thus for instance the development of competitive and acceptable synthetic rubber left unstable economic conditions in Malaya and Borneo, while synthetic cordage fibers posed problems for the Philippines, an important exporter of abaca. Also, development of synthetic diamond bort threatened the diamond industries of the Congo, Brazil, and South Africa; the appearance of mylar film reduced the income of India's mica industry; and synthetic quartz crystals jeopardized Brazil's key export. The relevant policy question, then, appeared to be how to plan the orderly introduction of new materials technology so that economic disruption in less-developed nations was limited.[74]

Meanwhile the Kennedy administration made plans to sell off portions of the stockpile inventory. Political and budgetary considerations, along with the new strategic calculations, prompted this course. The new president had heard reports that his predecessor used the stockpile as "an economic assistance device to specific metals or minerals or industry groups," and the name of former Secretary of the Treasury George Humphrey figured prominently in speculation about wrongdoing. Kennedy undoubtedly found it convenient to investigate Republican policies, a ploy familiar in national and state government to discredit political opponents. But more than this, Kennedy recognized that holding approximately $8 billion in materials inventories represented a wasteful use of taxpayers funds and it served as an impediment to capital expansion in the metals industry.[75]

While administration aides conducted one review, Senator Stuart Symington launched his own investigation, and it soon concluded that materials accumulations exceeded reasonable requirements for a three-year limited war. Consequently, the Senate committee recommended abandoning stockpile purchases to support domestic mining. Interestingly, Kennedy's cabinet-level review recognized "the possibility that in a mobilization situation short of war, sources of raw materials may be denied to us," a statement acknowledging how resource inventories might fulfill an important role as a cushion against dislocations short of actual war. Incidentally, Elliott, the single-minded cold warrior, also believed existing stocks could protect the American economy against disruptions from "guided revolutions" and "blackmail," situations that actually emerged a decade later.[76]

In the Kennedy review, defenders of large stockpiles lost the policy battle. Influential economic advisers, specifically Walter Heller and Kermit Gordon, argued effectively against adoption of this "new stockpiling concept—protection against possible peacetime interruptions of supplies, through Soviet subversion, strikes in foreign mines . . ." Acceptance of this principle, they argued, would bring astronomical costs and invite additional pressures from domestic miners to purchase more strategic materials. Over the next decade three U.S. presidents did sell off large quantities of stockpiled materials, implementing a policy inaugurated by Kennedy's aides. President Johnson, in particular, used stockpile sales of copper and aluminum to quench inflationary pressures during the Vietnam War as well as to generate more revenue for the Treasury, thus reducing public criticism of his costly Great Society programs. For the Treasury these materials sales yielded a tidy profit. During the years of acquisitions the U.S. had spent $6 billion on strategic materials. Disposals over the 1958–1975 period generated $7 billion in revenue. In 1974 alone the sales amounted to $2 billion.[77]

In the 1960s, then, although competition with the Soviet Union remained a crucial strategic reality, officials no longer feared the

Chapter Nine
The Scramble for Resources Renewed

ANOTHER international scramble for minerals took shape in the 1970s—and it promised to redefine the global power struggle of the late twentieth century. For about twenty years after the Korean War broke out, policymakers had little occasion to focus on raw-materials issues. Prices of these industrial commodities remained relatively stable and supplies were adequate to satisfy rising world consumption. Suddenly, in 1973–1974 circumstances changed. Materials prices soared, shortages appeared, and national competition intensified. An Arab-dominated oil cartel successfully quadrupled petroleum prices and embargoed energy shipments temporarily. Other minerals prices climbed precipitously—zinc and tin more than doubled, copper increased 50 percent. In political capitals around the industrial world there was concern other raw-material cartels might imitate the successful oil exporters and use coercion for economic and political advantage.[1]

What were the implications of these events? Some knowledgeable officials offered somber forecasts. For instance, Charles W. Robinson, president of the Marcona Corporation and soon to be a top State Department official responsible for economic diplomacy, told a congressional committee that 1973 was a "chronological watershed—the beginning of a new era in which our concern over access to markets gives way to a new and growing concern over the availability of the resources required to maintain our rising standards of living." He called for adjusting to a new era of resource scarcity and accelerating inflation, a future quite different from the resource abundance and relatively stable prices characterizing the preceding two decades. And, from a different perspective Lester Brown of the Overseas Development Council predicted that many would "remember 1973 more for its energy and food scarcities than for Watergate and the Arab-Israeli War."[2]

A number of key questions emerged—and they resembled issues raised in discussions after both world wars. Did the shortages and price hikes signal resource exhaustion and perhaps a future breakdown of the global economy? Were the problems temporary, or likely to prove enduring? Was it likely other export cartels would emerge, using their dominance of rich mineral deposits to coerce importing nations so as to achieve political objectives or promote a major redistribution of world income? Would these conditions breed intense competition among industrial nations already heavily reliant on foreign sources of supply? How could the U.S., unilaterally or jointly with other nations, protect its economy from future supply dislocations?

In the U.S. these trends were often misunderstood. The public, for instance, generally blamed large oil companies for higher energy prices and overlooked the implications of excessive reliance on Arab oil exporters. Actually, the 1973–1974 dislocations had deepseated origins and represented a culmination of several significant changes in the world economic and political environment. For one thing, soaring demand for raw materials spread from the established industrial nations to developing countries, and simultaneously Western Europe and Japan recuperated rapidly from World War II devastation. From 1950 to 1970 Japanese output climbed better than 9 percent yearly while Western European countries grew about 5 percent annually. By contrast, the U.S. and Great Britain both grew more slowly—3.6 percent and 3 percent respectively—but even this moderate growth multiplied their total consumption of raw materials in only 20 years. By the early 1970s, then, global raw material consumption had reached unprecedented levels, and appeared certain to climb higher. From 1950 to 1970 world consumption of raw steel increased 315 percent, aluminum went up 666 percent, copper climbed 231 percent, and zinc tonnage rose 247 percent. Foreign consumption of these materials increased at an even higher rate than in the U.S. as Europe and Japan revived from World War II.[3]

Danger loomed on the supply side; new capacity expanded more slowly than demand in the late 1960s and early 1970s. From the Korean War until the Vietnam military buildup, commodity prices generally had remained low, reflecting the war-induced overexpansion and subsequent unutilized capacity. With excess capacity, the marketplace discouraged additional expansion. Profits lagged in the metals industry, and this in turn depressed stock prices, handicapping efforts to raise investment capital to expand facilities for future needs. For instance, from 1966 to 1973, while other industries averaged a 3.1 percent annual growth in capital investment, the metals processing industry rose only 2 percent each year.[4]

A combination of other negative economic and political factors impeded new investments in minerals. Higher interest rates to contain inflation and protect a weakened dollar in world currency markets, late in the 1960s, discouraged capital investments, and so did a variety of domestic and foreign political obstacles. In the U.S. federal stockpile sales created uncertainty in commodity markets, while new environmental and occupational safety regulations increased capital costs and extended the lead time required to bring new mines into operation. For copper mines, for instance, there is now a ten- to fifteen-year lead time between discovery and first production.[5]

Abroad a resurgence of nationalism and a hostile climate for minerals operations in underdeveloped countries further retarded expansion on the supply side. Many newly independent and underdeveloped countries adopted a more militant, ideological tone. Convinced that traditional international law, which provided some protection of foreign investors, cloaked imperialism, the dissatisfied governments challenged traditional practice. They disputed the concept of "prompt, adequate and effective compensation" for expropriated property, and proceeded to nationalize foreign investments, especially mining operations. Between January 1961 and January 1975, governments seized 128 investments in petroleum, mining and processing. At the United Nations and in other international meetings the underdeveloped bloc used its numerical advantage to redefine standards governing foreign investments. A 1962 U.N. General Assembly resolution had asserted permanent national sovereignty over natural resources of developing countries. Now in 1974 the U.N. adopted a "Charter of Economic Rights and Duties of States," which spelled out the limited rights of foreign investors and asserted that compensation for expropriation must be determined by the host country's domestic laws. Other governments must refrain from applying economic and political measures limiting the rights of producing states to regulate foreign investments.[6]

This erosion of traditional international law had a demonstrable effect on global investment patterns, as did the mounting intrusion of government in the investment process, with its restrictions on currency, taxes, and other surveillance. In the early 1950s underdeveloped nations received about 60 percent of U.S. direct investments in foreign mining, but by 1976 the figure was only 33 percent. Now U.S. minerals investments concentrated in several stable developed countries—Canada, Australia, and South Africa. This shift undoubtedly affected the growth and flow of world trade in primary products. The importance of less developed nations as suppliers of primary commodities in total world exports dropped from 40.5 percent in 1955 to 34.7 percent in 1973. It seemed that the uncertain investment climate in some militant Third World countries was hampering export expansion—while private mining companies flocked to the more predictable environs of Canada, Australia, and South Africa.[7]

In these circumstances, conditions were ripe for a price explosion. It came in 1973 and 1974. Governments of major industrial countries elected to synchronize their economic growth plans, partly to reduce stress on currencies in the uncertain period after the Bretton Woods international monetary system collapsed in 1971. This economic stimulus strategy quickly ran into trouble, for there was no longer sufficient unutilized capacity to accommodate the surging demand for industrial raw materials—and as a result, prices soared. What exacerbated the situation was a shortage mentality among businessmen. Pessimistic that existing supplies would prove inadequate for their needs, and anticipating even higher prices, purchasing agents decided to boost inventories. This type of panic buying had the inevitable result—it pushed prices even higher.[8]

Not all analysts explained the upward price movements as a cyclical phenomenon resulting from overheated demand and supply bottlenecks. Economic historian Walt W. Rostow interpreted the price surge as indicating the arrival of a fifth Kondratieff long wave in real commodity prices, one that might continue into the 1980s. He observed that previous upswings extended from 1898 through World War I, and then began in the late 1930s, lasting through World War II into the Korean War. While Kondratieff himself never presented a coherent theory of long waves, Rostow suggests a satisfactory explanation must embrace major trend phenomena such as population increase, growth of industrial output, technology, and the rate of family formation. He anticipates that the higher materials prices will continue because the "global pace of population increase and industrialization suggests that the pressure of demand on the supply of foodstuffs and raw materials will not prove to be a short-term phenomenon."[9]

For the U.S. and other market-oriented industrial nations the Organization of Petroleum Exporting Countries (OPEC) petroleum embargo and the subsequent proliferation of cartel arrangements among nations producing bauxite, copper, and other materials had disturbing implications. There was, of course, the possibility, however remote, that these new minerals cartels would emulate OPEC and embargo shipments for political and economic reasons. But other types of supply dislocations seemed even more likely. Producing countries might withhold production so as to preserve natural resources for future use, or they might employ collusive bargaining power in order to boost prices of commodities to uneconomic levels. Or internal turmoil might disrupt shipments, as had occurred to copper from Chile and Zambia as well as cobalt from Zaire.

Any of these moves could disrupt the economic stability of major industrial powers, for they all had become increasingly reliant on foreign supplies. Japan, of course, had always lacked an adequate materials base for industrialization, but now relied even more on imports while building a major export-oriented industrial economy on the rubble of World War II devastation. Western European nations had been more self-sufficient before the world wars, but now they, too, looked outward for high-grade minerals and fuels. Their individual dependence on imports ranged from 70 to 100 percent. But for the U.S. loss of material self-sufficiency was a relatively new phenomenon. In 1900, the U.S. had reveled in the luxury of self-reliance, producing 15 percent more materials (not including food and gold) than it consumed, while exporting substantial quantities of copper, iron, and petroleum. That export surplus gradually disappeared, so that by the early 1950s the U.S. experienced a 9 percent deficit. In the late 1970s the materials deficit approached 25 percent—or, excluding petroleum, about 15 percent.[10]

Early in this century the industrial powers had utilized military force and diplomatic influence to protect vital foreign investments, such as raw materials. For instance, Britain and the U.S. generally sponsored an open international economy in which trade and capital flowed easily among nations, while parent governments stood ready to maintain international order and enforce respect for property rights. When smaller, politically unstable countries defaulted on international obligations, London and Washington acted firmly and effectively. Presidents Theodore Roosevelt, William Howard Taft, and Woodrow Wilson used the marines or navy to protect Caribbean commercial interests, and this type of "gunboat diplomacy" reached its zenith before World War I. But unilateral enforcement fell into disfavor, partly because it contradicted the sovereign rights assured each nation in such international legal instruments as the Charter of the United Nations. For a while the two powerful English-speaking allies would rely on covert forces to achieve stability. One spectacular success for covert action occurred in 1953 when these forces helped overturn a radical Iranian regime that had expropriated foreign oil holdings.[11]

Germany and Japan took a different approach to remedy their resource deficiencies in the interwar period. Each sought to achieve a self-reliant empire—Germany in Eastern Europe and Japan in Southeast Asia. Also the Germans displayed considerable ingenuity and prowess in developing synthetics and utilizing low-grade domestic ores so as to reduce dependence on vulnerable overseas supplies. Japan also relied on bilateral trading agreements to bind supplying nations more closely to Tokyo (as did the Nazi German regime), but Japan's limited scientific base did not permit the extensive development of substitution or alternative technology.[12]

Along with the emerging militance of Third World nations, another political consideration helped shape the industrial countries' approaches to materials issues. It was the continuing competition with the Soviet Union for world influence. This contest cooled temporarily after the October 1962 missile crisis; and with the deployment of intercontinental ballistic missiles carrying nuclear warheads it seemed for a time that raw materials would have only a minor role in any future war between the giant powers. In a nuclear war stockpiles would not be needed to sustain essential defense production—rather they might facilitate reconstruction.

But within a decade stockpiles acquired new relevance to military planners. As the Soviets achieved strategic parity, and continued to build a large warm-water navy, the prospects rose that the Kremlin might successfully employ a less dangerous strategy than nuclear war to achieve world dominance. It might continue to sponsor "wars of national liberation," using proxy forces where appropriate. And it could use superior naval forces to dominate merchant shipping and control geographical choke points. Evidence began accumulating that Soviet backing for revolutionary forces in Africa and the Middle East had such an ulterior purpose—destabilization of the Western world economy and access to Middle East crude oil to satisfy Soviet needs. Events in Angola, Zaire, South Africa, and especially in Africa's Eastern Horn all revived the concern William Y. Elliott and other economic warfare specialists voiced in the 1960s. A consistent Soviet objective, where circumstances permitted, was to gain leverage over vital raw-material deposits, not simply to cannibalize the international economy but also to enhance Kremlin bargaining power and world influence. The threat was credible to import-dependent Western industrial economies: a Soviet-sponsored revolutionary movement might disrupt raw-material shipments at times of its own choosing.[13]

How could the U.S. and other industrial nations respond effectively? Early in the 1970s specialists hastened to reconsider materials policies designed for a less complicated era. Older materials plans had aimed to protect the U.S. from major wartime interruptions in the physical flow of materials, such as occurred when German and Japanese naval forces disrupted overseas supply routes in 1942. Policymakers also had considered the self-sufficiency option, but rejected it, realizing that this country lacked adequate ferroalloy deposits for efficient economic production. Instead, with stockpiles of chromium, tungsten, vanadium, and other such materials, the U.S. hoped to meet defense requirements until sea lanes could be reopened or substitute materials developed with technology. Partly because the domestic mining industry enjoyed disproportionate influence in Congress, federal stockpile policy tended to encourage high-cost domestic production of some materials, like lead and zinc in the 1950s. These preparations seemed best designed for unambiguous national emergencies, such as a global war fought with conventional weapons, not for restraining national cartels or coping with rapid price fluctuations. Nor had industrial countries generally prepared for the contingency when politically-active underdeveloped countries devised common marketing strategies, discouraged private investors from developing new minerals supplies, and zealously promoted a global redistribution of income.[14]

Public sensitivity to environmental deterioration ignited interest in another comprehensive Paley-type study of resource endowments and future needs before the events of 1973–1974 added a tone of urgency. In October 1970 President Richard Nixon signed legislation creating a National Commission on Materials Policy (NCMP). This commission was instructed to report no later than June 1973 with recommendations designed to "utilize present resources and technology more efficiently and to anticipate future materials requirements of the Nation and the world."[15]

To a degree this study did reiterate some of the unimplemented recommendations made in the Paley Report twenty years earlier. It called for better public planning and a reorganization of government agencies so as to integrate materials, energy, and environmental policies. In particular, the sections on international minerals policy merit attention both because they echoed the Paley Commission and anticipated, correctly as it turned out, future supply disruptions. Like Paley, NCMP firmly rejected the isolationist option of national self-sufficiency. It said: "Here the message of the Paley Report rings true: self-sufficiency is either physically impossible or so costly in diverted manpower and capital expenditures in the cost of not pursuing other desirable goals, that it has no reality." Anticipating that petroleum-exporting nations might soon employ a resource embargo for political and financial advantage, as in fact they did four months after the report was released, the report warned that national materials policy should avoid overdependence on a few countries for items lacking in America's domestic resource base. "The interest of national security will be served by maintaining access to a reasonable number of diverse suppliers for as many materials as possible," it reiterated. Where import problems were foreseen, the U.S. should foster the expansion of domestic production, diversify sources of supply, develop special relations with more reliable suppliers, and devise substitutes or synthetics. All these were practical and orthodox remedies for a vulnerable supply situation.[16]

An important and insightful study, the NCMP report and its recommendations were soon sidetracked when events abroad shifted policymaking priorities. The Mideast war and petroleum embargo tended to subordinate environmental considerations to national security concerns. And, despite its many strengths, this updated materials study had not given extensive attention to vital defense implications, nor had it set to rest the alarmist warnings of resource pessimists who forecast materials exhaustion and social breakdown. Now policymakers wanted some direct answers to a different set of questions. Did the traumatic events of 1973 and 1974 signal that the world was actually running short of resources at a dangerous rate? Did the depletion of high-quality and accessible materials warrant urgent measures of conservation and control? Did the bold success of the OPEC cartel encourage other cartels to employ raw-materials embargoes for price-gouging or political concessions?[17]

To evaluate policy options, Congress encouraged several investigations, including research within its Office of Technology Assessment, the General Accounting Office, and in a series of materials conferences held at New England College, Henniker, New Hampshire. The latter were organized in conjunction with the important Federation of Materials Societies, and brought together scientists, federal officials, and representatives of industry, to consider key policy issues. Other relevant research took place in the executive branch, especially in the Interior Department. While each contributed to the evolving discussion of materials issues, the work of another important study commission, the National Commission on Supplies and Shortages (NCSS) sought to synthesize the relevant conclusions for policy.[18]

Importantly, this 1976 study soundly rejected the pessimistic resource-exhaustion thesis, advanced in the controversial Club of Rome study released in 1972. "Resource exhaustion is not a serious possibility within the foreseeable future," the government study asserted. The doomsday argument had underestimated prospects for technological advance promoting a more efficient use of resources and substitution among materials. Over the preceding century, the report noted, mineral resources and agricultural products had exhibited a long-run price stability, partly the result of technological advances which made lower quality resources usable in production processes. The study also discounted concern that America had become overly dependent on foreign suppliers. Actually, in the twenty years following 1950, the "net increase in American dependence on foreign materials sources . . . can reasonably be said to have been quite modest."

Petroleum, however, was the conspicuous exception to this conclusion.[19]

Still the constant danger of sudden and severe supply disruptions, resulting either from concerted political action such as another OPEC embargo, or internal instability, warranted official preparations. The report favored using government materials stockpiles as insurance against these economic dislocations, although not as a device to stabilize commodity prices. With this recommendation the thinking in Washington had completed a circle on the usefulness of stockpiles. In the 1950s these official inventories seemed to offer only short-term insurance against war-produced supply disruptions, and then in the 1960s the view gained support that stockpiles could safely be reduced in size. Renewed interest in government supplies mirrored renewed appreciation that these could cushion the U.S. economy temporarily against pressures from government cartels, much in the way defense stockpiles could cushion the war economy against a disruption of merchant shipping in a conventional war.[20]

Out of these discussions and experiences, U.S. officials began to anticipate three distinctly different types of materials problems in the 1980s. First, there was a continuing danger of materials shortages—the product of rising world consumption and insufficient development of new mines. Second, there was the danger of temporary supply disruptions, stemming from wars, revolutions, or cartel embargoes. And, finally, there was concern about unreasonable price hikes imposed by foreign suppliers.[21]

Whether materials supply satisfied growing demand depended in part on the pace of economic growth. From 1951 to 1975 world gross domestic product had increased 4.7 percent annually, an unusually high rate, and projections made in the early 1970s tended to assume this would continue at about 5 percent or above. This meant world output of major metals would need to triple in thirty years. But new estimates completed in 1977 offered an appreciably lower projection. It was now forecast that world gross domestic product would grow by an average of 3.3 percent to the year 2000. This lower estimate suggests that the output of major metals must only double, not triple, to meet world demand.[22]

The lower projections for economic growth seemed more attainable, but even so the question remained whether the minerals industry would successfully double production, or treble it if the growth

rate accelerated. With depressed prices returning after the 1973–
1974 surge, the international minerals industry faced different conditions—oversupply of copper, zinc, and nickel. In numerous instances new price levels fell below the working costs of producers.
At one time when a few private concerns dominated the minerals
trade, production cutbacks would have restored order to markets.
But, interestingly, some national governments responded differently—for they sought to maximize foreign exchange earnings, not
profits. Chile, for instance, resisted urging from Zambia, Zaire, and
Peru to cut back copper production moderately, because its low production costs enabled Chile to make money even at depressed prices.
However the intense competition forced the closing of copper mines
in the U.S. and Canada. The squeeze on high-cost producers during a
period of overcapacity, plus the uncertainty of investments in underdeveloped nations, threatened to pose severe long-term problems.
According to the International Monetary Fund, the reduced investment in new productive capacity could lead to "serious supply shortages" in the 1980s, "even without abnormal demand growth."[23]

Initial anxiety that a series of Third World producer cartels
might imitate OPEC and use their stranglehold on vital materials to
coerce industrial nations proved a remote possibility rather than an
immediate reality. Most materials producers lacked a common political objective, as the Arab-dominated oil cartel did, and it was unlikely
exporters of nonfuel minerals would resort to a total embargo for
punitive purposes. Even if a common political objective emerged, such
as a concerted southern hemisphere drive to create a new international economic order, the loss of export revenues was unlikely to be
acceptable to all producers. An important reason for doubting Third
World governments would use raw-materials pressure successfully
was that Australia, Canada, and South Africa were major suppliers
of metals which the U.S. lacked (except for bauxite where U.S. imports came predominantly from Caribbean countries). These relatively developed materials-exporting nations had a different set of political interests than did the militant southern hemisphere bloc that
railed against existing world arrangements from the U.N. and its
affiliate agencies.[24]

A more likely cause of import interruptions was civil war resulting either from racial strife in southern Africa or Soviet-backed
subversion. In the southern tier of Africa, a region including the

Union of South Africa and Southern Rhodesia as well as confrontation states like Zaire and Zambia, delicate political and strategic issues intertwined. On the one hand, the U.S. identified with the efforts of Africa's black majority to overthrow the last vestiges of minority white rule in Rhodesia and South Africa. On the other, American policymakers worried that violent change would either produce Marxist regimes hostile to development of minerals reserves for export, or periods of anarchy and civil strife. In Western Europe and North America there was growing concern that Africa had become the West's Achilles heel. From 1973 to 1976 the U.S. was heavily dependent on southern tier sources of supply. Forty-seven percent of America's cobalt came from Zaire, 33 percent of platinum and 56 percent of vanadium from South Africa, and 58 percent of ferrochromium from South Africa and Rhodesia. For the Western industrial world South Africa was a major minerals supplier—providing 88 percent of platinum, 74 percent of mined gold, 58 percent of vanadium, and 47 percent of chrome ore. Also, it supplied 31 percent of the non-Communist countries' antimony, 22 percent of asbestos and 13 percent of uranium.[25]

The spread of Soviet influence in Africa worried Western strategists, for a fundamental shift in the global balance of power was at stake. While a direct assault on Western Europe presented an extremely high danger of a nuclear war, with the destruction of society, the Soviet Union and its Cuban surrogates could expect to achieve their ideological objectives and world dominance through a less risky initiative—one designed to undermine the economic strength of the West in Africa. They could hope to deny it key raw materials or severely interrupt the trade routes around southern Africa. And any general denial of Western access to foreign resources could "suspend economic growth in Western Europe and Japan for many years, pending radical improvements in the technology for exploiting indigenous resources," reported Dr. William Schneider of the Hudson Institute. This type of severe economic setback would likely result in serious socio-political upheavals in the affected countries.[26]

Finally, there was the prospect of future price hikes by other producers' cartels emulating the OPEC success. After the Arab petroleum price boost, there were other similar moves—an effort to control world coffee prices, a tripling of phosphate prices, and concerted actions by bauxite and copper exporters. How this political action would fare later when industrial nations achieved a high level of economic activity was speculative, but a legitimate point of concern. Even without other successful price pushups, the U.S. seemed certain to find growing import dependence a costly burden for the dollar to support. This country's nonenergy minerals gap was expected to rise from $9.5 billion in 1974 to $40 billion by the year 2000. While domestic resources or substitutes might alter the composition of imports, shortfalls of aluminum, iron ore, and copper appeared likely to account for much of this deficit. When taken in conjunction with a $40 billion net energy deficit in 1977, this trend continued to augur trouble for the embattled American dollar unless the U.S. managed to expand substantially its exports of industrial and consumer products as well as foodstuffs.[27]

Among policy-oriented minerals specialists several approaches won favor as ways to reduce U.S. vulnerability to import dislocations and persistent shortages. One underlying assumption remained intact, however: the U.S. could not realistically pursue either a policy of imperial expansion to obtain secure sources of supply, or adopt a program of national self-sufficiency. Public opinion would not back nineteenth-century style territorial expansion. The isolation option was technologically possible with adequate preparation time and expenditures, but it would require unacceptable levels of planning and involve unacceptably high costs in terms of prices passed along to consumers and damage to foreign trade. The goal in each case had to be attainment of a sustainable pattern of consumption, efficiently utilizing all resources, including natural resources, manpower, technology and capital.[28]

Stockpiling attracted new interest, for official inventories offered a critical first line of defense to exogenous interruptions. In theory these stockpiles could be used to smooth out price discontinuities and to discourage suppliers from resorting to embargoes or abrupt price hikes. While stockpiles could buy time for scientists and policymakers to develop other more durable solutions to supply shortages, the chief defect was the high cost of effective stockpiles. It was estimated that to keep the price of nonferrous materials within 15 percent of their 1973–1974 trend lines would require stockpile inventories equal to about 9 percent of total U.S. consumption. To maintain this percentage of copper, tin, and zinc would involve a commitment of an estimated $526 million for inventories. Moreover, if government inventories were employed to stabilize the private market, they could be unavailable to meet emergency requirements stemming from a disruption of supplies during a war or embargo. Industry sources, remembering how government stockpile sales had disrupted orderly commodity markets and discouraged development of new mining capacity, criticized proposals for economic stockpiling.[29]

While the latter approach lacked adequate domestic political backing, the Ford and Carter administrations did move to expand national security stockpiles. In 1973 President Nixon began to reduce official inventories drastically when planners concluded the country could safely stockpile for only a one-year war, but this questionable decision was soon reversed. In 1976, the old three-year contingency plan was restored, and President Gerald Ford asked congressional permission to buy $183 million worth of items as part of a plan to increase stockpile holdings to a value exceeding $10 billion in the 1980s. At that time the stockpile had about $7.4 billion in materials— some 91 different items ranging from feathers to zinc. Soon the Carter administration reviewed these recommendations and reaffirmed the targets. Washington was expected to become a buyer of copper, nickel, zinc, certain kinds of manganese, refractory bauxite, as well as jewel bearings and feathers.[30]

This expansion of defense stocks did not involve creation of an economic stockpile, but the two were interrelated. Often in the past officials used defense inventories for ad hoc economic stabilization, and this backdoor approach seemed likely to continue unless Congress specifically forbade that practice. During the Vietnam War President Lyndon Johnson had sold copper to depress high prices, and both he and President Nixon used sales to make budget deficits look smaller. In 1975 Secretary of State Henry Kissinger reportedly even found a way to use stockpile sales for foreign aid. Israel was allowed to buy industrial diamonds from the government supply on credit and then sell these diamonds in Europe at a profit. The Senate Armed Services Committee later criticized the deal, stating that national security inventories were not "to be manipulated for economic or political reasons."[31]

Stockpiles offered only a short-term cushion. For protection against protracted embargoes and to place a ceiling on the prices paid for commodity imports, Washington and the private sector looked to technology for answers. In this direction the possibilities were "virtually limitless," concluded Franklin P. Huddle, a Library of Congress materials specialist. "Given time, the United States could learn to do without almost any except the very large tonnage materials, and could achieve economies even with these." Research focused on improving discovery and extraction techniques along with the substitution and recycling of materials. According to the U.S. Geological Survey, new techniques of geochemical and geophysical investigation offered considerable promise for discovering blind ore deposits. Until recently major deposits were discovered largely from surface outcroppings, and the new techniques of subsurface prospecting opened a fascinating new dimension to minerals exploration. Also there were still vast areas of the U.S. not adequately explored with existing tools and techniques—and these included most of Alaska as well as the continental shelves and some government lands in the western U.S.[32]

In materials substitution scientists made important strides. Previously aluminum had replaced wood and metals in hundreds of uses, and now scientists have begun looking for new economical ways to obtain alumina from Georgia and Alabama clays. While alternate sources of aluminum remained expensive, perhaps $40 per ton as opposed to Caribbean bauxite delivered in the U.S. for $19 to $27 a ton, the research discouraged bauxite-producing countries from escalating their demands to the point where they were priced out of the market. Other substitution efforts also proved successful. Plastics and glass fibers now compete with steel in car parts, and plastic pipe has cut into the market for copper pipe. Other new alloys have reduced the use of expensive palladium and silver. Materials technology even advanced to the point where scientists could give a material a required property by implanting ions. This could "give a plentiful material the properties it needs to supplant a scarce one, and give the scarce one the qualities that enable it to stand up longer in use," said Thomas Falkie, director of the U.S. Bureau of Mines.[33]

Recycling scrap offered many other opportunities to save primary materials from needless extraction, to conserve on energy uses, and to protect the environment. While U.S. government policies (including depletion allowances and other tax policies, purchasing practices, and freight rates) tended to discourage the use of secondary materials, that usage is growing—and offers enormous future potential. Most minerals can be reused, although petroleum cannot. In the mid-1970s the U.S. was already recycling about half of its antimony scrap as well as 25 percent of iron and copper. Twenty percent of nickel and tin were reused, while about 10 percent of aluminum, zinc, and chromium saw secondary usage.[34]

Two other unilateral approaches—resource conservation and deep-sea mining—suggested ways for the U.S. to hold down its reliance on imports and prevent acute shortages. With greater public backing for efforts to utilize materials efficiently, it seemed the U.S. could cut its minerals appetite substantially. As V. E. McKelvey, former director of the U.S. Geological Survey, observed bluntly: "We have been wasting our resource capital on a massive scale." Consumers used energy and minerals for frivolous, nonproductive purposes. "Who needs a 5,000 pound car that can go 120 miles an hour?" he asked.[35]

But unless political leaders convince Americans to pursue a more austere lifestyle, it seems likely that efforts to mine the sea offer the greatest promise. In every world ocean ferromanganese nodules were found to exist at depths below 2,000 meters, and these contain four principal elements—nickel, copper, manganese, and cobalt. Much attention has focused on the commercial use of deepsea nickel and copper, not so much on the manganese and cobalt which are more readily available from conventional sources. Despite the promise, there were several major obstacles for scientists and public officials to overcome. Seabed mining technology needed further refinement, and governments wanted to negotiate an international agreement governing ocean mining. Nonetheless, should a world accord emerge or the U.S. opt to pursue deepsea mining ventures alone, the nodules are believed to offer a viable alternative supply, permitting the U.S. to diversify away from possible cartels and place a limit on materials prices. It is believed that by 1985 the U.S. could process four to five million tons of seabed ore annually, and this could provide 92 percent of America's cobalt consumption, 33 percent of ferromanganese, 18 percent of nickel, and 1.5 percent of copper. But private sea-mining companies were reluctant to take the enormous risks involved in 1978 until the prices of nickel and copper improved and until Congress either approved an international treaty or licensed U.S. firms.[36]

A second basic approach open to the U.S. and other industrial nations was to seek a political accommodation with dissatisfied Third

World countries—either through bilateral deals or multilateral arrangements. Despite the sometimes virulent language and the nationalistic excesses, there was an overriding reason for industrial nations to seek a workable compromise. The developed countries had only 35 percent of the world's major nonfuel mineral reserves, while the centrally-planned economies had another 25 to 30 percent. The less-developed countries had an estimated 40 to 45 percent of all minerals reserves—and for some materials such as tin, bauxite and phosphate they held the principal deposits.[37]

Southern hemisphere nations had ideas of their own. Eager to emulate the sudden gains of oil producers, other developing nations pushed extravagant claims. Not only did they want preferential access to markets for their semiprocessed exports, and more international economic assistance, but also they sought debt relief and international commodity agreements to stabilize raw-materials prices, protecting these exports against the downward pressure of oversupply. While the U.S. wanted to see commodity accords as means to stabilize prices around long-term trends for the mutual benefit of producers and consumers, some developing countries had another purpose—achieving a concealed transfer of income from rich to poor nations. For a group of seventy-seven nations who composed UNCTAD, the United Nations Conference on Trade and Development, these issues gained a momentum of their own—especially commodity price stabilization with a common fund to finance buffer stocks. The goals were utopian, involving global equity and income redistribution. But it was doubtful the political leaders of developed countries could accommodate these demands without alienating their own domestic electorates.[38]

Initially, Presidents Nixon and Ford sought to block additional commodity agreements, fearful these would achieve redistribution rather than price stability. Although the Ford administration did persuade Congress to permit U.S. participation in the international tin agreement, there was a noticeable reluctance to encourage this pattern. Rather U.S. policymakers pushed for new arrangements to protect private investors and stimulate minerals exploration in backward nations. At the fourth ministerial meeting of UNCTAD in Nairobi, Kenya during May 1976, Secretary of State Henry Kissinger proposed creation of an International Resources Bank with a $1 billion capital fund. It would mobilize capital for resources development projects and support guarantees of both investor and host country performance. As an affiliate of the World Bank Group this mechanism would reduce risk and promote private investment while protecting the host government's interests. But the plan fell on deaf ears. Less-developed countries suspected the U.S. wanted to expand resource production in order to lower commodity prices, while less-developed nations sought to boost their export prices, not increase production.[39]

When the Carter administration took office, it pursued a different tack in negotiations on commodities. Whereas Secretary Kissinger had approached the contentious issues on a case-by-case basis, proposing that consumer-producer groups be set up for every raw material in order to consider ways of promoting efficiency, growth, and stability in the market, Carter's aides offered a more specific commitment to commodity agreements. The U.S., they said, will join and help finance arrangements that stabilize commodities around underlying market trends providing the agreements balance interests of consumers and producers and permit both parties to share responsibility for managing the accords. Also, instead of pushing Kissinger's resources bank, Carter's aides sought to "scramble the eggs" differently. The new policy rested on encouraging the World Bank and the Overseas Private Investment Corporation, a U.S. agency that insures private foreign investments, to encourage foreign minerals developments projects. OPIC would offer to guarantee loans of up to $50 million for mining and oil ventures, and it wanted congressional authority to make direct loans for minerals development.[40]

Also the Carter administration announced in December 1977 that it was beginning a cabinet-level review of nonfuel minerals policies. Within fifteen months the taskforce would have recommendations for the president. The group, chaired by Interior Secretary Cecil Andrus, would consider "whether the trends toward international interdependence and the politicization of certain minerals markets are increasing U.S. vulnerability to foreign supply curtailments and price manipulations." Also, it would examine whether "U.S. reserves, production capacity, and inventories are adequate to deal with possible supply/price interruptions, or with the economic and social consequences of such disruptions."[41]

This initiative resembled President Eisenhower's reconsideration of government policies in 1953 in the aftermath of the Paley Report.

Before implementing policies prescribed in studies conducted during the previous administration, Carter, like Eisenhower, wanted new policymakers to conduct their own review. From a different standpoint, continued interest in issues of minerals supply emphasized how policy priorities of the late 1970s diverged from those in the 1960s when abundance kept most materials prices relatively stable. In the years ahead, as world demand continued to climb and as industrial nations continued to rely heavily on foreign sources of supply, materials questions seemed likely to remain high on the list of foreign policy priorities. The U.S. was too dependent on other nations for the commodities needed to sustain an advanced industrial society for policymakers to ignore external events that might jeopardize economic security.

Epilogue

SUFFICIENT time has not elapsed to give the latest events and trends adequate historical perspective. Nor does the outside researcher enjoy unrestricted access to important national security documents for the 1950s and more recent times, in order to assess fully the evolution of U.S. policy. For these reasons, the present account does not attempt an exhaustive assessment of contemporary policies, leaving those to a future historical researcher. Rather, this volume concentrates on the fascinating period from World War I to the early 1960s—a period for which official documentation is generally rich.

In emphasizing how natural resource considerations have helped shape U.S. foreign policy during the twentieth century, this study seeks to redress partially a conspicuous shortcoming of academic writings in history—the absence of any systematic consideration of how resource endowments affected American history. While an earlier generation of historians and social scientists, like Brooks Adams and Ellen Semple, did note how environmental factors influenced the U.S. experience, recent writings neglect this consideration. Instead scholarly writings tend, at the present, to converge on social history, including studies of blacks, women, ethnics, urbanization, and other people-related topics. Certainly until the 1973 petroleum embargo resurrected materials issues, even basic college textbooks ignored energy and resource questions. For instance, textbook discussions of American economic development in the late nineteenth century usually mentioned the robber barons, government backing for transcontinental railroads and other themes, but ignored a vital factor: America's fortuitous endowment with the key natural resources required for economic development—especially iron, coal, copper, and manganese. More often than not, until recently the only reference to iron in basic textbooks appeared under the index heading "Iron Curtain."[1]

One explanation for this seeming neglect comes from Marxist historian Gabriel Kolko who suggests that textbook writers often avoid the "main questions and the exceedingly difficult basic problems . . . largely because the murky reflective banalities of conventional liberal thought have encouraged myopia." As Kolko says, written history should serve another important function; it should "assess the main institutional and social forces in a society over time and how they interacted."[2]

There are several distinct emphases among writers who do seek to explain how underlying forces shape society. Marxist historians, for instance, stress that America's global expansion was an inevitable function of the capitalist system, and its supposedly inherent tendencies to overproduce and underconsume. From my own vantage point, the uneven natural distribution of high-quality ore deposits and the inherent drive for power among nation-states deserve greater consideration. Implicit in my own analysis is the thesis that the uneven distribution of natural resources among nations, not the type of economic organization within nations, has greater bearing on an economy's propensity to import raw materials. It is at least arguable that a socialist America would need to obtain foreign raw materials to supplement inadequate domestic reserves, and that a capitalist Soviet Union could pursue the same autarkic foreign economic policies, choosing to develop internal resources rather than import from abroad. Indeed, with a rational, efficient domestic system for allocating resources it is possible to question whether a Soviet regime would need to look abroad for new petroleum reserves—as the Kremlin soon must do, according to a provocative Central Intelligence Agency study, because it is unable to recover abundant domestic reserves.[3]

From a different perspective this book identifies, and seeks to explain, how national competition for mineral resources underlay twentieth century international relations. Too often orthodox diplomatic histories ignore substantive economic issues, like access to raw materials, perhaps because these themes frequently do not interest professional diplomats with a traditional bias toward political affairs. Such a correction is overdue. From World War I, when industrial nations awoke abruptly to the realization they lacked sufficient domestic minerals to satisfy the industrial requirements of modern warfare, the quest for secure foreign supplies has been a major consideration of great-power diplomacy. For Great Britain, Germany, and Japan, in particular, access to foreign minerals was, and remains, crucial to national prosperity and security. For the U.S. foreign materials offered an important supplement to a rich domestic resource base lacking only a few ferroalloys. After World War II depletion of these deposits would heighten American reliance on high-grade foreign ores. Similarly, the quest for industrial raw materials, especially items used in steel-making, was an underlying source of discord in the interwar period. The desire to achieve greater materials self-sufficiency was, as Chapter 3 shows, an important reason why Germany and Japan launched campaigns to extend their territory. But to attain autarky the two Axis powers also needed to seize sufficient war materials—and so the quest for raw materials proved both a long-term objective and an immediate necessity for the dissatisfied powers who triggered World War II.

Since that time the competition for raw materials has broadened and intensified. Depletion of many high-quality ore deposits in the Atlantic region—such as American iron, copper, lead, zinc, and petroleum—encouraged extractive firms to look abroad, to Africa, Asia and Latin America, for other high-quality ore deposits. At the same time the diffusion of industrialism has multiplied global demand for basic materials. And both of these trends occurred as decolonization brought to power nationalist leaders hostile to foreign investments and determined to change the rules of the game. They wanted to exploit resource endowments for the state's direct benefit, ostensibly to effect a redistribution of income from rich nations to Third World nations. In this turbulent period, extractive firms experienced nationalization, a new militance emerged among Southern Hemisphere nations, and by the 1970s the commodity exporters were banding together in cartels to set prices and regulate production.

Superimposed on the widening North-South rift between developed and less-developed nations was the continuing East-West struggle. In this contest control of primary materials remained both a weapon and a strategic objective. First, while both the Soviet Union and the U.S. enjoyed comparative materials self-sufficiency, at least in relation to other industrial nations, each had serious vulnerabilities. Moscow lacked secure supplies of tin and rubber. The U.S. lacked both of these and most ferroalloys. And for both, growing petroleum needs dictated a new interest in access to Middle East petroleum in the late 1970s. As competition continued between the two super-powers, some American policymakers perceived that a major Soviet goal remained to isolate this country, along with Western Europe and Japan, from high-quality ore deposits in Southeast Asia, Africa, and the Middle East. Disturbances in Indochina, Zaire (the former Belgian Congo), Rhodesia, and South Africa all provided a measure of confirmation. So did the Soviet takeover of the Cuban revolution and Moscow's support for socialist political elements in copper-rich Chile. In each instance far more than minerals was at stake, and the present study does not mean to exaggerate raw-materials considerations when competing ideologies, political interests, and security concerns influenced decisions in the Kremlin and Washington. Nonetheless, planners in Moscow, it can reasonably be inferred, were as sensitive to America's mineral deficiencies as were the minerals specialists in Washington. Any move that deprived the Western world of significant supplies served to improve the Soviet position in world politics.

While political conflicts and security needs spurred the quest for stable materials supply, fortuitous circumstances and shifting technology altered this struggle in important ways. The random distribution of high-grade ore deposits around the world more than anything else had influenced the initial approach to minerals questions. Up until World War II, for instance, the North Atlantic region served as the principal mining region, and the U.S. exported large quantities of petroleum, coal, iron, copper, lead, and zinc. Germany, Japan, and Great Britain to varying degrees lacked bountiful deposits of these materials, and invariably looked beyond their own borders. Had nature endowed Germany and Japan, the two later-comers to industrialization and empire, with an ample, diversified resources base, it is doubtful these two nations would have challenged the Anglo-American global system so recklessly and desperately. Certainly the foreign policy moves of Adolph Hitler and militarist Japan sprang from a sense of national despair, partly the result of growing population and limited materials endowments.

If the asymmetrical distribution of material resources stirred national rivalries, technology helped liberate foreign policy from the expansionist imperative. During World War I the Haber process for fixing nitrogen from the air enabled Germany to escape a blockade of Chilean nitrogen; and similar technological developments permitted the U.S. to substitute Arkansas bauxite for high-quality bauxite from Dutch Guiana in aluminum production when Nazi submarines disrupted Caribbean supply routes during 1942. Technology provided a synthetic rubber to replace the natural rubber shut off when Japan conquered Malaya in 1942. Synthetics, substitutes, and even recycling previously used raw materials all served to ease pressure on national decisionmakers during World War II, and later these techniques would give the U.S. economy flexibility during the cold war. These options, plus new supplies from deep-sea nodules, promised to liberate the materials-using industries from the future pressures of resource depletion and rising costs, as well as from supply dislocations and coercion.

Although improved technology permits a flexible response to adverse changes in the flow of materials, rising demand periodically has exceeded available supplies—and both shortages and abrupt price hikes resulted. Near the close of World War I, during the Korean War, and again in the 1970s, minerals prices soared, and governments worried about the implications of resource exhaustion and rising costs, two concerns expressed in the writings of economists Thomas Malthus and David Ricardo. Perhaps it was only coincidence, but these three periods of intense public concern coincided with the final phases of a Kondratieff long wave—and once prices began to ease, problems of materials supply faded from public view.

Despite gloomy forecasts of exhaustion and scarcity, minerals prices remained relatively stable in constant dollars over the long term. For example, copper and lead reached pre–World War I peaks higher than price heights in the 1970s. Zinc and petroleum were within 15 percent of their pre-1914 levels in 1976. From a different perspective economist William Nordhaus shows, by comparing prices of minerals and labor, that "there has been a continuous decline in resource prices for the entire century" before 1970. Why was the evidence of rising prices inconclusive when modern industry consumed and wasted such vast quantities of nonrenewable materials? The pessimistic forecasts erred, in part because government studies underestimated actual reserves. Often officials failed to appreciate fully that private mining companies seldom hold reserves for more than ten years projected requirements. Also, forecasts neglected to anticipate how supplies would expand as commodity prices surged upward during periods of high demand for raw materials. And they overlooked technology as a dynamic force to lower costs. Technology enabled mining companies to extract lower quality ores profitably. In this area copper offers an excellent illustration. At the opening of this century, ore containing 3 percent copper was the poorest that could be mined efficiently, but in the 1970s the cutoff level was down to 0.2 percent.[4]

Another factor working to hold down costs was international trade. As the U.S. exhausted high-grade domestic ores, it looked increasingly to accessible, quality deposits in other countries. Appendix 2 shows how U.S. imports of metals and minerals have increased as a percent of consumption, particularly for iron ore, petroleum, and zinc. Growing reliance on foreign supplies did not mean that the U.S. was exhausting its domestic resources, for large quantities of low-grade ore remained, though often in areas less accessible to industry than foreign ores which might be transported cheaply by sea.

Determined to maintain secure access to foreign reserves in an uncertain world, threatened by German and Japanese expansionism and then by Soviet ambitions, policymakers sought to stabilize supply relationships through international cooperation and unilateral action. During the interwar period, when German and Japanese desires collided head-on with the interests of other industrial powers, efforts to protect the status quo centered on the League of Nations. But neither the open-door policy, which sought to assure general access to mineral reserves, or the minerals sanction, received adequate support to prove effective. Sanctions did not halt Italian aggression in Ethiopia, nor did the American oil and scrap iron embargo arrest Japanese expansionism in 1941. Part of the problem stemmed from the inherent weakness of the League of Nations, which lacked the support of the U.S.

After World War II international law and institutions exhibited different shortcomings. Newly independent nations successfully challenged traditional concepts which assured foreign investors compensation for nationalization, and they used United Nations machinery to pass resolutions that strengthened the hand of materials-exporting nations. More recent efforts to negotiate mutually agreed codes of conduct governing foreign investments, an international resources development bank, and a treaty governing seabed resources, foundered in political and ideological differences. Despite the setbacks, some existing international machinery, especially the World Bank Group, was increasing its support for raw-material development projects, and over a period of time it was quite probable new relationships would evolve to expand and regularize the flow of international raw materials.

For the U.S. several unilateral strategies emerged to secure supplies of foreign resources and to cushion against supply disruptions. Washington articulated the doctrine of equal access to the raw materials of less-developed nations, and used diplomatic leverage to gain concessions for American petroleum companies in the Middle East and Dutch East Indies after World War I. During World War II the federal government encouraged the expansion of American copper companies in Chile and mining companies in Mexico. In one conspicuous instance the U.S. even built and operated a mining facility abroad—the Nicaro nickel project in Cuba. As the cold war intensified, American leaders again took an active interest in protecting key overseas installations from sabotage. These included copper mines in Chile, cobalt facilities in the Congo, petroleum refineries in Indonesia and the Caribbean, among others. While advancing the interest of U.S.–based mining firms, Washington's policies were not based solely on promoting the nation's self-interest. As economist Raymond Mikesell has shown, U.S. investments in foreign mining tend to increase world minerals supplies, not simply the availability of those resources specifically to the U.S. Interestingly, although the U.S. government encouraged overseas expansion of American mining firms, it proved reluctant to back these same firms against nationalization, except to insist on application of the doctrine of prompt and adequate compensation. Without forceful backing in Washington and without effective international law, the minerals companies expanded their investments rapidly in areas outside the volatile Third World. Australia, Canada, and South Africa, nations rich in raw materials and adhering to established concepts of international law, were the prime beneficiaries in the 1960s.[5]

From Theodore Roosevelt's first interest in a conservation conference to Charles K. Leith's investigation for the Minerals Inquiry, the Paley Commission, and the National Commission on Materials Policy, U.S. officials discussed components of a national minerals policy. Insofar as a formal policy evolved, it rested on encouraging the importation of high-quality foreign materials and on discouraging development of high-cost domestic minerals, except in wartime. Leith's investigation, the Paley Report, and the National Commission on Materials Policy all reiterated the economic wisdom that cost considerations warranted obtaining the least expensive materials. This principle justified expanding imports, despite potential dangers to national security from excessive reliance on them. In Congress, where domestic mining interests exerted clout, this policy ran into frequent opposition, and as a result government spent billions of dollars establishing a sheltered market for some American materials—especially lead and zinc during the 1950s. Interestingly, although government encouraged scientists and policymakers to explore resource-related issues thoroughly, it made inadequate preparation for implementing specific recommendations. This gap between planning and policy implementation remained a serious problem, as did poor coordination and a lack of information for effective public and private decision-making.[6]

To avoid supply disruptions in wartime, the federal government gradually adopted a stockpiling program, but serious policy errors marred that effort. Government moved too slowly in obtaining necessary materials for World War II and the Korean War, despite abundant lessons from the past. Then, as if it sought to avoid repeating earlier mistakes, the federal government allowed materials purchases to overexpand in the 1950s, when the Eisenhower administration used these purchases to assist the depressed mining industry. Sales in the 1960s and 1970s would again cut stockpiles sharply. Mining industry leaders would claim, with some justification, that government stockpiling first encouraged private industry to overexpand, and then discouraged necessary minerals development in the 1960s with inventory sales.

From a different perspective, however mistaken and shortsighted official policies sometimes seemed, American commitment to the principle of equal access, its vigorous opposition to autarkic solutions, and its support for international institutions and collective security undoubtedly contributed to the evolution of a stable and bountiful international order after World War II. Had Japan and Western Europe not found political advantage in an open trading world, these economies, both far more dependent on overseas raw materials than the U.S., might again have resorted to military expansionism, as they had in the 1930s. For a quarter century after World War II U.S. political and economic leadership made the world a safer and more prosperous place to live for all nations, and this atmosphere helped subordinate the competition for natural resources.

Inevitably, the forces of change would create a new environment for national policymakers. Soaring world demand, depletion of known deposits, a new militance among less developed nations possessing rich materials resources, and the waning of American influence all eroded the old order. So did the rise of Soviet power, and its apparent aspiration to use materials as a pawn in the struggle for world influence. These factors, and others, promised to make the competition for raw materials more intense in the 1980s.

Appendix ɪ   Average Annual U.S. Producer Price (Cents per Pound)

Year	Copper Actual Price	Copper 1972 Constant	Lead Actual	Lead 1972	Zinc Actual	Zinc 1972
1900	16.55	68.22	4.41	18.18	4.30	17.72
1901	16.40	68.53	4.36	18.22	4.00	16.72
1902	11.97	46.90	4.10	16.07	4.76	18.65
1903	13.62	52.83	4.26	16.52	5.25	20.36
1904	13.11	50.70	4.32	16.71	5.00	19.33
1905	15.98	61.39	4.70	18.06	5.90	22.67
1906	19.77	73.58	5.66	21.06	6.20	23.07
1907	20.86	73.94	5.35	18.96	5.50	19.50
1908	13.39	49.23	4.23	15.55	4.20	15.44
1909	13.11	44.74	4.30	14.68	5.40	18.43
1910	12.88	42.15	4.49	14.69	5.40	17.67
1911	12.55	44.61	4.46	15.85	5.70	20.26
1912	16.48	55.14	4.48	14.99	6.90	23.08
1913	15.52	51.34	4.40	14.56	5.60	18.52
1914	13.31	45.04	3.87	13.10	5.10	17.26
1915	17.47	58.12	4.67	15.54	14.20	47.24
1916	28.46	76.86	6.83	18.44	13.60	36.73
1917	29.19	57.37	8.71	17.12	8.90	17.49
1918	24.68	43.48	7.46	13.14	8.00	14.09
1919	18.90	31.53	5.81	9.69	7.00	11.68
1920	17.50	26.19	8.08	12.09	7.80	11.67
1921	12.65	29.96	4.55	10.77	4.70	11.13
1922	13.56	32.36	5.71	13.63	5.70	13.60
1923	14.61	33.53	7.25	16.64	6.70	15.38
1924	13.16	31.04	8.08	19.06	6.30	14.86
1925	14.16	31.64	9.02	20.16	7.66	17.12
1926	13.93	32.16	8.42	19.44	7.37	17.01
1927	13.05	31.53	6.75	16.31	6.25	15.10

[a] Deflator derived from wholesale price index.

Tin		Petroleum ($/bbl.) (U.S. Wellhead)		Iron Ore (Av. Value per Long Ton)		
Actual	1972	Actual	1972	Actual	1972	Deflator[a]
29.9	123.25	1.19	4.91	2.42	9.98	24.26
16.7	69.79	.96	4.01	1.71	7.15	23.93
26.8	105.02	.80	3.13	1.84	7.21	25.52
28.1	109.00	.94	3.65	1.89	7.33	25.78
28.0	108.28	.86	3.32	1.56	6.03	25.86
31.4	120.63	.62	2.38	1.77	6.80	26.03
39.8	148.12	.73	2.72	2.11	7.85	26.87
38.2	135.41	.72	2.55	2.55	9.04	28.21
29.5	108.46	.72	2.64	2.27	8.35	27.20
29.7	101.36	.70	2.38	2.15	7.34	29.30
34.1	111.58	.61	1.99	2.47	8.08	30.56
42.3	150.37	.61	2.16	2.11	7.50	28.13
46.1	154.23	.74	2.47	1.88	6.29	29.89
44.3	146.54	.95	3.14	2.19	7.24	30.23
34.3	116.07	.81	2.74	1.81	6.13	29.55
38.6	128.41	.64	2.13	1.83	6.09	30.06
43.5	117.47	1.10	2.97	2.34	6.32	37.03
61.8	121.46	1.56	3.06	3.15	6.19	50.88
88.8	156.45	1.98	3.48	3.39	5.97	56.76
63.3	105.59	2.01	3.35	3.50	5.84	59.95
48.3	72.27	3.07	4.59	4.11	6.15	66.83
29.9	70.80	1.73	4.09	3.37	7.98	42.23
32.6	77.80	1.61	3.84	3.12	7.45	41.90
42.7	98.00	1.34	3.08	3.45	7.92	43.57
50.2	118.40	1.43	3.37	2.91	6.86	42.40
57.9	129.38	1.68	3.75	2.52	5.63	44.75
65.3	150.74	1.88	4.34	2.51	5.79	43.32
64.4	155.59	1.30	3.14	2.47	5.97	41.39

Year	Copper Actual Price	Copper 1972 Constant	Lead Actual	Lead 1972	Zinc Actual	Zinc 1972
1928	14.68	34.97	6.31	15.03	6.03	14.36
1929	18.23	44.23	6.83	16.57	6.49	15.74
1930	13.11	35.01	5.52	14.74	4.56	12.18
1931	8.24	26.10	4.24	13.43	3.64	11.53
1932	5.67	20.10	3.18	11.27	2.88	10.21
1933	7.15	25.04	3.87	13.56	4.03	14.12
1934	8.53	26.32	3.86	11.91	4.16	12.84
1935	8.76	25.27	4.06	11.71	4.33	12.49
1936	9.58	27.36	4.71	13.45	4.90	14.00
1937	13.27	35.52	6.01	16.09	6.52	17.45
1938	10.10	29.71	4.74	13.94	4.61	13.56
1939	11.07	33.12	5.05	15.11	5.12	15.32
1940	11.40	33.53	5.18	15.24	6.34	18.65
1941	11.87	31.34	5.79	15.29	7.48	19.75
1942	11.87	27.78	6.48	15.16	8.25	19.31
1943	11.87	26.52	6.50	14.52	8.25	18.44
1944	11.87	26.38	6.50	14.44	8.25	18.33
1945	11.87	25.89	6.50	14.18	8.25	18.00
1946	13.92	26.61	8.11	15.50	8.73	16.69
1947	21.15	32.93	14.67	22.84	10.50	16.35
1948	22.20	31.93	18.04	25.95	13.58	19.53
1949	19.36	29.30	15.36	23.25	12.15	18.39
1950	21.46	31.25	13.30	19.36	13.88	20.21
1951	24.37	31.86	17.49	22.86	17.99	23.52
1952	24.37	32.76	16.47	22.14	16.21	21.79
1953	28.92	39.41	13.48	18.37	10.86	14.80
1954	29.82	40.54	14.05	19.10	10.69	14.53

a Deflator derived from wholesale price index.

Tin		Petroleum ($/bbl.) (U.S. Wellhead)		Iron Ore (Av. Value per Long Ton)		
Actual	1972	Actual	1972	Actual	1972	Deflator[a]
50.4	120.06	1.17	2.79	2.46	5.86	41.98
45.2	109.66	1.27	3.08	2.61	6.33	41.22
31.7	84.65	1.19	3.18	2.64	7.05	37.45
24.5	77.61	.65	2.05	2.60	8.24	31.57
22.0	77.99	.87	3.08	2.42	8.58	28.21
39.1	136.95	.67	2.35	2.59	9.07	28.55
52.2	161.06	1.00	3.09	2.58	7.96	32.41
50.4	145.37	.97	2.80	2.48	7.15	34.67
46.4	132.53	1.09	3.11	2.56	7.31	35.01
54.3	145.34	1.18	3.16	2.87	7.68	37.36
42.3	124.41	1.13	3.32	2.81	8.26	34.00
50.3	150.51	1.02	3.05	2.89	8.65	33.42
49.8	146.47	1.02	3.00	2.51	7.38	34.00
52.0	137.31	1.14	3.01	2.68	7.08	37.87
52.0	121.69	1.19	2.78	2.63	6.15	42.73
52.0	116.20	1.20	2.68	2.70	6.03	44.75
52.0	115.56	1.21	2.69	2.70	6.00	45.00
52.0	113.44	1.22	2.66	2.77	6.04	45.84
54.5	104.19	1.41	2.70	3.07	5.86	52.31
77.9	121.28	1.93	3.00	3.44	5.36	64.23
99.3	142.84	2.60	3.74	3.91	5.62	69.52
99.3	150.30	2.54	3.84	4.50	6.81	66.07
95.5	139.05	2.51	3.65	4.99	7.27	68.68
127.1	166.16	2.53	3.31	5.46	7.14	76.49
120.5	161.98	2.53	3.40	6.09	8.19	74.39
95.8	130.55	2.68	3.65	6.76	9.21	73.38
91.8	124.81	2.77	3.76	6.99	9.50	73.55

Year	Copper Actual Price	Copper 1972 Constant	Lead Actual	Lead 1972	Zinc Actual	Zinc 1972
1955	37.51	50.88	15.14	20.54	12.30	16.68
1956	42.00	55.15	16.01	21.02	13.49	17.72
1957	30.17	38.52	14.66	18.72	11.40	14.55
1958	26.31	33.12	12.11	15.25	10.31	12.98
1959	30.99	38.94	12.21	15.34	11.46	14.40
1960	32.34	40.59	11.95	15.00	12.95	16.25
1961	30.32	38.22	10.87	13.70	11.55	14.56
1962	31.00	38.95	9.63	12.10	11.63	14.61
1963	31.00	39.07	11.14	14.04	12.01	15.14
1964	32.35	39.56	13.62	16.66	13.57	16.60
1965	35.36	43.60	16.00	19.73	14.50	17.88
1966	36.00	42.96	15.12	18.04	14.50	17.31
1967	38.10	45.38	14.00	16.67	13.85	16.50
1968	41.17	47.84	13.21	15.35	13.50	15.69
1969	47.43	53.04	14.93	16.70	14.65	16.38
1970	58.07	62.65	15.69	16.93	15.32	16.53
1971	52.09	54.47	13.89	14.52	16.13	16.87
1972	51.44	51.44	15.03	15.03	17.75	17.75
1973	59.53	52.64	16.29	14.40	20.66	18.27
1974	77.06	57.33	22.53	16.76	35.95	26.74
1975	64.53	43.94	21.53	14.66	38.96	26.53
1976	69.62	45.31	23.10	15.03	37.01	24.09

[a] Deflator derived from wholesale price index.

Sources: All data, except petroleum, obtained from U.S. Bureau of Mines. Petroleum from U.S. Department of Commerce, *Historical Statistics of the United States*, I:593–594. Also, U.S. Department of Energy, *Annual Report to Congress, 1977.*

Tin		Petroleum ($/bbl.) (U.S. Wellhead)		Iron Ore (Av. Value per Long Ton)		
Actual	1972	Actual	1972	Actual	1972	Deflator[a]
94.7	128.46	2.77	3.76	7.12	9.66	73.72
101.4	133.16	2.79	3.66	7.47	9.76	76.15
96.3	122.94	3.09	3.89	8.31	10.60	78.33
95.1	119.73	3.01	3.79	8.59	10.81	79.43
102.1	128.28	2.90	3.64	8.69	10.92	79.59
101.4	127.26	2.88	3.61	8.73	10.96	79.68
113.3	142.80	2.89	3.64	8.99	11.33	79.34
114.6	143.99	2.90	3.64	8.84	11.11	79.59
116.6	146.96	2.89	3.64	9.22	11.62	79.34
157.7	192.86	2.88	3.52	9.52	11.64	81.77
178.2	219.73	2.86	3.53	9.53	11.75	81.10
164.0	195.73	2.88	3.44	9.49	11.33	83.79
153.4	182.71	2.92	3.48	9.92	11.82	83.96
148.1	172.09	2.94	3.42	10.21	11.86	86.06
164.4	183.85	3.09	3.46	10.34	11.56	89.42
174.1	187.83	3.18	3.43	10.80	11.65	92.69
167.3	174.94	3.39	3.54	11.55	12.08	95.63
177.5	177.50	3.39	3.39	12.20	12.20	100.00
227.6	201.26	3.89	3.44	12.84	11.35	113.09
396.3	294.82	6.87	5.11	16.34	12.16	134.42
339.8	231.39	7.67	5.22	21.41	14.58	146.85
379.8	247.18	8.19	5.33	24.28	15.80	153.65

Appendix 2   **Net U.S. Imports of Selected Metals and Minerals as a Percentage of Apparent Consumption** (Based on net imports of metals, minerals, ores, and concentrates; net imports = imports − exports +/− government stockpile and industry stock changes)

Minerals and Metals	1900	1913	1918	1920	1929
Copper	E	E	E	E	0
Iron ore	3	2.4	E	0.2	2.5
Lead	E	0.7	E	12.5	3.9
Manganese	96	99	62	86	92
Nickel	100	100	100	100	100
Petroleum	E	E	E	6.2	E
Zinc	E	E	E	E	E

E: net exports.
Source: U.S. Bureau of Mines; data before 1950 computed from Neal Potter and Francis T. Christy, Jr., *Trends in Natural Resource Commodities.*

1939	1943	1950	1955	1960	1965	1970	1975
E	22.6	31	17	E	15	E	E
2.5	E	11	18	18	32	30	30
1.	35	40	39	33	31	22	11
96	88	77	79	89	94	95	98
100	100	90	84	72	73	71	72
E	E	8	10	16	19	21	35
7.4	35.4	41	51	46	53	54	61

Notes

Introduction

1. Statistics appear in U.S. President, Council of Economic Advisers, *Economic Report of the President, 1974*, p. 307. Other background material is in U.S. National Commission on Supplies and Shortages, *The Commodity Shortages of 1973–1974: Case Studies*.
2. "The Scramble for Resources," *Business Week*, June 30, 1973, p. 56.
3. Donella H. Meadows, et al., *The Limits to Growth*, quotations on back cover and p. 23.
4. "The Scramble for Resources," *Business Week*, June 30, 1973, p. 56.
5. Lester Brown, "Rich Countries and Poor in a Finite, Interdependent World," *Daedalus* 102 (Fall 1973): 158; C. Fred Bergsten, "The Threat from the Third World," *Foreign Policy* 11 (Summer 1973): 108.
6. Political scientists, more than historians, have emphasized minerals considerations. See Harold and Margaret Sprout, *Foundations of International Politics*, pp. 365–391, and Robert Strausz-Hupe, *The Balance of Tomorrow*, pp. 119–121.

1. World War I and the Global Scramble for Resources

1. Brooks Adams, *The New Empire*, pp. 3–4 (quotation), 198–199.
2. Environmental determinism gained a wide following during the interwar period, especially among students of political geography. For an introduction to geopolitics, read Russell H. Fifield and G. Etzel Pearcy, *Geopolitics in Principle and Practice*, and Johannes Mattern, *Geopolitik: Doctrine of National Self-Sufficiency and Empire*. Hitler's familiarity with these principles appears in *Mein Kampf*, pp. 935–937, and *Hitler's Secret Book*, pp. 13–16, 46–52. See also Werner Maser, *Hitler's Mein Kampf*, p. 122. On American revisionism, consult Warren Cohen, *The American Revisionists*.
3. On "foundations of power," see Secretary of the Interior Franklin Lane's *Report of the Secretary of the Interior*, 1915, 1:5–9. T. A. Rickard, *Man*

and Metals, 2:1049. Mineral determinism appears in the following basic texts: William Smith Culbertson, *International Economic Policies*, pp. 304–340; John Donaldson, *International Economic Relations*, pp. 427–431; Erich W. Zimmermann, *World Resources and Industries*, pp. 429–430.

4. On Leith, the standard biography is Sylvia Wallace McGrath, *Charles Kenneth Leith: Scientific Adviser.*

5. Among their important writings are these: Leith, *The Economic Aspects of Geology*; Smith, ed., *The Strategy of Minerals*; and Spurr, ed., *Political and Commercial Geology and the World's Mineral Resources.*

6. Spurr, *Political and Commercial Geology*, p. vi.

7. Charles K. Leith, "Exploitation of Foreign Minerals," *Economic Geology* 22 (August 1927): 518–520, quote on p. 519.

8. Harold J. Barnett and Chandler Morse, *Scarcity and Growth*, pp. 51–97. On Turner's link to "environmental determinism" note Ray A. Billington, *Frederick Jackson Turner*, pp. 108–131.

9. Frank Vanderlip, *The American 'Commercial Invasion' of Europe*, p. 95; U.S. National Conservation Commission, *Report, S. Doc. 676*, 60th Cong., 2nd sess., p. 2.

10. U.S. National Conservation Commission, *Report*, p. 546. A good summary of this report is Charles R. Van Hise, *The Conservation of Natural Resources in the United States.* Also valuable is Samuel P. Hays, *Conservation and the Gospel of Efficiency.*

11. Barnett and Morse, *Scarcity and Growth*, pp. 72–97.

12. League of Nations, *Statistical Yearbook*, 1928, pp. 94–99; Joseph B. Umpleby, "The Position of the United States among the Nations" in *Strategy of Minerals*, edited by George Otis Smith, p. 288.

13. George Otis Smith, *Our Mineral Reserves* (U.S. Geological Survey Bulletin No. 599), pp. 5, 9–10.

14. Ibid., p. 6.

15. B. R. Mitchell, *European Historical Statistics, 1750–1970*, pp. 378, 381, 388, 424–425.

16. Hans J. Morgenthau, *Politics among Nations*, pp. 114–115; Thomas Holland, "International Relationship of Minerals," *Nature* 124 (August 3, 1929): 189; Alan Bateman, "Can the Western Hemisphere Be Self-Contained Industrially?" undated memorandum, President's Materials Policy Commission (hereafter PMPC), Box 58.

17. David S. Landes, "Technological Change and Development in Western Europe, 1750–1914," in *Cambridge Economic History of Europe*, edited by H. J. Habbakkuk and M. Postan, 6:477–496; W. H. Dennis and William Herbert, *Foundations of Iron and Steel Metallurgy*, pp. 223–225.

18. Holland, "International Relationship," pp. 189–190.

19. Leo Grebler and Wilhelm Winkler, *The Cost of the World War to Germany and to Austria-Hungary*, pp. 12–13.

20. Fritz Fischer, *Germany's Aims in the First World War*, pp. xi, 538–539,

585, 589, 591, 607–608. John Bakeless, *The Economic Causes of Modern War*, pp. 141–176.

21. Margaret P. Doxey, *Economic Sanctions and International Enforcement*, pp. 17–19; Marion C. Siney, *The Allied Blockade of Germany, 1914–1916*, pp. 245–258; Daniel T. Jack, *Studies in Economic Warfare*, pp. 82–145; Arthur Salter, *Allied Shipping Control: An Experiment in International Administration*, pp. 88–97, 117–130; Chester G. Gilbert, "Nitrogen," in *Political and Commercial Geology*, edited by Spurr, pp. 429–430.

22. Frank F. Grout, "A Case of National Dependence: Germany," in *Strategy of Minerals*, edited by Smith, pp. 307–313; D. F. Hewett, "Manganese," in *Political and Commercial Geology*, edited by Spurr, pp. 107–108; Louis Guichard, *The Naval Blockade, 1914–1918*, pp. 270–273; and F. G. Tryon, "How Germany Met the Raw Materials Blockade, 1914–1918," in *Boycotts and Peace*, edited by Evans Clark, pp. 338–349.

23. Guichard, *Naval Blockade*, pp. 272–274; Alex Skelton, "Copper," in *International Control in the Non-Ferrous Metals*, edited by William Y. Elliott et al., pp. 408–409.

24. Skelton, "Nickel," in *International Control*, edited by Elliott et al., pp. 141–143; Mira Wilkins, *The Maturing of Multinational Enterprise*, pp. 11–12.

25. W. N. Medlicott, *The Economic Blockade*, 1:34–35; William K. Hancock, *Four Studies in War and Peace in This Century*, pp. 4–5; Doxey, *Economic Sanctions*, pp. 18–19.

26. Neal Potter and Francis T. Christy, Jr., *Trends in Natural Resource Commodities*, pp. 318, 342; G. A. Roush, ed., *The Mineral Industry: Its Statistics, Technology and Trade During 1914*.

27. John A. DeNovo, "The Movement for an Aggressive American Oil Policy Abroad, 1918–1920," *American Historical Review* 61 (July 1956): 856; Skelton, "Copper," in *International Control*, edited by Elliott et al., pp. 399–400; Council on Foreign Relations, *Mineral Resources and Their Distribution as Affecting International Relations*, pp. 16–19. An authoritative survey is Grosvenor B. Clarkson, *Industrial America in the World War*, pp. 315–386.

28. Walt Whitman Rostow, "Kondratieff, Schumpeter, and Kuznets: Trend Periods Revisited," *Journal of Economic History* 35 (December 1975): 719–753.

29. Skelton, "Zinc," in *International Control*, edited by Elliott et al., pp. 696–700; Frederick B. Hyder, "Zinc," in *Political and Commercial Geology*, edited by Spurr, pp. 294–316.

30. U.S. Tariff Commission, *Industrial Readjustments of Certain Mineral Industries Affected by the War*, pp. 128–138; Edson Bastin, "Minor Metals," in *Strategy of Minerals*, edited by Smith, pp. 186–187; Bernard Baruch, *American Industry in the War*, pp. 150–151; Clarkson, *Industrial America*, pp. 377–378.

31. U.S. Tariff Commission, *Industrial Readjustments*, pp. 53–57; G. A. Roush, *Strategic Mineral Supplies*, p. 126.

32. Charles K. Leith, "War Problems in Minerals: II—Overseas War Mineral Movements," *Engineering and Mining Journal* 112 (October 8, 1921): 573–574; J. E. Spurr, "War Minerals Problems: III—The War Minerals Investigations of the Bureau of Mines," *Engineering and Mining Journal* 112 (October 22, 1921): 651.

33. Spurr, "War Minerals Problems," p. 651. For the War Industry Board perspective, see Clarkson, *Industrial America*, pp. 379–381.

34. Clarkson, *Industrial America*, p. 381.

35. Hubert Work to Calvin Coolidge, September 15, 1926, file 3618, Coolidge Papers, Film 1881, series 1. For a contemporary account, note Philip N. Moore, "War Minerals Relief Commission, 1919–1921," *Engineering and Mining Journal* 112 (November 5, 1921): 730–736.

36. Spurr, "War Minerals Problems," p. 653. A published version of these studies appears as Spurr, *Political and Commercial Geology*, quotations on p. 544.

37. Leith, "War Problems in Minerals: II," p. 575.

38. Charles K. Leith, "International Control of Metals," in U.S. Geological Survey, *Mineral Resources of the United States, 1917*, 1:9A–16A. Quote, p. 13A.

39. Ibid., p. 14A.

40. Ibid., p. 15A.

41. C. K. Leith to Mrs. Leith, January 17, 1919, files of Andrew Leith, Leith Papers.

42. "Notes by C. K. Leith on Paris Conference," files of Andrew Leith, Leith Papers.

43. Ibid.

44. Ibid.

45. Ibid.

2. Dependent America and the Quest for Mineral Self-Sufficiency

1. Ernest R. May, *"Lessons" of the Past*.

2. For data, see Appendix 1.

3. League of Nations, *Raw Material Problems and Policies*, pp. 21–32.

4. Ibid., p. 31.

5. Ibid., pp. 32–34; Corrado Gini, *Report on Problem of Raw Materials and Foodstuffs*.

6. League of Nations, *Raw Material Problems*, p. 35.

7. Ibid., p. 36. See also Dean E. Traynor, *International Monetary and Financial Conferences in the Interwar Period*.

8. On the interwar world economy, consult: Alfred E. Eckes, Jr., *A Search for Solvency*; Charles P. Kindleberger, *The World in Depression, 1929–*

1939; and John W. F. Rowe, *Primary Commodities in International Trade.*

9. League of Nations, *Memorandum on the Iron and Steel Industry*, p. 6; National Industrial Conference Board, *Rationalization of German Industry*, pp. 79–105; Charles K. Leith, J. W. Furness, and Cleona Lewis, *World Minerals and World Peace*, pp. 170–173; Hajo Holborn, *A History of Modern Germany*, pp. 752–753; and G. A. Roush, ed., *The Mineral Industry; Its Statistics, Technology and Trade* (annual volumes, 1920–1929).

10. Charles K. Leith, *World Minerals and World Politics*, pp. 60–61, 91; Roush, *The Mineral Industry* (annual volumes); Leith, Furness, and Lewis, *Minerals and Peace*, pp. 173–174.

11. Josiah E. Spurr, "Russian Manganese Concessions," *Foreign Affairs* 5 (April 1927): 506–507; Charles K. Leith, "The World Manganese Situation," *Mining and Metallurgy* 8 (May 1927): 206–207; Mira Wilkins, *The Maturing of Multinational Enterprise*, pp. 107–108.

12. Leith, *Minerals and Politics*, p. 70; H. Foster Bain, "Minerals in Relation to Possible Development in the Far East," *Economic Geology* 22 (May 1927): 213–229.

13. U. K. Parliamentary Papers. "Dominions Royal Commission: Final Report," p. 63.

14. Ibid., pp. 70, 72, 74, 75.

15. Elizabeth S. May, "The International Tin Cartel," in *International Control in the Non-Ferrous Metals*, edited by William Y. Elliott et al., pp. 288–292; Benjamin B. Wallace and Lynn R. Edminster, *International Control of Raw Materials*, pp. 219–235, 244–246.

16. J. Henry Richardson, *British Economic Foreign Policy*, pp. 130–155; Leith, Furness, and Lewis, *Minerals and Peace*, pp. 177–178; William S. Culbertson, *International Economic Policies*, pp. 265–303; and quotation in E. Mackay Edgar, "Great Britain's Grip on Reserve Oil Supplies of the World," *Engineering and Mining Journal* 109 (May 22, 1920): 1173.

17. Benjamin H. Williams, *Economic Foreign Policy*, pp. 60–70; quotation in State Department memorandum to Dr. Arthur N. Young, May 23, 1925, FW 800.63/683, National Archives, RG 59.

18. Leith, *Minerals and Politics*, pp. 80–98.

19. Ibid., pp. 76–101; Wilkins, *Maturing of Enterprise*, pp. 113–122, 159–162; Herbert Feis, *The Diplomacy of the Dollar*, pp. 18–38, 48–60.

20. William C. Redfield, *Dependent America*, pp. vii, 13, 209. Quote on p. 13.

21. Sylvia W. McGrath, *Charles Kenneth Leith*, pp. 160–162; Council on Foreign Relations, *Mineral Resources and Their Distribution as Affecting International Relations*; "Notes on Mineral Round Table," Institute of Politics, Williamstown, Massachusetts, July–August 1926, Box 85, National Archives, RG 107.

22. Mining and Metallurgical Society of America, *International Control of Minerals*, pp. 7–15. This report had support from the prestigious Mining and Metallurgical Society of America and the American Institute of Mining and Metallurgical Engineers.
23. Ibid., pp. 9–10.
24. Ibid., pp. 18–19.
25. Ibid., pp. 37–42, quotation on p. 42.
26. Ibid., pp. 85–86, quotation on p. 86.
27. McGrath, *Leith*, pp. 169–171.
28. G. A. Roush, *Strategic Mineral Supplies*, pp. 60–61, 231; quotation on p. 60.
29. Ibid., pp. 155–156.
30. Charles T. Harris, "Strategic Commodities," March 26, 1934, Raw-Materials-Strategic 912, National Archives, RG 107; Elmer W. Pehrson, "What are Strategic and Critical Materials?" *Mining and Metallurgy* 25 (July 1944): 339–341.
31. C. B. Robbins to Charles K. Leith, March 30, 1928, Raw-Materials-Minerals 907, National Archives, RG 107; Leith to Arthur Dwight, January 15, 1929, Leith Papers; Harris memorandum, "Notes on Procurement and Distribution of Strategic and Critical Materials," August 23, 1933, Raw-Materials-Strategic 912, National Archives, RG 107. For a general discussion of war plans, see Louis Morton, "Germany First: The Basic Concept of Allied Strategy in World War II," in *Command Decisions*, edited by Kent Roberts Greenfield, pp. 11–47.
32. Jacob Viner, "National Monopolies of Raw Materials," *Foreign Affairs* 5 (July 1926): 585; League of Nations, *Raw Material Problems*, p. 41.
33. Quotation in League of Nations, *Raw Material Problems*, p. 42; on U.S. export restrictions, consult Wallace and Edminster, *International Control*, pp. 260–266. On copper-export association, see U.S. Federal Trade Commission, *Report on the Copper Industry*, and Alex Skelton, "Copper," in *International Control*, edited by Elliott et al., pp. 415–459. A more recent interpretation is Rowe, *Primary Commodities*, pp. 125–126.
34. Wallace and Edminster, *International Control*, pp. 76–121; Walter H. Voskuil, *Minerals in Modern Industry*, pp. 297–311.
35. Voskuil, *Modern Industry*, pp. 273–278; Wallace and Edminster, *International Control*, pp. 26–56.
36. Wallace and Edminster, *International Control*, pp. 172–218. See also, Williams, *Economic Foreign Policy*, pp. 395–399.
37. U.S. House of Representatives, Interstate and Foreign Commerce Committee, *Crude Rubber, Coffee, Etc., Hearings*, pp. 1–7, quotation on p. 2.
38. Herbert Hoover, *The Memoirs of Herbert Hoover: The Cabinet and the Presidency, 1920–1933*, pp. 81–84. Quotation on p. 84. An important secondary account written before the opening of Hoover's presidential papers is Joseph Brandes, *Herbert Hoover and Economic Diplomacy: Department of Commerce Policy, 1921–1928*.
39. *Wall Street Journal*, January 1, 1926; "Statement by Secretary Hoover

Regarding Foreign Monopolies," January 4, 1926, Box 211, Hoover-Commerce Papers, Hoover Papers; J. Henry Schroder Banking Corp., memorandum, January 4, 1926, Box 224, Hoover-Commerce Papers, Hoover Papers; and W. L. Schurz to Julius Klein, January 13, 1926, Box 226, Hoover-Commerce Papers, Hoover Papers; Viner, "National Monopolies," p. 593.

40. League of Nations, *Raw Material Problems*, pp. 45–47.

41. Computed from figures in Vivian E. Spencer, *Raw Materials in the United States Economy, 1900–1969*, pp. 14–23. See also Eugene Cameron, "The Contribution of the United States to National and World Mineral Supplies," in *The Mineral Position of the United States, 1975–2000*, edited by Eugene N. Cameron, pp. 9–27.

42. Leith, *Minerals and Politics*, pp. 3–5, quotation on p. 4.

43. Ibid., pp. 7–8.

44. Leith, *Minerals and Politics*, pp. 9–11, quotation on p. 11. G. A. Roush, "The Mineral Industry, 1892–1941," in *The Mineral Industry: Its Statistics, Technology and Trade During 1941*, edited by G. A. Roush, pp. xxi–lxx.

45. Leith, *Minerals and Politics*, pp. 12–13, quotation on p. 12; William P. Rawles, *The Nationality of Commercial Control of World Minerals*; and Rawles, "Control of the Principal Minerals by the World Powers," in American Institute of Mining and Metallurgical Engineers, Mineral Inquiry, *Elements of a National Mineral Policy*, pp. 25–29.

46. Wilkins, *Maturing of Enterprise*, pp. 55–59; Cleona Lewis, *America's Stake in International Investments*, pp. 583–587.

47. Leith, *Minerals and Politics*, pp. 13–18, quotation on p. 15; Elliott et al., *International Control*, pp. 3–21. For material on other minerals, consult Voskuil, *Modern Industry*, and Roush, *Strategic Mineral Supplies*. On manganese, note J. W. Furness, *The Marketing of Manganese Ore*.

48. "World Minerals and World Politics," *Mining and Metallurgy* 12 (February 1931), 74–75; McGrath, *Leith*, pp. 173–175; Charles K. Leith, "Elements of a National Mineral Policy," *Mining and Metallurgy* 14 (May 1933): 224–226, quotation on p. 224.

49. Leith, "Elements," p. 226; AIMME, Mineral Inquiry, *Mineral Policy*, pp. 21–22.

50. Leith, Furness, and Lewis, *Minerals and Peace*, pp. 18–22.

51. Ibid., pp. 23–31. For more information on these trends, consult the annual volumes of Roush, *Mineral Industry*.

3. Minerals and the Origins of World War II

1. For a brief introduction to these different interpretations, consult: Hans W. Gatzke, *European Diplomacy between Two Wars, 1919–1939*; E. M. Robertson, ed., *The Origins of the Second World War*; and John L. Snell, ed., *The Outbreak of the Second World War: Design or Blunder?*

2. In his excellent new synthesis, Alan S. Milward also concludes the three Axis powers "were influenced in their decisions for war by the conviction that war might be an instrument of economic gain." See his *War, Economy and Society 1939–1945*, p. 4. On trade disruption and autarky, Charles P. Kindleberger, *The World In Depression, 1929–1939*, pp. 281–282. Also Charles K. Leith in the Geological Society of America, *Minerals in the Peace Settlement*, p. 3.

3. Thomas Holland, *The Mineral Sanction*, pp. 38–41, 50–51.

4. Charles K. Leith, J. W. Furness, and Cleona Lewis, *World Minerals and World Peace*, pp. 44–55; Brooks Emeny, *The Strategy of Raw Materials: A Study of America in Peace and War*, pp. 12–25.

5. Denis Mack Smith, *Mussolini's Roman Empire*, pp. 3, 18–19.

6. Cited in Herbert W. Schneider, *Making the Fascist State*, p. 34.

7. Smith, *Roman Empire*, pp. 15–16.

8. On Mussolini see Ivone Kirkpatrick, *Mussolini*. Quotation in George W. Baer, *The Coming of the Italian-Ethiopian War*, p. 35. On Italian colonialism, Maxwell H. H. Macartney and Paul Cremona, *Italy's Foreign and Colonial Policy, 1914–1937*, and Smith, *Roman Empire*, pp. 32–43, 107–123.

9. On sanctions, see Margaret P. Doxey, *Economic Sanctions and International Enforcement*, pp. 46–58. On the U.S. position, see Brice Harris, Jr., *The United States and the Italo-Ethiopian Crisis*, and Herbert Feis, *Seen From E. A.*, pp. 193–308. Mussolini quoted in Paul Schmidt, *Hitler's Interpreter*, p. 60.

10. Doxey, *Economic Sanctions*, pp. 46–58. The best account of League of Nations actions is F. P. Walters, *A History of the League of Nations*, pp. 623–691.

11. Charles K. Leith, "The Role of Minerals in Recent International Affairs," April 9, 1938, unpublished paper, Leith Papers. For Holland's view, *Mineral Sanction*, pp. 9–12.

12. Smith, *Roman Empire*, pp. 92, 107, 109, 122. Italy's birthrate declined from 28.4 per thousand in 1925 to 23.4 in 1935. During the same period the death rate dropped from 17.1 per thousand to 14. Compared to Britain and France, Italy had a high birthrate, however. For complete statistics, B. R. Mitchell, *European Historical Statistics, 1750–1970*, p. 117.

13. Norman Rich, *Hitler's War Aims*, 1:xix–xliii. On geopolitics, Russell H. Fifield and G. Etzel Pearcy, "The History and Development of Political Geography," in *World Political Geography*, edited by Fifield and Pearcy, pp. 22–36. Also Johannes Mattern, *Geopolitik*.

14. Rich, *Hitler's War Aims*, 1:xix–xliii; Gerhard L. Weinberg, *The Foreign Policy of Hitler's Germany*, pp. 5–7; Adolf Hitler, *Mein Kampf* and *Hitler's Secret Book*. Louis P. Lochner, ed., *The Goebbels Diaries*, p. 148.

15. Berenice A. Carroll, *Design for Total War*, p. 104.

16. Ibid., p. 138; Amos E. Simpson, *Hjalmar Schacht in Perspective*, pp. 128–130; Hjalmar Schacht, "Germany's Colonial Demands," *Foreign*

Affairs 15 (January 1937): 233; Earl R. Beck, *Verdict on Schacht*, p. 110; William E., Jr., and Martha Dodd, eds., *Ambassador Dodd's Diary, 1933–1938*, p. 377.

17. Schacht, "Germany's Colonial Demands," p. 229.

18. Ibid., p. 229. Schacht, a conservative banker acceptable to German industrialists and highly regarded in foreign banking circles, eventually resigned in November 1937, having failed to persuade Hitler to emphasize exports in place of autarky and armaments. For discussion of this episode, see Simpson, *Schacht in Perspective*, pp. 134–159.

19. Simpson, *Schacht in Perspective*, pp. 128–129; Ian Colvin, *The Chamberlain Cabinet*, pp. 36–37, 39–40, 42–43, 53–54, 87–88, 90; Edgar B. Nixon, ed., *Franklin D. Roosevelt and Foreign Affairs*, 3:586–588; Rich, *Hitler's War Aims*, 2:404–409. A fascinating picture of British politics in the 1930s emerges in Maurice Cowling, *The Impact of Hitler*.

20. Hitler, *Hitler's Secret Book*, p. 99.

21. Weinberg, *Foreign Policy*, pp. 353–354.

22. Carroll, *Total War*, p. 103.

23. Weinberg, *Foreign Policy*, pp. 353–354; Rich, *Hitler's War Aims*, 1:64–66; Carroll, *Total War*, pp. 102, 176–177.

24. Carroll, *Total War*, p. 177. For a discussion of the comparative mineral status of major powers, consult G. A. Roush, *Strategic Mineral Supplies*, pp. 454–469.

25. Quotations in Holland, *Mineral Sanction*, p. 59; H. Foster Bain, "Minerals in Relation to Possible Development in the Far East," *Economic Geology* 22 (May 1927): 221. Leith held a similar view, see Leith, *World Minerals and World Politics*, pp. 69–72. Charles E. Neu explores the expansion theme in his *The Troubled Encounter*.

26. On U.S. relations with Japan, see Akira Iriye, *Across the Pacific* and *After Imperialism*. Also valuable is Neu, *The Troubled Encounter*. James B. Crowley deals with *Japan's Quest for Autonomy*, as does Christopher Thorne, *The Limits of Foreign Policy*, pp. 16–77. An older, insightful study of economic dimensions is Albert E. Hindmarsh, *The Basis of Japanese Foreign Policy*. Statistics come from G. C. Allen, *A Short Economic History of Modern Japan, 1867–1937*, pp. 104–105, 150–151.

27. Hindmarsh, *Japanese Foreign Policy*, pp. 28–88.

28. John E. Orchard, *Japan's Economic Position*, pp. 1–3. See also, E. B. Schumpeter, ed., *The Industrialization of Japan and Manchukuo, 1930–1940*.

29. Allen, *Economic History*, p. 179.

30. The most recent account is Thorne, *Limits of Foreign Policy*. On the value of Manchuria, see Francis C. Jones, *Manchuria Since 1931*, pp. 140–166. Also important is Roy H. Akagi, "Japan's Economic Relations with China," *Pacific Affairs* 4 (June 1931): 471–478. Joseph C. Grew, *Ten Years in Japan*, pp. 128–130, 302–304.

31. Herbert von Dirksen, *Moscow, Tokyo, London: Twenty Years of German Foreign Policy*, pp. 138–140.
32. Elmer W. Pehrson, "Minerals in National and International Affairs," in *Economics of the Mineral Industries*, edited by Edward H. Robie, pp. 501–503. On Holland and Leith, note these: Holland, *Mineral Sanction*, and Leith, Furness, and Lewis, *Minerals and Peace*, pp. 199–206. Leith's paper to International Studies Conference in Paris, July 1937, Leith Papers; also, Charles Wright to Leith, May 31, 1938, Leith Papers.
33. Quotes from State Department memorandum, March 8, 1937, 500.C 1112/115 National Archives, RG 59; League of Nations, *Raw Material Problems and Policies*, pp. 57–58.
34. State Department memorandum, November 4, 1936, 500.C 1112/77, National Archives, RG 59; Veatch to Feis, October 6, 1936, 500.C 1112/55 1/2, National Archives, RG 59; Hull to State Department, December 14, 1936, 500.C 1112/85, National Archives, RG 59; League of Nations, *Raw Material Problems*, p. 58.
35. Unidentified State Department memorandum, July 29, 1937, 500.C 1112/150, and Grew to Hull, March 3, 1937, 500.C 1112/106, National Archives, RG 59. The Japanese view appears in Seizaburo Takahashi, *Japan and World Resources*, pp. 42–43.
36. League of Nations, *Raw Material Problems*, p. 58; Howard Bucknell to Secretary of State, September 9, 1937, 500.C 1112/153; and Bucknell to Secretary of State, October 14, 1937, both National Archives, RG 59.
37. League of Nations, *Raw Material Problems*, p. 66.
38. Sylvia W. McGrath, *Charles Kenneth Leith*, pp. 177–186; U.S. National Resources Board, *A Report on National Planning and Public Works in Relation to Natural Resources and Including Land Use and Water Resources with Finding and Recommendation*, pp. 444–447.
39. Brooks Emeny, *The Strategy of Raw Materials*, pp. 92, 174, quotation on p. 174. On War Department support for this research, see J. K. Crain memorandum, June 27, 1934, Box 86, National Archives, RG 107.
40. Roosevelt to Secretary of Interior, May 29, 1934, 811.24/1027; Feis to Phillips, June 4, 1934, F.W. 811.24/1027; memorandum, May 9, 1935, 811.24/1035, all National Archives, RG 59.
41. Feis memorandum, May 17, 1935, 811.24/1034, and Feis to Hull, December 12, 1935, 811.24/1041, both National Archives, RG 59; David E. Lockwood, *The Stockpiling of Strategic and Critical Materials*, pp. 7–8.
42. The best analysis of Roosevelt's actions appears in Robert A. Divine, *Roosevelt and World War II*. D. W. Bell to Hull, June 3, 1938, 811.24/1115, RG 59.
43. On the silver mine lobby, consult Allan Seymour Everest, *Morgenthau, the New Deal, and Silver*.
44. Feis to Hull, February 5, 1937, 811.24/1058, National Archives, RG 59.
45. Feis to Hull, October 14, 1938, 811.24 Raw Materials/2; Hull to Roosevelt, December 23, 1938, 811.24 Raw Materials/24A; Welles to Feis,

January 16, 1939, 811.24 Raw Materials/31; Feis to William Y. Elliott, March 21, 1939, 811.24 Raw Materials/62, all in National Archives, RG 59.

46. *American Metal Market*, February 1, 1939; Press Release, April 10, 1939, 811.24 Raw Materials/67; Senator Henry C. Lodge, Jr., to State Department, April 11, 1939, 811.61321/127, both in National Archives, RG 59; *American Metal Market*, April 15, 1939.

47. U.S. Department of State, *Foreign Relations of the United States* (hereafter abbreviated FR), 1940, 2:250–252; Roy Veatch memorandum, August 8, 1939, 811.24 Raw Materials/270, National Archives, RG 59; War Production Board, "Evolution of the Metals and Minerals Policy of the War Production Board," September 2, 1943, National Archives, RG 179.

48. Charles K. Leith, "The Role of Minerals in Recent International Affairs," unpublished paper presented to Missouri School of Mines, April 9, 1938, Leith Papers; Rich, *Hitler's War Aims*, pp. 100, 118, 181–182; Charles Will Wright, "Germany's Drive for Mineral Self-Sufficiency," *Mining and Metallurgy* 20 (May 1939): 241–247; "The Copper in Germany's War Chest," *American Metal Market*, March 23, 1939; "Germany Negotiates for Mineral Materials from Southeastern Europe," *American Metal Market*, March 11, 1939; Harold L. Ickes to William J. Donovan, January 21, 1942, #10248, National Archives, RG 226. See also Antonin Basch, *The Danube Basin and the German Economic Sphere*, p. 214; Glenn T. Harper, *German Economic Policy in Spain*, pp. 18–19, 113–114; Hans Peter Krosby, *Finland, Germany and the Soviet Union, 1940–1941*.

49. Rich, *Hitler's War Aims*, 2:134. See also, Earl F. Ziemke, "The German Decision to Invade Norway and Denmark," in *Command Decisions*, edited by Kent Roberts Greenfield, pp. 49–72.

50. Rich, *Hitler's War Aims*, 2:206–207. For an analysis of Germany's reliance on Swedish iron ore, see Alan S. Milward, *War, Economy and Society 1939–1945*, pp. 308–312.

51. Ibid., 2: 207–208; "The Economic Effects of the German-Soviet Pacts," *American Metal Market*, August 30, 1939. Also, Milward, *War, Economy*, pp. 326–327.

52. Nobutaka Ike, ed., *Japan's Decision for War: Records of the 1941 Policy Conferences*, p. 11.

53. Dickover memorandum, June 27, 1939, 811.24/RM/221, National Archives, RG 59.

54. Robert Burnett Hall, "American Raw-Material Deficiencies and Regional Dependence," *Geographical Review* 30 (April 1940): 177–186. Quote on p. 185. See also, Russell D. Buhite, "The Open Door in Perspective: Stanley K. Hornbeck and American Far Eastern Policy," in *Makers of American Diplomacy*, edited by Frank J. Merli and Theodore A. Wilson, p. 448.

55. Ike, ed., *Japan's Decision for War*, pp. 148, 222.

56. Ibid., p. 191. For circumstances of World War II, see Jerome B. Cohen, *Japan's Economy in War and Reconstruction*, pp. 104–107.
57. Ike, ed., *Japan's Decision for War*, p. 188.
58. Elmer W. Pehrson, "The Axis and Strategic Minerals," *Engineering and Mining Journal* 143 (May 1942): 42.
59. Ibid.
60. Milton Van Slyck, "Have-Nots Now the Haves as a Result of Upsets in War," *Newsweek*, September 7, 1942, p. 39.
61. "The Race for Metals," *Fortune* 25 (March 1942): 85–86; "1942—The Year to Win or Lose," *Business Week*, March 14, 1942, pp. 34, 37.

4. Resources for Victory

1. For a discussion of economic warfare from the British perspective, consult W. N. Medlicott, *The Economic Blockade*, 2 vols. A topical treatment is Yuan-Li Wu, *Economic Warfare*.
2. Quote, Medlicott, *Economic Blockade*, 1:47; Margaret P. Doxey, *Economic Sanctions and International Enforcement*, pp. 19–21.
3. Medlicott, *Economic Blockade*, 2:633–639.
4. There is a voluminous literature on American involvement, and the scholarly reader should begin with the authoritative William L. Langer and S. Everett Gleason, *The Challenge to Isolation*, which discusses the "moral embargo" in 1:330–331. A scholarly reinterpretation is Robert A. Divine, *Roosevelt and World War II*. A recent book, based on newly released documents, is Joseph Lash, *Roosevelt and Churchill, 1939–1941*. For Henry Morgenthau's actions to embargo molybdenum, see John Morton Blum, *From the Morgenthau Diaries*, 2:126–129.
5. Divine, *Roosevelt*, pp. 30–31; Medlicott, *Economic Blockade*, 1:471–472.
6. David Horton, *Import Policies and Programs of the War Production Board and Predecessor Agencies: May 1940 to November 1945*, pp. 9–10; War Production Board (hereafter WPB) Policy Analysis and Records Branch, "Evolution of the Metals and Minerals Policy of the War Production Board," September 2, 1943, National Archives, RG 179, pp. 6–7.
7. WPB, "Evolution of Minerals Policy," pp. 6–7.
8. Medlicott, *Economic Blockade*, 2:125; Langer and Gleason, *Challenge to Isolation*, 2:607–637; Sumner Welles to President Roosevelt, May 1, 1940, Official File 932, Roosevelt Papers (hereafter FDR); Elliott quoted in memo to Edward R. Stettinius, October 17, 1940, Box 15, Council of National Defense, Advisory Commission (hereafter NDAC), Roosevelt Library, RG 220.
9. Langer and Gleason, *Challenge to Isolation*, 2:631–632; Henry Wallace to President Roosevelt, May 15, 1940, Official File 932, FDR; WPB, "Evolution of Minerals Policy," pp. 6–7.

10. Horton, *Import Policies*, pp. 13–14.
11. Ibid.
12. Ibid.; Jesse Jones defends his procedures in *Fifty Billion Dollars*, pp. 396–401.
13. WPB, "Evolution of Minerals Policy," p. 9; Roosevelt to Jesse Jones, December 2, 1940, Official File 401, FDR; Melvin G. deChazeau to Leon Henderson, September 19, 1941, Box 32, Henderson Papers.
14. William S. Culbertson, "War Trade," address November 12, 1940, to Army Industrial College, Washington, D.C., Box 964, Foreign Economic Administration (FEA), RG 169.
15. On Roosevelt's administrative style, note Dean Acheson's trenchant comment in *Present at the Creation*, p. 43.
16. NDAC to President Roosevelt, November 27, 1940, FEA Papers, RG 169.
17. Ibid.; John E. Hamm to Harry Hopkins, December 2, 1940, Box 301, Hopkins Papers.
18. NDAC to President, November 27, 1940, FEA, RG 169.
19. Medlicott, *Economic Blockade*, 1:496–497; Reconstruction Finance Corporation (RFC), "Memorandum for the Board of Economic Warfare on Activities of RFC in Elimination of Axis Influences in Latin America," May 18, 1942, Box 117, Wallace Papers, Roosevelt Library.
20. Quote in W. Y. Elliott to W. A. Harriman, January 10, 1941, file 112.03, WPB, RG 179; WPB, "Evolution of Minerals Policy," p. 9.
21. Horton, *Import Policies*, pp. 29–33.
22. Eliot Janeway, "A Job for a Business Man," *Asia* 41 (May 1941): 212. See also Michael Straight, "Jesse Jones, Bottleneck," *New Republic* 105 (December 29, 1941): 881–882. On the Jones-Wallace controversy, note Jones, *Fifty Billion Dollars*, pp. 485–510, and John Morton Blum, ed., *The Price of Vision*, pp. 210–226; Edward L. and Frederick H. Schapsmeier, *Prophet in Politics*, pp. 50–71.
23. Isador Lubin to Harry Hopkins, January 19, 1942, Box 221, Hopkins Papers.
24. A good summary of American experiments with economic warfare appears as V. L. Horoth, "Our Economic War Against the Axis," *Current History and Forum* 53 (June 1941): 38–40.
25. "No Shortages—Stettinius," *Business Week*, July 20, 1940, p. 24; "We Can Go Ersatz, Too," *Business Week*, July 6, 1940, p. 20.
26. "Strategic Quest," *Business Week*, September 20, 1941, pp. 57–58; "The Race for Metals," *Fortune* 25 (March 1942): 84–87; WPB, "Evolution of Minerals Policy," pp. 13–14.
27. Frank T. Sisco, "Metal and Mineral Shortages and Substitutions in National Defense," *Mining and Metallurgy* 22 (October 1941): 483–487.
28. WPB, "Evolution of Minerals Policy," p. 13.
29. Hitler's Balkan policy and his thrust into the Caucasus were oriented to attaining petroleum, indicates Paul Carell, *Hitler's War on Russia*, pp. 536–537. U.S. Joint Staff Planners Directive (JPS. 5), February 3, 1942,

Box 1, President's Secretary's File, FDR; an excellent introduction to strategic issues appears in Maurice Matloff and Edwin M. Snell, *Strategic Planning for Coalition Warfare, 1941–1942*, p. 158.

30. "Japan: Present and Future Logistic Situation," March 20, 1942, Naval Intelligence Report, Office of Strategic Services (OSS), RG 226.

31. Max Dixon and E. S. Taub to Morris Rosenthal, March 7, 1942, Box 112, RFC, RG 234.

32. Roosevelt showed interest in the geopolitical thinking of Isaiah Bowman, president of Johns Hopkins University. See FDR to Bowman, November 18, 1939, President's Personal File, 5575, FDR; Nicholas John Spykman, *America's Strategy in World Politics*, pp. 299–300, 446–448, 468.

33. Spykman, *America's Strategy*, p. 468.

34. WPB, "Evolution of Minerals Policy," p. 16; E. A. Locke, Jr., to Donald M. Nelson, December 24, 1942, Box 327, Hopkins Papers; L. W. Douglas to Harry L. Hopkins, October 14, 1942, Box 133, Hopkins Papers.

35. William Donovan to President Roosevelt, February 17, 1942, President's Secretary's File, Box 164, FDR; Federal Bureau of Investigation, "Axis Aspirations through South America," April 1942, Box 144, Hopkins Papers.

36. Federal Bureau of Investigation, "Axis Aspirations through South America," April 1942, Box 144, Hopkins Papers.

37. Bolivia memorandum, undated, Box 962, FEA, RG 169.

38. Wallace Diary, December 31, 1942, Wallace Papers, Iowa; quote in Wallace Diary, October 31 and November 11, 1942, Wallace Papers, Iowa.

39. J. Edgar Hoover to Harry Hopkins, December 21, 1943, Box 141, Hopkins Papers; Víctor Andrade, *My Missions for Revolutionary Bolivia, 1944–1962*, p. 29. Adolph Berle, an assistant secretary of state, wrote later that this coup was planned in Buenos Aires with Nazi assistance, see Beatrice Bishop Berle and Travis Beal Jacobs, eds., *Navigating the Rapids*, p. 449.

40. WPB, "Evolution of Minerals Policy," pp. 16–25, quotes on pp. 16, 24.

41. Alan M. Bateman, "The F.E.A. Metals and Minerals Program and Procedure," December 1945, Box 2, Bateman Papers; Bateman, "Report on Minerals and Metals Mission to Mexico," B-317, Bateman Papers. Statistics from U.S. Department of Commerce, *Historical Statistics of the United States*, 2:905. See also Marvin D. Bernstein, *The Mexican Mining Industry*, pp. 223–234.

42. Bateman, "F.E.A. Metals," and Earl M. Irving to Alan Bateman, "History of Foreign Nickel Procurement by U.S. Government Agencies, 1941–1945," October 10, 1945, Box 5, Bateman Papers.

43. Irving to Bateman, "History of Foreign Nickel Procurement," Box 5, Bateman Papers; U.S. Bureau of Mines, *Minerals Yearbook, 1945*, pp. 624–626.

44. WPB, "Evolution of Minerals Policy," p. 19. For details of the premium price plan in operation, see George R. Kinzie, *Copper Policies of the War Production Board and Predecessor Agencies*, pp. 48–55; Horton, *Import Policies*; and Charles M. Wiltse, *Lead and Zinc Policies of the War Production Board and Predecessor Agencies*, pp. 54–57.

45. WPB, "Evolution of Minerals Policy," pp. 20–21. For the best account of British-American materials cooperation, consult Joel Hurstfield, *The Control of Raw Materials*.

46. WPB, "Evolution of Minerals Policy," p. 26.

47. Ibid., pp. 27–28; Roosevelt to Sen. James Murray, April 24, 1943, WPB Doc. 214, WPB, RG 179; Horton, *Import Policies*, pp. 90–92.

48. Donald H. McLaughlin, "Government's Role in a National Mineral Policy," *Mining Engineering* 1 (April 1949): 19.

49. Charles K. Leith, "Review of Technologic Effort in Metals and Minerals," March 25, 1943, Leith Papers. For aluminum statistics, U.S. Dept. of Commerce, *Historical Statistics*, 1:605.

50. On economic warfare programs, see Medlicott, *Economic Blockade*.

51. Jesse Jones to President Roosevelt, February 23, 1942, Minutes of U.S. Commercial Company, vol. 1, Reconstruction Finance Corporation (RFC), RG 234.

52. Minutes of U.S. Commercial Company, March 27, 1942, vol. 1, RFC, RG 234; Robert K. Warner, "Report on Preclusive Operations in Metals and Minerals During the Period, January 1, 1942, to June 30, 1944," July 4, 1944, RFC, RG 234.

53. Warner, "Report on Preclusive Operations," RFC, RG 234; Albert Speer, *Inside the Third Reich*, p. 316.

54. Warner, "Report on Preclusive Operations," RFC, RG 234. See also Medlicott, *Economic Blockade*, 2:582–610; David Gordon and Royden Dangerfield, *The Hidden Weapon*, pp. 105–115.

55. Warner, "Report on Preclusive Operations," RFC, RG 234; Medlicott, *Economic Blockade*, 2:547–581; Gordon and Dangerfield, *Hidden Weapon*, pp. 105–115.

56. Speer, *Inside the Third Reich*, p. 316; Warner, "Report on Preclusive Operations," RG 234; Blanche Britt Armfield, "Preclusive Operations in the Neutral Countries in World War II," undated, Box 890, RG 169; Medlicott, *Economic Blockade*, 2:525–546.

57. Medlicott, *Economic Blockade*, 2:417–418, 630–662. Alan S. Milward notes in *War, Economy and Society, 1939–1945* that the German "conquest of territory was a highly effective riposte to economic blockade" (p. 312).

5. "Have Not" America and the Debate over Postwar Minerals Policy

1. L. S. Cates, "Clouds Over Mining," *Mining and Metallurgy* 27 (Decem-

ber 1946): 579–582; Alan M. Bateman, "Wartime Dependence on Foreign Minerals," *Economic Geology* 41 (June–July 1946): 308–327. Other figures from Neal Potter and Francis T. Christy, Jr., *Trends in Natural Resource Commodities*, pp. 370, 376, 378. Quote in U.S. House of Representatives, Committee on Public Lands, *Strategic and Critical Minerals and Metals, Hearings*, 80th Cong., 2nd sess., pts. 4 and 5, p. 986.

2. See Appendix 1.

3. Potter and Christy, Jr., *Trends*, pp. 456, 458, 464; Bateman, "Wartime Dependence," p. 309, for quote.

4. Bateman, "Wartime Dependence," p. 314.

5. Edgar B. Nixon, ed., *Franklin D. Roosevelt and Conservation*, 2:599, 644–646. Quote on p. 599. Pinchot to William D. Hassett, April 17, 1945, White House Subject File, Box 158, Truman Papers.

6. Ickes to President Truman, May 31, 1945, White House Subject File, Box 158, Truman Papers.

7. Harold Ickes, "The War and Our Vanishing Resources," *American Magazine* 140 (December 1945): 20.

8. U.S. Department of the Interior, *Annual Report for the Year ending June 30, 1945*, pp. v–vii; Ickes, "Vanishing Resources," pp. 22 (quote), 128.

9. Cited in S. G. Lasky, "Ore-Reserve Viewpoints," *Mining and Metallurgy* 27 (September 1946): 466. See also, "Let Them Give Us Something," *Mining and Metallurgy* 25 (March 1944): 171.

10. Elmer W. Pehrson, "The Mineral Position of the United States and the Outlook for the Future," *Annual Report of the Board of Regents of the Smithsonian Institution 1945*, pp. 175–199. Quotes, pp. 176, 181.

11. " 'Have' Versus 'Have Not'," *Mining Congress Journal* 32 (March 1946): 23; "Metals and Minerals: Has the World Enough?" *Mining and Metallurgy* 26 (April 1945): 196.

12. "Making America 'Mineral Conscious'," *Mining Congress Journal* 31 (December 1945): 19; "Don't Belittle Our Mineral Resources," *Mining Congress Journal* 31 (February 1945): 26.

13. Evan Just, "A National Mineral Policy," *Engineering and Mining Journal* 146 (April 1945): 86–91. Further discussion of tax incentives appears in Harvey S. Mudd, "Postwar Demand and Supply of Minerals," *Mining and Metallurgy* 27 (January 1946): 22–24.

14. W. E. Wrather, "Mineral Resources and Mineral Resourcefulness," *Mining and Metallurgy* 27 (August 1946): 427–428. Quote, p. 428.

15. Clyde Williams, "Metals, Minerals, and Research," *Mining and Metallurgy* 28 (March 1947): 140–143. Quote, p. 143.

16. U.S. Dept. of the Interior, *Annual Report, 1946*, pp. 6–7. Quote, p. 6.

17. Ibid., pp. 7–8. Quote, p. 8.

18. Ibid., p. 8. For a full list of these projects together with results, consult U.S. House of Representatives, *Strategic Minerals*, pp. 1472–1479.

19. Interior, *Report, 1946*, pp. 8–9; Harry S. Truman, *Public Papers of the Presidents, 1947*, pp. 378–379.

20. Bateman, "Wartime Dependence," p. 325.

21. Charles K. Leith, "Principles of Foreign Mineral Policy of the United States," *Mining and Metallurgy* 27 (January 1946): 14.

22. William Y. Elliott, "Strategy and Politics of Raw Materials in Peace and War," unpublished paper, May 5, 1945, Box 233, Office of War Mobilization and Reconversion, RG 250.

23. Ibid.

24. For an introduction to this debate over postwar stockpiles, consult Glenn H. Snyder, *Stockpiling Strategic Materials*, and the official account by David Horton, *Import Policies and Programs of the War Production Board and Predecessor Agencies*, pp. 109–132. For the mining industry, "Stockpiling—Freezing Metal Stocks," *Mining Congress Journal* 30 (January 1944): 15.

25. Leahy to Nelson, September 17, 1943, 811.24/1943, State Department, RG 59; Elliott cited in Horton, *Import Policies*, p. 114; Ball's letter to Rostow, January 4, 1944, 811.24/1952, State Department, RG 59.

26. Memorandum for Paul Nitze, September 17, 1943, 811.24/1891, State Department, RG 59.

27. Memorandum for meeting of War Mobilization Committee, January 3, 1944, 112.02, War Production Board (WPB), RG 179; and Donald Nelson's protest to Byrnes, January 1, 1944, 112.02, WPB, RG 179. Elliott played a key role in boosting Nelson's resistance, January 1, 1944, 112.02, WPB, RG 179.

28. For a discussion of specific bills, see Horton, *Import Policies*, p. 128.

29. Ibid.; Fortas to Harold Smith, August 17, 1943, 811.24/1890, State Department, RG 59.

30. Memorandum, February 10, 1944, 811.24/1964, State Department, RG 59. For testimony on the Scrugham proposal, see U.S. Senate, *Stock Piles of Strategic Minerals, Hearings* on S. 1160, 78th Cong., 1st sess.

31. Snyder, *Stockpiling*, pp. 16–20; Horton, *Import Policies*, pp. 128–132.

32. Ickes to Hull, February 7, 1944, 11-34 Strategic Materials, and Michael W. Strauss to Sec. Ickes, February 8, 1944, 11-34 Strategic Materials, both in Interior Department, RG 48.

33. David E. Lockwood, *The Stockpiling of Strategic and Critical Materials: Legislative History and Analysis of Pertinent Developments 1939–1973*, p. 15; stockpiling provisions of PL 457 appear in U.S. House, *Strategic Minerals*, pp. 983–984.

34. Army-Navy Munitions Board, *A Report to Congress on Strategic Materials*, 79th Cong., 1st sess., pp. 1–15. Quotes on pp. 1, 4.

35. Ickes to James V. Forrestal, January 1, 1945, 11-34 Strategic Minerals-General, Interior Department, RG 48.

36. Ickes to J. G. Scrugham, February 22, 1945, 11-34 General, Interior Department, RG 48; memorandum, Burns to A. Z. Gardner, January 9, 1945, 811.24/1-945, State Department, RG 59.

37. Burns to Gardner, January 9, 1945, 811.24/1-945, State Department,

RG 59. For State Department testimony on S. 1160, Senator Scrugham's proposal, see U.S. House, *Strategic Minerals*, pp. 1074–1076.

38. *Congressional Record*, March 31, 1946, p. 3610. For the text, U.S. House, *Strategic Minerals*, pp. 1232–1235.

39. U.S. Congress, *Conference Report to Accompany S. 752 on Strategic and Critical Materials for National Defense Purposes*, 79th Cong., 2nd sess.

40. Ibid.

41. Ibid. For text of "Buy American" Act, see U.S. House, *Strategic Minerals*, pp. 1235–1236. Truman's statement of July 23, 1946, appears on pp. 1236–1237.

42. Julius A. Krug, "National Mineral Policies," *Mining Congress Journal* 32 (October 1946): 24–27. Quote on p. 27.

43. Harry J. Evans, "The Stock-piling Bill—S. 752," *Mining and Metallurgy* 27 (August 1946): 434–436. Quote on p. 436. *Congressional Record*, May 24, 1946, p. 5679, quote on p. 5682.

44. U.S. House, *Strategic Minerals*, pp. 1232–1235. Paine quoted on p. 933. On war materials, p. 1523.

45. U.S. House, *Strategic Minerals*, pp. 923, 1507–1509.

46. National Security Resources Board Minutes, December 4, 1947, Box 13; and NSRB R-3, December 5, 1947, Box 17, both in NSRB, RG 304.

47. U.S. House, *Strategic Minerals*, pp. 1528–1529. Paine quoted p. 932.

48. Krug to Senator O'Mahoney, May 15, 1947, 11-34 Strategic Materials-General, Interior Department, RG 48; U.S. House, *Strategic Minerals*, p. 1491.

49. U.S. Department of the Interior, *Annual Report, 1948*, pp. 42–49.

50. Ibid., pp. 43, 44. Additional material on Geological Survey and Bureau of Mines activities appears in U.S. House of Representatives, Committee on Appropriations, *Operations of the Interior Department, Hearings*, 80th Cong., 2nd sess., pt. 1, pp. 54–63.

51. Krug Report, May 19 and 20, 1948, Croston files, Box 14, NSRB, RG 304.

52. Ibid.

53. Ibid.

54. Ibid.

6. Minerals and the Cold War

1. *Foreign Relations of the U.S.: 1950 (FR)*, 1:238 (quote), 280; Alan M. Bateman, "America's Stake in World Mineral Resources," *Mining Engineering* 1 (July 1949): 25.

2. For minerals prices, see Appendix 1; President's Materials Policy Commission (PMPC), *Resources for Freedom*, 1:6; Bateman, "America's Stake," p. 25. Trade figures from Neal Potter and Francis T. Christy, Jr., *Trends in Natural Resource Commodities*.

3. Walter Millis, ed., *The Forrestal Diaries*, p. 387.

4. *FR:* *1948*, 1:546, 667.
5. Hillenkoetter to Daniel Fahey, March 8, 1950, Box 123, National Security Resources Board (NSRB), RG 304. For earlier statements, see National Security Council (NSC) 20/4, November 23, 1948, in *FR:* *1948*, 1:667; *FR:* *1949*, 1:294–339.
6. *FR:* *1948*, 1:663, 666.
7. Charles Cortez Abbott, "Economic Warfare—the Defense," unpublished paper presented to Naval War College, November 9, 1948, NSRB, RG 304.
8. Elmer W. Pehrson, "Mineral Economics," *Mining Engineering* 1 (March 1949): 50; Pehrson, "Problems of United States Mineral Supply," *Annals of the American Academy of Political and Social Science*, 278 (November 1951): 177. Another minerals specialist, Charles Will Wright, warned of Soviet moves in "Mineral Consolidation," *Mining Engineering* 1 (July 1949): 53.
9. *FR:* *1948*, 8:506. For information on Soviet-oriented Communist parties, see Robert J. Alexander, *Communism in Latin America*, pp. 83–84, 200–205. Bowers comments on his experiences, *Chile through Embassy Windows: 1939–1953*, pp. 166–170. For Bowers' letter to President Truman, see Bowers to Truman, July 18, 1950, White House Subject File, Truman Papers.
10. *FR:* *1948*, 9:759–766. "Security of Strategically Important Industrial Operations in Foreign Countries," (August 26, 1948), NSC 29, National Archives, Modern Military Records.
11. "Security of Strategically Important Industrial Operations in Foreign Countries," (October 24, 1953), NSC 163/1, Eisenhower Library.
12. Thomas Curtis to Henry Brodie, May 15, 1952, Croston files, NSRB, RG 304. See also *FR:* *1949*, 1:343.
13. John R. Steelman to James Forrestal, December 24, 1948, NSRB, RG 304; Pehrson to Bateman, December 30, 1948, Box 2, Bateman Papers.
14. "U.S. Policy toward Southeast Asia," (July 1, 1949), NSC 51, National Archives, Modern Military Records; *FR:* *1950*, 6:42–44.
15. "Areas to Which Access by the United States is Essential," June 12, 1950, Box 18, NSRB, RG 304.
16. Ibid.
17. For policymakers' concerns, see *FR:* *1948*, 1:510–529, 541–542, 546–550. As background to the Marshall Plan, Herbert Feis, *From Trust to Terror*, pp. 225–264.
18. *FR:* *1948*, 4:490, 510. Kennan memorandum quoted, p. 490.
19. U.S. Bureau of Mines memorandum on chromite, May 26, 1948, and memorandum on manganese, May 26, 1948, both NSRB, RG 304; U.S. House of Representatives, Committee on Public Lands, *Strategic and Critical Minerals and Metals, Hearings*, 80th Cong., 2nd sess., 1948.
20. Bureau of Mines, chromite memorandum, May 26, 1948, NSRB, RG 304. For public testimony on the chromite situation, see U.S. House, *Strategic Minerals*, pp. 499–665.

21. Bureau of Mines, manganese memorandum, May 26, 1948, NSRB, RG 304. For public testimony, see U.S. House, *Strategic Minerals*, pp. 1–497.
22. NSRB, Minutes, June 15, 1948, NSRB, RG 304.
23. Ibid.; see also *FR: 1948*, 4:552–554.
24. *FR: 1948*, 4:563–564, 569, 575–585; Arthur Hill to D. F. Carpenter, December 8, 1948, NSRB, RG 304.
25. Memorandum of manganese and chrome task group, December 30, 1948, RG 304; James Boyd, "The Unseen Keystone of Steel," February 21, 1950, Box 13, Boyd Papers; U.S. Bureau of Mines *Minerals Yearbook, 1949*, pp. 234–242, 741–757; "Manganese Deficit Averted," *Mining Engineering* 4 (November 1952): 1030.
26. Executive Committee on Economic Foreign Policy, Working Group on Strategic Materials, "Strategic Materials for U.S. Stockpiles under the European Recovery Program," October 27, 1947, State Department, RG 353.
27. U.S. House, *Strategic Materials*, pp. 1432–1433; Working Group on Strategic Materials, "Strategic Materials," RG 353.
28. *FR: 1947*, 1:777–778.
29. Ibid.; Working Group on Strategic Materials, "Strategic Materials," RG 353.
30. Tom Falco, "ECA's Strategic Materials Division," *Engineering and Mining Journal* 149 (September 1948): 70–74; "Your Stake in the ECA," *Engineering and Mining Journal* 149 (September 1948): 67. Quote on p. 67.
31. U.S. Mutual Security Program, *First Report to Congress* (December 31, 1952), p. 42; U.S. Mutual Security Program, *Second Report to Congress* (June 30, 1952), p. 46; Charles Will Wright, "An Accounting of World Mining for 1949," *Mining World* 12 (April 15, 1950): 24. For other information on ECA minerals projects, see U.S. Bureau of Mines, *Minerals Yearbook*, 1949, p. 22; and ibid., 1950, p. 21.
32. U.S. Department of State, *Bulletin*, January 30, 1949, p. 123. For State Department discussion of this pledge, see *FR: 1949*, 1:757–788. Other useful accounts: Bruce Carlton Netschert, "Point Four and Mineral Raw Materials," *Annals of the Association of American Geographers* 41 (June 1951): 133–145; Alan Probert, "Point IV—Medieval Mining Frontiers Pushed Back," *Mining Engineering* 4 (July 1952): 661–671.
33. Mira Wilkins, *The Maturing of Multinational Enterprise*, pp. 304–308. Howland Bancroft, "The Broadening Road to Foreign Investment," *Mining Engineering* 4 (July 1952): 666–668.
34. Marina von Neumann Whitman, *Government Risk-Sharing in Foreign Investment*, pp. 39–120. See also E. R. Barlow and Ira T. Wender, *Foreign Investment and Taxation* and Peggy Brewer Richman, *Taxation of Foreign Investment Income*.
35. Whitman, *Government Risk-Sharing*, pp. 69–120.
36. "Foreign Minerals—Our Security," *Mining Engineering* 4 (July 1952):

655. "Private Capital Outflows to Foreign Countries," *Survey of Current Business*, December 1951, p. 14.

37. "Wanted: A Foreign Mineral Policy," *Engineering and Mining Journal* 153 (October 1952): 71. For other criticisms of the State Department, see Charles Will Wright, "Mineral Consolidation," *Mining World* 15 (March 1953): 52–54.

38. "Review of the National Stockpile Program," June 21, 1950, NSRB, RG 304; Shannon to Symington, June 22, 1950, NSRB, RG 304. On stockpiling financing problems, see *FR: 1949*, 1: 364.

39. Quote in "The Threat to Raw Materials," *Intelligence Digest* 12 (October 1950): 7. See also "Drifts and Crosscuts," *Mining World* 12 (August 1950): 9; "Economic Importance of the Far East," National Intelligence Estimate 56 (March 1952), NSRB, RG 304. On reasons for U.S. intervention, see *FR: 1950*, 1 and 7.

40. Shannon to Symington, July 5, 1950, NSRB, RG 304.

41. Ibid.

42. NSRB, Board Minutes, July 21, 1950, NSRB, RG 304; U.S. President, Council of Economic Advisers, *Mid Year Economic Report, July 26, 1950*; U.S. Bureau of Mines, *Minerals Yearbook, 1951*, pp. 24–25.

43. Simon D. Strauss, "Nonferrous Metals," *Mining Engineering* 3 (February 1951): 110–112; U.S. Director of Defense Mobilization, *Building America's Might* (Report to the President, April 1, 1951), p. 30; Glenn H. Snyder, *Stockpiling Strategic Materials*, pp. 178–180.

44. "Report of the Chairman of the NSRB (January 1951)," President's Secretary's Files, Box 146, Truman Papers.

45. Willard L. Thorp, "The New International Economic Challenge," Department of State *Bulletin* 25 (August 13, 1951): 245–248. See also periodic reports of the Director of the Office of Defense Mobilization.

46. Thorp, "New Challenge," p. 247; International Materials Conference, *Report on Operations of the International Materials Conference, February 26, 1951, to March 1, 1952*, pp. 1–3.

47. Nichols to Mikesell, "Summary of Current Experience of the International Materials Conference," May 30, 1951, Box 125, PMPC.

48. H. H. Liebhafsky, "The International Materials Conference in Retrospect," *Quarterly Journal of Economics* 71 (May 1957): 267–288. Quotes appear on pp. 277, 286.

49. U.S. Senate, Committee on Interior and Insular Affairs, *Accessibility of Strategic and Critical Materials to the United States in Time of War and for Our Expanding Economy*, Report No. 1627, 83rd Cong., 2nd sess., p. 7.

50. U.S. Bureau of Mines, *Minerals Yearbook*, 1951, pp. 22–23; "Outstanding Commitments of the Federal Government under Materials Purchase Programs," undated, Box 2, Whitman Cabinet Papers, Eisenhower Papers; U.S. Senate, *Accessibility of Strategic Materials*, pp. 23–27.

51. "Economic Importance of South Asia," National Intelligence Estimate 56 (March 1952), NSRB, RG 304.

52. Ibid.
53. "Economic Importance of the Far East," National Intelligence Estimate 56 (March 1952), NSRB, RG 304.
54. "Latin American Metals and Minerals," National Intelligence Estimate 56 (July 1952), NSRB, RG 304.
55. Thomas Curtis to Henry Brodie, memorandum, May 15, 1952, NSRB, RG 304.
56. "Economic Importance of the Near and Middle East," National Intelligence Estimate 56 (March 1952), NSRB, RG 304.
57. U.S. House of Representatives, Committee on Armed Services, *United States–Vietnam Relations, 1945–1967*, 9:186, 191. This document is NSC 162/2 on "Basic National Security Policy."

7. The Paley Report: A Mid-Century Minerals Survey

1. Symington to Truman, December 27, 1950, Official File 3035, Truman Papers.
2. Minutes, U.S. President's Materials Policy Commission (hereafter cited as PMPC), January 30, 1951, Box 3, PMPC. Quote, "Background of Staff Members Is Needed," *Mining World* 14 (September 1952): 34–35. On Symington's role, see J. D. Ratcliff, "What's Left in Uncle Sam's Pantry?" *Collier's* 131 (January 10, 1953): 34–35.
3. Harry S. Truman, *Public Papers of the Presidents, 1951*, p. 118.
4. Minutes, PMPC, January 30, 1951, Box 3, PMPC.
5. PMPC, *Resources for Freedom*, 1:3.
6. Ibid.
7. Ibid., 1:5.
8. Ibid., 1:4–5.
9. Ibid., 1:2, 6; U.S. Bureau of Mines, *Minerals Yearbook, 1973*, 1:2–7.
10. PMPC, *Resources for Freedom*, 1:9.
11. For recent consumption figures and other data, see U.S. Bureau of Mines, *Commodity Data Summaries*, 1977. For commentary on projections, see Warren E. Morrison and Robert E. Johnson, Jr., "The Evolving Minerals Economy," in U.S. Bureau of Mines, *Mineral Facts and Problems*, 1970 edition, pp. 1–11.
12. PMPC, *Resources for Freedom*, 1:7–14. Quotes on pp. 10, 14.
13. On scarcity and exhaustion concepts, see Harold J. Barnett and Chandler Morse, *Scarcity and Growth*, pp. 1–13. PMPC, *Resources for Freedom*, 1:13.
14. PMPC, *Resources for Freedom*, 1:21.
15. Ibid., 1:23–26. Quote, p. 25.
16. Ibid., 1:13–14.
17. Ibid., 1:27.
18. Ibid., 1:29; 5:1–3.
19. Ibid., 1:30–32.

20. Ibid., 1:79.
21. Ibid., 1:33–35; 5:10–17.
22. Ibid., 1:33–36, quotes on pp. 33, 36.
23. Ibid., 1:59–60, quote on p. 60.
24. Ibid., 1:61, 63–64, quote p. 64.
25. Ibid., 1:64–67.
26. Ibid., 1:68–69.
27. Ibid., 1:70.
28. Ibid., 1:73–74.
29. Ibid., 1:75–77.
30. Ibid., 1:83–90, quote on p. 90.
31. Ibid., 1:163–167, quote on p. 163.
32. Bateman quote, "Meeting with Mining Geologists," May 10, 1951, pp. 49–50, Box 6, PMPC.
33. Joralemon quote, ibid., p. 52.
34. Coombs quote, ibid., p. 53.
35. Ibid., pp. 29–30, 37.
36. Ibid., pp. 41–42.
37. Feis memorandum, "Government Measures to Stimulate the Development of Raw Materials in Foreign Countries," undated, Box 124, PMPC.
38. "Summary of Minutes," February 27, 1951, Box 3, PMPC.
39. D. H. Allen, "Ways to Increase U.S. Imports of Strategic Materials from Latin America," February 20, 1951, Box 123, PMPC.
40. *Fortune* 46 (August 1952): 3; Paley to Stuart Symington, June 13, 1952, Box 1, PMPC.
41. Truman, *Public Papers, 1952*, pp. 454–455.
42. *Time*, June 30, 1952, pp. 78–80; *New Republic* 127 (July 7, 1952): 10.
43. *New York Times*, June 28, 1952; *Wall Street Journal*, June 25, 1952.
44. Henry Hazlitt, " 'Planning' for 1975," *Newsweek* 40 (September 1, 1952): 57.
45. *Congressional Record*, June 23, 1952, pp. 7839–7840, and June 28, 1952, pp. 8455–8457.
46. "Don't Let It Die," *Mining Engineering* 4 (September 1952): 855; "There'll Be Some Changes Made," *Engineering and Mining Journal* 153 (September 1952): 87.
47. "Mining Industry Spokesmen Give Their Views on 'Paley Report'," *Mining World* 14 (September 1952): 61–63. Also, Otto Herres, "What the Paley Report Means to U.S. Miners," *Engineering and Mining Journal* 153 (December 1952): 72–75.
48. S. H. Williston in "Comments on the Paley Report," *Engineering and Mining Journal* 153 (September 1952): 95.
49. Simon Strauss' comments appear in "That Paley Report," *Mining Congress Journal* 38 (December 1952): 40–42; Andrew Fletcher's comments in "Comments on Paley Report," *Engineering and Mining Journal* 153 (September 1952): 94.
50. "Chasm or Gap?" *Economist* 165 (November 22, 1952): 582.

51. James Boyd suggested how documents reveal a change in national policy in U.S. Congress, Joint Committee on Defense Production, *Federal Materials Policy, Part I*, pp. 15–16.

8. From Scarcity to Plenty—President Eisenhower and Cold War Minerals Policy, 1953–1963

1. Paley to Eisenhower, December 15, 1952, Box 922, President's Materials Policy Commission (PMPC); Eisenhower to Horace Albright, October 2, 1952, Official File 134-G, Eisenhower Papers (hereafter DDE).
2. Office of Defense Mobilization, "Staff Report on Major Problems in the Strategic and Critical Materials Area, with Emphasis on the Principal Ferro-alloys," July 14, 1952, National Security Resources Board (NSRB), RG 304.
3. "A Time of Crisis," *Engineering and Mining Journal* 154 (February 1953): 71. On conditions in the minerals industries, consult annual volumes of U.S. Bureau of Mines, *Minerals Yearbook*, and annual surveys in the February issue of *Engineering and Mining Journal*, especially 1953 and 1954.
4. See Chapter 7.
5. Hans H. Landsberg, Leonard L. Fischman, and Joseph L. Fisher, *Resources in America's Future*, pp. 3–12, 488–496. Quote on p. 10.
6. On minerals prices, see Appendix 1.
7. Eisenhower Diary, July 2, 1953, Box 5, DDE. Quotations in the following paragraph are from the same source.
8. James T. Patterson, *Mr. Republican: A Biography of Robert A. Taft*, pp. 474–496, considers the Ohio senator's shifting position, which was critical of troop commitments to Western Europe and sympathetic to use of U.S. airpower to win the Korean War.
9. Hauge to Eisenhower, July 28, 1956, Whitman Administrative files, Box 19, DDE; Hauge to Lincoln Gordon, June 30, 1953, Official File 116-M, DDE.
10. Gerald Morgan to Hauge, April 24, 1953, Official File 116-M, DDE; Hauge to Sherman Adams, April 25, 1953, Box 1, Hauge Papers; U.S. Commission on Foreign Economic Policy (hereafter CFEP), *Report to the President and the Congress* (January 1954), pp. 91–93, quotation on pp. 92–93.
11. CFEP, *Report*, pp. 12–27. Quotations on pp. 17, 18.
12. Ibid., p. 35.
13. "Mineral Raw Materials in Defense and Foreign Trade Policies," Report Area 8, No. 6 (December 12, 1953), Box 47, CFEP Papers, Eisenhower Library; CFEP, *Report*, p. 40.
14. CFEP, *Report*, p. 80.
15. C. E. Wilson to Gabriel Hauge, "Preliminary Department of Defense

Views on the Randall Commission Report," February 12, 1954, Official File 116-M, DDE; CFEP, *Staff Papers*, p. 223.

16. *Life*, June 21, 1954, p. 130.

17. U.S. Senate, Committee on Interior and Insular Affairs, *Accessibility of Strategic and Critical Materials to the United States in Time of War and for Our Expanding Economy*, Report No. 1627, 83rd Cong., 2nd sess., pp. 1, 13, 30.

18. Ibid., p. 14.

19. Ibid., pp. 4–5.

20. Ibid., p. 156.

21. Ibid., pp. 17, 21.

22. U.S. Senate, Committee on Interior and Insular Affairs, *Stockpile and Accessibility of Strategic and Critical Materials to the United States in Time of War, Hearings pursuant to S. Res. 143*, 83d Cong., 1st sess., 1:35–45. For recent supply characteristics, U.S. Department of the Interior, *Mining and Minerals Policy, 1976*, pp. 24–25. Even Elmer W. Pehrson, prominent exponent of the so-called "have-not" thesis, allowed that for purposes of security the U.S. "should stimulate the production of those minerals in the Western Hemisphere for which we are now dependent on the Eastern Hemisphere." See Senate, *Stockpile Hearings*, 1:242–245. For a recent assessment, note International Economic Studies Institute, *Raw Materials and Foreign Policy*, p. 104.

23. E. H. Weaver to George Landry, undated memorandum, lot 63A-199, Office of Civil and Defense Mobilization (OCDM), RG 304.

24. Dwight D. Eisenhower, *Public Papers of the Presidents, 1953*, pp. 713–714.

25. U.S. Senate, Committee on Armed Services, *Inquiry into the Strategic and Critical Material Stockpiles of the United States, Hearings*, 87th Cong., 2nd sess., 4:1080–1085.

26. Ibid.

27. Ibid.

28. Ibid.

29. Leslie S. Wright to Franklin M. Aaronson and William N. Lawrence, March 8, 1957, lot 72A-6638, Office of Emergency Preparedness (OEP), RG 396.

30. Legislative Leadership Meeting, March 22, 1954, Supplementary Notes, Whitman Legislative Meetings, Box 1, DDE.

31. U.S. Bureau of Mines, *Minerals Yearbook, 1954*, 1:12–13. On the State Department view, see Senate, *Inquiry*, 4:1092–1097, quotations on pp. 1092, 1094; Hauge to General Persons, August 23, 1954, Box 11, Areeda Papers. Herbert Hoover also favored stockpile purchases, Eisenhower to Arthur Flemming, July 1, 1954, Whitman Administrative File, Box 15, DDE.

32. U.S. Senate, Committee on Armed Services, *Inquiry into the Strategic and Critical Material Stockpiles of the United States, Draft Report*, 88th Cong., 1st sess., pp. 36–44.

33. Glenn H. Snyder, *Stockpiling Strategic Materials*, pp. 196–209; Wilton B. Persons to Rep. James T. Patterson, October 14, 1955, Official File 134-E-2, DDE; *Minerals Yearbook, 1955*, pp. 387, 420.
34. *Minerals Yearbook, 1955*, pp. 141–143, 841; *Minerals Yearbook, 1956*, pp. 869–870.
35. Eisenhower Diary, July 24, 1953, Box 5, DDE; Eisenhower Diary, January 11, 1956, Box 5, DDE.
36. Cabinet Paper (CP-57-60/1), February 1, 1957, Whitman Cabinet Files, Box 8, DDE; Kestnbaum memorandum of conversation with Broadbent, May 22, 1957, Box 11, Kestnbaum Papers; Legislative Leadership Meeting, July 2, 1957, Supplementary Notes, Whitman Legislative Meetings, Box 2, DDE.
37. Snyder, *Stockpiling Strategic Materials*, pp. 227–232.
38. Ibid., pp. 105–108, 227–232.
39. Report of Special Stockpile Advisory Committee, January 28, 1958, Official File 133-J, Box 663, DDE.
40. Cabinet Paper (CP-58-78/1), April 22, 1958, Whitman Cabinet File, Box 11, DDE; Senate, *Inquiry, Draft*, pp. 12–14, 18.
41. Cabinet Paper (CP-58-78/1).
42. The next stockpile reassessment began early in 1962 when President John Kennedy ordered the director of the Office of Emergency Preparedness to chair an executive review. It recommended a study to consider stockpile requirements for postnuclear war reconstruction, a problem recognized earlier. Also the executive task force urged consideration of including a reserve for allied war production needs in the U.S. strategic and critical materials stockpile. Significantly, this review recommended retaining the three-year planning period as the base for tabulating stockpile objectives.
43. Senate, *Inquiry, Draft*, pp. 17, 61. Quotation on p. 61.
44. Ibid., pp. 62–66. Quotation on p. 66. The Eisenhower administration was aware of problems with the Defense Production Act inventory. In an internal study it found that $244 million of the $632 million supply in December 1958 did not meet stockpile specifications. Low-quality tungsten, metallurgical manganese and chromite made up much of the unsatisfactory material. OCDM Staff Report on the Program for Strategic Materials, Cabinet Paper (CP-58-78/2), August 20, 1959, Whitman Cabinet File, Box 7, DDE.
45. On Benson, see his *Cross Fire*. Eisenhower quotation from Legislative Leadership Meeting, July 2, 1957, Supplementary Notes, Whitman Legislative Meetings, Box 2, DDE; Memorandum to Council on Foreign Economic Policy (CFEP 542/1), November 13, 1956, Box 1, Francis Papers; Senate, *Inquiry, Draft*, pp. 32–33.
46. Senate, *Inquiry, Draft*, p. 18.
47. Ibid., p. 121.
48. For details, consult annual volumes of *Minerals Yearbook*.

49. Thorsten V. Kalijarvi to Arthur Flemming, June 12, 1955, Box 680, DDE; American Smelting and Refining Company, *Annual Report*, 1954, p. 2.

50. Charles R. Ince, "Zinc," *Engineering and Mining Journal* 160 (February 1959): 107; Robert L. Ziegfeld, "Lead," *Engineering and Mining Journal* 160 (February 1959): 110.

51. Eisenhower to Sherman Adams, May 16, 1958, Box 11, Areeda Papers.

52. Joseph Rand to Clarence B. Randall, July 29, 1958, Box 1, Rand Papers.

53. Benson's opposition helped kill the proposal, *Cross Fire*, pp. 397–399; Eisenhower disagreed with Benson in Eisenhower to Benson, May 17, 1958, Diary, Box 20, DDE. "The New Subsidy Plan," *Engineering and Mining Journal* 159 (June 1958): 661. American Smelting and Refining Company, *Annual Report, 1959*, p. 9; *Wall Street Journal*, May 12, 1958.

54. "President Suspends Consideration of Lead and Zinc Tariffs," U.S. Department of State *Bulletin*, July 14, 1958, p. 69.

55. "President Limits Imports of Lead and Zinc," U.S. Department of State *Bulletin*, October 13, 1958, pp. 579–580.

56. *El Comercio* (Lima, Peru), September 23, 1958; *Melbourne Herald* (Australia), September 24, 1958; *London Times*, September 25, 1958; *American Metal Market*, September 27, 1958.

57. Paul Cullen to Gordon Gray, October 23, 1958, Box 6, Paarlberg Papers; Council on Foreign Economic Policy, *Handbook Foreign Economic Policy of the United States*, December 31, 1958, lot 63A-263, OCDM, RG 304.

58. For background on commodity agreements, consult John W. F. Rowe, *Primary Commodities in International Trade*, pp. 155–183. An interesting Latin American perspective appears in Víctor Andrade, *My Missions for Revolutionary Bolivia, 1944–1962*, a book written by a former Bolivian ambassador to the U.S. On Malayan tin, see "Report of the U.S. Tin Mission to Malaya," November 22, 1951, Lot 63A-199, OCDM, RG 304.

59. Hauge to Adams, November 16, 1953, Box 1, Hauge Papers; Walter B. Smith to Douglas McKay, June 8, 1953; Wormser to George Humphrey, September 15, 1953; and Wormser to Thorsten V. Kalijarvi, October 22, 1953, all 11-34 Tin, Official Files, DDE. Also, Council on Foreign Economic Policy, *Handbook Foreign Economic Policy of the United States*, and Memo to Council (CFEP 531), June 28, 1958, in Lot 63-A-263, OCDM, RG 304.

60. Joseph Rand to Colonel Cullen, September 23, 1959, Box 6, Rand Papers; Royce A. Hardy remarks to Council on Foreign Economic Policy, October 8, 1959, Lot 63-A-263, OCDM, RG 304.

61. "Note on Lead and Zinc Meeting," July 19, 1960, DDE; "Lead and Zinc," August 5, 1960, Box 6, Paarlberg Papers.

62. Thomas C. Mann to Phillip Areeda, Official File 99-Z, Box 680, DDE.

63. Dwight D. Eisenhower, *Public Papers of the Presidents, 1960*, pp. 671–672.

64. *Minerals Yearbook, 1961*, 1:766–767; *Minerals Yearbook, 1962*, 1:754.

65. Samuel C. Waugh to Edmund Mansure, September 22, 1954, Lot 73-A-1051, OEP, RG 396; Senate, *Inquiry, Draft*, p. 71; Douglas Dillon to Clarence B. Randall, April 30, 1960, Lot 63-A-263, OCDM, RG 304.

66. "Will the Momentum of the 50's Carry Over into the 60's?" *Engineering and Mining Journal* 161 (February 1960) : 89; for official assessments of trends, see U.S. Bureau of Mines, *Mineral Facts and Problems, 1960*.

67. U.S. Congress, Joint Committee on Defense Production, *Federal Materials Policy, Part I*, p. 148; Mira Wilkins, *The Maturing of Multinational Enterprise*, pp. 329–331, 392.

68. Theodore C. Sorensen, *Kennedy*, p. 228; Nixon and Dulles quotes in Edwin H. Arnold, "Mobilizing America for Free World Economic Development," July 7, 1958, Box 7, Rand Papers. Similar interpretations emerge in Walt Whitman Rostow, *The Diffusion of Power, 1957–1962*, pp. 21–27, 54–55.

69. U.S. Senate, Committee on Armed Services, *Inquiry, Hearings*, 9:3238–3239; William Y. Elliott, undated memorandum, Lot 72A-2036, OEP, RG 396.

70. Sorensen, *Kennedy*, p. 636; see also Arthur Schlesinger, Jr., *A Thousand Days*, p. 575.

71. Leo A. Hoegh to Gen. Andrew Goodpaster, July 15, 1960, Lot 73A-1051, OEP, RG 396.

72. Lyman Kirkpatrick to Edward McDermott, September 23, 1963, Lot 72A-2036-4; Edward A. McDermott to G. Griffith Johnson, August 31, 1962, Lot 72A-6638, OEP, RG 396.

73. Frank Huddle to Elliott, undated memorandum, and "Planning a National Materials Policy for the Cold War," August 17, 1962, both in Lot 72A-2036, OEP, RG 396.

74. Huddle to Elliott, undated memorandum, both in Lot 72A-2036, OEP, RG 396.

75. Quote from Edward McDermott oral interview, May 22, 1964, Kennedy Library, p. 31.

76. Report of the Executive Stockpile Committee, March 19, 1962, Box 16, White Papers; Elliott quoted in Franklin P. Huddle, "The Evolving National Policy For Materials," *Science* 191 (February 20, 1976) : 656.

77. Walter Heller and Kermit Gordon memorandum to Lee C. White and Carl Kaysen, December 22, 1962, Box 372, Kaysen Papers. International Economic Studies Institute, *Raw Materials*, pp. 258–273. For a discussion of stockpile sales see U.S. Congress, Office of Technology Assessment, *An Assessment of Alternative Economic Stockpiling Policies*, pp. 241–251.

9. The Scramble for Resources Renewed

1. On price changes, see Appendix 1.
2. U.S. House of Representatives, Committee on Foreign Affairs, *Global Scarcities in an Interdependent World, Hearings,* 93d Cong., 2nd sess., pp. 231, 240.
3. International Economic Studies Institute (IESI), *Raw Materials and Foreign Policy,* p. 15; U.S. National Commission on Materials Policy (NCMP), *Material Needs and the Environment Today and Tomorrow: Final Report,* pp. 2–17.
4. U.S. National Commission on Supplies and Shortages (NCSS), *Government and the Nation's Resources,* pp. 50–62; U.S. Congress, Congressional Budget Office, *U.S. Raw Materials Policy: Problems and Possible Solutions,* pp. 27–29. See also economist Otto Eckstein's comments on the shortage of primary processing capacity in U.S. Senate, Committee on Government Operations, *Material Shortages, Hearings,* 93d Cong., 2nd sess., pp. 105–111.
5. NCMP, *Material Needs,* pp. 4B-19; U.S. Department of Interior, *Mining and Minerals Policy, 1977: Annual Report of the Secretary of the Interior under the Mining and Minerals Policy Act of 1970,* pp. 84–85.
6. IESI, *Raw Materials,* pp. 350–374; U.S. Comptroller General, *Domestic Policy Issues Stemming from U.S. Direct Investment Abroad,* p. 61. The Interior Department calculates 150 complete or partial nationalizations of foreign mining enterprises between 1960 and 1974. See U.S. Department of Interior, *Mining and Minerals Policy, 1977,* p. 144.
7. IESI, *Raw Materials,* p. 22; U.S. Comptroller General, *Domestic Policy Issues,* p. 61; NCSS, *Nation's Resources,* pp. 37–38.
8. NCSS, *Nation's Resources,* pp. 47–62.
9. Walt Whitman Rostow, "Kondratieff, Schumpeter, and Kuznets: Trend Periods Revisited," *Journal of Economic History* 35 (December 1975): 719–753, quote on p. 750. See also Rostow, *The World Economy: History and Prospect,* pp. 287–298.
10. IESI, *Raw Materials,* pp. 14–22, 81; Eugene Cameron, "The Contribution of the United States to National and World Mineral Supplies," in *The Mineral Position of the United States, 1975–2000,* edited by Eugene Cameron, pp. 10–12. On the current minerals deficit, see U.S. Congress, Office of Technology Assessment, *Engineering Implications of Chronic Materials Scarcity,* p. 11.
11. On investments and international law, IESI, *Raw Materials,* pp. 350–374. Mira Wilkins, *The Maturing of Multinational Enterprise,* pp. 321–323, discusses briefly the Iranian intervention.
12. IESI, *Raw Materials,* pp. 34–37.
13. Concern about Soviet ambitions in Africa emerges in Robert L. Schuettinger, ed., *South Africa—The Vital Link,* and Walter F. Hahn and Alvin J. Cottrell, *Soviet Shadow Over Africa.* David Rees discusses the strategy of denying resources to the West in "Soviet Strategic Penetra-

tion of Africa," *Conflict Studies* 77 (November 1976): 2–3. And, from the Soviet side E. A. Tarabrin, an African specialist with the Soviet Academy of Sciences, notes how African nations can nationalize resources to prevent foreign capital from inflicting "additional damage on the economy of a young country" and in the process weaken global imperialism. "The government policies of Algeria, Zambia and Guinea, where specific measures have been adopted to see that the raw material resources serve the country's own interests and where use has been made of the factor of the inter-imperialist struggle, show what opportunities in this direction lie open to a developing country." Tarabrin, *The New Scramble for Africa*, p. 195.

Growing concern about a Soviet arms buildup and expansionist activity in Africa has precipitated a series of warnings from influential specialists and former policymakers. The Committee on Present Danger issued a statement April 4, 1977, "What Is the Soviet Union Up To?" claiming that the ultimate Soviet objective remained a "Communist world order." In pursuit of that goal Moscow sought to undercut "the economic links connecting the 'capitalist' world, and especially the United States, with the countries of the Third World, on the assumption that lack of access to the raw materials, labor and markets available in these countries would throw the industrialized democracies into a series of fatal convulsions." Another warning appears in Patrick Wall, ed., *The Southern Oceans and the Security of the Free World: New Studies in Global Strategy.*

14. U.S. Congress, Congressional Budget Office, *Raw Materials Policy*, pp. 9–18; IESI, *Raw Materials*, pp. 91–110.
15. On the origins of NCMP, see Franklin P. Huddle, "The Evolving National Policy for Materials," *Science* 191 (February 20, 1976): 654–659. On NCMP goals, see NCMP, *Material Needs*, p. 9.
16. NCMP, *Material Needs*, pp. 9–24, 9–26.
17. Huddle, "Evolving National Policy," p. 657; NCSS, *Nation's Resources*, pp. ix–xii.
18. Huddle, "Evolving National Policy," pp. 654–659.
19. NCSS, *Nation's Resources*, p. ix, 28.
20. Ibid., pp. 127–154.
21. U.S. Congress, Congressional Budget Office, *Raw Materials Policy*, pp. 13–17; Nelson A. Rockefeller, *Critical Choices for Americans: Vital Resources—Reports on Energy, Food & Raw Materials*, pp. 151–153.
22. U.S. Bureau of Mines, *Mineral Facts and Problems* (Bulletin 650), pp. 1–4; "Slower Growth Projected for Mining," *Engineering and Mining Journal* 179 (January 1978): 63–68.
23. "The 'Price' of Oil," *Mining Journal* 289 (August 26, 1977): 153; "Outlook for Metal Markets Brighter in 1978," *IMF Survey*, February 6, 1978, p. 34. On Chilean copper, "False Dawn for Copper?" *Mining Journal* 290 (April 7, 1978): 250.

24. IESI, *Raw Materials*, pp. 111–127; NCSS, *Nation's Resources*, pp. 28–29.

25. U.S. Bureau of Mines, *Mineral Commodity Summaries 1978*, pp. 34, 42, 126, 184; "Contest in Africa," *Mining Journal* 289 (July 8, 1977): 21–23.

26. "Contest in Africa," *Mining Journal* 289 (July 8, 1977): 22.

27. Rockefeller, *Vital Resources*, 1:145–151.

28. Ibid., 1:162–163.

29. U.S. Congress, Congressional Budget Office, *Raw Materials Policy*, p. 36; criticisms of economic stockpiling include "Commodities: American Stockpiles, Reserves and Buffers," *Economist*, December 25, 1976, p. 77.

30. *Wall Street Journal*, February 16 and October 10, 1977.

31. *Wall Street Journal*, February 16, 1977; "New Attractions for Stockpiles," *Mining Journal* 283 (July 12, 1974): 30–31.

32. Franklin P. Huddle discussed materials substitution in an interview on March 14, 1977. U.S. Congress, Office of Technology Assessment, *Engineering Implications*, pp. 8–16. On new techniques of exploration for copper, see Lyman H. Hart, "Mineral Science and the Future of Metals," *Mining Engineering* 25 (April 1973): 57–63.

33. *Wall Street Journal*, April 2 and June 14, 1976; "Strength in Substitutes," *Barron's*, January 7, 1974, p. 11; U.S. Congress, Office of Technology Assessment, *Engineering Implications*, p. 25; Rockefeller, *Vital Resources*, 1: 158–160.

34. U.S. Congress, Office of Technology Assessment, *Engineering Implications*, p. 24.

35. Ibid., p. 15.

36. IESI, *Raw Materials*, pp. 231–257; U.S. Department of Interior, *Mining and Minerals Policy 1977*, pp. 133–137. Interior estimates ocean mineral capacity could reach ten million tons of annual recovery by 1985, p. 134; *Wall Street Journal*, July 31, 1978.

37. Bension Varon and Kenji Takeuchi, "Developing Countries and Non-Fuel Minerals," *Foreign Affairs* 52 (April 1974): 508; IESI, *Raw Materials*, p. 38.

38. IESI, *Raw Materials*, pp. 38–96.

39. "Bankrolling World Resources," *Business Week*, April 26, 1976, p. 33; Henry A. Kissinger, "UNCTAD IV: Expanding Cooperation for Global Economic Development," in U.S. Department of State, *Bulletin* 74 (May 31, 1976): 657–672.

40. "A Push To Tap New Resources," *Business Week*, July 18, 1977, p. 18; Julius L. Katz, "International Commodity Policy," U.S. Department of State, *Bulletin* 78 (March 1978): 1–6; C. Fred Bergsten, "The Policy of the United States toward International Commodity Agreements," U.S. Treasury news release, February 21, 1978.

41. "Shaping U.S. Minerals Policy," in Jimmy Carter, *Weekly Compilation of Presidential Documents*, December 19, 1977, p. 1854.

Epilogue

1. Brooks Adams, *The New Empire*, pp. 3–4; Ellen Churchill Semple, *American History and Its Geographic Conditions*. Harold and Margaret Sprout display a keen sensitivity to environmental factors in *Toward a Politics of the Planet Earth*, pp. 284–296. On history textbooks, see Eckes, "American History Textbooks and the New Issues of Trade, Payments, and Raw Materials," *History Teacher* 11 (February 1978): 237–246.

2. Gabriel Kolko, *Main Currents in Modern American History*, pp. viii–ix.

3. U.S. Central Intelligence Agency, *The International Energy Situation: Outlook to 1985*, pp. 12–13.

4. James Frederick McDivitt and Gerald Manners, *Minerals and Men*, p. 78; U.S. Bureau of Mines, *Mineral Facts and Problems* (Bulletin 667), p. 350; William D. Nordhaus, "Resources as a Constraint on Growth," *American Economic Review* 64 (May 1974): 22–27, quote p. 24. For a brief history of pessimistic government predictions on oil and gas, see *Congressional Record*, June 10, 1977, p. E 3669.

5. Raymond F. Mikesell, *Nonfuel Minerals: U.S. Investment Policies Abroad*, p. 10.

6. U.S. Congress, Joint Committee on Defense Production, *Federal Materials Policy (Part I)*, p. 16.

Bibliography

Manuscript Collections

Areeda, Phillip E., Papers. Eisenhower Library, Abilene, Kansas.

Army-Navy Munitions Board. National Archives, Record Group 225.

Assistant Secretary of War, Planning Branch, 1921–1941. National Archives, Record Group 107.

Bateman, Alan M., Papers. Sterling Library, Yale University, New Haven, Connecticut.

Blaisdell, Thomas C., Papers. Truman Library, Independence, Missouri.

Blough, Roy, Papers. Truman Library, Independence, Missouri.

Boyd, James, Papers. Truman Library, Independence, Missouri.

Bureau of Foreign and Domestic Commerce. National Archives, Record Group 151.

Bureau of Mines. Washington National Records Center, Record Group 70.

Califano, Joseph A., Office Files. Johnson Library, Austin, Texas.

Chapman, Oscar, Papers. Truman Library, Independence, Missouri.

Clayton, Will, and Thorp, Willard L., Office Files. Truman Library, Independence, Missouri.

Combined Boards. National Archives, Record Group 179.

Commerce Department. National Archives, Record Group 40.

Coolidge, Calvin, Papers. Microfilm available in Ohio State University Library, Columbus, Ohio.

Council of National Defense, Advisory Commission, Records. Roosevelt Library, Hyde Park, New York.

Cox, Oscar, Papers. Roosevelt Library, Hyde Park, New York.

Culbertson, William S., Papers. Library of Congress.

Dodge, Joseph M., Papers. Eisenhower Library, Abilene, Kansas.

Edminster, Lynn R., Papers. Truman Library, Independence, Missouri.

Eisenhower, Dwight D., Papers. Eisenhower Library, Abilene, Kansas.

Feldman, Myer, Staff Files. Kennedy Library, Waltham, Massachusetts.

Foreign Economic Administration. Washington National Records Center, Record Group 169.

Francis, Clarence, Papers. Eisenhower Library, Abilene, Kansas.

Harding, Warren, Papers. Ohio Historical Society, Columbus, Ohio.

Hauge, Gabriel, Papers. Eisenhower Library, Abilene, Kansas.
Henderson, Leon, Papers. Roosevelt Library, Hyde Park, New York.
Hoover, Herbert, Papers. Hoover Library, West Branch, Iowa.
Hopkins, Harry, Papers. Roosevelt Library, Hyde Park, New York.
Interior Department. National Archives, Record Group 48.
Jacoby, Neil, Papers. Eisenhower Library, Abilene, Kansas.
Johnson, Lyndon B., Papers. Johnson Library, Austin, Texas.
Jones, Jesse, Papers. Library of Congress.
Kaysen, Carl, Files. Kennedy Library, Waltham, Massachusetts.
Kennedy, John F., Papers. Kennedy Library, Waltham, Massachusetts.
Kestnbaum, Meyer, Papers. Eisenhower Library, Abilene, Kansas.
Krug, Julius, Papers. Library of Congress.
Leith, Charles K., Papers. University of Wisconsin, Madison, Wisconsin.
Morgan, Gerald, Papers. Eisenhower Library, Abilene, Kansas.
National Security Resources Board. National Archives, Record Group 304.
Office of Civil and Defense Mobilization. Washington National Records Center, Record Group 304.
Office of Emergency Preparedness. Washington National Records Center, Record Group 396.
Office of Strategic Services. National Archives, Record Group 226.
Office of War Mobilization and Reconversion. National Archives, Record Group 250.
Paarlberg, Don, Papers. Eisenhower Library, Abilene, Kansas.
President's Commission on Foreign Economic Policy (Randall Commission). Eisenhower Library, Abilene, Kansas.
President's Materials Policy Commission (Paley Commission). Truman Library, Independence, Missouri.
Rand, Joseph, Papers. Eisenhower Library, Abilene, Kansas.
Reconstruction Finance Corporation. National Archives, Record Group 234.
Redfield, William C., Papers. Library of Congress.
Roosevelt, Franklin D., Papers. Roosevelt Library, Hyde Park, New York.
Snyder, John W., Papers. Truman Library, Independence, Missouri.
State Department. National Archives. Record Groups 59 and 353.
Truman, Harry S., Papers. Truman Library, Independence, Missouri.
Wallace, Henry A., Papers. Roosevelt Library, Hyde Park, New York.
Wallace, Henry A., Papers. University of Iowa, Iowa City, Iowa.
War Production Board. National Archives, Record Group 179.
Waugh, Samuel, Papers. Eisenhower Library, Abilene, Kansas.
White, Lee, Files. Kennedy Library, Waltham, Massachusetts.
Wilbur, Ray L., Papers. Hoover Library, West Branch, Iowa.
Wilson, Hugh, Papers. Hoover Library, West Branch, Iowa.

Dissertations and Unpublished Papers

Allen, Dan Charles. "Franklin D. Roosevelt and the Development of an

American Occupation Policy in Europe." Ph.D. dissertation, Ohio State University, 1976.

Chalk, Frank. "The United States and the International Struggle for Rubber, 1914–1941." Ph.D. dissertation, University of Wisconsin, 1970.

Christman, Calvin Lee. "Ferdinand Eberstadt and the Economic Mobilization for War, 1941–1943." Ph.D. dissertation, Ohio State University, 1971.

Official Documents

Bergsten, C. Fred. "The Policy of the United States toward International Commodity Agreements." U.S. Treasury news release, February 21, 1978.

Carter, Jimmy. *Weekly Compilation of Presidential Documents.* December 19, 1977.

Eisenhower, Dwight D. *Public Papers of the Presidents of the United States.* 8 vols. Washington: Government Printing Office, 1960–1961.

Furness, J. W. *The Marketing of Manganese Ore* (U.S. Department of Commerce Trade Information Bulletin 599). Washington: Government Printing Office, 1929.

Gini, Corrado. *Report on Problem of Raw Materials and Foodstuffs.* Geneva: League of Nations, 1921.

Horton, David. *Import Policies and Programs of the War Production Board and Predecessor Agencies: May 1940 to November 1945.* Washington: War Production Board, 1947.

International Labor Office, Geneva. *Papers Relating to Schemes of International Organization for the Distribution of Raw Materials and Foodstuffs.* Geneva: International Labor Office, 1920.

International Materials Conference. *Report on Operations of the International Materials Conference, February 26, 1951, to March 1, 1952.* Washington: International Materials Conference, 1952.

Johnson, Lyndon B. *Public Papers of the Presidents of the United States.* 10 vols. Washington: Government Printing Office, 1965–1970.

Katz, Julius L. "International Commodity Policy." In U.S. Department of State *Bulletin* 78 (March 1978): 1–6.

Kennedy, John F. *Public Papers of the Presidents of the United States.* 3 vols. Washington: Government Printing Office, 1962–1964.

Kinzie, George R. *Copper Policies of the War Production Board and Predecessor Agencies: May 1940 to November 1945.* Washington: War Production Board, 1947.

Kissinger, Henry A. "UNCTAD IV: Expanding Cooperation for Global Economic Development." In U.S. Department of State *Bulletin* 74 (May 31, 1976): 657–672.

League of Nations. *Statistical Yearbook.* Geneva: League of Nations, annual, 1927–1938.

———. *World Economic Survey, 1939–1941.* Geneva: League of Nations, 1941.

———. Economic and Financial Section. *Memorandum on the Iron and Steel Industry.* Geneva: League of Nations, 1927.

———. Secretariat. Economic, Financial and Transit Department. *Raw Material Problems and Policies.* Geneva: League of Nations, 1946.

Nixon, Richard M. *Public Papers of the Presidents of the United States.* 6 vols. Washington: Government Printing Office, 1971–1975.

Spencer, Vivian Eberle. *Raw Materials in the United States Economy, 1900–1969.* Washington: Bureau of the Census, 1972.

Truman, Harry S. *Public Papers of the Presidents of the United States.* 8 vols. Washington: Government Printing Office, 1961–1966.

United Kingdom. *Parliamentary Papers.* "Dominions Royal Commission: Final Report," Cd. 8462, 1917–1918, vol. 10.

U.S. Army-Navy Munitions Board. *A Report to Congress on Strategic Materials.* 79th Cong., 1st sess., 1945.

U.S. Bureau of Mines. *Commodity Data Summaries, 1977.* Washington: Bureau of Mines, 1977.

———. *Mineral Commodity Summaries, 1978.* Washington: Bureau of Mines, 1978.

———. *Mineral Facts and Problems.* (Bulletin 585) 3d ed. Washington: Government Printing Office, 1960.

———. *Mineral Facts and Problems.* (Bulletin 650) 4th ed. Washington: Government Printing Office, 1970.

———. *Mineral Facts and Problems.* (Bulletin 667) Bicentennial ed. Washington: Government Printing Office, 1976.

———. *Mineral Raw Materials: Survey of Commerce and Sources in Major Industrial Countries.* New York: McGraw-Hill, 1937.

———. *Mineral Resources of the United States.* Washington: Public Affairs Press, 1948.

———. *Minerals Yearbook.* Washington: Government Printing Office, annual.

U.S. Central Intelligence Agency. *The International Energy Situation: Outlook to 1985.* Washington: CIA, April 1977.

U.S. Commission on Foreign Economic Policy. *Report to the President and the Congress.* Washington: Government Printing Office, 1954.

———. *Staff Papers.* Washington: Government Printing Office, 1954.

U.S. Commission on Population Growth and the American Future. *Population, Resources and the Environment, Research Report 3,* edited by Ronald Ridker. Washington: Government Printing Office, 1972.

U.S. Comptroller General. *Deep Ocean Mining—Actions Needed to Make It Happen.* Washington: U.S. General Accounting Office, June 28, 1978.

———. *Domestic Policy Issues Stemming from U.S. Direct Investment Abroad.* Washington: U.S. General Accounting Office, January 16, 1978.

U.S. Congress. *Conference Report to Accompany S. 752 on Strategic and Critical Materials for National Defense Purposes.* 79th Cong., 2nd sess., 1946.

———. *Congressional Record.* 75th–95th Cong. (1937–1978).

——. Congressional Budget Office. *Commodity Initiatives of Less Developed Countries: U.S. Responses and Costs.* Washington: Government Printing Office, May 1977.

——. ——. *U.S. Raw Materials Policy: Problems and Possible Solutions.* Washington: Government Printing Office, December 28, 1976.

——. Joint Committee on Defense Production. *Federal Materials Policy, Part 1: Recommendations for Action, 1952–1976.* Washington: Government Printing Office, 1976.

——. Office of Technology Assessment. *An Assessment of Alternative Economic Stockpiling Policies.* Washington: Government Printing Office, August 1976.

——. ——. *Engineering Implications of Chronic Materials Scarcity.* Washington: Government Printing Office, 1977.

U.S. Department of Commerce. Bureau of the Census. *Historical Statistics of the United States, Colonial Times to 1970.* 2 vols. Washington: Government Printing Office, 1975.

U.S. Department of Energy. Energy Information Administration. *Annual Report to Congress, 1977.* Washington: Government Printing Office, May 1978.

U.S. Department of the Interior. *Annual Report of the Secretary of the Interior.* Washington: Government Printing Office, annual.

——. *Mining and Minerals Policy. Annual Report of the Secretary of the Interior under the Mining and Minerals Policy Act of 1970.* Washington: Government Printing Office, annual.

——. *National Resources and Foreign Aid.* Washington: Government Printing Office, 1947.

U.S. Department of State. *Bulletin.* Vols. 1–78. (1939–1978).

——. *Foreign Relations of the United States.* (Annual volumes 1913–1950). Washington: Government Printing Office, 1920–1976.

U.S. Director of Defense Mobilization. *Building America's Might.* (Report to the President, April 1, 1951.) Washington: Government Printing Office, 1951.

U.S. Federal Trade Commission. *Report on the Copper Industry.* Washington: Government Printing Office, 1947.

U.S. Geological Survey. *Preliminary Report on the Mineral Resources of the United States in 1918.* Washington: Government Printing Office, 1918.

——. *Report upon Certain Deficient Strategic Materials.* Washington: Government Printing Office, 1940.

U.S. House of Representatives. Committee on Appropriations. *Operations of the Interior Department, Hearings.* 80th Cong., 2nd sess., 1948.

——. Committee on Armed Services. *United States–Vietnam Relations, 1945–1967.* 92nd Cong., 1st sess., 1972, 12 vols.

——. Committee on Foreign Affairs. *Global Scarcities in an Interdependent World, Hearings.* 93rd Cong., 2nd sess., May 1974.

——. Committee on Public Lands. *Hearings on National Minerals Act of 1949.* 81st Cong., 1st sess., 1949.

————. ————. *Strategic and Critical Minerals and Metals, Hearings.* 80th Cong., 2nd sess., 1948.

————. Interstate and Foreign Commerce Committee. *Crude Rubber, Coffee, Etc., Hearings.* 69th Cong., 1st sess., January 1926.

————. Select Committee on Foreign Aid. *Final Report on Foreign Aid, H.R. 1845.* 80th Cong., 2nd sess., 1948.

U.S. Mutual Security Program. *Reports to Congress.* Washington: Government Printing Office, 1951–1960.

U.S. National Commission on Materials Policy. *Material Needs and the Environment Today and Tomorrow: Final Report.* Washington: Government Printing Office, 1974.

U.S. National Commission on Supplies and Shortages. *The Commodity Shortages of 1973–1974: Case Studies.* Washington: Government Printing Office, 1976.

————. *Government and the Nation's Resources.* Washington: Government Printing Office, December 1976.

U.S. National Conservation Commission. *Report, S. Doc. 676.* 60th Cong., 2nd sess., 1910.

U.S. National Resources Board. *A Report on National Planning and Public Works in Relation to Natural Resources and Including Land Use and Water Resources with Finding and Recommendation.* Washington: Government Printing Office, 1934.

U.S. National Security Resources Board. *Materials Survey, Copper, 1952.* Washington: Government Printing Office, 1952.

————. *Materials Survey on Tin.* Washington: Government Printing Office, 1953.

U.S. President. Council of Economic Advisers. *Economic Report of the President.* Washington: Government Printing Office, annual.

————. Council on International Economic Policy. *International Economic Report of the President.* Washington: Government Printing Office, annual volumes 1971–1977.

U.S. President's Materials Policy Commission. *Resources for Freedom.* 5 vols. Washington: Government Printing Office, 1952.

U.S. Senate. Committee on Armed Services. *Inquiry into the Strategic and Critical Material Stockpiles of the United States. Draft Report,* 88th Cong., 1st sess. Washington: Government Printing Office, 1963.

————. ————. *Inquiry into the Strategic and Critical Material Stockpiles of the United States, Hearings.* 87th Cong., 2nd sess., 1962.

————. Committee on Government Operations. *Materials Shortages, Hearings,* 93d Cong., 2nd sess., 1974.

————. Committee on Interior and Insular Affairs. *Accessibility of Strategic and Critical Materials to the United States in Time of War and for Our Expanding Economy.* Report No. 1627, 83rd Cong., 2nd sess., 1954.

————. ————. *Hearings on Mineral Resources Development.* 81st Cong., 1st sess., 1949.

————. ————. *Stockpile and Accessibility of Strategic and Critical Mate-*

rials to the United States in Time of War, Hearings pursuant to S. Res. 143. 83rd Cong., 1st sess., 1953.

————. Committee on Public Lands. *Hearings on Investigation of the Factors Affecting Minerals, Fuels, Forestry, and Reclamation Projects.* 80th Cong., 1st sess., 1947.

————. Mines and Mining Committee. *Stock Piles of Strategic Minerals, Hearings* on S. 1160. 78th Cong., 1st sess., 1943.

U.S. Tariff Commission. *Colonial Tariff Policies.* Washington: Government Printing Office, 1922.

————. *Industrial Readjustments of Certain Mineral Industries Affected by the War.* (Trade Information Series, No. 21).

Wiltse, Charles M. *Lead and Zinc Policies of the War Production Board and Predecessor Agencies: May 1940 to March 1944.* Washington: War Production Board, 1946.

Books and Articles

Abbott, Charles C. "Economic Defense of the United States." *Harvard Business Review* 26 (September 1948): 613–626.

————. "Economic Penetration and Power Politics." *Harvard Business Review* 26 (July 1948): 410–424.

Acheson, Dean. *Present at the Creation: My Years in the State Department.* New York: Norton, 1969.

Adams, Brooks. *The New Empire.* 1st pub. 1902. New York: Bergman Publishers, 1969.

Adler-Karlsson, Gunnar. *Western Economic Warfare 1947–1967: A Case Study in Foreign Economic Policy.* Stockholm: Almquist & Wiksell, 1968.

Aitchison, Leslie. *A History of Metals.* 2 vols. New York: Interscience Publishers, 1960.

Akagi, Roy H. "Japan's Economic Relations with China." *Pacific Affairs* 4 (June 1931): 471–478.

Alexander, Robert J. *Communism in Latin America.* New Brunswick: Rutgers University Press, 1957.

Allen, G. C. *A Short Economic History of Modern Japan, 1867–1937.* London: G. Allen & Unwin, 1946.

American Institute of Mining and Metallurgical Engineers. Mineral Inquiry. *Elements of a National Mineral Policy.* New York: AIMME, 1933.

Anderson, Irvine H., Jr. *The Standard-Vacuum Oil Company and United States East Asian Policy, 1933–1941.* Princeton: Princeton University Press, 1975.

Anderson, Thornton. *Brooks Adams: Constructive Conservative.* Ithaca: Cornell University Press, 1951.

Andrade, Víctor. *My Missions for Revolutionary Bolivia, 1944–1962.* Pittsburgh: University of Pittsburgh Press, 1976.

Angell, Norman. *Raw Materials, Population Pressure and War*. Boston: World Peace Foundation, 1936.

Asahi, Isoshi. *The Economic Strength of Japan*. Tokyo: Hokuseido Press, 1939.

Aziz, Muhammed Abdul. *Japan's Colonialism and Indonesia*. The Hague: M. Nijhoff, 1955.

Baer, George W. *The Coming of the Italian-Ethiopian War*. Cambridge: Harvard University Press, 1967.

Bain, H. Foster. "Minerals in Relation to Possible Development in the Far East." *Economic Geology* 22 (May 1927): 213–229.

————. *Ores and Industry in the Far East*. New York: Council on Foreign Relations, 1933.

————. "The Third Kingdom: Some Reflections on Our Mineral Heritage." *Geographical Review* 18 (April 1928): 177–195.

————, and Read, Thomas Thornton. *Ores and Industry in South America*. New York: Harper, 1934.

Bakeless, John. *The Economic Causes of Modern War: A Study of the Period 1879–1918*. New York: Moffat, Yard, 1921.

Baldwin, Hanson. "Hitler Can Be Defeated: Economic Measures." *New York Times Magazine*, June 15, 1941, p. 5.

Bancroft, Howland. "The Broadening Road to Foreign Investment." *Mining Engineering* 4 (July 1952): 666–668.

Bannerman, H. M. "The Search for Mineral Raw Materials." *Mining Engineering* 9 (September 1957): 1103–1108.

Barger, Harold, and Schurr, Sam H. *The Mining Industries, 1899–1939: A Study of Output, Employment and Productivity*. New York: National Bureau of Economic Research, 1944.

Barlow, E. R., and Wender, Ira T. *Foreign Investment and Taxation*. Englewood Cliffs: Prentice-Hall, 1955.

Barnett, Harold J., and Morse, Chandler. *Scarcity and Growth: The Economics of Natural Resource Availability*. Baltimore: Johns Hopkins University Press, 1963.

Baruch, Bernard. *American Industry in the War*. New York: Prentice-Hall, 1941.

————. *Making of the Reparation and Economic Sections of the Treaty*. New York: Harper, 1920.

Basch, Antonin. *The Danube Basin and the German Economic Sphere*. New York: Columbia University Press, 1943.

————. *The New Economic Warfare*. New York: Columbia University Press, 1941.

Bateman, Alan. "America's Stake in World Mineral Resources." *Mining Engineering* 1 (July 1949): 23–27.

————. *Economic Mineral Deposits*. New York: John Wiley, 1942.

————. "Foreign Minerals for the War Program." *Engineering and Mining Journal* 144 (April 1943): 59.

———. "Minerals: Supply and Demand." *Bulletin of Atomic Scientists* 17 (October 1961): 331–335.

———. "Our Future Dependence on Foreign Minerals." *Annals of the American Academy of Political and Social Science* 281 (May 1952): 25–32.

———. "Wartime Dependence on Foreign Minerals." *Economic Geology* 41 (June–July 1946): 308–327.

Batt, William L. "Raw Materials Solvency." *Mining and Metallurgy* 24 (July 1943): 308–309.

Becht, J. Edwin, and Belzung, L. D. *World Resource Management: Key to Civilizations and Social Achievement.* Englewood Cliffs: Prentice-Hall, 1975.

Beck, Earl R. *Verdict on Schacht: A Study in the Problem of Political "Guilt."* Tallahassee: Florida State University Press, 1955.

Bengston, Nels A., and Van Royen, Willem. *Fundamentals of Economic Geography.* New York: Prentice-Hall, 1942.

Benson, Ezra Taft. *Cross Fire: The Eight Years with Eisenhower.* Garden City: Doubleday, 1962.

Bergsten, C. Fred. "The Threat from the Third World." *Foreign Policy* 11 (Summer 1973): 102–124.

Berle, Beatrice Bishop, and Jacobs, Travis Beal, eds. *Navigating the Rapids, 1918–1971: From the Papers of Adolf A. Berle.* New York: Harcourt Brace Jovanovich, 1973.

Bernstein, Marvin D. *The Mexican Mining Industry, 1890–1950: A Survey of Politics, Economics and Technology.* Albany: State University of New York Press, 1964.

Bidwell, Percy Wells. *Raw Materials: A Study of American Policy.* New York: Council on Foreign Relations, 1958.

Billington, Ray Allen. *Frederick Jackson Turner: Historian, Scholar, Teacher.* New York: Oxford University Press, 1973.

Blum, John Morton. *From the Morgenthau Diaries: Years of Urgency, 1938–1941.* Boston: Houghton Mifflin, 1965.

———, ed. *The Price of Vision: The Diary of Henry A. Wallace, 1942–1946.* Boston: Houghton Mifflin, 1973.

Borg, Dorothy. *The United States and the Far Eastern Crisis of 1933–1938: From the Manchurian Incident through the Initial Stage of the Undeclared Sino-Japanese War.* Cambridge: Harvard University Press, 1964.

Borkenau. F. *The New German Empire.* New York: Viking, 1939.

Bowers, Claude G. *Chile through Embassy Windows: 1939–1953.* New York: Simon and Schuster, 1958.

Bowman, Isaiah. *The New World: Problems in Political Geography.* 4th ed. New York: World, 1928.

Boyd, James. "Mineral Stocks Necessary for National Defense." *Mining and Metallurgy* 29 (December 1948): 663–665.

Boyle, John Hunter. *China and Japan at War, 1937–1945: The Politics of Collaboration.* Stanford: Stanford University Press, 1972.

Brandes, Joseph. *Herbert Hoover and Economic Diplomacy: Department of Commerce Policy, 1921–1928.* Pittsburgh: University of Pittsburgh Press, 1962.

Brookings, Robert S. "The Relations of Raw Materials to Peace and Prosperity." *Academy of Political Science Proceedings* 12 (July 1926): 113–115.

Brooks, David B., and Anderson, P. W. "Mineral Resources, Economic Growth and World Population." *Science* 5 (July 1974): 13–18.

Brown, Harrison. "How Vulnerable Are We?" *Bulletin of Atomic Scientists* 13 (November 1957): 318–322.

Brown, Lester. "Rich Countries and Poor in a Finite, Interdependent World." *Daedalus* 102 (Fall 1973): 153–164.

Bryant, Farris. "National Defense through the Acquisition and Stockpiling of Strategic and Critical Materials." *Journal of Public Law* 16 (1967): 345–358.

Burns, James M. *Roosevelt: The Lion and the Fox.* New York: Harcourt, Brace and World, 1956.

———. *Roosevelt: The Soldier of Freedom.* New York: Harcourt Brace Jovanovich, 1970.

Cameron, Eugene N., ed. *The Mineral Position of the United States, 1975–2000.* Madison: University of Wisconsin Press, 1973.

Campbell, Robert F. *The History of Basic Metals: Price Control in World War II.* New York: Columbia University Press, 1948.

Campbell, Thomas M., and Herring, George C., eds. *The Diaries of Edward R. Stettinius, Jr., 1943–1946.* New York: New Viewpoints, 1975.

Carell, Paul. *Hitler's War on Russia.* London: George C. Harrap, 1964.

Carroll, Berenice A. *Design for Total War: Arms and Economics in the Third Reich.* The Hague: Mouton, 1968.

Cates, L. S. "Clouds over Mining." *Mining and Metallurgy* 27 (December 1946): 579–582.

Clark, Evans, ed. *Boycotts and Peace.* New York: Harper, 1932.

Clarkson, Grosvenor B. *Industrial America in the World War: The Strategy behind the Line, 1917–1918.* Boston: Houghton Mifflin Co., 1923.

Clawson, Marion, ed. *Natural Resources and International Development.* Baltimore: Johns Hopkins University Press, 1964.

Cohen, Jerome B. *Japan's Economy in War and Reconstruction.* Minneapolis: University of Minnesota Press, 1949.

Cohen, Warren I. *The American Revisionists: The Lessons of Intervention in World War I.* Chicago: University of Chicago Press, 1967.

Cole, D. H. *Imperial Military Geography.* 9th ed. London: Sifton Praed, 1938.

Colvin, Ian. *The Chamberlain Cabinet.* New York: Taplinger, 1971.

Committee on Present Danger. "What Is the Soviet Union Up To?" Washington: CPD, April 4, 1977.

Connelly, Philip, and Perlman, Robert. *The Politics of Scarcity: Resource Conflicts in International Relations.* London: Oxford University Press, 1975.

Council on Foreign Relations, Inc. *Mineral Resources and Their Distribution As Affecting International Relations.* New York: CFR, 1922.

Cowling, Maurice. *The Impact of Hitler: British Politics and British Policy, 1933–1940.* London: Cambridge University Press, 1975.

Crowley, James B. *Japan's Quest for Autonomy: National Security and Foreign Policy, 1930–1938.* Princeton: Princeton University Press, 1966.

Cuff, Robert D. *The War Industries Board: Business-Government Relations during World War I.* Baltimore: Johns Hopkins University Press, 1973.

Culbertson, William Smith. *International Economic Policies: A Survey of Economics of Diplomacy.* New York: D. Appleton, 1925.

———. "Raw Materials and Foodstuffs in the Commercial Policies of Nations." *Annals of the American Academy of Political and Social Science* 112 (1924): 21–26.

Daily, Arthur F. "Economic Aspects of Interruption of Diamond Production in Congo Republic." *Mining Engineering* 13 (May 1961): 475–479.

DeMille, John B. *Strategic Minerals: A Summary of Uses, World Output, Stockpiles, Procurement.* New York: McGraw-Hill, 1947.

Dennis, W. H. *Metallurgy in the Service of Man.* London: MacDonald, 1961.

———, and Herbert, William. *Foundations of Iron and Steel Metallurgy.* Amsterdam: Elsevier, 1967.

Denny, Ludwell. *America Conquers Britain: A Record of Economic Strife.* New York: Knopf, 1930.

DeNovo, John A. "The Movement for an Aggressive American Oil Policy Abroad, 1918–1920." *American Historical Review* 61 (July 1956): 854–875.

Dewhurst, J. Frederic. *America's Needs and Resources.* New York: Twentieth Century Fund, 1947.

deWilde, John C. "Raw Materials in World Politics." *Foreign Policy Reports* 12 (September 15, 1936): 162–176.

Dirksen, Herbert von. *Moscow, Tokyo, London: Twenty Years of German Foreign Policy.* Norman: University of Oklahoma Press, 1952.

Divine, Robert A. *Roosevelt and World War II.* Baltimore: Johns Hopkins University Press, 1969.

Dodd, William E., Jr., and Dodd, Martha, eds. *Ambassador Dodd's Diary: 1933–1938.* New York: Harcourt, Brace, 1941.

Donaldson, John. *International Economic Relations: A Treatise on World Economy and World Politics.* New York: Longmans, Green, 1928.

Doxey, Margaret P. *Economic Sanctions and International Enforcement.* London: Oxford University Press, 1971.

Eckel, E. C. *Coal, Iron and War.* New York: Henry Holt, 1920.

Eckes, Alfred E., Jr. "American History Textbooks and the New Issues of Trade, Payments, and Raw Materials." *History Teacher* 11 (February 1978): 237–246.

———. *A Search for Solvency: Bretton Woods and the International Monetary System, 1941–1971.* Austin: University of Texas Press, 1975.

Edgar, E. Mackay. "Great Britain's Grip on Reserve Oil Supplies of the World." *Engineering and Mining Journal* 109 (May 22, 1920): 1173.

Einzig, Paul. *Economic Warfare, 1939–1940.* London: Macmillan, 1941.

Elliott, William Y.; May, Elizabeth S.; Rowe, J.W.F.; Skelton, Alex; and Wallace, Donald H. *International Control In the Non-Ferrous Metals.* New York: Macmillan, 1937.

Emeny, Brooks. *The Strategy of Raw Materials: A Study of America in Peace and War.* New York: Macmillan, 1934.

Emerson, Rupert. "The Dutch East Indies Adrift." *Foreign Affairs* 18 (July 1940): 735–741.

Ethridge, Mark. "The Economic Consequences of a Hitler Victory." *International Conciliation* 370 (May 1941): 549–563.

Evans, Harry J. "The Stock-piling Bill—S. 752." *Mining and Metallurgy* 27 (August 1946): 434–436.

Everest, Allan Seymour. *Morgenthau, the New Deal, and Silver.* New York: King's Crown Press, 1950.

Falco, Tom. "ECA's Strategic Materials Division." *Engineering and Mining Journal* 149 (September 1948): 70–74.

Feis, Herbert. *The Diplomacy of the Dollar: First Era, 1919–1932.* Baltimore: Johns Hopkins University Press, 1950.

———. *From Trust to Terror: The Onset of the Cold War, 1945–1950.* New York: Norton, 1970.

———. *The Road to Pearl Harbor.* Princeton: Princeton University Press, 1950.

———. *Seen From E.A.: Three International Episodes.* New York: Knopf, 1947.

Fifield, Russell H., and Pearcy, G. Etzel. *Geopolitics in Principle and Practice.* Boston: Ginn, 1944.

———. *World Political Geography.* New York: Crowell, 1949.

Fischer, Fritz. *Germany's Aims in the First World War.* New York: Norton, 1967.

Fisher, Joseph L., and Potter, N. *World Prospects for Natural Resources.* Baltimore: Johns Hopkins University Press, 1974.

Flawn, Peter T. *Mineral Resources: Geology, Engineering, Economics, Politics, Law.* New York: John Wiley, 1966.

———. "Minerals: A Final Harvest or An Endless Crop?" *Engineering and Mining Journal* 166 (May 1965): 106–108.

Frasché, Dean F. *Mineral Resources.* (A Report to the Committee on Natural Resources of the National Academy of Sciences—National Research Council.) Washington: NAS-NRC, 1962.

Gaddis, John Lewis. *The United States and the Origins of the Cold War, 1941–1947.* New York: Columbia University Press, 1972.

Gann, L. H. "The Northern Rhodesian Copper Industry and the World of

Copper: 1923–1952." *Rhodes-Livingston Institute Journal* 18 (1955): 1–18.

Gatzke, Hans W. *European Diplomacy between Two Wars, 1919–1939.* Chicago: Quadrangle Books, 1972.

Geological Society of America. *Minerals in the Peace Settlement.* New York: The Society, 1940.

Goodman, Bernard. *Industrial Materials in Canadian-American Relations.* Detroit: Wayne State University Press, 1961.

Gordon, David. "How We Blockaded Germany." *Harpers* 190 (December 1944): 14–22.

———, and Dangerfield, Royden. *The Hidden Weapon: The Story of Economic Warfare.* New York: Harper, 1947.

Grebler, Leo, and Winkler, Wilhelm. *The Cost of the World War to Germany and to Austria-Hungary.* New Haven: Yale University Press, 1940.

Green, David. *The Containment of Latin America: A History of the Myths and Realities of the Good Neighbor Policy.* Chicago: Quadrangle Books, 1971.

Greenfield, Kent Roberts, ed. *Command Decisions.* Washington: Department of the Army. Office of Military History, 1960.

Gregory, J. W. "The Geological Factors Affecting the Strategy of the War." *Contemporary Review* 108 (December 1915): 769–779.

Grew, Joseph C. *Ten Years in Japan.* New York: Simon and Schuster, 1944.

Grieve, Muriel. "Economic Sanctions: Theory and Practice." *International Relations* 3/6(October 1968): 431–443.

Guichard, Louis. *The Naval Blockade, 1914–1918.* New York: D. Appleton, 1930.

Hahn, Walter F., and Cottrell, Alvin J. *Soviet Shadow Over Africa.* Miami: Center for Advanced International Studies, University of Miami, 1976.

Hall, Robert Burnett, "American Raw-Material Deficiencies and Regional Dependence." *Geographical Review* 30 (April 1940): 177–186.

Hancock, William K. *Four Studies in War and Peace in This Century.* Cambridge: Cambridge University Press, 1961.

Harper, Glenn T. *German Economic Policy in Spain: During the Spanish Civil War, 1936–1939.* The Hague: Mouton, 1967.

Harris, Brice, Jr. *The United States and the Italo-Ethiopian Crisis.* Stanford: Stanford University Press, 1964.

Harris, Seymour E. *The Economics of Mobilization and Inflation.* New York: Norton, 1951.

Hart, Lyman H. "Mineral Science and the Future of Metals." *Mining Engineering* 25 (April 1975): 57–63.

Hawtrey, R. G. *Economic Aspects of Sovereignty.* 2nd ed. London: Longmans, Green, 1952.

Hays, Samuel P. *Conservation and the Gospel of Efficiency: The Progressive Conservation Movement, 1890–1920.* Cambridge: Harvard University Press, 1959.

Hazlitt, Henry. " 'Planning' for 1975." *Newsweek* 40 (September 1, 1952): 57.

Henderson, Hubert Douglas. *Colonies and Raw Materials.* Oxford: The Clarendon Press, 1939.

Herres, Otto. "What the Paley Report Means to U.S. Miners." *Engineering and Mining Journal* 153 (December 1952): 72–75.

Hess, Gary R. *America Encounters India, 1941–1947.* Baltimore: Johns Hopkins University Press, 1971.

Hindmarsh, Albert E. *The Basis of Japanese Foreign Policy.* Cambridge: Harvard University Press, 1936.

Hitler, Adolf. *Hitler's Secret Book.* New York: Grove Press, 1961.

———. *Hitler's Secret Conversations, 1941–1944.* New York: Farrar, Straus and Cudahy, 1953.

———. *Mein Kampf.* Boston: Houghton Mifflin, 1939.

Holborn, Hajo. *A History of Modern Germany.* New York: Knopf, 1969.

Holland, Thomas. "The International Relationship of Minerals." *Nature* 124 (August 3, 1929): 187–194.

———. *The Mineral Sanction as an Aid to International Security.* London: Oliver and Boyd, 1935.

———. "Relation of Mineral Resources to World Peace." *Nature* 150 (September 26, 1942): 364–366.

Holman, Eugene. "Our Inexhaustible Resources." *Atlantic* 189 (June 1952): 29–32.

Holmes, Harry. *Strategic Materials and National Strength.* New York: Macmillan, 1942.

Hoover, Herbert. *The Memoirs of Herbert Hoover: The Cabinet and the Presidency, 1920–1933.* New York: Macmillan, 1952.

Horoth, V. L. "Our Economic War against the Axis." *Current History and Forum* 53 (June 1941): 38–40.

Hotchkiss, William O. "Our Declining Mineral Reserves." *Yale Review* 37 (September 1947): 68–79.

Huddle, Franklin P. "The Evolving National Policy for Materials." *Science* 191 (February 20, 1976): 654–659.

Hurstfield, Joel. *The Control of Raw Materials.* London: H. M. Stationery Office, 1953.

Ickes, Harold. "The War and Our Vanishing Resources." *American Magazine* 140 (December 1945): 20–22.

Ike, Nobutaka, ed. *Japan's Decision for War: Records of the 1941 Policy Conferences.* Stanford: Stanford University Press, 1967.

Ince, Charles R. "Zinc." *Engineering and Mining Journal* 160 (February 1959): 107–109.

International Economic Studies Institute. *Raw Materials and Foreign Policy.* Washington: IESI, 1976.

Inui, Kiyosue. "Japan's Fundamental Trade Problem." *Far Eastern Review* 33 (July 1937): 256–261.

Iriye, Akira. *Across the Pacific: An Inner History of American–East Asian Relations*. New York: Harcourt, Brace and World, 1967.

————. *After Imperialism: The Search for a New Order in the Far East, 1921–1931*. Cambridge: Harvard University Press, 1965.

Jack, Daniel T. *Studies in Economic Warfare*. New York: Chemical Publishing Co., 1941.

Janeway, Eliot. "A Job for a Business Man." *Asia* 41 (May 1941): 212.

Jones, Francis C. *Japan's New Order in East Asia: Its Rise and Fall, 1937–1945*. London: Oxford University Press, 1954.

————. *Manchuria since 1931*. London: Royal Institute of International Affairs, 1949.

Jones, Jesse. *Fifty Billion Dollars: My Thirteen Years with the RFC (1932–1945)*. New York: Macmillan Co., 1951.

Joralemon, Ira B. "Control of Mineral Supplies, Peace by Force." *Mining and Metallurgy* 25 (May 1944): 253.

————. "The 'Have-Not' Theory and Metal Prices." *Mining Congress Journal* 32 (June 1946): 54–57.

Just, Evan. "Foreign Private Investment—A Boon to Developing Countries." *Mining Engineering* 9 (June 1957): 641–645.

————. "A National Mineral Policy." *Engineering and Mining Journal* 146 (April 1945): 86–91.

Kahn, Herman; Brown, William; and Martel, Leon. *The Next 200 Years: A Scenario for America and the World*. New York: Morrow, 1976.

Kapp, Karl William. *The League of Nations and Raw Materials, 1919–1939*. Geneva: Geneva Research Centre, 1941.

Karlbom, Rolf. "Sweden's Iron Ore Exports to Germany, 1933–1944." *Scandinavian Economic History Review* 13 (1965): 65–73.

Keynes, J. M. "The Control of Raw Materials by Governments." *The Nation and the Atheneum* 39 (June 12, 1926): 267–269.

————. "The Policy of Government Storage of Foodstuffs and Raw Materials." *Economic Journal* 48 (September 1938): 449–460.

Killough, Hugh Baxter, and Killough, Lucy W. *Raw Materials of Industrialism*. New York: Crowell, 1929.

Kindleberger, Charles P. *The World in Depression, 1929–1939*. Berkeley: University of California Press, 1973.

King, Alwyn H., and Cameron, John R. "Materials and the New Dimensions of Conflict." In *New Dynamics in National Strategy*. New York: Crowell, 1975.

Kirkpatrick, Ivone. *Mussolini: A Study in Power*. New York: Hawthorn Books, 1964.

Klochkovsky, L. L. *Economic Neocolonialism: Problem of South-East Asian Countries' Struggle for Economic Independence*. Moscow: Progress Publishers, 1975.

Kolko, Gabriel. *Main Currents in Modern American History*. New York: Harper and Row, 1976.

Kolko, Joyce. *America and the Crisis of World Capitalism*. Boston: Beacon Press, 1974.

————, and Kolko, Gabriel. *The Limits of Power: The World and United States Foreign Policy, 1945–1954*. New York: Harper and Row, 1972.

Krosby, Hans Peter. *Finland, Germany and the Soviet Union, 1940–1941: The Petsamo Dispute*. Madison: University of Wisconsin Press, 1968.

Krug, Julius A. "National Mineral Policies." *Mining Congress Journal* 32 (October 1946): 24–27.

Landes, David S. "Technological Change and Development in Western Europe, 1750–1914." In *The Cambridge Economic History of Europe*, edited by H. J. Habbakkuk and M. Postan, 6:477–496. Cambridge: Cambridge University Press, 1965.

Landsberg, Hans H; Fischman, Leonard L.; and Fisher, Joseph L. *Resources in America's Future: Patterns of Requirements and Availabilities, 1960–2000*. Baltimore: Johns Hopkins University Press, 1963.

Langer, William L. *Our Vichy Gamble*. New York: Norton, 1947.

————, and Gleason, S. Everett. *The Challenge to Isolation, 1937–1940*. New York: Council on Foreign Relations, 1952.

————. *The Undeclared War, 1940–1941*. New York: Council on Foreign Relations, 1953.

Lash, Joseph. *Roosevelt and Churchill, 1939–1941*. New York: Norton, 1976.

Lasky, S. G. "Economics, Foreign Pressures, Depleted Mines—Determine Mineral Self-Sufficiency." *Mining Engineering* 13 (August 1961): 971–973.

————. "Ore-Reserve Viewpoints." *Mining and Metallurgy* 27 (September 1946): 466–468.

Leith, Charles K. *The Economic Aspects of Geology*. New York: Holt, 1921.

————. "Elements of a National Mineral Policy." *Mining and Metallurgy* 14 (May 1933): 224–226.

————. "Exploitation of Foreign Minerals." *Economic Geology* 22 (August 1927): 518–520.

————. "International Control of Metals." In U.S. Geological Survey, *Mineral Resources of the United States, 1917*, 1:9A–16A. Washington: Government Printing Office, 1921.

————. "Principles of Foreign Mineral Policy of the United States." *Mining and Metallurgy* 27 (January 1946): 6–17.

————. "War Problems in Minerals: II—Overseas War Mineral Movements." *Engineering and Mining Journal* 112 (October 8, 1921): 570–575.

————. "The World Iron and Steel Situation in Its Bearing on the French Occupation of the Ruhr." *Foreign Affairs* 1 (June 15, 1923): 136–151.

————. "The World Manganese Situation." *Mining and Metallurgy* 8 (May 1927): 206–207.

————. *World Minerals and World Politics: A Factual Study of Minerals in Their Political and International Relations*. New York: McGraw-Hill, 1931.

———; Furness, J. W.; and Lewis, Cleona. *World Minerals and World Peace*. Washington: Brookings Institution, 1944.

Lewis, Cleona. *America's Stake in International Investments*. Washington: Brookings Institution, 1938.

———. *Nazi Europe and World Trade*. Washington: Brookings Institution, 1941.

Liebhafsky, H. H. "The International Materials Conference in Retrospect." *Quarterly Journal of Economics* 71 (May 1957): 267–288.

Lippmann, Walter. "The Economic Consequences of a German Victory." *Life* 9 (July 22, 1940): 64–69.

Lochner, Louis P., ed. *The Goebbels Diaries, 1942–1943*. Garden City, N.Y.: Doubleday, 1948.

Lockwood, David E. *The Stockpiling of Strategic and Critical Materials: Legislative History and Analysis of Pertinent Developments, 1939–1973*. Washington: Library of Congress, Congressional Research Service, May 8, 1974.

Loewenheim, Francis L.; Langley, Harold D.; and Jonas, Manfred, eds. *Roosevelt and Churchill: Their Secret Wartime Correspondence*. New York: Saturday Review Press, 1975.

Lovering, T. S. *Minerals in World Affairs*. New York: Prentice-Hall, 1943.

Macartney, Maxwell H. H., and Cremona, Paul. *Italy's Foreign and Colonial Policy, 1914–1937*. London: Oxford University Press, 1938.

McClure, Wallace. *World Prosperity As Sought through the Economic Work of the League of Nations*. New York: Macmillan, 1933.

MacCormac, John. "Diplomat of Global Economics." *New York Times Magazine*, November 7, 1943, p. 14.

McDivitt, James Frederick, and Manners, Gerald. *Minerals and Men: An Exploration of the World of Minerals and Metals, Including Some of the Major Problems That Are Posed*. Baltimore: Johns Hopkins University Press, 1974.

McGrath, Sylvia W. *Charles Kenneth Leith: Scientific Adviser*. Madison: University of Wisconsin Press, 1971.

Mackinder, Halford J. *Democratic Ideals and Reality*. New York: Holt, 1919.

McLaughlin, Donald H. "Government's Role in a National Mineral Policy," *Mining Engineering* 1 (April 1949): 19.

McLellan, David S. *Dean Acheson: The State Department Years*. New York: Dodd, Mead, 1976.

Maier, Charles S. *Recasting Bourgeois Europe: Stabilization in France, Germany, and Italy in the Decade after World War I*. Princeton: Princeton University Press, 1975.

Malenbaum, Wilfred. *Materials Requirement in the United States and Europe in the Year 2000*. Washington: National Commission on Materials Policy, 1973.

Maser, Werner. *Hitler's Mein Kampf: An Analysis*. London: Faber and Faber, 1970.

Mason, Edward S. "American Security and Access to Raw Materials." *World Politics* 1 (January 1949): 147–160.

————. *Controlling World Trade: Cartels and Commodity Agreements.* New York: McGraw-Hill, 1946.

————. "Nationalism and Raw Materials." *Atlantic* 191 (March 1953): 61–65.

————. "Natural Resources and Environmental Restrictions to Growth." *Challenge* 20 (January–February, 1978): 14–20.

————. "Raw Materials, Rearmament, and Economic Development." *Quarterly Journal of Economics* 66 (August 1952): 327–341.

Matloff, Maurice, and Snell, Edwin M. *Strategic Planning for Coalition Warfare, 1941–1942.* Washington: Department of the Army, Office of Military History, 1953.

Mattern, Johannes. *Geopolitik: Doctrine of National Self-Sufficiency and Empire.* Baltimore: Johns Hopkins University Press, 1942.

May, Ernest R. *"Lessons" of the Past: The Use and Misuse of History in American Foreign Policy.* New York: Oxford University Press, 1973.

Meadows, Donella H.; Meadows, Dennis L.; Randers, Jorgen; and Behrens, William W. III. *The Limits to Growth.* New York: Universe Books, 1972.

Medlicott, W. N. *The Economic Blockade.* 2 vols. London: H.M. Stationery Office, 1952, 1959.

Mehl, Robert F. *A Brief History of the Science of Metals.* New York: American Institute of Mining and Metallurgical Engineers, 1948.

Merli, Frank J., and Wilson, Theodore A., eds. *Makers of American Diplomacy: From Benjamin Franklin to Henry Kissinger.* New York: Scribner's, 1974.

Meyerhoff, Howard A. "Mineral Raw Materials in the National Economy." *Science* 135 (February 16, 1962): 510–516.

————. "Some Social Implications of Natural Resources." *Annals of the American Academy of Political and Social Science* 249 (January 1947): 20–31.

Mikdashi, Zuhayr. *The International Politics of Natural Resources.* Ithaca: Cornell University Press, 1976.

Mikesell, Raymond Frech, et al. *Foreign Investment in the Petroleum and Mineral Industries.* Baltimore: Johns Hopkins University Press, 1971.

————. *Nonfuel Minerals: U.S. Investment Policies Abroad.* Beverly Hills: Sage Publications, 1975.

Millis, Walter, ed. *The Forrestal Diaries.* New York: Viking, 1951.

Milward, Alan S. "Could Sweden Have Stopped the Second World War?" *Scandinavian Economic History Review* 15 (1967): 127–138.

————. *War, Economy and Society, 1939–1945.* London: Allen Lane, 1977.

Mining and Metallurgical Society of America. *International Control of Minerals.* New York: The Society, 1925.

Mitchell, B. R. *Abstract of British Historical Statistics.* Cambridge: Cambridge University Press, 1962.

————. *European Historical Statistics, 1750–1970.* New York: Columbia University Press, 1975.

Moon, Parker T. *Imperialism and World Politics.* New York: Macmillan, 1942.

Moore, Philip N. "War Minerals Relief Commission, 1919–1921." *Engineering and Mining Journal* 112 (November 5, 1921): 730–736.

Morgan, John Davis. *The Domestic Mining Industry of the United States in World War II: A Critical Study of the Economic Mobilization of the Mineral Base of National Power.* Washington: Government Printing Office, 1949.

————. "U.S. Strategic Materials Stockpiles and National Strategy." *Mining Engineering* 12 (August 1960): 925–928.

Morgenthau, Hans J. *Politics among Nations: The Struggle for Power and Peace.* New York: Knopf, 1948.

Morley, James William, ed. *Dilemmas of Growth in Prewar Japan.* Princeton: Princeton University Press, 1971.

Mudd, Harvey S. "Postwar Demand and Supply of Minerals." *Mining and Metallurgy* 27 (January 1946): 22–24.

National Industrial Conference Board. *Rationalization of German Industry.* New York: NICB, 1931.

Netschert, Bruce Carlton. "Point Four and Mineral Raw Materials." *Annals of the Association of American Geographers* 41 (June 1951): 133–145.

Neu, Charles E. *The Troubled Encounter: The United States and Japan.* New York: John Wiley, 1975.

Nixon, Edgar B., ed. *Franklin D. Roosevelt and Conservation, 1911–1945.* New York: Arno Press, 1975.

————. *Franklin D. Roosevelt and Foreign Affairs.* 3 vols. Cambridge: Harvard University Press, 1969.

Norcross, F. S., Jr. "Cuban Development May Solve U.S. Manganese Problem." *Mining and Metallurgy* 20 (August 1939): 380–383.

Nordhaus, William D. "Resources as a Constraint on Growth." *American Economic Review* 64 (May 1974): 22–27.

Offner, Arnold A. *American Appeasement: United States Foreign Policy and Germany, 1933–1938.* Cambridge: Harvard University Press, 1969.

Okita, Saburo. "Natural Resource Dependence and Japanese Foreign Policy." *Foreign Affairs* 52 (July 1974): 714–724.

Oliver, John W. *History of American Technology.* New York: Ronald Press, 1956.

Olund, Henning E., and Gustavson, Samuel A. "The Premium Price Plan—Its Cost and Its Results." *Engineering and Mining Journal* 149 (December 1948): 72–78.

Orchard, John E. *Japan's Economic Position: The Progress of Industrialization.* New York: McGraw-Hill, 1930.

Paley, William S. "Not Enough Materials for U.S." *U.S. News and World Report,* August 15, 1952, pp. 44–50.

Parsons, A. B., ed. *Seventy-Five Years of Progress in the Mineral Industry,*

1871–1946. New York: American Institute of Mining and Metallurgical Engineers, 1947.

Patterson, James T. *Mr. Republican: A Biography of Robert A. Taft.* Boston: Houghton Mifflin, 1972.

Pearson, Roger, ed. *Sino-Soviet Intervention in Africa.* Washington: Council on American Affairs, 1977.

Pehrson, Elmer W. "The Axis and Strategic Minerals." *Engineering and Mining Journal* 143 (May 1942): 42.

————. "Mineral Economics." *Mining Engineering* 1 (March 1949): 50–54.

————. "The Mineral Position of the United States and the Outlook for the Future." *Annual Report of the Board of Regents of the Smithsonian Institution,* 1945.

————. "Our Mineral Resources and Security." *Foreign Affairs* 23 (July 1945): 644–657.

————. "Problems of United States Mineral Supply." *Annals of the American Academy of Political and Social Science* 278 (November 1951): 166–178.

————. "What are Strategic and Critical Materials?" *Mining and Metallurgy* 25 (July 1944): 339–341.

Peyret, Henry. *La Guerre de Matières Premières.* 3rd ed. Paris: Presses Universitaires de France, 1946.

Pogue, Forrest C. *George C. Marshall.* 3 vols. New York: Viking, 1963–1973.

Potter, Neal, and Christy, Francis T., Jr. *Trends in Natural Resource Commodities, Statistics of Prices, Output, Consumption, Foreign Trade, and Employment in the United States, 1870–1957.* Baltimore: Johns Hopkins University Press, 1962.

Probert, Alan. "Point IV—Medieval Mining Frontiers Pushed Back." *Mining Engineering* 4 (July 1952): 661–671.

Prunty, Merle, Jr. "Strategic Metallic Alloys and United States Dependence." *Economic Geography* 17 (October 1941): 380–388.

Ratcliff, J. D. "What's Left in Uncle Sam's Pantry?" *Collier's* 131 (January 10, 1953): 34–35.

Rawles, William P. *The Nationality of Commercial Control of World Minerals.* New York: American Institute of Mining and Metallurgical Engineers, 1933.

Redfield, William C. *Dependent America: A Study of the Economic Bases of Our International Relations.* Boston: Houghton Mifflin, 1926.

Rees, David. "Soviet Strategic Penetration of Africa." *Conflict Studies* 77 (November 1976): 1–19.

Requa, Mark L. *The Relation of Government to Industry.* New York: Macmillan, 1925.

Rich, Norman. *Hitler's War Aims.* 2 vols. New York: Norton, 1973–1974.

Richardson, J. Henry. *British Economic Foreign Policy.* New York: Macmillan, 1936.

Richman, Peggy Brewer. *Taxation of Foreign Investment Income: An Economic Analysis.* Baltimore: Johns Hopkins University Press, 1963.
Rickard, T. A. *Man and Metals: A History of Mining in Relation to the Development of Civilization.* 2 vols. New York: McGraw-Hill, 1932.
———. *Retrospect: An Autobiography.* New York: McGraw-Hill, 1937.
Robertson, E. M., ed. *The Origins of the Second World War: Historical Interpretations.* New York: St. Martin's Press, 1971.
Robie, Edward H., ed. *Economics of the Mineral Industries.* New York: American Institute of Mining and Metallurgical Engineers, 1959.
Rockefeller, Nelson. *Critical Choices for Americans: Vital Resources—Reports on Energy, Food & Raw Materials.* Lexington, Mass.: D. C. Heath, 1977.
Rosen, S. McKee. *The Combined Boards of the Second World War: An Experiment in International Administration.* New York: Columbia University Press, 1951.
Rostow, Walt Whitman. *The Diffusion of Power, 1957–1962.* New York: Macmillan, 1972.
———. "Kondratieff, Schumpeter and Kuznets: Trend Periods Revisited." *Journal of Economic History* 35 (December 1975): 719–753.
———. *The World Economy: History and Prospect.* Austin: University of Texas Press, 1978.
Roush, G. A., ed. *The Mineral Industry: Its Statistics, Technology and Trade.* New York: McGraw-Hill, annual, 1914–1940.
———. *Strategic Mineral Supplies.* New York: McGraw-Hill, 1939.
Rowe, John W. F. *International Control in the Non-Ferrous Metals.* New York: Macmillan, 1937.
———. *Primary Commodities in International Trade.* Cambridge: Cambridge University Press, 1965.
Royal Institute of International Affairs. *Raw Materials and Colonies.* London: Royal Institute, 1936.
Salter, Arthur. *Allied Shipping Control: An Experiment in International Administration.* Oxford: Clarendon Press, 1921.
———. *Memoirs of a Public Servant.* London: Faber and Faber, 1961.
———. *Slave of the Lamp: A Public Servant's Notebook.* London: Weidenfeld and Nicolson, 1967.
Schacht, Hjalmar. *Account Settled.* London: Weidenfeld and Nicolson, 1949.
———. "Germany's Colonial Demands." *Foreign Affairs* 15 (January 1937): 223–234.
Schapsmeier, Edward L., and Schapsmeier, Frederick H. *Ezra Taft Benson and the Politics of Agriculture: The Eisenhower Years, 1953–1961.* Danville, Ill.: Interstate Printers and Publishers, 1975.
———. *Prophet in Politics: Henry A. Wallace and the War Years, 1940–1965.* Ames: Iowa State University Press, 1970.
Schiller, Herbert. "Access to Raw Materials." *Bulletin of Atomic Scientists* 18 (October 1962): 16–19.

Schlesinger, Arthur, Jr. *A Thousand Days: John F. Kennedy in the White House.* Boston: Houghton Mifflin, 1965.

Schlesinger, James R., et al. *Defending America: Toward a New Role in the Post-Detente World.* New York: Basic Books, 1977.

Schmidt, Paul. *Hitler's Interpreter.* London: William Heinemann, 1950.

Schmokel, Wolfe W. *Dream of Empire: German Colonialism, 1919–1945.* New Haven: Yale University Press, 1964.

Schneider, Herbert W. *Making the Fascist State.* New York: Oxford University Press, 1928.

Schuettinger, Robert L., ed. *South Africa—The Vital Link.* Washington: Council on American Affairs, 1976.

Schumpeter, E. B. *The Industrialization of Japan and Manchukuo, 1930–1940: Population, Raw Materials and Industry.* New York: Macmillan, 1940.

Schweitzer, Arthur. *Big Business in the Third Reich.* Bloomington: Indiana University Press, 1964.

Semple, Ellen Churchill. *American History and Its Geographic Conditions.* Boston: Houghton Mifflin, 1903.

Simonds, Frank H., and Emeny, Brooks. *The Great Powers in World Politics: International Relations and Economic Nationalism.* New York: American Book Company, 1935.

Simpson, Amos E. *Hjalmar Schacht in Perspective.* The Hague: Mouton, 1969.

Siney, Marion C. *The Allied Blockade of Germany, 1914–1916.* Ann Arbor: University of Michigan Press, 1957.

Sisco, Frank T. "Metal and Mineral Shortages and Substitutions in National Defense." *Mining and Metallurgy* 22 (October 1941): 483–487.

Smith, Denis Mack. *Mussolini's Roman Empire.* New York: Viking, 1976.

Smith, Gaddis. *Dean Acheson.* New York: Cooper Square Publishers, 1972.

Smith, George Otis. *Our Mineral Reserves: How to Make America Industrially Independent.* (U.S. Geological Survey Bulletin 599) Washington: Government Post Office, 1914.

———, ed. *The Strategy of Minerals: A Study of the Mineral Factor in the World Position of America in War and in Peace.* New York: D. Appleton, 1919.

———. "War Problems in Minerals: United States Geological Survey, 1914–1918." *Engineering and Mining Journal* 112 (December 3, 1921): 892–894.

Smith, George Otis; Summers, L.L.; Durand, E. Dana; Moon, Parker T.; and Earle, Edward M. *Raw Materials and Their Effect upon International Relations.* Worcester, Mass.: Carnegie Endowment for International Peace, 1926.

Snell, John L., ed. *The Outbreak of the Second World War: Design or Blunder?* Boston: D. C. Heath, 1962.

Snyder, Glenn H. *Stockpiling Strategic Materials: Politics and National Defense.* San Francisco: Chandler Publishing Co., 1966.

Sorensen, Theodore C. *Kennedy*. New York: Harper and Row, 1965.

Speer, Albert. *Inside the Third Reich, Memoirs*. New York: Macmillan, 1970.

Sprout, Harold, and Sprout, Margaret. *Foundations of International Politics*. Princeton: Van Nostrand, 1962.

———. *Toward a Politics of the Planet Earth*. New York: Van Nostrand Reinhold, 1971.

Spurr, Josiah E. "Russian Manganese Concessions." *Foreign Affairs* 5 (April 1927): 506–507.

———. "War Problems in Minerals." *Engineering and Mining Journal* 112 (September 24, 1921): 500–502, and (October 22, 1921): 651–656.

———, ed. *Political and Commercial Geology and the World's Mineral Resources*. New York: McGraw-Hill, 1920.

Spykman, Nicholas John. *America's Strategy in World Politics: The United States and the Balance of Power*. New York: Harcourt, Brace, 1942.

Staley, Eugene. *Raw Materials in Peace and War*. New York: Council on Foreign Relations, 1937.

———. *War and the Private Investor: A Study in the Relations of International Politics and International Private Investment*. Garden City: Doubleday, Doran, 1935.

Stein, Emanuel, and Backman, Jules, eds. *War Economics*. New York: Farrar and Rinehart, 1942.

Stocking, George W., and Watkins, Myron W. *Cartels in Action: Case Studies in International Business Diplomacy*. New York: Twentieth Century Fund, 1946.

Stolper, Gustav. *German Economy, 1870–1940: Issues and Trends*. New York: Reynal and Hitchcock, 1940.

Straight, Michael. "Jesse Jones, Bottleneck." *New Republic* 105 (December 29, 1941): 881–882.

Strauss, Simon D. "Nonferrous Metals." *Mining Engineering* 3 (February 1951): 110–112.

Strausz-Hupe, Robert. *The Balance of Tomorrow: Power and Foreign Policy in the United States*. New York: G. P. Putnam's, 1945.

———, and Possony, Stefan T. *International Relations: In the Age of the Conflict between Democracy and Dictatorship*. New York: McGraw-Hill, 1950.

Sullivan, George F. "U.S. Ready to Prove It Can Do without Russian Manganese." *Iron Age* 163 (March 10, 1949): 151–152.

Sutulov, A. *Minerals in World Affairs*. Salt Lake City: University of Utah Press, 1972.

Takahashi, Seizaburo. *Japan and World Resources*. Tokyo: The Foreign Affairs Association of Japan, September, 1937.

Tarabrin, E. A. *The New Scramble for Africa*. Moscow: Progress Publishers, 1974.

Thorne, Christopher. *The Limits of Foreign Policy: The West, the League and the Far Eastern Crisis of 1931–1933.* London: Hamish Hamilton, 1972.

Thorp, Willard L. "The New International Economic Challenge." U.S. Department of State *Bulletin* 25 (August 13, 1951): 245–248.

Traynor, Dean E. *International Monetary and Financial Conferences in the Interwar Period.* Washington: Catholic University of America Press, 1949.

Tryon, F. G., and Eckel, E. C. *Mineral Economics: Lectures under the Auspices of the Brookings Institution.* New York: McGraw-Hill, 1932.

Tuchman, Barbara W. *The Zimmermann Telegram.* New York: Viking, 1958.

Tufts, Robert W. "Preparedness for Economic Warfare in the Light of the World War Experience of the Allies and the United States." New York: Council on Foreign Relations, December 17, 1940.

Tulchin, Joseph S. *The Aftermath of War: World War I and U.S. Policy toward Latin America.* New York: New York University Press, 1971.

Vance, Maurice M. *Charles Richard Van Hise: Scientist Progressive.* Madison: State Historical Society of Wisconsin, 1960.

Vanderlip, Frank. *The American 'Commercial Invasion' of Europe.* Reprint, New York: Arno Press, 1976.

Van Gelderen, J. *The Recent Development of Economic Foreign Policy in the Netherlands East Indies.* London: Longmans, Green, 1939.

Van Hise, Charles R. *The Conservation of Natural Resources in the United States.* New York: Macmillan, 1910.

Van Mook, H. J. *The Netherlands Indies and Japan: Their Relations, 1940–1941.* London: G. Allen and Unwin, 1944.

Van Slyck, Milton. "Have-Nots Now the Haves As a Result of Upsets in War." *Newsweek* 20 (September 7, 1942): 39.

Varon, Bension, and Takeuchi, Kenji. "Developing Countries and Non-Fuel Minerals." *Foreign Affairs* 52 (April 1974): 497–510.

Villari, Luigi. *Italian Foreign Policy under Mussolini.* New York: Devin-Adair, 1955.

Viner, Jacob. "National Monopolies of Raw Materials." *Foreign Affairs* 5 (July 1926): 585–600.

Voskuil, Walter H. *Minerals in Modern Industry.* New York: John Wiley, 1930.

———. "The Search for Mineral Adequacy." *The Journal of Geography* 58 (November 1959): 385–399.

Wall, Patrick, ed. *The Southern Oceans and the Security of the Free World: New Studies in Global Strategy.* London: Stacey International, 1977.

Wallace, Benjamin Bruce, and Edminster, Lynn Ramsey. *International Control of Raw Materials.* Washington: Brookings Institution, 1930.

Wallace, Henry A. "The Silent War: Battle for Strategic Materials." *Collier's* 108 (November 22, 1941): 14–15.

Walters, F. P. *A History of the League of Nations.* London: Oxford University Press, 1965.

Watkins, Myron W. "Scarce Raw Materials: An Analysis and a Proposal." *American Economic Review* 34 (June 1944): 227–260.

Weigert, Hans W. *Generals and Geographers: The Twilight of Geopolitics.* New York: Oxford University Press, 1942.

Weinberg, Gerhard L. *The Foreign Policy of Hitler's Germany: Diplomatic Revolution in Europe, 1933–1936.* Chicago: University of Chicago Press, 1970.

Weissman, Stephen R. *American Foreign Policy in the Congo, 1960–1964.* Ithaca: Cornell University Press, 1974.

Whitman, Marina von Neumann. *Government Risk-Sharing in Foreign Investment.* Princeton: Princeton University Press, 1965.

Whittlesey, Derwent. *The Earth and the State: A Study of Political Geography.* New York: Holt, 1939.

———. *German Strategy of World Conquest.* New York: Farrar and Rinehart, 1942.

Wilkins, Mira. *The Emergence of Multinational Enterprise: American Business Abroad from the Colonial Era to 1914.* Cambridge: Harvard University Press, 1970.

———. *The Maturing of Multinational Enterprise.* Cambridge: Harvard University Press, 1974.

Williams, Benjamin H. *Economic Foreign Policy of the United States.* New York: McGraw-Hill, 1929.

Williams, Clyde. "Metals, Minerals, and Research." *Mining and Metallurgy* 28 (March 1947): 140–143.

Wilson, Joan Huff. *American Business and Foreign Policy, 1920–1933.* Lexington: University of Kentucky Press, 1971.

Wrather, W. E. "Mineral Resources and Mineral Resourcefulness." *Mining and Metallurgy* 27 (August 1946): 427–428.

Wright, Charles Will. "An Accounting of World Mining for 1949." *Mining World* 12 (April 15, 1950): 19–26.

———. "Communist Activities in the Battle for Industrial Supremacy." *Mining Engineering* 16 (January 1964): 52–54.

———. "Foreign Mining Investments Require Government Support." *Engineering and Mining Journal* 147 (April 1946): 80–81.

———. "Germany's Drive for Mineral Self-Sufficiency." *Mining and Metallurgy* 20 (May 1939): 241–247.

———. "Mineral Consolidation." *Mining Engineering* 1 (July 1949): 53.

———. "Mineral Consolidation." *Mining World* 15 (March 1953): 52–54.

Wu, Yuan-Li. *Economic Warfare.* New York: Prentice-Hall, 1952.

———. *Raw Material Supply in a Multipolar World.* New York: Crane, Russak, 1973.

Ziegfeld, Robert L. "Lead." *Engineering and Mining Journal* 160 (February 1959): 110–112.

Zimmermann, Erich W. *World Resources and Industries: A Functional Appraisal of the Availability of Agricultural and Industrial Resources.* New York: Harper, 1933.

Periodicals

American Economic Review.
American Metal Market.
American Political Science Review.
Annals of the American Academy of Political and Social Science.
Barron's.
Bulletin of Atomic Scientists.
Business History Review.
Business Week.
Christian Science Monitor.
Columbus Dispatch.
El Comercio (Lima, Peru), 1958.
Economist (London).
Economic Geography.
Economic Geology.
Engineering and Mining Journal.
Foreign Affairs.
Foreign Policy.
Fortune.
Geographical Review.
Harvard Business Review.
IMF Survey.
Iron Age.
Journal of American History.
London Times, 1958.
Melbourne Herald (Melbourne, Australia), 1958.
Mining and Metallurgy.
Mining Congress Journal.
Mining Engineering.
Mining Journal.
Mining World.
New Republic.
Newsweek.
New York Times.
Quarterly Journal of Economics.
Scandinavian Economic History Review.
Science.
Time.
Vital Speeches.
Wall Street Journal.
Washington Post.

Corporate Reports

American Metal Company, Ltd. (AMAX), 1946–1974.
American Smelting and Refining Company (ASARCO), 1945–1974.

Oral History Interviews

Bean, Louis. Truman Library, Independence, Missouri.
Bell, David E. Truman Library, Independence, Missouri.
Chartener, William H. Johnson Library, Austin, Texas.
Elsey, George. Truman Library, Independence, Missouri.
Fox, Lawrence. Johnson Library, Austin, Texas.
Hauge, Gabriel. Eisenhower Library, Abilene, Kansas.
Jacoby, Neil. Eisenhower Library, Abilene, Kansas.
McDermott, Edward. Kennedy Library, Waltham, Massachusetts.
Miller, Raymond W. Truman Library, Independence, Missouri.
Salant, Walter. Truman Library, Independence, Missouri.
Solomon, Anthony. Johnson Library, Austin, Texas.
Dr. Franklin P. Huddle, Senior Specialist in Science and Technology with the Library of Congress, and a former Defense Department official concerned with stockpile-related issues, discussed issues with the author on March 14, 1977.

Index